The Tenacity of the Couple-Norm

The Tenacity of the Couple-Norm

Intimate citizenship regimes in a changing Europe

Sasha Roseneil, Isabel Crowhurst, Tone Hellesund,
Ana Cristina Santos and Mariya Stoilova

First published in 2020 by
UCL Press
University College London
Gower Street
London WC1E 6BT
Available to download free: www.uclpress.co.uk

A CIP catalogue record for this book is available from The British Library.

ISBN: 978-1-78735-891-1 (Hbk.)
ISBN: 978-1-78735-890-4 (Pbk.)
ISBN: 978-1-78735-889-8 (PDF)
ISBN: 978-1-78735-892-8 (epub)
ISBN: 978-1-78735-893-5 (mobi)
DOI: https://doi.org/10.14324/111.9781787358898

Contents

Part IV: The tenacity of the couple-norm

Part V: Methodological appendix

List of figures

Preface and acknowledgements

This book is one of many publications to flow from the FEMCIT project, and first and foremost we wish to thank all our colleagues in this remarkable collective endeavour, a research project that involved 45 feminist social scientists across 13 European countries. Beatrice Halsaa, Sevil Sümer and Solveig Bergman were the scientific leaders of the project, along with two of us – Sasha Roseneil and Tone Hellesund. Siren Hogtun was the Administrative Coordinator. Nicky LeFeuvre, Line Nyhagen Predelli, Joyce Outshoorn and Monica Threlfall were the other members of the FEMCIT Steering Committee. The European Commission 6th Framework provided the funding that enabled us to carry out this ambitious programme of research. We acknowledge the support of the universities at which we have worked whilst undertaking the research and writing the book, in particular Birkbeck, University of London, where the project was based, and the Rokkan Centre and the University of Bergen, the University of Essex, the Centre for Social Studies at the University of Coimbra and, latterly, UCL.

At Birkbeck, Miriam Zukas always took a keen interest in our research on intimate citizenship, as did colleagues in the Department of Psychosocial Studies and the Birkbeck Institute for Social Research: Lisa Baraitser, Matt Cook, Rosie Cox, Stephen Frosh, Gail Lewis, Joni Lovenduski, Daniel Monk, Lynne Segal and Bruna Seu. Carly Guest, Robert Kulpa, Katherine Ludwin, William Potter, Sharon Shoesmith, Mahnaz Sekechi and Ceren Yalcin engaged creatively with our interview data as participants in our interpretation workshops, offering invaluable challenge and insightful contributions to our analysis. Heather Elliott, Prue Chamberlyne and Tom Wengraf spent five days training us in the biographical-narrative interpretive method at the start of the research; we did not follow their guidance to the letter, but this book is unimaginable without their work. Tom's dedication to the development of the biographical-narrative interpretive method was particularly inspirational. We are hugely grateful to Jenny Bredull, who provided patient and painstaking editorial and research assistance at various stages in the project. We also thank all of those who form part of our own intimate circles, who lived with the idea, and writing, of the book for a very long time.

But above all, we acknowledge the generous contribution of the people in London, Sofia, Oslo and Lisbon whose accounts of living with and against the couple-norm are the heart of this book.

PART I

Identifying the couple-norm

1
Introduction

The couple remains one of the most potent objects of normativity in contemporary European societies. Over recent decades, people have been spending longer periods of their lives outside the heterosexual cohabiting couple-form. Everyday practices of intimacy and the cultures, laws and policies that frame them have been undergoing profound change. As the extended family has tended to recede from daily life and the nuclear family has been losing its hold on individuals, intimate life choices have proliferated. Women's greater economic and social independence and the profound reshaping of cultural expectations and personal desires by feminist and lesbian and gay movements have fore-grounded the ideals of equality, self-actualization and individual rights and freedom. This has contributed to the rising numbers of people who are living alone, remaining unmarried, divorcing, de-domesticating their sexual and love relationships, living openly with, marrying and divorcing same-sex partners. Yet amidst these radical upheavals in personal life there are significant continuities in norms and lived experience, even amongst those most embodying and affected by them. It is against the backdrop of these changes that the *tenacity of the couple-norm* comes sharply into focus.

This book is about the ongoing strength of the couple-norm and the insidious grip it exerts on our lives as it defines what it is to be a citizen, a fully recognized and rights-bearing member of society. It exposes the construction of *coupledom* – the condition or state of living as a couple – as the normal, natural and superior way of being an adult,[1] in order to offer an anatomy of the couple-norm – an analysis of its structure, organization and internal workings. It explores how the couple-norm is lived and experienced, how it has changed over time and how it varies between places and social groups. Our aim is to make explicit, to literalize (Strathern, 1992), the couple-norm in order to understand its tenacity and ubiquity across changing landscapes of law, policy and everyday life in four contrasting national contexts: the United Kingdom, Bulgaria, Norway and Portugal.

Our central argument is that the couple-norm is at the heart of how intimate life is organized, regulated and recognized by regimes of intimate citizenship.[2] The couple-form has historically been valorized and conventionalized, so that it is the very essence of 'normal'. Whether a person is coupled or not is fundamental to their experience of social recognition and belonging:[3] the good citizen is the coupled citizen, and the socially integrated, psychologically developed and well-functioning person is coupled. Being part of a couple is widely seen and felt to be an achievement, a stabilizing status characteristic of adulthood, indicative of moral responsibility and bestowing full membership of the community. To be outside the couple-form is, in many ways, to be outside, or at least on the margins of, society.

In the book we explore how the *couple-form* – the structure of affinity that is composed of an intimate/sexual dyad – is institutionalized, supported and mandated by a plethora of legal regulations, social policies and institutions, cultural traditions and everyday practices.[4] We use the concept of the *couple-form* to make clear the distinction between the structural formation and the lived experience of actual couples. Often prefacing the term 'couple-form' with an adjective in order to specify a particular type of couple structure, such as the married, the heterosexual or the cohabiting couple-form, we identify the multifarious ways in which the couple-form is assumed, promoted and sometimes even enforced, and how this serves to shape the intimate life choices and trajectories, the subjectivities, deepest longings and desires, of those who seem to be living aslant to the conventional heterosexual cohabiting couple-form. We argue that these processes serve to establish and repeatedly reconstitute and re-enact the couple-norm, and we refer to this powerful social and cultural mandating and promotion of the couple-form as *couple-normativity*.

But the book also attends to practices and moments that challenge couple-normativity. Both consciously chosen and explicit, as well as circumstantial, unconscious and implicit, such practices and moments emerge as people grapple with the vicissitudes of intimate life. We present vivid examples of how the couple-norm is experienced by people whose intimate lives are ostensibly 'unconventional', people who are living at the forefront of societal transformations in personal life through being single, lesbian/gay/bisexual/in a same-sex relationship, living in shared housing and/or in a living-apart relationship. Drawing on a body of in-depth biographical-narrative – or life story – interviews with people in Lisbon, London, Oslo and Sofia, our *case studies of the couple-norm in action* illustrate similarities and differences in the operation of the couple-norm across national borders and cultural contexts, and amongst both majority and minoritized groups. These case studies offer exemplifications as well as exceptions, demonstrating how people live in complicated, often ambivalent relationships to the couple-norm – adjusting themselves to its demands, investing hope in its achievement, actively resisting and more or less consciously struggling with it, as well as remaking it in myriad variations that they imagine will better suit the particularity of their hopes, desires and situations.

Notes

1   In *coupledom*, the suffix *-dom* conjures the sense of a domain/an authority or jurisdiction (e.g. kingdom), a rank or status (e.g. earldom) and a general condition (e.g. martyrdom, freedom).
2   The concept of 'intimate citizenship regime' is fully explained in Chapter 3.
3   We use the gender-neutral pronoun 'their' throughout the book, as is increasingly common in English.
4   We use the phrase 'intimate/sexual dyad' to acknowledge the dynamic and sometimes fraught relationship between intimacy and sexuality within coupledom.

2
Questioning the couple-form

Both mainstream social science and public political discourse have historically failed to register the extent to which attachment to the couple-form is the assumed basis of citizenship, and how systematically the heterosexual intimate/sexual dyad is privileged as the generative centre and affective heart of the social formation and the body politic. However, it is possible to trace, through a scattered set of writings – polemic, political and research-based – a long-standing and increasingly influential thread of thinking, largely rooted in feminism, which places the unassailable social and political position of the couple-form into question.

An implicit critique of the institutionalization of the couple-form and its normativity runs through several centuries of feminist writing about marriage and men's control of women through domesticity, familial ideology and heterosexuality. As early as the beginning of the eighteenth century Mary Astell's anonymously published work *Some Reflections upon Marriage* (1700) offered a powerful critique of the inequities that forced women to marry, that required their deference within marriage and that meant that happy marriages were few and far between. Later in the eighteenth century, Mary Wollstonecraft's treatise in support of women's equal citizenship, *A Vindication of the Rights of Woman* (2004 [1792]), argued that no woman could truly be free to marry until she was economically able to remain single. A similar line was taken by Norwegian writer Camilla Collett in her novel *The District Governor's Daughters* (2017 [1854/5]), in which she critiqued arranged and forced marriages and the reality that marriage was the only route for middle- and upper-class women to a secure livelihood.

In the 1880s and 1890s, 'first wave' feminist campaigners across Europe embarked upon struggles to release women from the economic necessity of marriage, seeking to secure access to higher education and the labour market for the increasing number of unmarried women of bourgeois backgrounds who had no male wage to support them. Josephine Butler, for example, challenged compulsory matrimony and the devastating psychosocial consequences of failing to secure a husband: 'I cannot believe it is every woman's duty to marry, in this age of the world. There is abundance of work to be done which needs men and women detached from domestic ties; our unmarried women will be the greatest blessing to the community when they cease to be soured by disappointment or driven by destitution to despair' (1869: xxxv).

Moving beyond a critique of women's exclusion from education, professional work and skilled trades, a more radical analysis of marriage as central to women's oppression and as comparable to prostitution emerged in the early twentieth century. British suffragette Christabel Pankhurst, for instance, stated in 1913 that she regarded it as 'the man's instinctive endeavour [...] to keep the woman in a state of economic dependence'. She continued: 'This desire to keep women in economic subjection to themselves – to have women, as it were, at their mercy – is at the root of men's opposition to the industrial and professional employment of women. If a woman can earn an adequate living by the work of her hand or brain, then it will be much harder to compel her to earn a living by selling her sex' (2001: 204). With dependence seen as inherent in the status of the wife, and marriage regarded by some as the sale of sex in return for a living (e.g. Hamilton, 1981 [1901]), many first wave feminists saw paid work as the primary route to emancipation, but also emphasized the rights and needs of independent women, particularly for education and housing (Hellesund, 2003; Melby et al., 2006a; Moksnes, 1984).

Demands for women's liberation from the confines of marriage, the family and compulsory heterosexuality became a driving force amongst elements of the 'second wave' women's movement in western Europe in the late 1960s, 1970s and 1980s. The writings of activists and scholars echoed and intensified the concerns of earlier feminists, developing a trenchant critique of the institutionalization of marriage as the dominant form of intimate relationship, and of women's restriction and oppression within the private sphere and their inability to earn a living wage.[1] Marriage and the family were understood as a material social structure that produces and sustains women's dependency on men (Delphy and Leonard, 1992) and as an oppressive ideal that fixes gender roles (Chodorow, 1978), and love itself came to be seen as 'the pivot of women's oppression today' (Firestone, 1970: 113). In this context, feminists sought liberation in opposing the nuclear family and advocating the de-privatization of social reproduction by establishing communal households in which childcare and housework would be shared (Barrett and McIntosh, 1982; Greer, 2006 [1970]; Millett, 1970; Smart, 1984). Such alternative living arrangements were seen as making family structures 'less necessary' for women (Barrett and McIntosh, 1982: 159). The oppression and exploitation of female sexuality (Greer, 2006 [1970]; Millett, 1970) and the institution of 'compulsory heterosexuality' (Rich, 1980; Raymond, 2001 [1986]), which were understood as serving to divide women from each other (Radicalesbians, 1970), were also a major concern of the more radical thinkers. Seeking sexual freedom, autonomy and pleasure for women, they challenged marriage, monogamy and romantic fantasies of hetero-sexual love. The practice of 'consciousness-raising' – finding words to speak about gendered experiences of selfhood and intimate rela-tionships, and their disappointments and oppressions, within a small, mutually supportive group of women – was seen as a revolutionary method by which subjectivities and lives could be transformed and by which women might be able to move beyond the possessiveness and emotional dependency of the conventional couple (Hesford, 2009). In many circles of feminists and lesbians during this period, monogamy was subject to trenchant critique, and non-monogamy and communal living were valorized as properly feminist, post-patriarchal practices (Jackson and Scott, 2004; Rosa, 1994; Roseneil, 2016).

In parallel, and often in a critical relationship with white feminism, black and minoritized/racialized feminists were, during the same 'second wave' period, exploring racialized experiences of family, intimacy and sexuality (Carby, 1982; Parmar, 1982; Anthias and Yuval-Davis, 1983; Smith, 1983). In drawing attention to histories and legacies of slavery and migration, to the prevalence of lone parenting by African-Caribbean mothers and the related importance of female support networks, as well as to the role of the family in resistance to racist oppression, a range of different perspectives on key feminist concerns about repro-duction, home, family and the couple-form were developed.[2] The voice of black lesbian-feminism and its powerful critique of racist, patriarchal heteronormativity was also being articulated in the poetry and prose of American activist-writers Pat Parker and Audre Lorde, posing a challenge to white and heterosexual feminism that became, and remains, influential beyond the United States in the development of intersectional and queer thinking about intimate relationships.[3]

In tandem with the concerns of feminist writers and activists outside the academy, there has been increasing recognition in the social sciences of the historicity, diversity and diversification of relationship forms. As the scholarly focus on the family and marriage[4] has broadened into a wider exploration of intimacy and personal life,[5] attention has increasingly been drawn to the couple as a social institution. Erving Goffman, in his study of stigma, was one of the first sociologists to highlight the normative deviation enacted by 'the metropolitan unmarried and merely married who disavail themselves of the opportunity to raise a family, and instead support a vague society that is in rebellion, albeit mild and shortlived, against the family system' (1963: 144). In the mid-1980s, as part of his overarching theorization of modernity, Niklas Luhmann (1986) identified the emergence of the intimate couple as a particular type of sexual relationship in the eighteenth century, a 'structure of relationship' that he understood as characterized by the affirmation of each individual person's sense of self in an increasingly differentiated and less stable social system. Anthony Giddens (1992) followed with his work on the transformation of intimacy in the late twentieth century, which, influentially but controversially, posited the democratization and the increasing contingency and plasticity of intimate couple relationships.[6] More recently, the anthropologist Elizabeth Povinelli argued that the western couple-form is fundamentally tied to the emergence of individualism that followed the Reformation, as the 'genealogical grid slowly contracted around the conjugal couple and their immediate filial relations' (2006: 214).

There is now a significant corpus of sociological, psychological and historical literatures on life *outside the conventional couple*. One of the strongest threads in this body of work is research on singleness. More often than not focusing on women, and exploring both experiences of social marginalization and agentic attempts to construct positive single identities in the context of social disapprobation, singleness research points to the powerful social and discursive pressures to couple.[7] The increasing prevalence of solo-living[8] has also attracted the attention of social researchers as have 'living apart together' relationships,[9] practices of non-familial shared housing,[10] and, more recently, consensual non-monogamy, including polyamory,[11] and asexuality.[12] These strands of research, along with the contributions of theorists (and critics) of the 'transformation of intimacy' (Giddens, 1992), individualization (Beck and Beck-Gernsheim, 1995, 2002), and liquid modernity

(Bauman, 2000) theses, and those writing about love and romance as social institutions,[13] together serve to identify the modern romantic couple-form, rooted in love and 'disclosing intimacy' (Jamieson, 1998), as a historically contingent social formation that is compelling in its ubiquity, yet also contested and in transition.

It has been in sexuality studies and queer theory that the most explicitly critical analysis of the couple-form has been developed. In the English-speaking West, the gay liberation politics of the 1970s (Altman, 1971; Weeks, 1985; D'Emilio, 1992), like the women's liberation movement, posed an explicit challenge to family, monogamy and what some saw as the tyranny and oppressions of the couple-form. Emerging from this context and drawing on the historical construc- tionism of the first generation of critical sexuality scholars – Mary McIntosh (1968), Jeffrey Weeks (1977, 2012 [1981]), Michel Foucault (1978) and Judith Walkowitz (1982) – Gayle Rubin's (1993 [1984]) influential 'Notes for a Radical Theory of the Politics of Sex' points to the centrality of the couple-form in the religious, psychiatric and popular 'hierarchical system of sexual value' that operates in modern western societies. Rubin argues that this system positions marital reproductive heterosexuals 'at the top of the erotic pyramid', beneath whom are 'unmarried monogamous heterosexuals in couples, followed by most other heterosexuals' (Rubin, 1993 [1984]: 11). She posits the existence of a 'charmed circle' of 'sexuality that is "good", "normal", and "natural"', 'ideally [...] heterosexual, marital, monogamous, repro- ductive and non-commercial [...] coupled, relational, within the same generation and occur[ing] at home' (1993 [1984]: 13). In contrast, 'bad, abnormal, unnatural, damned sexuality' takes place at 'the outer limits' and is 'homosexual, unmarried, promiscuous, commercial, alone or in groups, casual, cross-generational, in public, involves pornography, manufactured objects or is sadomasochistic'. Rubin's work, along with Leo Bersani's argument in 'Is the Rectum a Grave?' (1987) that sexuality is fundamentally antisocial and challenging of normativity, have seeded the anti-normativity that is foundational to queer theory.[14]

Amongst queer theorists, the critique of normative forms of intimacy, particularly the romantic love-based couple-form, is a defining theme. Lauren Berlant and Michael Warner's (1998) disquisition on how US national public culture revolves around 'a love plot of intimacy and familialism' (1998: 318) offers a potent and influential exposition of the operations of heteronormativity, whilst also pointing to the intimate innovations involved in 'queer world making':

Queer and other insurgents have long striven, often dangerously or scandalously, to cultivate what good folks used to call criminal intimacies. We have developed relations and narratives that are only recognized as intimate in queer culture: girlfriends, gal pals, fuckbuddies, tricks. Queer culture has learned not only how to sexualize these and other relations, but also to use them as a context for witnessing intense and personal affect while elaborating a public world of belonging and transformation. Making a queer world has required the development of kinds of intimacy that bear no necessary relation to domestic space, to kinship, to the couple form, to property, or to the nation. (Berlant and Warner, 1998: 558)

In later work, Berlant (2000: 5) develops the argument that 'desires for intimacy that bypass the couple or the life narrative it generates have no alternative plots, let alone few laws or stable spaces of culture in which to clarify or to cultivate them'. She offers a critique of how love has come to be regarded as 'the ligament of patriotism and the family' (2000: 440), and romantic love as the fundamental attachment of humans, in which optimistic investments are made, which are, cruelly, bound to disappoint (2011). In a similar vein, although with differing trajectories, Laura Kipnis's (2003) polemic 'against love' seeks a radical politics of adultery, and Michael Cobb's queer treatise on singleness tackles head-on 'the toxic, totalitarian prominence of the couple' (2012: 24) and 'a world slavishly devoted to the supremacy of the couple' (2012: 8), promoting an 'ethics of distance' rather than of intimacy.[15]

But increasingly it has been through the mode of negative critique that a queer perspective on coupledom has been advanced. The 'good homosexual' (Smith, 1994), the monogamously coupled 'normal gay' (Seidman, 2002) and the struggle for same-sex marriage and equality in coupled citizenship have come to be the primary object of queer critique.[16] Understood as retrogressive, 'privatized, deradicalized, de-eroticized, confined' (Bell and Binnie, 2000: 3), these practices and politics have been critiqued as embodying, variously: normality and respectability (Warner, 1999), 'neo-conservativism' (Patton, 1993), 'homonormativity' and 'the sexual politics of neoliberalism' (Duggan, 2002), 'assimilationism' (Cover, 2006), 'queer liberalism' (Eng, Muñoz and Halberstam, 2005) and 'homonationalism' (Puar, 2007). Much of this work rests upon a narrative of the history of lesbian and gay politics that sees radical, community-oriented gay liberation politics giving way, by the mid-1980s, to a more liberal, state-focused set of claims relating first to AIDS/HIV and later to same-sex relationship recognition, family-building and equal marriage.[17] Cindy Patton, for instance, argues that in the United States the response to AIDS and the resurgence of right-wing politics was to seek the inclusion of lesbian and gay couples and families rather than to challenge the power of the rhetoric of family values. She sees this move 'from smash the family to family values' as having been articulated through 'the sentimental representation of the dyad of buddy-victim, or lifetime companion and dying partner' (1999: 369). More reparatively, Robyn Wiegman suggests that the marriage movement might be seen as a 'broad compensatory response' to the historical trauma of the AIDS epidemic in which 'stories are now legend of lover and partners denied access to medical decisions, hospital visitations, funerals, and the remains of shared households, including children' (2012: 340). But, however interpreted, whilst there has undoubtedly been a significant shift in emphasis in lesbian and gay movements towards a politics of recognition and inclusion and the emergence of a clearly articulated desire for the security of state and cultural recognition of couple relationships, there has also always been a grassroots ambivalence about seeking state sanction for same-sex rela-tionships. Anarchist, queer and radical feminist activists and writers, in particular, have actively challenged this focus.[18] Moreover, 'ordinary' lesbians and gay men continue to engage in complex everyday nego-tiations that complicate the binary positioning of 'liberal complicity' versus 'queer antinormative rebellion' that queer studies often sets up (Wiegman, 2012: 340; see also Heaphy et al., 2013). Whether they are understood as forming 'families of choice' (Weston, 1991; Stacey, 2004), engaging in 'queer counterintimacies' (Berlant and Warner, 1998) or performing 'life experiments' (Weeks, Heaphy and Donovan, 2001), in which lovers and ex-lovers,[19] friendship,[20] and non-monogamy/polyamory[21] might play an important role, lesbians and gay men can be seen as charting their life courses with a greater degree of reflexive consideration and awareness of normativity than is called forth for those whose intimate desires and practices pose no challenge to traditional ideals of love and family.

This book builds on the work of these activists, writers and researchers to develop deeper understandings of the mechanisms by which what we are calling 'the couple-norm' operates, attending particularly to its variability, but also to its persistence, across time and place.

Notes

1 For example, Barrett and McIntosh (1982), Firestone (1970), Friedan (1963), Millett (1970), Mitchell (1966), Oakley (1974) and Smart (1984).

2 There was a particularly intense debate within British socialist-feminism about racism, ethnocentrism and theorization of the family. See Carby (1982), Barrett and McIntosh (1985) and Bhavnani and Coulson (1986).

3 See the work of both Parker and Lorde in the anthology *Home Girls* (Smith, 1983) and Lorde (2012 [1984]). On their influence in the development of queer theory, see Garber (2001).

4 Classic sociological studies of marriage and marital couple relationships focus particularly on the tension between continuity and change in marriage as a social institution. These include Gillis (1985, 1996), Finch and Summerfield (1991), Mansfield and Collard (1988), Finch and Morgan (1991), Duncombe and Marsden (1993, 1995), Lewis (2001a, 2001b, 2001c), Coontz (2004, 2005), Carter and Duncan (2018), Davis (2010), Stacey (2011), Eekelaar and Maclean (2013) and Cherlin (2004, 2005, 2010).

5 Different approaches to intimacy and personal life are developed by Luhmann (1986), Giddens (1992), Jamieson (1998), Roseneil and Budgeon (2004), Roseneil and Ketokivi (2016) and Smart (2007).

6 There have been many critiques of Giddens's transformation of intimacy thesis, for instance: Jamieson (1998, 1999), Ribbens McCarthy and Edwards (2002), Ribbens McCarthy, Edwards and Gillies (2003), Skeggs (2003), Silva and Smart (1999), Smart (2000) and Smart and Neale (1999). Roseneil (2007) and Roseneil and Budgeon (2004) find more value in the thesis than many feminist sociologists, taking up the challenge of studying transformations in non-normative intimacies.

7 See, for example, Adams (1976), Chandler (1991), Chasteen (1994), Gordon (1994), Lewis and Moon (1997), Hellesund (2003), Reynolds and Wetherell (2003), Reynolds (2008), Reynolds and Taylor (2005), Byrne and Carr (2005), Trimberger (2005), Holden (2007), DePaulo and Morris (2005), DePaulo (2006), MacVarish (2006), Simpson (2006), Budgeon (2008), Reynolds (2008), Vicinus (2010), Zajicek and Koski (2003), Rufus (2003), Israel (2002), Cargan (2007) and Moran (2004).

8 Hall and Ogden (1999, 2003), Chandler et al. (2004), Jamieson, Wasoff and Simpson (2009), Klinenberg (2012), Jamieson and Simpson (2013).

9 See Levin (2004), Haskey (2005), Roseneil (2006), Duncan et al. (2012, 2013) and Stoilova et al. (2014).

10 See Heath (2004, 2009) and Heath et al. (2017).

11 See Jamieson (2004), Jackson and Scott (2004), Klesse (2006, 2007a, 2007b), Barker and Langridge (2010), Willey (2015), and Santos et al. (2019).

12 See Carrigan (2011a, 2011b), Carrigan, Gupta and Morrison (2013), Dawson, McDonnell and Scott (2016) and Rothblum and Behony (1993).

13 See Langford (1999), Evans (2003), Illouz (1997), Swindler (2003) and Kaufmann (2011).

14 Warner (1991) first deployed the concept of heteronormativity, but it was through the early work of Judith Butler (1990) and Eve Sedgwick (1991) that normativity really took its place at the heart of queer theory's conceptual apparatus for thinking about power and governmentality. For a discussion and critique of queer theory's anti-normativity, see Wiegman (2012).

15 See also Riley (2002) on the right to be lonely.

16 See Bell and Binnie (2000), Richardson (2005, 2018), Cover (2006), Patton (1998).

17 Arguments for same-sex marriage emanating from a range of different political positions include Pierce (1995), Sullivan (1997), Eskridge (1996), Signorile (1997) and Kitzinger and Wilkinson (2004). More ambivalent/historical discussions include Ferguson (2007), Calhoun (2008), Rydstrøm (2011) and Chauncey (2004).

18 For instance: Homocult (1992), the 2006 'Beyond Marriage' statement, https://mronline.org/2006/08/08/beyond-same-sex-marriage-a-new-strategic-vision-for-all-our-families-relationships/; Against Equality (2017), Conrad (2010), Polikoff (2008), Barker (2013) and Heckert (2010).

19 See Duggan (2012) on registering a domestic partnership in New York City with her ex-lover in the wake of 9/11.

20 See Nardi (1992, 1999), Weinstock and Rothblum (1996), Roseneil (2000a, 2000c, 2006b) and Roseneil and Budgeon (2004).
21 See Munson and Stelboum (1999), Rothblum (1999), Worth, Reid and McMillan (2002), Jamieson (2004), Ritchie and Barker (2006), Klesse (2006, 2007a, 2007b), Barker and Langdridge (2010), Adam (2010), Stacey (2004), Emens (2004), Robinson (2013), Heckert (2010).

3
Approach and core concepts

Our approach draws on both analytical and interpretivist traditions in social science: it seeks to identify and specify social processes and practices in action and to understand the stories, experiences and subjectivities of people in their everyday lives. Linking macro and micro, social and psychic, public and private, we draw on literatures, theoretical lenses and methods from feminist research, sociology, citizenship studies, comparative social policy analysis, sexuality studies and queer theory, and psychosocial studies. In particular, the book is concerned with macro-level processes of social change as worked through the state and with the specificity of lived biographical experience and personal meanings in particular times and places.

Specificities of time and place

We take history seriously, recognizing that the power of tradition and the legacies of the past that are carried forward in laws, cultures, habits and psyches mean that we are never only living in the current moment of citizenship.[1] We take social transformation equally seriously, identifying the importance of legal and policy changes and attending carefully to the inventiveness of everyday life, to the agentic and energetic remaking of life-worlds in which people engage, both with conscious intent to challenge the status quo and in less thought-out, pragmatic practices of bricolage.[2]

   We also believe that place matters. Even in the context of cultural globalization, economic neo-liberalization and over half a century of political 'Europeanization', the local and the national persist as powerful generators of attachment and shapers of opportunity. Whilst we acknowledge the danger of 'methodological nationalism' – of assuming 'that the nation, the state or the society is the natural social and political form of the modern world' (Wimmer and Glick Schiller, 2002: 301) – culture, including critical thought, 'remains related to places' (Chakrabarty, 2008 [2000]: xvi). It matters that our research project was led from the United Kingdom, that most of our team meetings took place in London and that our shared, working language is English.[3] The dominance of English in the global social sciences means that this book is fundamentally shaped by anglophone literatures, even as we read and conducted empirical research in the majority languages of three non-anglophone countries.[4] As a research team, our *collective* 'base-line' (Schneider, 1984: 268) academic culture is anglophone and, more specifically, British. But it is also important that our *individual* base-line cultures and languages, from which we engage in acts of comprehension and comparison, are diverse, including amongst them the four countries we have studied here. We have attempted to recognize, as postcolonial theorist Dipesh Chakrabarty (2008 [2000]) argues, that 'we think out of particular histories that are not always transparent to us' and that these histories are both spatially specific and structured through ideas about Europe and European modernity. Hence the foundational concepts through which we have thought this work – citizenship, intimacy, state, civil society, the individual, public and private, equality and human rights, for instance – 'bear the burden of European thought and history' (Chakrabarty, 2008 [2000]: 4). These concepts also have differing resonance and valence across a Europe which carries a history of division between east and west, north and south, democracy and totalitarianism, liberalism and social democracy, Catholicism and Protestantism, amongst many other social, cultural and political cleavages and conflicts. We understand 'Europe' to be a highly diverse and fractured space – a contested geopolitical territory that is being constantly reshaped from within and from without. Thus we maintain that the nation states of Europe remain crucial in understanding intimate life, but also that each nation-state is internally highly differentiated in terms of intimate practices and values, particularly as a consequence of histories of colonialism and im/migration.

The book ranges across Europe, encompassing lives led in very different parts of the continent, although always in capital cities. We seek to remain close to – to remember and foreground – the historical and geographical specificities of the stories told to us by our interviewees, rather than abstracting them from their contexts in order to make a generalized argument about 'Europe', the 'global north' or 'western societies'. We are aware that there is a very real problem of 'asymmetric ignorance' (Chakrabarty, 2008 [2000]: 28) about non-anglophone countries, which means that those without English as a native language tend to know far more about the English-speaking world than vice versa. It is also a reality that the literature is highly uneven: there is much more relevant research available on the UK than on the other countries.[5] Thus we seek actively to 'provincialize' the UK,[6] placing it alongside other diverse and complex multicultural nations, with differing relationships to colonialism, democracy and liberalism, and varying degrees of economic prosperity and in/equality.

Within our discussion of each of the four countries, we endeavour to de-centre the white, Christian, Anglo middle-class, heterosexual, conventionally coupled majorities that have overwhelmingly been the reference point for previous studies of both intimacy[7] and citizenship.[8] This is a study of those living at the edges of convention, a sample of people from the national majority ethnic populations and from two ethnic groups in each country that are minoritized/racialized: people from the Pakistani and Turkish-speaking communities in London,[9] from Roma and Turkish communities in Sofia, the Pakistani and Sami communities in Oslo, and from the Roma and the Cape Verdean communities in Lisbon.[10] We have attempted to take into account (some of) the diversity that characterizes our four case study countries, whilst also recognizing that the small number of people we interviewed cannot and should not stand as representatives of their communities of identity and belonging. We do not refrain from re-presenting stories of our interviewees that speak of negative and violent experiences from both within and beyond their own families and communities, and we recognize that intra-group oppression and practices of exclusion are characteristics of all social groups.

Our approach rests on a recognition of the social, cultural and political importance of boundaries and borders, both those that delineate nation states and ethnic groups and those that serve to categorize particular intimate practices and identities – as lesbian, gay, heterosexual, single, coupled, normal, abnormal, for instance. We draw from queer theory a deconstructionist, anti-categorical impulse to identify and understand boundary violations and challenges to rigid delineations of the intimate and sexual status quo.[11] This means that we both appreciate the different histories and realities that pertain to those living in particular countries and communities and with and through particular identity categories, and at the same time we resist their reification. Hence we do not engage in systematic comparisons between nations, members of social groups and intimate or sexual identity categories.

Intimate citizenship

This book comes out of the large, cross-national, multidisciplinary research project 'Gendered Citizenship in Multicultural Europe: the impact of contemporary women's movement' (FEMCIT).[12] FEMCIT set out to understand the difference that women's movements have made to the full inclusion, participation and recognition of women in political, social and cultural life across Europe in the period since the late 1960s. We started from a feminist position that asserts that citizenship as a normative ideal is about 'full membership of community', as citizenship theorist T. H. Marshall (1950) famously asserted. But we also posited that citizenship research must look beyond Marshall's classic delineation of three spheres of citizenship – civil, political and social – to encompass all arenas in which the three 'key elements of citizenship – rights and responsibilities, belonging and participation' (Lister et al., 2007: 1) – are exercised and contested. Thus, we developed an approach to citizenship that was both more expansive and wide-ranging and more intensively focused on the everyday, the experiential and the micro-sociological than classic theorizations of citizenship. Attentive to the scope and diversity of feminist struggles, we designed a research programme composed of six empirical studies, each addressing a dimension of citizenship: political, social, economic, religious/cultural, bodily and intimate. In common with a growing body of critical citizenship studies, these six strands of the FEMCIT research sought to move beyond narrow understandings of citizenship as formal membership of a nation state, to inquire more broadly into questions of belonging, recognition and participation in relation to state and civil society.[13] We were concerned both with the structures and regulations that constitute citizenship and, equally, with how citizenship is lived and practised.

The point of departure for our study is the claim that citizenship cannot be understood without attention to the sphere of intimacy. Historically and conventionally, the domain of close personal relationships that emerged in modernity with the individualization of personhood (Luhmann, 1986) has been regarded as the opposite of the public, civic world in which citizenship activities are seen to reside.[14] But informed by the radical rethinking of politics and personal life that was set in train by the second wave feminist argument that 'the personal is political', we start from a position that regards 'public' and 'private' as mutually entangled, with no clear, real or ultimate distinction to be drawn between them.[15] Whom we are close to and how we conduct our personal, sexual, familial and love relationship are always, unavoidably, political matters, the product of power relations and processes of social and cultural shaping.

From this perspective, citizenship always necessarily incorporates an intimate dimension. From one angle, when looking at formal membership of the nation state, familial practices of reproduction and birthright grant citizenship to the newborn (Stevens, 1999): the child born of a citizen of x becomes a citizen of x. Relatedly, as part of what political theorist Carole Pateman (1989) calls 'the fraternal social contract', nation states have historically assumed and promoted particular forms of intimate relationship and family form within which their citizens should be born and raised – 'national heterosexuality', in Lauren Berlant and Michael Warner's (1998) terminology. From a different, more sociological angle, Ken Plummer's conceptualization of intimate citizenship focuses on the less formal aspects of citizenship: the ability to be an active agent who exercises control and choice over 'all those matters linked to our most intimate desires, pleasures and ways of being in the world' (1995: 151).[16] He describes intimate citizenship as concerned with 'decisions around the *control (or not) over* one's body, feelings, relationships; *access (or not) to* representations, relationships, public spaces, etc; and *socially grounded choices (or not)* about identities, gender experiences, erotic experiences' (1995: 151; italics in the original).

Drawing these strands of thinking together, we suggest that the study of intimate citizenship should involve attention both to the everyday experiences of inclusion and exclusion, recognition and misrecognition, freedom and oppression, choice and constraint, autonomy, dependence and interdependence that are associated with particular intimate life practices, and to the laws and policies, social relations and cultures that regulate and shape these intimate life practices, and experiences. This means expanding the study of citizenship beyond the formal, the legal and the rational, to encompass the affective realm of love, attachment, desire and belonging.

With this conceptual backdrop, we set out to explore the relationship between these various elements of intimate citizenship in four countries. Using what is often referred to as a 'most different' comparative methodology (Przeworski and Teune, 1970), we chose the countries to provide a range of welfare regimes and histories of civil society–state relations: the UK, a late liberal welfare state; Bulgaria, a post-communist state; Norway, a social democratic welfare state; and Portugal, a post-dictatorship southern European welfare state. The research addressed three spheres of intimate citizenship – civil society action, state activity and everyday life – and in each of the countries we conducted:

- an historical study of the claims and demands of movements for gender and sexual equality and change in relation to intimate life (from 1968 to 2008);[17]
- a critical analysis of law and policy concerning intimate life (see Roseneil et al., 2008, 2013); and
- a biographical-narrative study of everyday experiences of intimate citizenship (see Roseneil et al., 2012).

Intimate citizenship regimes

Central to our analysis in this book is attention to the historically, spatially and culturally varying ways in which intimate life is organized, regulated and recognized. Our approach identifies the importance of real and meaningful differences in law, policy and culture at nation state level that impact upon intimate life, with national welfare regimes sanctioning different social relations of family and work.[18] This approach owes much to the comparative sensibility fostered by social policy analysts, particularly those who have theorized welfare regimes, gender regimes and citizenship regimes.[19] The importance of the idea of 'welfare regime' is that it proposes that the organization of welfare in any given country, and the historical compromises, political ideologies and institutional relationships between state, market and family that structure the provision of welfare, play a dynamic role in the construction of intimate relationships. Particularly salient to our concerns here is the extent to which welfare regimes facilitate the possibility of living outside the couple-form.[20] The book is also fundamentally dependent upon the critical problematics of feminism, sexuality studies and queer theory, which have historicized sexuality and intimate relations, their gendered power relations and normativities, and that have traced the relationship between (hetero)sexuality and nation.[21] Existing literature on welfare regimes, mainstream and feminist, has paid scant attention to issues of sexuality or same-sex relationships, being largely, and unreflexively, concerned with the heterosexual family and the relationship between men, women, the state and the market, in the work of hetero-sexual social reproduction (Roseneil et al., 2013).

We use the notion of *intimate citizenship regime* (Roseneil, 2010) to refer to the particular constellation of legal, social and cultural conditions of intimate citizenship that prevail in a particular nation state, at a particular time. We are building here on Jane Jenson's (2007) concept of citizenship regime, which she sees as a 'set of norms and practices in motion' (2007: 53) and specifically as 'the institutional arrangements, rules and understandings that guide and shape concurrent policy decisions and expenditures of states, problem definitions by states and citizens, and claims-making by citizens' (2007: 55).[22] Thus, an intimate citizenship regime might be thought of as *a set of norms and practices related to intimate life, in motion*. These norms and practices regulate and construct closeness between people, laying down the framework and conditions within which personal relationships take place. Operating largely through normative power, contemporary intimate citizenship regimes work through popular consent, or hegemony, in Antonio Gramsci's terms (1971), by shaping our innermost desires and life expectations, rather than by force, although sanctions, coercion and their threat are never completely absent. Historically contingent, intimate citizenship regimes develop over time in relation to already existing law and policy, demonstrating considerable 'path dependence'.[23] But they are also always in motion, responding to the civil society activism and claim-making of social movements and the decisions of political actors, and changing in the context of the longue durée of cultural transformation and processes of modernization, democratization and individualization. New directions are opened up for intimate citizenship regimes at critical historical junctures – such as the end of a period of dictatorship or totalitarian rule, or accession to the European Union.

Our cross-national analysis of how intimate citizenship law and policy have changed in the UK, Bulgaria, Norway and Portugal, particu-larly in the wake of challenges from women's and lesbian and gay movements, suggests that intimate citizenship regimes differ along a number of dimensions: they can be more or less patriarchal or gender-equal; more or less familial or individualized; more or less heteronor-mative or sexuality-equal. During the past 50 years, the overarching direction of social change has been largely from the former to the latter, although the situation in post-communist Bulgaria in relation to gender and sexual equality is complex. More specifically, we found that, despite their very different political histories and legal and welfare systems, all four states have historically operated with highly constrained gendered and heteronormative assumptions about the form and nature of legitimate intimate relationships, intervening in a wide range of ways to define the parameters of their citizens' intimate lives. We found that the legal and policy privileging of marriage as the 'gold standard' intimate relationship has declined significantly in recent years, and recognition of diversity in intimate life has increased. Most notably, there has been a remarkable shift – one that might even be called a revolution – in law and policy in relation to same-sex sexuality and relationships (although this is uneven across the four countries), as lesbians and gay men are increasingly included within the 'charmed circle' (Rubin, 1993 [1984]) of intimate citizenship, with a radical shift towards a new European norm of 'homotolerance' and a process of 'homonormalization' (Roseneil et al., 2012).[24] However, cohabiting, procreative coupledom remains the privileged and normative form of intimate life: the good and proper intimate citizen is no longer necessarily married or heterosexual, but they are living in a long-term, stable, sexually exclusive, co-residential partnership.

Norms and normativity

We did not embark on our research on intimate citizenship with an intention to focus on the couple-norm, or indeed with the concept in our lexicon. Whilst we were well versed in the Foucauldian-inspired critique of normativity that has been fundamental to queer theory,[25] our initial concerns were framed less by a post-structuralist interest in disciplinary society and its modes of governmentality,[26] and more by an agentically and sociologically oriented approach to the study of social movements and contemporary forms of citizenship. We wished to understand the practice and lived experience of intimate citizenship and the extent to which these have been influenced by the interventions of social movements. Indeed, the legacy of sociology's historic attachment to both an 'oversocialized' conception of personhood and an 'overintegrated' view of society (Wrong, 1961), in both of which the unconflicted internalization of norms is key, made some of us sceptical about the overweening emphasis placed on norms and normativity in queer theory.[27] The concept of 'norm', so central to queer theory, had fallen firmly out of fashion in sociology due to its tarnished association with Parsonian structural functionalism.[28] As Andrew Sayer (2011: 155–6) has pointedly noted, 'reductionist sociological descriptions of people as norm-fulfilling have a bland, demeaning and alienated character'.

However, the analysis that we carried out of intimate citizenship law and policy, and our in-depth biographical-narrative interviews with people living outside the conventional couple-form, impressed upon us the importance of norms and normativity within the current intimate citizenship regimes that we were studying. As we met together regularly to discuss the findings of our investigations into the history and current state of law and policy governing intimate life, and as we proceeded through the collective process of analysing our interviews (see Part V, the Methodological appendix), we were struck, over and over again, by how certain principles of 'oughtness' and valorization and 'the play of oppositions between the normal and the abnormal or pathological' (Ewald, 1990: 140) – what might best be described as norms – were working to shape the conditions of intimate citizenship in each of our case study countries,[29] defining membership and belonging and simultaneously ensuring exclusion and marginalization.

The four core norms of intimate citizenship

As our analysis proceeded, we came to understand intimate citizenship regimes as operating as normative systems. Anthropologist David Schneider describes a normative system as consisting of 'the rules and regulations which an actor should follow if his behaviour is to be accepted by his community or his society as proper' (2004: 261).[30] We were able to distinguish four core norms of intimate citizenship at work across the countries we were studying and hence as central to their intimate citizenship regimes: the gender-norm, the hetero-norm, the procreative-norm and the couple-norm. Each of these has historically been seen, in both lay and scientific understandings, as universal, as given by nature rather than as culturally constructed by human practice as a norm.

Firstly, the gender-norm – the norm of differentiation, complementarity and hierarchy between men and women – was clearly apparent. This is the norm of intimate citizenship that divides humanity into two genders, set in a hierarchical and necessarily interdependent binary relationship with each other, and that organizes legal and social membership and belonging on the basis of adherence to recognizable performances and practices of normative gender. Historically, the gender-norm has operated as a patriarchal gender-norm, with masculinity and men clearly privileged over and dominating of femininity and women. Secondly, we found the hetero-norm sharply in evidence in the law and policy that we analysed and in the life stories of the people we interviewed.[31] The hetero-norm deems forms of intimate life structured around 'opposite-sex' relationships to be natural, necessary and recognizable, and has been identified by queer theory as central to modern western societies. Thirdly, we identified what we have called the procreative-norm – the assumption, expectation and cultural demand that biological procreation should sit at the heart of the social formation, and that intimate relationships, sexuality and the wider organization of the social should be driven by and structured around a naturalized notion of a primary, fundamental, procreative imperative.[32] And, finally, the couple-norm, our focus in this book, which mandates that the intimate/sexual dyad is the basic unit of social life, impressed upon us its potency and its ubitquity.[33] Whilst analytically distinguishable, these norms are powerfully entangled with each other – so that, for instance, the gender-norm of differentiation, complementarity and hierarchy suffuses and gives meaning to the hetero-norm, whilst the couple-norm is imbued with expectations of heterosexuality and procreation, and so on. Together, overlaid and interwoven, these norms are a fundamental part of the tapestry of our intimate imaginaries.

Our research found these norms to be constitutive as well as regulative of intimate life,[34] actively shaping intimate desires, possibilities and practices. They operate in multiple ways: politically, via state power – through legal prohibition and regulation, and administratively, through social and public policy; socially – through clusters of injunctions and expectations in social institutions, practices and everyday relationships between family, friends, neighbours, colleagues and wider communal connections; and through cultural expectations, representations and idealizations of the right, the good and the desirable.[35] As François Ewald suggests of norms in general, these norms are not the product of any single body or group; they are 'created by the collectivity without being willed by anyone in particular', and they operate more horizontally than vertically, with no individual holding 'the power to declare […] or establish [them]' (Ewald, 1990: 155). We identified how intimate citizenship norms are enforced by a range of social sanctions, such as marginalization and ostracism by people and groups who matter, and positive reinforcers, such as celebration, gift-giving and social inclusion. These sanctions and reinforcers serve to imbue conforming intimate practices with a 'sense of rightness' (Berlant and Warner, 1998) and make non-conforming intimate practices personally risky and sometimes even dangerous.[36] But importantly, intimate citizenship norms do not just operate upon us, from outside: they are internalized and become part of who we are.[37] Our interview material led us to a psychosocial understanding that these norms are woven into subjectivities, forming what, drawing on the work of Lynne Layton (2002), we might call the 'normative unconscious',[38] so that non-conformity can be productive of shame, guilt and anxiety – emotions that tend to be experienced as internal sanctions, potentially generating psychological distress and inner conflict.[39]

However, because no intimate citizenship regime is entirely hegemonic, and because subjectivity and desire are never entirely stable and without conflict, there is always resistance to dominant norms; counter-normative agency is always pressing against the established order.[40] Norms are far from contiguous with behaviour, and we found that intimate citizenship norms are anything but static and absolute in their power. We came to see them as tenacious, but also as contingent. As Judith Butler emphasizes in her psychoanalytically informed theorization of sexual and gender norms, norms never quite succeed in 'totaliz[ing] the social field' (1993: 191) or completely defining identity or desire.[41] They are always open to change, constantly in movement and subject to challenge, negotiation and reworking in everyday life. On the one hand, there are the explicit, reflexively self-aware, non-conformist practices and political challenges of individuals, social movements and other collective actors who are seeking to modify or change the norms; this is a central element of the intimate reflexivity and increased exercise of agency and choice in matters of love and sexuality that Anthony Giddens (1992) identifies as characteristic of late modernity. On the other hand, there are implicit, non-reflexively self-aware departures from normative expectations by individuals and groups, who might seek to hide their aberrant behaviour, or who, within particular communal, ethnic or local contexts, might creatively establish their own norms of intimacy and personal life which run against mainstream norms, as they find themselves, for a range of reasons, unable or unwilling to live according to the norms that characterize the currently/locally prevailing intimate citizenship regime. Deviation from dominant intimate citizenship norms is widespread, and feelings of failure and emotional distress consequent on not living up to cultural ideals torment many. As psychoanalysis suggests, conflict between adherence and rebellion structures psychic life for everyone, not only for those who are conscious of their struggles with normativity, for as these norms are woven into the fabric of subjectivity, they can provoke first an itch, then deeper discomfort, and ultimately, resistance and rebellion, as they are tugged at, tweaked, twisted and remade. Many individuals in our study, each with their own singular history of love, desire and attachment, came up against collectively established norms and often felt profoundly out of kilter, isolated, even exiled from their social group. Moreover, our research found that democratic societies are rarely entirely unified and consistent in how they operationalize these norms.[42] Spaces can be found and opened up for the reworking of intimate citizenship norms within, and sometimes at the edges of, state institutions, as well as in activist milieux, and spaces of 'voluntary', civic engagement, and in the realm of commercial exchange.[43]

All this means that the strength and salience of these norms vary significantly over time and place and between different individuals and social groups, and that they are backed up by differing degrees of moral obligation and 'oughtness'. At one end of the continuum there are systematically formulated, mandatory versions of the norms. Then there are preferential versions, enacted via informal sanctions of communal inclusion/exclusion, through gossip, censure and social ostracism. And at the other end of the continuum, there are permissive versions, backed by positive reward, particularly in the form of esteem and praise.[44]

Relating to and researching the couple-norm

The rootedness of this book in the lives and stories of the people we interviewed, and our commitment to understanding their realities, means that we seek to approach our subject matter with 'humane sympathy' (Abbott, 2007: 96). There is a danger, identified by Biddy Martin (1996) and Robyn Wiegman (2012), that a relentless anti-normativity, such as that sometimes embraced within queer theory, can produce a somewhat superior, even contemptuous, hypercritical gaze that 'fears ordinariness' (Martin, 1996) and 'names and shames' 'those normalities that are inhabited, desired and pursued within gay, lesbian, trans and queer discourses as well as outside them' (Wiegman, 2012: 334), whilst idealizing practices that are regarded as transgressive of dominant norms. Although this book conceptually foregrounds normativity, arguing that the couple-norm is central to regimes of intimate citizenship, we do not wish to be read as thereby condemning or criticizing our interviewees, whose lives we describe as shaped by this norm. We are not 'against' couples or being part of a couple, just as we are not 'against' gender, heterosexuality or procreation, the other normativities that structure intimate citizenship regimes. We *all* (the authors included) live our lives in relation to the couple-norm and the possibilities of cultural recognition, social membership and belonging, intimacy and security it offers. No one can exist entirely outside the framing power of the couple-norm, or beyond its lure, and hence our approach here is to seek not to align moral worth or cultural kudos with either active or implicit resistance or embrace of couple-normativity.[45] Like Wiegman and Wilson (2015), we are sceptical of the idea that norms have a readily identifiable outside, and we consider norms to be 'more capacious' and 'intricate' in their dynamics than might sometimes be suggested in anti-normative critique. Our approach emphasizes the 'motility and relationality' (Wiegman and Wilson, 2015) of norms and recognizes that 'wherever there is life there are norms' (Canguilhem, 1994: 351).

The couple-norm in operation

In the next two parts of the book, we present our understanding and analysis of the operation of the couple-norm in four European countries. Part II examines the historical institutionalization of the couple-norm as part of the national intimate citizenship regimes of the United Kingdom, Bulgaria, Norway and Portugal. Part III explores how people living in the capital cities of these countries experience the couple-norm in their intimate lives in the early years of the twenty-first century. We discuss how the couple-norm operates through state power, via law and policy, in social relationships and interactions, particularly within the social groups that matter to people, their primary reference groups (families, friendship groups and communities of identity and belonging) and, more diffusely, through cultural expectations and injunctions, and the pressure and stigma they produce. We show how there has been a general diminution in the legal mandating and policy support of particular versions of the couple-form (married and heterosexual) over recent decades, but how the social enforcement and cultural promotion of the couple-form, as the right and desirable way to live, are more impactful than legal sanctions.[46] The presentation of case studies from amongst our interviewees illustrates how the couple-norm is experienced from 'within' – as internal pressure to find and keep a partner in order to achieve 'normal', respectable adulthood – and from 'without' – as social and cultural pressure exerted by people who matter (family, friends, wider social networks) and by society more diffusely, to live within the couple-form in order to achieve social recognition and validation.

The couple-norm has many facets. At its core is the construction of coupledom as the normal, natural and superior state of being an adult. Around this core is a complexly composed array of – sometimes contradictory – value-laden expectations and injunctions about the ideal couple-form and the right and proper way to be in a couple. Rather than distinguishing definitively between the social and cultural pressure exerted through and by *expectations* that mould and shape, and the stronger, more rigid, law-like control of *injunctions* that demand and insist, we coin the notion of *expectation↔injunction* to capture the continuum on which the constituent components of the couple-norm exist. Binding together 'expectation' and 'injunction', whilst holding in mind the relationship but also the difference between the two terms, the bi-directional arrow seeks to highlight, through its continually jarring presence, the complex interplay between the more subtle shaping and the more explicit regulation of intimate life.

Our research identified a number of powerful expectation↔injunctions about the couple: firstly, that the couple should be subject to family approval, that it should be a family matter – of concern and interest to wider kin, not just to the couple itself;[47] secondly, that the couple should be alike in ways that pertain to culture, social status and identity (homogamous/endogamous), particularly regarding ethnicity, religion and age;[48] thirdly, that the couple should be married (or en route to marriage) and life-long; fourthly, that the couple should be based (at least initially) on romantic love; fifthly, that the couple should be sexually intimate and sexually exclusive (see van Hoof, 2017); and sixthly, that the couple should be the subject of dedicated work, to maintain and improve its functioning.

These expectation↔injunctions about the normative couple-form vary over time and place, and between social groups, and do not all apply at any one time to everyone. For instance, the traditional *injunction* to marriage, that strongly privileged the heterosexual married couple-form, has diminished very significantly over recent decades and might now be regarded more as a weaker *expectation* in many, although certainly not all, contexts. The expectation↔injunction that the couple should be based on romantic love is currently culturally hegemonic in western and European societies, but amongst communities of ethnic belonging with strongly collectivist orientations, marriage, and thus the couple relationship, is often seen as being about building and extending the family. Romantic love is not necessarily seen as a starting point or as a sensible base for such a union.[49] The interests of the family are often regarded as coming before the interests of the individual, and parents and the rest of the family are an integral part of the marriage from its first conceptualization, including often 'arranging it'.[50]

The expectation↔injunctions surrounding the couple-form and how it is lived are fundamentally entangled with other norms of intimate citizenship – the gender-norm, the hetero-norm and the procreative-norm. They often have different salience and potency for men and women, for heterosexuals, lesbians, gay men and bisexuals, and at different times in people's lives, particularly in relation to the idea of the reproductive 'biological clock', youth and ageing.[51] They tend to become visible when they are challenged in some way, or when there is tension or conflict between contradictory expectation↔injunctions, such as between those that see the couple-form as a space of romance and privacy, and those that regard it as a parental/family matter, of interest and concern to wider kin.[52] Moreover, these expectation↔injunctions continue to prevail even though they are far from fully realized in everyday life, as seen, for instance, in the failure of the injunction to monogamy to eradicate sexual 'infidelity'.

In Part II, we discuss how the couple-norm has come to be such a salient feature of contemporary intimate citizenship regimes, by exploring the history of its institutionalization, and the changes that have taken place in its specification in the law and policy of our four case study countries.

Notes

1 Chakrabarty's (2008 [2000]: 243) identification of the 'problem of the temporal heterogeneity of the "now"', of 'the plurality that inheres in the "now"', is apposite.
2 Duncan (2011) develops an argument about contemporary personal life as the outcome of a process of non-reflexive, pragmatic and habitual bricolage. See also Carter and Duncan (2018).
3 It is for this reason that we start with the UK in our discussion of both intimate citizenship regimes (Part II) and case studies of the couple-norm in action (Part III).
4 The five of us as a research team were born and brought up in five different countries (the UK, Italy, Norway, Portugal and Bulgaria).
5 Herzog (2011) makes a similar point about literature on sexuality in Europe, suggesting that Portugal and Norway are amongst the countries that are under-researched. She does not mention Bulgaria.
6 Here we echo Chakrabarty's (2008 [2000]) efforts to 'provincialize Europe', which he is clear does not mean rejecting or discarding English language perspectives 'to which one largely owes one's intellectual existence' (16).
7 The nadir of research on intimate life in which generalization was made from a study of the white Anglo middle class was perhaps Schneider's (1968) *American Kinship*.
8 Citizenship is undoubtedly a concept with its roots in the European Enlightenment with 'an unavoidable – and in a sense indispensable – universal and secular vision of the human' (Chakrabarty, 2008 [2000]: 4).

9   It is important to note that these and other minoritized groups are far from internally homogeneous and are necessarily something of a construction of the research. 'British Pakistani', for instance, is an ambiguous category (Shaw, 1988, 2000), and the Turkish-speaking community in London includes people with roots in Turkey and Cyprus, and who identify as Kurdish (Atay, 2010).

10 Our interviewees were all living in the capital cities of their countries, although many of them had moved there from other places, and whilst we do not systematically focus on the capital city contexts within they are living, they do undoubtedly shape their experiences. These are urban lives, lived in the most cosmopolitan and diverse parts of the four countries.

11 See foundational contributions to queer theory's deconstruction of sexual identity categories: Fuss (1991) on the necessity of questioning the stability of the heterosexual–homosexual binary and its construction 'on the foundation of another related opposition: the couple "inside" and "outside"'; Butler on identity categories as 'instruments of regulatory regimes, whether as the normalizing categories of oppressive structures or as the rallying points for a liberatory contestation of that very oppression' (1991: 13–14); and Berlant and Warner's (1998: 316) critique of how the category of heterosexuality 'consolidates as a sexuality widely differing practices, norms and institutions'.

12 FEMCIT was an Integrated Project, funded by the European Union Framework 6 initiative (2007–11), under the thematic priority 'citizens and governance' (project number: 028746). For more information about FEMCIT see Halsaa, Roseneil and Sümer (2011, 2012) and Roseneil et al. (2012).

13 Feminist work on citizenship that inspired and/or paralleled the FEMCIT approach includes Werbner and Yuval-Davis (1999), Somers (2008), Orloff (1993, 1996), Lister (1989, 1997), Hall and Williamson (1999), Siim (2000) and Yuval-Davis (2008).

14 Luhmann's (1986) theorization of intimacy suggests that the radical societal differentiation that characterizes modernity means that individual persons need to have affirmation 'at the level of their respective personality systems' from a 'close world' (15–16).

15 Hanisch, the author of the women's liberation movement paper 'The Personal is Political' (1970), which is the first time the slogan appeared in print, states on her website that the title was given to the paper by editors Firestone and Koedt. See http://www.carolhanisch.org/CHwritings/PIP.html (accessed 20 September 2020).

16 The notion of 'intimate citizenship' has a broader referent than that of 'sexual citizenship' (Evans, 1993; Weeks, 1998; Bell and Binnie, 2000; Richardson, 2000).

17 We use the phrase 'movements for gender and sexual equality and change' to encompass women's movements, feminist movements and lesbian and gay movements/LGBT movements, both in their autonomous formations and as elements within other movements, political parties and non-governmental organizations. For brevity, we also refer to these movements as women's and/or lesbian and gay movements, as appropriate (see Roseneil et al., 2010, 2011). Transgender politics and identities were not a major focus of the research, although we did review the history of gender recognition legislation in each country as part of our critical analysis of law and policy. Recognizing both our focus on lesbian and gay politics and identities, and that of the movements we were studying during the period 1968–2008, we tend to refer to 'lesbian and gay movements' unless other terminology, such as LGBT, or LGBTQI+, for example, was used by the movement itself, or by a cited author, commentator or individual. We recognize that terminology and identities are in flux, and we have sought, as much as possible, to stay close to the self-identifications of the individual and collective actors at the time of the research. We have, therefore, not sought to impose uniformity across the book through the adoption of currently favoured (but often also contested) terminology.

18 On national welfare regimes, family and work, see Lewis (1992), Sainsbury (1994, 1996), Daly (2000), Daly and Rake (2003), Knijn and Komter (2004) and Saraceno (2014).

19 'Regime thinking' in comparative social science owes its prevalence to the influence of Esping-Andersen's (1990) typology of social democratic, conservative and liberal welfare regimes through which he defined ideal typical relations between state and economy (politics and markets). Esping-Andersen's work spawned a veritable industry of regime analysis and was extended by feminist critics to bring into play relations between state, economy and family. Key regime theorists include: on welfare regimes, Esping-Andersen

(1990) and Schierup, Hansen and Castles (2006); on gender systems, Duncan (1995), and on gender regimes, Pascall and Lewis (2004) and Walby (2004); and on citizenship regimes, Jenson and Phillips (1996).

20   This point is made by a number of feminist social policy analysts, including Orloff (1993), O'Connor (1993) and Lister (1997). Lister specifies the need for 'a socially acceptable standard of living, independently of family relationships, either through paid work or social security provisions' (1997: 173), echoing early twentieth-century feminist claims.

21   On the historicity of sexuality see Smith-Rosenberg (1975), Faderman (1985), Foucault (1978), Weeks (1977, 1985, 1991, 2012 [1981]); Traub (1994), Sedgwick (1985), Bray (1982), Goldberg (1992), Halperin (1998) and Berlant and Warner (1998).

22   However, the notion of intimate citizenship poses a challenge to Jenson's understanding of citizenship, which differentiates between the spaces of 'citizenship', 'markets' and 'families'.

23   The notion of path dependence is widely used in historical sociology to refer to 'historical sequences in which contingent events set into motion institutional patterns or event chains that have deterministic properties' (Mahoney, 2000: 507).

24   The intimate citizenship recognition of trans and non-binary people remains highly contested across Europe. See, for example, Hines and Santos (2018), Kuhar, Monro and Takács (2018) and Monro and Van de Ros (2018).

25   It is in the work of Foucault (1978) that the emphasis on norms and normativity that has come to define queer theory originates, with Butler serving as his primary mediator and reinterpreter (1990, 1993, 1997, 2004). On anti-normativity in queer studies, see Hall and Jagose (2012), Wiegman (2012) and Wiegman and Wilson (2015). Wiegman (2012: 305) discusses the move from queer theory to queer studies, which she regards as 'an institutionalized project of antinormativity'.

26   Foucault (1991 [1977], 1978) argues that the norm emerged, in the nineteenth century, as a means of social regulation, replacing the negative restraints of the juridical system of law with more positive controls of normalization: 'The judges of normality are present everywhere. We are in the society of the teacher-judge, the doctor-judge, the educator-judge, the "social worker"-judge; it is on them that the universal reign of the normative is based; and each individual, wherever he may find himself, subjects to it his body, his gestures, his behaviour, his attitudes, his achievements' (1991 [1977]: 304). An opposing view of norms is offered by sociologist Finley Scott (1971), who suggests that there has been an increase in the proportion of norms that are codified in law in modern societies.

27   Wrong's (1961) excoriating critique of 'the oversocialized conception of man in modern sociology', which set dominant trends in (American) sociology against the more complex perspective on socialization and internalization offered by Freud, was important in turning the tide against Durkheimian (2014 [1893])/Parsonian (1951) structural functionalism and approaches which regarded people basically as passive norm-followers. Wrong argued for the importance of attention to inner conflict, as well as to the 'desire for material and sensory satisfactions' (1961: 190) and for power, and for a dialectical understanding of the relationship between 'conformity and rebellion, social norms and their violation, man and social order' (1961: 191). In subsequent decades, the concept of norm went out of fashion in sociology with the emergence of critical/Marxist sociology's emphasis on struggle and social conflict, interpretivist and interactionist emphases on knowledgeable actors and their interpretation of norms in concrete action situations, and a 'postmodern' emphasis on the complexity, diversity and fluidity of meanings and values. It is striking that discussions about norms and normativity in queer studies have taken place with seemingly no recognition of debates about the concepts in sociology and coincide with a rise in interest in norms amongst rational choice and game theorists in economics, political science and law.

28   One of the most significant (functionalist) sociological theorists of norms is Finley Scott (1971), who sees norms as 'patterns of sanctions' that function to ensure 'species viability'.

29   See Ewald on changing understandings of the norm over the past two centuries, in particular the move from 'norm' as simply another word for rule, to 'norm' referring to a particular variety of rules, a way of producing them and a principle of valorization (1990: 140).

30   Schneider, quite rightly, goes on to say: 'They [normative systems] should on no account be confused with patterns of behaviour which people actually perform. It is the rule "though shalt not steal" that is the norm, not the fact that many people do not steal; it is the rule

that a middle class father should earn the money to support his family, not the fact that many actually do' (2004: 261).

31   On the hetero-norm see Roseneil et al. (2012).

32   On the procreative-norm see Roseneil et al. (2016). We choose this term rather than 'repronormativity', as used, for example, by Collins, Leib and Markel (2008), in recognition of the feminist claim that the 'reproduction' of life extends far beyond the conceiving and bearing of children, which is the focus of what we call the procreative-norm.

33   We prefer the broader term 'couple-norm', which we have formulated through this body of research, to the concept of 'mononormativity' (Pieper and Bauer, 2006; Wilkinson, 2010), which focuses attention on one facet of the couple-norm – the injunction of monogamy. The notion of 'compulsory coupledom' (Wilkinson, 2012), which echoes Rich's (1980) concept of 'compulsory heterosexuality', overstates its case: coupledom is normative but certainly not systematically compulsory in most western contexts, and it is indeed possible to live, well and happily, outside the couple-form.

34   In this we are in line with both classical sociological (Durkheimian and Parsonian) and Freudian approaches to social norms (Wrong, 1961).

35   Durkheim (2014 [1893]) distinguished between custom and law as the two principal normative structures that define a way of life.

36   Emphasizing the role of social sanctions and positive reinforcers in upholding norms is in contrast with Parsons's focus on the internalization of norms in early childhood.

37   On the internalization of norms from a sociological perspective, see Finley Scott: 'A person "internalizes" or learns a norm to the extent that (other things being equal) he conforms to it at a spatial or temporal remove from sanctions. He learns it through sanctions applied by his social environment. Once the norm is learned, the emergence of deviant behaviour following termination of sanctions is slow. But the learning of norms is never complete and always involves expectations that sanctions will be applied. Thus even when norms are thoroughly learned, when moral commitment is strong and a sense of obligation is reported as keenly felt, the maintenance of both conscience and conformity depends on the exercise of sanctions' (1971: xiii).

38   On the operation of norms as psychic phenomena see Butler, who argues that they both restrict and produce desire, 'govern the formation of the subject and circumscribe the domain of liveable sociality', and yet are also 'vulnerable to both psychic and historical change' (1997: 21).

39   In holding that both internal and external sanctions are vital in the operation of norms, we are rejecting the relevance of any straightforward distinction between shame and guilt societies/cultures (Benedict, 1946).

40   Our emphasis on counter-normative agency poses an implicit and 'gentle critique' (Clarke et al., 2014) of the Foucauldian concept of governmentality. Like Clarke et al. we 'find ourselves working with a somewhat unfinished hybrid of Gramscian and Foucauldian views of power' (2014: 31), unable to accept that the subjects of governmentality 'come as and when summoned' (2014: 153) and holding that they are 'more troublesome' than Foucault tends to suggest. This is particularly so in the realm of sexuality and desire.

41   We echo Rose's (1987) and Butler's (1993, 1997, 2004) psychoanalytic understanding of the ways in which the unconscious thwarts norms, so that desire and sexuality are never entirely contained or determined by norms, which means that 'norms do not exercise a final or fatalistic control, at least, not always' (Butler, 2004: 15).

42   As Pringle and Watson (1992) argue, 'the state' is a contested space, in which political struggles play out and where interests, including feminist interests, may be productively mobilized. Clarke et al. (2014) suggest that states are 'ensembles', complex, composite, differentiated 'ensembles', shaped by contradictory practices and contested by political forces.

43   The increasing economic power of single women and lesbian and gay individuals and couples ('the pink pound' in the UK) has leveraged considerable change in, for instance, the provision and marketing of goods and services. For critical analyses of this, see Badgett (1997, 2003), Chasin (2001), Gardyn (2001), Sender (2004), Guidotto (2006) and DePaulo (2011).

44   We draw here on Gross, Manson and McEachern (1958) on the varying intensity of norms.

45 Anthropologist Daniel Miller (2007) makes a powerful argument for the importance of attending both to the flexibility and diversity of contemporary relationships at an experiential level and also to the formal aspects of kinship – 'the retained importance of normative formal expectations'. As he argues, 'evidence for complexity and diversity does not preclude an equal and abiding emphasis upon normativity and formal ideals' (no page number).

46 In 1971 Finley Scott argued that punishment by stigmatization and the loss of conventional middle-class status is more important for 'strong norms, such as those that prohibit fraud, grand larceny, homosexuality, child molestation and so forth: their violation not only entails legal sanctions but also the loss of the deviant's employment and his public reputation' (171). Indeed, he suggested that the informal sanctions are much stronger than the formal legal ones (199). He also argued that the societal threat to withdraw valuable status has less power over those 'who have no status to lose'.

47 As Shaw explains in relation to South Asians in the UK, 'obligations to one's immediate and more extended family have priority over personal self-interest', and hence 'decisions about marriage are a matter of corporate not individual concern' (2001: 325).

48 It is important to note that cross-class relationships did not emerge as a significant issue amongst our interviewees. We might speculate that these remain considerably less common than other mixed relationships. On age-gap relationships, see Lehmiller and Agnew (2008).

49 Collectivism 'pertains to societies in which people from birth onwards are integrated into strong, cohesive in-groups, which throughout people's lifetime continue to protect them in exchange for unquestioning loyalty', while 'individualism pertains to societies in which the ties between individuals are loose; everyone is expected to look after himself or herself and his or her immediate family' (Hofstede, 1991: 51).

50 See, for example, Bradby (1999), Bredal (2006), Hall (1995), Shaw (1988, 2000, 2001).

51 Roth's (1963) work on temporal norms and benchmarks – collective ideas about when certain events are expected to occur – is important here. See also Lahad (2017) on singlehood and waiting.

52 For instance, Shaw (2001) discusses how the South Asian tradition of arranged marriage means that 'obligations to one's immediate and more extended family have priority over personal self-interest', whereas in 'contemporary western ideology, by contrast, marriage is an expression of a fundamental liberty, the individual's right to choose a partner (even though choice is in practice constrained by such factors as social class, ethnic group, and parental interests' (2001: 325). 'Decisions about marriage are a matter of corporate not individual concern' (2001: 325).

PART II

Couple-normativity in European intimate citizenship regimes

4

Overview of couple-normativity in European intimate citizenship regimes

Across Europe, the couple-norm is a fundamental element of contemporary intimate citizenship regimes. One particular way of being and relating – the couple-form – is institutionalized and valorized, systematically expected, promoted and supported by nation states, in preference to non-coupled ways of living. Furthermore, particular versions of the couple-form are institutionalized and valorized, systematically expected, promoted and supported by nation states, in preference to other ways of living the couple-form. Living outside the couple-form, or in non-normative couple-forms, is made harder, economically, legally and socially, by the laws and policies of states. In Part II of the book, we discuss how couple-normativity operates within law and policy in each of our four case study countries. This necessarily means exploring the gendered regulation of family, sexuality and personal life more broadly, as it is with changes in these that the couple-norm emerges as a distinct element of the normative framework of intimate citizenship.

Whilst the history of couple-normativity in each country is unique, with different periodizations, processes and moments of transformation, there are some broad trends across European societies. Alongside the gradual demographic and cultural de-solidification of 'the family' as a patriarchal, heterosexual formation, the direct promotion and protection of the traditional family as an institution by law and policy has diminished, and increasingly the often differing needs and desires of individuals within the family and, to a lesser extent, beyond the family, are recognized. Indeed, there has been a 'de-patriarchalization' (Therborn, 2004) of intimate citizenship regimes throughout the twentieth century. At different times in different places, family law has moved towards supporting gender equality, overturning the historic civil incapacity of wives, liberalizing divorce laws and affirming women's autonomy and personhood within marriage (Gautier, 2005; Sutherland, 2012). Legal systems have moved away from overt discrimination against women (particularly married women) and towards supporting the equalization of life conditions for women.

These changes have been core demands of women's movements, and they have been realized as part of wider processes of democratization in western Europe, and began under communism in eastern Europe. This process has been variously supported, influenced and even compelled by the European Union, the Council of Europe and the emergent global human rights regime. Particularly important in this was the adoption, in 2000, of the European Union Charter of Fundamental Rights,[1] a rhetorically and politically significant statement about the meaning and reach of human rights within the Union, which became legally binding on member states with the Lisbon Treaty of 2007, impacting therefore on the three EU member states that were part of our study – the United Kingdom, Bulgaria and Portugal. Also significant was the Council of Europe's 2011 Istanbul Convention on preventing and combating violence against women and domestic violence. This established legally binding standards to protect women from violence, with the aims of contributing to the elimination of all forms of discrimination against women and promoting substantive equality between women and men.[2] The Convention has been signed by 46 countries, including all four of our case study countries, although neither the UK nor Bulgaria has ratified it. In the UK, cuts in government spending on domestic violence services under Conservative 'austerity politics' have contributed to the country's lack of readiness to ratify, whereas in Bulgaria opposition has been driven by both nationalist and Socialist Party politicians and by the Orthodox Church, critical of 'gender ideology', who have regarded the Convention as boding the introduction of same-sex marriage and 'third sex' recognition. Indeed, in 2018, the Constitutional Court of Bulgaria ruled that the Istanbul Convention contravenes the Bulgarian Constitution.[3]

Recent decades have also seen significant tendencies towards the de-familialization (Lister, 1994; Orloff, 2009) of welfare policy.[4] In the context of women's increased labour force participation and the demands of movements for gender and sexual equality and change, welfare states have increasingly, although unevenly, shifted from familial to more individualized policies that support and, in some cases demand, the labour market engagement of individuals qua individuals, rather than primarily targeting families. This implies the decline of state support for the male breadwinner–female homemaker couple-form in countries where this had been prevalent, and the emergence of a clear expectation of women's economic activity after childbearing. Heterosexual marriage, whilst still the 'gold standard' couple-form in terms of social status, in many countries is no longer the only form of intimate relationship receiving state recognition, leading to the suggestion that marriage has been de-institutionalized (Cherlin, 2004).

Over the past five decades, there have also been profound liberalizing changes in law and policy that have transformed norms about same-sex sexualities across Europe.[5] Same-sex sexual practice has been decriminalized and indeed legitimated. Lesbian, gay and bisexual people have been offered legal protection against discrimination and violence, and recognition of same-sex intimate relationships has been introduced in many countries, including the opening up of marriage. These changes, alongside a shift in the cultural representation and inclusion of lesbians and gay men to varying extents across the four countries, can be seen as constituting a process of homonormalization.

But beyond these broad transformational tendencies towards de-patriarchalization, individualization, liberalization, equalization and pluralization across Europe, there are very real differences in the intimate citizenship regimes of each of our four case study countries. Each has a distinctive history of politics and policy concerning gender, family and sexuality and has enacted different historic compromises between labour, capital and the state in the formulation of welfare policy, with specific implications for intimate citizenship and for the contemporary formulation and operation of the couple-norm.

The UK is historically a 'liberal' (Esping-Andersen, 1990) or 'liberal collective' (Ginsburg, 1992) welfare state, orientated strongly towards the market and means-tested benefits and, under the Labour governments of 1997 to 2010, towards 'social investment' policies. This means that the post-Second World War welfare state, which had been grounded in an expectation of the male breadwinner–female homemaker couple-form, moved during these years towards an expectation that both men and women are economically active individuals, and a conceptualization of children as future productive citizens in whom social investment should be made for the sake of future national social and economic well-being (Williams and Roseneil, 2004). UK social policy combines individual and family-based benefits, but is becoming increasingly individualized (Millar, 2003). Whilst there is a long history of feminist activism in the UK, the women's movement has tended to be considerably more ambivalent about, and less successful at, entering the state and establishing a state gender policy machine than, for instance, the Norwegian women's movement.

Bulgaria is one of a cluster of post-communist European welfare regimes (Fenger, 2005) that combine characteristics of Gøsta Esping-Andersen's 'social democratic' and 'conservative', traditional family-orientated welfare regimes.[6] With a history of state familialism and strong pronatalist policies under communism that financially penalized those who did not have children (Roseneil and Stoilova, 2011) and favoured married couples (Therborn, 2004), under communism Bulgaria also had a constitutional commitment to gender equality and high levels of female employment (Koeva and Bould, 2007). It was the first communist country to declare marriage constitutionally equal and secular. The post-communist era has seen a diminution in welfare services and benefits (Heinen, 2009) and increasing poverty and inequality, particularly affecting women and minorities (Sotiropoulou and Sotiropoulos, 2007).

As a 'social democratic' (Esping-Andersen, 1990), 'woman-friendly' (Hernes, 1987) welfare state, Norway has a legacy of low 'conceptual polarization of genders' (Löfström, 1998). Part of the Nordic 'vanguard of the dismantling of explicitly patriarchal marriage' (Therborn, 2004: 80), it has a long tradition of legal individualism and 'egalitarian marriage' (Melby et al., 2006b; Therborn, 2004). The social democratic state, influenced significantly by feminist activism, has been character-ized by commitments to both 'progressive maternalism' (Hagemann, 2007) and gender equality. Norwegian welfare policy exhibits a high degree of universalism, with most benefits defined without reference to family status, meaning that policy is, in Ruth Lister's (1994) terms, de-familialized, or individualized. At the same time, there is consider-able policy emphasis on granting safe and secure childhoods to children and on supporting families to that end.

Portugal transitioned to democracy after the overthrow of the Estado Novo dictatorship (1926–74), which had promoted the values of colonial nationalism, rural life, Catholicism, and the patriarchal family. It is one of a group of southern European welfare regimes characterized by the prevalence of the informal economy and a historic lack of resources for welfare expenditure.[7] This means that much welfare provision is familial rather than delivered through the state (Ferrera, 1996; Trifiletti, 1999; Ferreira, 2005; Ferreira, 2014; Flaquer, 2000).[8] With significant involvement of the Catholic Church in welfare provision and policy-making (Ferreira, 2005), at the same time as there is a socialist-influenced focus on workers' rights as part of the legacy of the Carnation Revolution of 1974, there has been a strong symbolic and rhetorical investment in 'the family'. As in other southern European welfare regimes, divorce rates, fertility rates and the political representation of women are low, and young people leave the parental home late. But Portugal stands out from other 'southern European' countries in having a female employment rate closer to Nordic, former communist countries and liberal welfare regimes (Walby, 2001) than to other southern European countries, and in having a higher proportion of births outside marriage (Coelho, 2005). Whilst the impact of movements for gender and sexuality equality and change is still largely unacknowledged (Tavares, 2010; Santos, 2013), Portuguese culture and politics are increasingly influenced by principles which were at the heart of the collective demands of the women's and LGBT movements. These include equality between women and men, and autonomy, choice and protection from violence for women and sexual minorities (Neves, 2008).

In the rest of Part II, we explore the place of the couple-norm in the intimate citizenship regime of each country in turn. We offer a historical exploration of the changes in law and policy that have led to the current landscape of intimate citizenship, focusing particularly on how the couple-form has been regulated and institutionalized, and we conclude each national discussion with an overview of changing patterns of coupling and uncoupling which point to significant transformations in 'normal' ways of living and loving in that country.

Notes

1   Article 21 of the Equality chapter states: 'Any discrimination based on any ground such as sex, race, colour, ethnic or social origin, genetic features, language, religion or belief, political or any other opinion, membership of a national minority, property, birth, disability, age or sexual orientation shall be prohibited.' The text is available at: http://www.europarl.europa.eu/charter/pdf/text_en.pdf (accessed 25 July 2020).
2   The Istanbul Convention: https://www.coe.int/fr/web/conventions/full-list/-/conventions/rms/090000168008482e (accessed 28 October 2019).
3   On the Bulgarian Constitutional Court decision, see https://ohrh.law.ox.ac.uk/promoting-gender-ideology-constitutional-court-of-bulgaria-declares-istanbul-convention-unconstitutional/ (accessed 28 October 2019).
4   Lister (1994) and many subsequent feminist scholars of social policy have used the notion of de-familialization to refer to the 'capacity for individual adults to uphold a socially acceptable standard to living independently of family relationships, either through paid work, or social security provisions' (1994: 37). This does not necessarily mean that family relations are no longer socially, culturally or politically salient. Esping-Andersen (1999) responded to feminist critics of his work by adopting the notions of familialism and nonfamilialism, with a familialist regime assuming that households and families are responsible for their members' welfare, whereas a defamilializing regime provides policies

that reduce the dependence of individuals on families. On these trends in law and policy, see Esping-Andersen (1999), Ostner (2004), McLaughlin and Glendinning (1994), Daly (2011), Orloff (1996, 2009) and Mathieu (2016).

5 See Roseneil et al. (2013) for a detailed discussion of the regulation and normalization of same-sex sexualities in our four case study countries.

6 In his classic 1990 book theorizing 'the three worlds of welfare capitalism', Esping-Andersen did not include communist/post-communist countries. According to his typology, which was based on a comparative historical analysis of social policy in 18 OECD countries in the period up to the end of the 1980s, social democratic welfare regimes are the Scandinavian states; conservative/corporatist welfare regimes are continental European nations, such as Austria, France and Germany, as well as Japan; and the liberal welfare model is seen in Anglophone countries, namely the UK, Australia, Canada and the United States.

7 In addition to neglecting communist countries, Esping-Andersen (1990) did not consider the specificities of the provision of welfare in southern European countries. In response, Ferrera (1996) sought to outline the characteristic features of southern European welfare states.

8 This has led to the suggestion that southern European states might be seen as 'welfare societies' (Wall et al., 2001) rather than welfare states.

5
The United Kingdom's intimate citizenship regime

Introduction

The contemporary intimate citizenship regime in the United Kingdom has developed through the increasing intervention of the state in intimate life and the gradual diminution of the power of the established church during the twentieth century.[1] The UK has a long liberal tradition of refraining from giving the state an *explicit* role in family matters (Land, 1979; Lewis et al., 2008; Mätzke and Ostner, 2010) and lacked a named field of 'family policy' until the Labour governments of 1997–2010. Nonetheless, law and policy have historically served to promote and defend the heterosexual couple-form and the family based on it. Both have been naturalized in social policies and through informal processes of interaction within local communities, religious and ethnic groups and other peer groups and social networks, which have exerted a heavy ingerence on people's lives (Weeks, 2012 [1981]).

The new middle classes of the nineteenth century had sanctified the domestic sphere as the domain of married women and mothers (Davidoff and Hall, 1987), claiming the superiority of their own intimate life arrangements and establishing a clear moral boundary between their respectability and 'the profligacy and excesses of the aristocracy and the dangers of the undomesticated working classes' (Wright and Jagger, 1999: 19). Thus 'the ideology of family life embedded in the wider notion of "respectability"' (Weeks, 2012 [1981]: 37) came to be central to the class-stratified British intimate citizenship regime that sought to bring the 'naturalness and stability that the bourgeois adhered to to the masses' (Weeks, 2012 [1981]: 39). The legacies of this are still felt, particularly by those whose intimate life practices do not meet the prescribed standards of middle-class respectability. Working-class lone mothers in particular have long been identified as the cause of crises of social cohesion and morality, and they were stigmatized and culturally vilified through the 1990s (Mann and Roseneil, 1999; Wright and Jagger, 1999) and continue to be in the twenty-first century (Tyler, 2008; Jensen and Tyler, 2012). This is despite the powerful force of feminist and lesbian and gay campaigning which fed into changing social attitudes and practices in relation to sexuality and relationships and the liberalizing legislation of the 1960s that addressed divorce, male homosexuality and abortion.

The privileging of the married heterosexual couple-form was deeply entrenched by the post-Second World War social and welfare reforms introduced by the Attlee Labour government. These were structured around, and served to support, the position of the male breadwinner and his dependent homemaker wife (Fink, 2000). In the ensuing decades, in the context of the country's shift from a manufacturing-based economy to a post-industrial, service sector-driven economy, the male breadwinner/female homemaker welfare model became increasingly obsolete and a new individualized and market-centred approach to citizenship contributed to the transformation to a 'liberal' welfare state (Esping-Andersen, 1990), which was firmly established when 'New Labour' came to power in 1997 (Taylor-Gooby, 2009).[2] In the period since then, there has been a shift in the model of intimate life assumed and promoted by welfare policy – from a 'male breadwinner' to an 'adult worker' model, which presumes that both adults in any committed couple, whether same-sex or hetero-sexual, are able and eager to enter the paid labour force (Carling, Duncan and Edwards, 2002). The financial imperative has become 'to get "people off welfare and into work" and the moral imperative has been to turn people into better citizens' (Williams and Roseneil, 2004: 185). Within this intimate citizenship regime, good citizens are implicitly those who are stably coupled and mutually committed (whether married or unmarried, heterosexual or homosexual), and who are thus able to be more economically productive, 'more responsible for the welfare outcomes they experience' and more inclined to behave 'as customers in a competitive market' (Taylor-Gooby, 2009: 128). In the wake of the financial crash of 2008, the Conservative–Liberal Coalition government (2010–15) and subsequent Conservative governments pursued a politics of 'austerity' for at least a decade,[3] involving deep cuts in local and central government welfare spending which have been predicated upon a further boosting, in discourse and policy, of the economically productive, stable and committed couple-form (Crossley, 2015; Hayton, 2015; Edwards and Gillies, 2016).

It is in the context of these transformations that we characterize the contemporary UK as 'late liberal', drawing on the work of Elizabeth Povinelli.[4] Povinelli (2011) suggests that the emergent combination, since the late 1960s, of the threats posed by (recurrent/ongoing) economic crises on the one hand, and social movements on the other, have been strategically and belatedly contained within the socio-political formation of 'late liberalism' through an economics of neo-liberalism (to solve the crises of liberal economics) and an instrumental politics of recognition (to solve crises of social legitimacy). These strategies have entailed the recognition and sanctioning of certain transformations in intimacy and 'alternative' intimate life arrangements and hence have produced a liberalization of the intimate citizenship regime. But they have also sidelined other, potentially more socially destabilizing, forms of intimacy outside the couple-form.

The grounding of the UK intimate citizenship regime

The UK intimate citizenship regime had at its heart – until the late twentieth century – a normative model of good and proper intimate life that was predicated on a set of rigid expectation↔injunctions relating to the married heterosexual couple-form. According to the middle-class Victorian ideal, the husband's role was that of economic provider, responsible for and representative of his family in the public world; the wife, as her husband's domestic dependent, maintained his home and raised his children. Although the 1839 and 1873 Custody of Infants Acts and the Married Women's Property Acts of 1870, 1882 (England and Wales) and 1881 (Scotland) allowed married women some access to custodial rights for their children and control of their own property, the cultural legacies of many centuries of common law that granted husbands custody of their children and control over their wives' personal property, land and wages (Lyndon Shanley, 1993) lasted long after the passing of this legislation.

The marital relationship was the only legally sanctioned site for sexual activity, the purpose of which was to produce children (Davidoff et al., 1999; Wright and Jagger, 1999). Spouses were expected to be both homogamous and monogamous and to procreate after marriage, not before. With the exception of homosexual men, who could be criminalized for 'homosexual offences' until 1967 in England and

Wales, women were consistently more harshly penalized, socially and legally, for defying these injunctions (Davidoff et al., 1999; Fink, 2000). Illegitimacy remained 'a disability, a legal, social and psychological blight' (Abbott, 2003: 16), for both mother and child, well into the second half of the twentieth century, and the term 'bastard' retains its status as an insult even now. Fatherhood, on the other hand, was not legitimated by the act of insemination, but exclusively by marriage, which rendered the mother 'guilty not only of producing an illegitimate child but also of being unable to name, legally, the child's father' (Fink, 2000: 181). It was only in the 1980s that almost all distinctions between children born in and out of wedlock were eliminated (Lowe, 1988; Thane, 2010).[5] The lateness of these policy changes reflects the interconnected strength of the couple-norm and the procreative-norm: proper, responsible parenthood and the production of future citizens required the parents to be married (Fink, 2000), and '"legitimacy" and "respectability" were treated as being more important than the child's existing relationships' (Eekelaar, 2013: 421). Nevertheless, already from the early 1960s, the number of children born outside marriage started to rise significantly, a trend that has remained unaltered since. In 1960 only 5.2 per cent of live births were outside marriage; in 1970 the figure was 8 per cent, and in 2017 it was 48.2 per cent (Eurostat, 2019).[6]

As a couple-form that defies the marital injunction, unmarried cohabitation was widely regarded as 'living in sin' through much of the twentieth century (Thane, 2010; Frost, 2008). Whilst a small minority of 'avant-garde' cohabiting couples made conscious decisions not to marry on political grounds, the majority were not able to marry, either due to parental opposition, particularly in the case of cross-class or mixed-heritage (race/ethnicity/faith) relationships, or legal impediments, such as a prior marriage that could not be dissolved (Frost, 2008). A policy climate adverse to any rupture in the bond of marriage was responsible for this situation: even after the Matrimonial Causes Act 1857 introduced judicial divorce in England and Wales, dissolution of marriage remained extremely difficult to obtain, especially for women. Whilst a petitioner husband only had to prove the adultery of the wife to get a divorce, a wife had to prove the husband's 'aggravated adultery'. The women's movement's pressure for divorce law reform contributed to gradual liberalization, and important new legislation was passed in the 1920s and 1930s.[7] However, this opening up of divorce on a wider set of grounds was justified by legislators and politicians as necessary in order to uphold the institution of marriage by enabling unmarried cohabitants to regularize their partnerships, as opposed to being represented as providing fairer, equal and accessible divorce for women (Thane, 2010). Similarly, when the Divorce Reform Act was passed in 1969, making it much easier to obtain a divorce in England and Wales, the official motivation emphasized that the proposed changes were aimed at reinforcing marriage, by rendering unmarried cohabitation unnecessary (Thane, 2010). In fact, quite the reverse came to pass, with an overall increase in divorce in the 1970s and a progressive decline in marriage that started at that same time.[8] Like births outside marriage, unmarried cohabitation has increased steadily since the early 1970s; the unmarried cohabiting couple-form is a common, often short-term, arrangement for adults without children (Thane, 2010),[9] and unmarried cohabiting couple families are the fastest-growing family type in the UK (ONS, 2017).

With these prescriptions about acceptable versions of the couple-form pertaining exclusively to the lives of heterosexuals, the intimate relationships of non-heterosexuals were largely outside the purview of law and policy-makers. To the extent that non-heterosexuals existed, they were seen as having sex, not relationships. Male homosexual acts had long been criminalized, but same-sex acts between women were unrecognized in the law. There were two moments in the 1920s when something of a moral panic about lesbianism broke through the cultural silence. In 1921 there was an attempt in Parliament to criminalize 'gross indecency between women', but this was ultimately halted for fear that the law would end up publicizing such acts.[10] In the same decade, the publication of Radclyffe Hall's lesbian-themed novel *The Well of Loneliness* (1928) led to an accusation of 'obscene libel' and a trial for obscenity which powerfully exposed social anxieties about the 'dangers of lesbianism' (Davidoff et al., 1999). As Lesley Hall (2000) notes, these two legal interventions against lesbianism illustrate a profound concern about the threat to the normative family of detaching sex from the heterosexual procreative couple-form. They took place against the backdrop of a vigorous and active women's movement which had been campaigning with increasing success for women's full political and economic citizenship and formed part of a wider cultural backlash against feminism (Weeks, 1977; Jeffreys, 1985; Doan, 2001).

Intimate citizenship after the Second World War

Public anxiety about threats to the family escalated soon after the end of the Second World War. The war years had brought about substantial disruption to the ordering of intimate life, with concern that the separation of married couples and the new roles and accompanying freedom experienced by women had opened a Pandora's box of promiscuity and extramarital sex that would permanently endanger marriage and the family (Fink, 2000). As a result, immediately after the end of the conflict, a strong political commitment emerged to restoring the pre-war gender order and the values of the 'traditional British family' (Fink, 2000; Hall, 2000; Herzog, 2011). However, Dagmar Herzog suggests that the post-war impetus to return to the conventional intimate order was more than the imposition of political and religious leaders: 'Sexuality had escaped from the marital framework in the years when the world turned upside down. Trying to repair ruptured relationships and restore a domesticated heterosexuality would become a project not only imposed from above by conservative governments and with the support of church leaders, but also a movement carried from the yearnings of countless ordinary people' (2011: 94).

The grounding of the post-war welfare settlement on the male breadwinner/female homemaker couple-form might be seen as resonant with the hopes and desires of many millions of British people for stability after the turmoil of the war years. A new model of 'companionate marriage', an optimistic view of the heterosexual couple-form characterized by intimacy, shared domestic life and egalitarian comradeship between a woman and her husband, tapped into this longing for conventional settled families, and was 'tirelessly advanced' (Herzog, 2011: 106) by the National Marriage Guidance Council during the 1950s.[11] As Leonore Davidoff et al. explain: 'it was a powerful ideal, which stressed the importance of romantic love, sexual attraction and mutual interests, while disguising realities of gendered inequalities of power and access to resources. Yet it set a standard by which it was believed all marriages would ultimately stand or fall' (Davidoff et al., 1999: 190). These modern ideals of coupledom demanded that intimacy be achieved and sustained through ongoing shared activities, rather than assumed through the act of marriage (Gillies, 2003), and in the following decades the association of heterosexual conjugal coupledom with exclusivity and romantic love became increasingly prevalent, as did the expectation that the relationship should be mutually satisfying.[12]

With the radical expansion and solidification of the welfare state under the 1945 Attlee Labour government, the post-war intimate citizenship regime was increasingly constituted of policies that were not ostensibly about regulating family and intimate relationships, but rather were framed as supporting families. But the introduction of social citizenship rights that assumed a working father and a home-based mother and that sought to support them and their children (Davidoff et al., 1999; Lewis, 1992) had the effect of excluding the single, separated, divorced or unmarried cohabitants from access to benefits (Fink, 2000). Indeed, the post-war welfare state offered more than a 'safety net' to married couples: it positively promoted marriage by funding the National Marriage Guidance Council from 1948 onwards, and by providing young married couples with much needed, affordable council housing. With the media, popular culture and fashion also promoting gender differentiation, procreation and coupledom, and with the gradual re-equalization of the ratio of men to women in the population, the marriage rate rose significantly and the age of first marriage fell steadily, until the 1970s (Abbott, 2003; Hall, 2000; Thane, 2010).

Changes and challenges to the couple-norm

The traditional yoking of sex and reproduction and the normative confinement of sex to the married, heterosexual couple were increasingly challenged by cultural, political and technological change from the late 1950s onwards. Pressure from professional and voluntary organizations and the work of women MPs resulted in the passing of the Legitimacy Act in 1959. This change in law brought the previously 'illegitimate' children of parents who had not been free to marry at the time of their birth but who had married subsequently into the definition of 'the family', dislodging assumptions about the unassailability and moral superiority of monogamous lifelong marriage from their central position in the UK intimate citizenship regime. Following the recommendation of the 1957 Wolfenden Report that male 'homosexual behaviour between consenting adults in private be no longer a criminal offence', a public discourse of tolerance of homosexuality and of non-intervention in the 'private lives' of citizens gradually started to emerge (Weeks, 1977, 1985; Roseneil et al., 2013). It took a decade of lobbying by the Homosexual Law Reform Society and the Albany Trust before the Sexual Offences Act of 1967 was passed by a Labour government, decriminalizing, in England and Wales, homosexual acts that took place between two men over 21 years of age 'in private'. In Scotland male homosexuality was decriminalized in 1980, two years later in Northern Ireland, and not until 1992 in the Isle of Man. The change in the law in Northern Ireland, where Christian religious authorities held much greater sway than in the rest of the UK, followed the first European Court of Human Rights case (*Dudgeon v UK*, 1981) to find that the criminalization of consenting sexual relations between adults in private was contrary to Article 8 of the European Charter of Human Rights.

In the early 1960s the advent of new technologies of contraception and developments in the legal and policy framework for reproductive rights marked the start of significant changes in sexual life for heterosexual women and men. The pill became available in 1961, and in 1967, with the passing of the Family Planning Act, local authorities were enabled to set up family planning clinics and to subsidize contraception, which was made free under the NHS in 1974 (Thane, 2010; Marks, 2001). The 1967 Abortion Act legalized abortion, under certain conditions, in England, Wales and Scotland.[13] As a result, as Hera Cook (2005: 123) notes, in England, women who 'had already begun to defer childbirth even when married [... now] did so in large numbers, producing a sexual lifestyle in which reproduction was separate from sexual activity and marriage was no longer a marker of either'. Both the couple-norm and the procreative-norm were changing form.

The rise of the women's and lesbian and gay movements in the 1970s exerted great influence on attitudes towards sexuality and personal relationships in the UK. The political campaigns and cultural activities of the movements challenged the hegemony of heterosexuality and the many social, economic and intimate inequalities to which women and non-heterosexuals were subjected, serving to radically de-privatize and politicize thinking about intimate life. By the 1980s, the prevalence of the idealized nuclear family of the post-war era was declining, and living arrangements were becoming, and being acknowledged to be, more complex, with single parents, separated parents, re-married partners and unmarried cohabiting heterosexual couples increasingly understood as constituting families (Cook, 2014; Jackson, 1998). After peaking in the early 1970s, marriage rates started their long-term decline, and age at first marriage continued to rise.[14]

In direct response to these changes, the Conservative governments of Margaret Thatcher (1979–90) and John Major (1990–7) drew together a politics of economic liberalism and the promotion of enterprise culture with a strong commitment to 'moral regeneration', the end of 'permissiveness' and a return to 'Victorian values'.[15] During this time, there was a political urgency to the project of 'rolling back' the post-Second World War welfare state (Hall, 1983; Gamble, 1988), and the family, conceptualized as properly the main source of welfare, 'was required to fill the space' (Maclean, 2002: 64). A traditionally gendered couple-form and family were regarded as 'the natural state of affairs' (Durham, 2001: 465) and as essential to the development of morality in children and health in the nation. Single mothers and absent fathers were identified as one of the country's main social problems, and family breakdown was regarded as being at the root of crime (Durham, 2001; Mann and Roseneil, 1999; Pascall, 1999).

At the same time, against the backdrop of the AIDS crisis and a virulent wave of homophobia stirred up by the media, the Conservative government moved to act against the increasing visibility of same-sex relationships and family-making and to oppose the support given to lesbian and gay communities by Labour local authorities in some of the major cities in the UK (Cooper, 1994, 1995). The passing of 'Section 28' of the 1988 Local Government Act prohibited local authorities from promoting 'the teaching in any maintained school of the acceptability of homosexuality as a pretended family relation-ship'. This was experienced by lesbians and gay men as an attack and a move against the progress that had been made in their social position and community development since the late 1960s. However, as Diane Richardson points out, despite this law's discriminatory treatment of homosexuality and its attempt to re-consign same-sex relationships to the privacy of the domestic sphere, 'what is interesting is how much it reveals about social change and the hegemony of heterosexuality, in terms of the felt necessity to legally reinscribe "family" as heterosexual' (2000: 3; Stacey, 1991). Whilst undoubtedly a major enactment of 'backlash politics', Section 28 might also be seen as evidence of the extent of cultural change in intimate life.

In fact, the reaction against feminism and the politics of lesbian and gay liberation embodied by Section 28, alongside the AIDS crisis, contributed to the reinvigoration of the lesbian and gay movement. Tens of thousands of people were mobilized for the first time to march for lesbian and gay rights, and both radical queer groups and more reformist lobbying organizations were formed, including the highly influential non-governmental organization Stonewall. Campaigns were launched for the equalization of the age of consent, the right of same-sex couples to adopt and the recognition of same-sex partner-ships (Roseneil et al., 2011). None of these demands were success-fully met under the Conservative governments that were so hostile to lesbian and gay rights during the late 1980s, but the stage was set for radical changes under the Labour government of Tony Blair (Waites, 2001, 2003).

New Labour and the pluralization of intimate citizenship

The end of 18 years of Conservative government in 1997 and the election of 'New Labour' (1997–2010) brought about substantial changes to the UK intimate citizenship regime, amounting to a pluralization of relationship recognition. The state became more active than ever before in 'refashioning family life and behaviour, [...] stabilizing family relations and recognizing stable family life as significant for social stability and social order' (Daly, 2010: 442). New Labour sought to develop a 'social investment state', in which welfare reforms foregrounded the centrality of paid work and an 'adult-worker', dual-career family, as opposed to the male breadwinner/female homemaker model of the post-Second World War welfare state. This new approach to social policy sought to develop both a flourishing economy and civil society through responsible, stable parenting and the improved well-being of children (Lister, 2003; Williams and Roseneil, 2004).[16]

Financial and social support for families increased significantly during the years of New Labour's 'social investment', whilst the meaning of 'family' in social policy also started to undergo significant change. According to social policy analyst Mary Daly, 'successive New Labour administrations had been sufficiently grounded in the realities of everyday life not to view family structure narrowly as the cereal packet family based on marriage' (2010: 441). In 1998, for example, the key message of the Green Paper *Supporting Families* – 'Britain's first formal governmental family policy statement' (Maclean, 2002: 64) – was that marriage was still the 'surest foundation for raising children and remains the choice of the majority of people in Britain' (Home Office, 1998: 4). At the same time, the Green Paper also stated that many lone parents and unmarried couples raise their children as successfully as married couples. In other public declarations following the Green Paper, the Home Secretary Jack Straw reiterated the message that marriage offers the best chance of stability for children, but also that what mattered was the quality of the relationship, not the institution itself (Durham, 2001). This dual messaging reflected the resistance within the Labour Party to pursuing a marriage-based pro-family stance that did not take into account that 'families come in all shapes and sizes', as the Minister for Employment and Women Tessa Jowell stated (Durham, 2001: 461). This recognition of the realities of social transformation in intimate life informed governmental policies and discourses in the years that followed. In 2008, the Cabinet Office produced an analytical document which stressed that 'families are the bedrock of our society',[17] that there is an 'increasing range of family structures' (Cabinet Office, 2008: 4) and that 'relationship types have become more fluid and family composition now changes more frequently over the life course' (2008: 22). Marriage, this paper stated, 'will remain of central importance' (2008: 4), but it is one option amongst other equal, 'alternative' relationships. Characterizing marriage as an option equal to other relationship arrangements meant that the latter were not only acknowledged, as the 1998 Green Paper had done, but were now given the same status and importance as marriage.

New Labour's socio-cultural agenda of inclusivity, social tolerance and recognition (Klett-Davies, 2012) manifested itself, arguably most prominently, in legislation and policy addressing the intimate relationships of non-heterosexuals. Before New Labour, the incorporation of lesbian and gay concerns within mainstream politics was rare, and political parties tended to maintain a careful distance from lesbians and gay men (Richardson, 2000). This changed with a raft of laws spurred by the social movement campaigns for lesbian and gay equality discussed earlier. Almost immediately after coming to power in 1997, changes in immigration law were introduced to allow a foreign member of an unmarried couple in a long-term relationship – whether heterosexual or same-sex – to apply to settle in Britain (Weeks, Heaphy and Donovan, 1999). The age of consent for gay men was equalized in 2000 (Waites, 2001, 2003). The Adoption and Children Act 2002 made it possible for same-sex couples to adopt a child jointly in England and Wales.[18] In 2003 Section 28 was abolished, and, in line with EU legislation, the Equality Act (Sexual Orientation) Regulations 2007 made discrimination against lesbians and gay men in the provision of goods and services illegal (Roseneil et al., 2011). The combination of these changes transformed the framework within which lesbians and gay men were able to couple and parent, challenging long-standing beliefs that 'homosexuals' posed a threat to children (Wilson, 2007).

Arguably the most significant enactment in the reshaping of the UK intimate citizenship regime by New Labour was the Civil Partnership Act of 2004. This introduced a distinctive legal institution – civil partnership – which gave same-sex couples who chose to enter into it the same rights, powers and duties as marriage. Civil partnerships can be seen as a major breakthrough in campaigns for lesbian and gay equality, offering for the first time full legal recognition of same-sex couples.[19] However, they were criticized by some activists and queer theorists as a liberal compromise that avoided challenging religious and conservative interests and that maintained the inherent superiority of the married couple-form as a heterosexual entity (Barker, 2006), whilst creating a 'parody of marriage' for lesbians and gay men (Stychin, 2006a: 903; Stychin, 2006b; Wilkinson and Kitzinger, 2005). Heterosexuality thereby retained its status as the norm, and non-heterosexuals remained different, if less unequal.

Another path-breaking step in the pluralization of the UK intimate citizenship regime and the recognition of diversity in intimate life was taken in 2008 with a set of amendments to the Human Fertilisation and Embryology Act (HFEA), which passed with little opposition.[20] These allowed for the recognition of both partners in a same-sex relationship as legal parents of children conceived through assisted conception and changed the requirement to consider the 'need for a father' to the 'need for supportive parenting' for children conceived by IVF.[21] However, the HFEA (2008) maintained the privileging of the legally sanctioned couple-form, introducing differential treatment of lesbian couples who were civil partnered from those who were not and re-inscribing the two-parent model of family (Wallbank, 2010; McCandless and Sheldon, 2010).

All in all, whilst New Labour brought a broader range of intimate relationships into the realm of legal recognition and policy support, the valuing of the committed, long-term, cohabiting couple-form as the best environment for the raising of children meant that couple-normativity remained at the heart of the UK intimate citizenship regime.

The new Conservative liberal intimate citizenship

The return to power of the Conservative Party in 2010, initially in coalition with the Liberal Democrats (2010–15), against the backdrop of deepening global economic crisis, marked a renewed emphasis on marriage in UK family policy, after the pluralizing intimate citizenship policies of New Labour. Prime Minister David Cameron repeatedly emphasized his commitment to marriage as the institution that gives couples 'a better chance at staying together', within a wider strategy of repairing 'broken Britain' (Kirby, 2009: 246; Lister and Bennett, 2010).

On the eve of the 2010 national general election, the Conservatives announced that, as part of their pro-marriage agenda, they would reintroduce tax breaks for married couples. Entering a coalition with the Liberal Democrats tempered the Conservatives' pro-marriage reforms but nonetheless limited tax breaks for married couples were introduced in 2015, in the form of the Marriage Allowance, which Cameron stressed was 'about far more than pounds and pence. It's about valuing commitment' (Gov.uk, 2015).

The introduction, in 2014, of the 'Family Test', which sought to recognize and address the potential impact of governmental policies on family relationships, was a further move to link stable families and couple relationships with desired policy outcomes (Edwards and Gillies, 2016).[22] The 'Family Test' guidance for government departments states that 'committed couple relationships bring significant benefits for the individuals themselves and children in those families' (DWP, 2014: 7) and therefore need to be protected. On the other hand, single mothers 'and their problematic, criminal children' were explicitly blamed by the Prime Minister in his speech on the 'fightback after the riots' of 2011,[23] which emphasized the contrast between the stable, heterosexual-couple family and the 'troubled families' that produced criminal behaviour and social disruption: 'I don't doubt that many of the rioters out last week have no father at home. Perhaps they come from one of the neighbourhoods where it's standard for children to have a mum and not a dad' (Gov.uk, 2011b). The emphasis on father-headed families and stable, working couples continued through the 2010s, driven forward with an 'austerity'-enacting programme of changes to welfare benefits that penalized lone mothers.

At the same time, Cameron's strategy of modernizing and 'detoxifying' a Conservative Party that was still remembered for Prime Minister Margaret Thatcher's Section 28, for 'family values' and Prime Minister John Major's notion of 'back to basics' meant that he did not roll back on the progressive legal changes introduced by the previous Labour governments. Cameron's Conservative Party demonstrated a far greater commitment to inclusivity in intimate citizenship than any of his predecessors. This meant that he pledged to include civil partnerships in any support given to marriage (Kirby, 2009), and he made a point of recognizing and valuing 'alternative' families. For instance, in a 2011 speech on 'families and relationships', Cameron stated: 'families are immeasurably important. And when I talk about families, I don't just mean the married with two children model. Yes, I am pro-commitment, back marriage and think it's a wonderful institution. But to me, a strong family is defined not by its shape, but by the love and support that's in it' (Gov.uk, 2011a). He continued to emphasize the importance of marriage/civil partnership as public commitments for couples that strengthen not only their relationship but also society at large, and at the Conservative Party conference in October 2011, he announced, to a far from enthusiastic audience, that a consultation had started on legalizing same-sex marriage. Despite the opposition to his proposal, in summer 2012 Cameron reiterated his commitment to gay marriage in a speech at an LGBT reception:

> I just want to say I am absolutely determined that this Coalition government will follow in that tradition [Labour's] by legislating for gay marriage in this parliament. I make that point not only as someone who believes in equality but as someone who believes passionately in marriage. I think marriage is a great institution – I think it helps people to commit, it helps people to say that they're going to care and love for another person.[24] It helps people to put aside their selfish interests and think of the union that they're forming. It's something I feel passionately about and I think if it's good enough for straight people like me, it's good enough for everybody and that's why we should have gay marriage and we will legislate for it. (Number10.gov.uk, 2012)

In January 2013, the Marriage (Same Sex Couples) Bill was introduced to Parliament. The debates that ensued in the following months, in and out of Parliament, were largely strongly supportive of the Bill and of marriage equality, and there was very little public opposition to the proposed legislation. In July 2013 the Marriage (Same Sex Couples) Act 2013 was passed and in December the government announced that same-sex couples would be able to marry in England and Wales from 29 March 2014 (Stonewall, 2014). In Scotland, the Marriage and Civil Partnership (Scotland) Act 2014 received Royal Assent in March 2014, and the first ceremonies took place on 31 December 2014. In Northern Ireland the Democratic Unionist Party consistently opposed the legalization of same-sex marriage in repeated debates in the Northern Ireland Assembly, but, in the context of the suspension of the Assembly, the UK Parliament approved its legalization, and in the absence of the reconvening of the Assembly, same-sex marriage has been legally recognized in Northern Ireland since January 2020.

The introduction of same-sex marriage entailed the elimination of the last legal instrument explicitly discriminating against lesbians and gay men in the UK. Whilst this has been regarded by some queer critics as instrumentally serving a right-wing government, because the stable couple-form 'provides the economic base to the nation and helps further the retrenchment of certain sections of the welfare state' (Wilkinson 2013: 211), it also signals the extent of the radical liberalization and pluralization of the UK intimate citizenship regime over recent decades. The equalization of legal frameworks for relationship recognition was completed in late 2019 with the introduction of the Civil Partnership (Opposite-sex Couples) Regulations. This followed a campaign for 'equal civil partnerships' and a Supreme Court ruling in 2018 that, by preventing heterosexual couples from entering into a civil partnership, the 2004 Civil Partnership Act was in breach of human rights. Prime Minister Theresa May committed the Conservative government to remove the 'unfairness' of the Act (Government Equalities Office, 2019), and 'opposite-sex civil partnerships' were introduced in England and Wales in December 2019 and in 2020 in Northern Ireland and Scotland. Looking ahead, as the UK has now exited the EU (as of 31 January 2020), new concerns have been raised (e.g. Dustin, Ferreira and Millns, 2019) about how EU regulations pertaining to jurisdictional issues in divorce proceedings, parental responsibility and maintenance will be amended, and with what consequences, and whether UK same-sex marriages will be recognized in all EU countries. It remains to be seen whether these developments will lead to new intimate citizenship exclusions, but at the time of writing, in 2020, same-sex and heterosexual couples in the United Kingdom had been granted equal access to the umbrella of state protection and legal recognition, leaving those living outside the couple-form comparatively less sheltered and effectively more marginalized than hitherto.

The landscape of coupledom in the contemporary UK

There has been a remarkable transformation in patterns of intimate life and a pluralization of household forms in the UK over recent decades. Marriage has become significantly less popular; marriage rates have fallen by almost 50 per cent, from 8.5 marriages per 1,000 population in 1970 to 4.4 per 1,000 in 2016 (Eurostat, 2019), and age at first marriage has risen significantly – from 22.4 for women in 1970 to 31.3 in 2015 (ONS, 2018). Divorce rates have more than doubled – from 0.7 per 1,000 population in 1966 and 1.0 in 1970, to a peak of 2.7 in 1990 and 1.8 in 2016 (Eurostat, 2019). Fewer women are having children: fertility rates have dropped from 1.9 in 1980, to a low of 1.64 in 2000, rising to 1.92 in 2010 and 1.7 in 2017 (Eurostat, 2019), and the average age at which women have a child has increased from 26.9 in 1980 to 30.5 in 2017 (Eurostat, 2019). Moreover, births outside marriage have soared, from 5.2 per cent of all births in 1960 to 48.2 per cent in 2017 (Eurostat, 2019).

Living outside the cohabiting couple-form has become increasingly common. There has been an increase in the proportion of one-person households, from 22 per cent of households in 1980 to 28.6 per cent in 2015 (UNECE, 2019). Accompanying this there has been a concomitant decline in the proportion of households comprised of couples with children, from 39 per cent in 1980 to 28.2 per cent in 2015 (UNECE, 2019), and of couple households overall, from 65 per cent in 1980 to 56.6 per cent in 2015 (UNECE, 2019). Whilst there is no longitudinal data on living-apart relationships, a 2011 survey found that 9 per cent of adults were in living-apart relationships (Duncan et al., 2014).

Notes

1   Our focus here is on the United Kingdom (as opposed to England more specifically) as the larger postcolonial and multicultural national context within which our London-based interviewees are situated. Policy differences across the four nations of England, Northern Ireland, Scotland and Wales are highlighted, where relevant, in the chapter. There are three legal jurisdictions in the UK: England and Wales, Northern Ireland and Scotland. The Anglican Church of England is the established church in England and the Church of Scotland is the national church of Scotland. The Anglican Church in Wales was disestablished in 1920. Writing about the first decades of the twentieth century, Weeks states that 'organised religion still counted in questions of marriage and divorce, in decision making on birth control, even in rituals of courtship' (2012 [1981]: 283); but as Britain has become more and more secularized, and is now 'one of the least religious countries in Europe' (416), the influence of the Anglican Church and of the Church of Scotland over matters of intimate citizenship has progressively waned. Northern Ireland, on the other hand, has remained, since its foundation in 1921, socially and religiously more conservative than the rest of the UK. However, the forces of secularization have also had an impact here, and the influence of both the Protestant and Catholic churches on intimate citizenship is being challenged (Evans and Tonge, 2018).
2   Esping-Andersen (1990) differentiates between welfare regimes on the basis of three principles: decommodification (the extent to which welfare is dependent on the market, particularly in relation to pensions, unemployment benefits and sickness benefits); social stratification (the extent to which the state maintains or challenges this); and the public–private mix (the role of state, market, family and the voluntary sector in welfare provision).
3   In October 2018, the then Conservative Prime Minister Theresa May pledged to bring an end to austerity.
4   It might be argued that there are problems with the designation of the UK either as 'late liberal', drawing on Povinelli (2011), or as 'liberal', following Esping-Andersen (1990), given the powerful influence of the social democratic politics and policies of key Labour governments (particularly Attlee's) which have, especially in relation to the National Health Service (NHS), become part of the UK's national sense of self. However, the differences

between the UK and 'fully' social democratic welfare states, such as Norway and Sweden, are, we believe, significant enough to warrant the use of the term (see Deeming, 2017 for further discussion of liberal welfare capitalism). We also consider 'late liberal' preferable to the designation 'neo-liberal' which is a widely used, if under-specified and multivalent, concept that 'has been stretched too far to be productive as a critical analytical tool' (Clarke, 2008: 135).

5   From the seventeenth century until the 1960s many illegitimate (as well as poor, disabled and orphaned) children were sent from Britain to its colonies (later Commonwealth countries), including Australia, Canada, New Zealand and Rhodesia, under the child migrant scheme, which was administered by religious and charitable organizations with government approval (Commonwealth of Australia, 2001; Gill, 1998).

6   There is some variation between the countries of the UK, with the highest proportion of children born outside marriage in Scotland, followed by England and Wales, and then Northern Ireland (ONS, 2018; NRS, 2018).

7   The Matrimonial Causes Act (1923) made it possible for women to obtain a divorce on the basis of their husband's adultery alone, as opposed to aggravated adultery (Probert, 1999). In 1925, the Poor Persons' Rules gave access to divorce to a wider population (Hall, 2000), and the Matrimonial Causes Act (1937) represented a watershed moment in divorce law by extending the grounds for divorce to unlawful desertion, cruelty and incurable insanity (Redmayne, 1993).

8   Divorce rates increased in England and Wales after the law came into effect in 1971 and continued to grow steadily, with a peak in 1993. In 2007 they started a slow decline, and since 2009 the number of divorces has fluctuated, with an increase in 2010, followed by two more years of stability, a decrease between 2013 and 2015 and then another increase in 2016 (ONS, 2019). In Scotland, following the introduction of a single ground for divorce with the Divorce (Scotland) Act 1976, the number of divorces also rose notably, then plateaued in the 1980s and 1990s and has been slowly declining since then (CRFR, 2002). In Northern Ireland, the Matrimonial Causes Order of 1978 (for Northern Ireland) introduced a single ground for divorce but retains more conservative procedures than the rest of the UK. The number of divorces has been increasing, but Northern Ireland has one of the lowest divorce rates in Europe, much lower than in England, Wales and Scotland, reflecting its more conservative and religious culture (Emery, 2013).

9   Ten years after first cohabiting, half of cohabiting couples have married, just under four in ten have separated and slightly over one in ten are still living together and are unmarried (Beaujouan and Ní Bhrolcháin, 2011). It should be noted that although unmarried couples who live together are sometimes called common-law partners, they do not have the same rights as married couples or civil partners.

10   The House of Lords rejected the move, with Lord Desart arguing persuasively: 'You are going to tell the whole world that there is such an offence, to bring it to the notice of women who have never heard of it, never thought of it, never dreamed of it. I think that is a great mischief' (quoted in Weeks, 1977: 106–7).

11   On post-war marriage, see Finch and Summerfield (1991), Gillies (2003) and Hall (2000).

12   Morgan (1991) argues that the shift from viewing marriage as a social institution at the core of the family unit to a personal relationship was also reinforced by professionals, including therapists and authors of therapeutic manuals.

13   Reproductive politics in Northern Ireland followed a different course. Local authorities were allowed to provide contraception in 1969 and a free family planning service was given official recognition in 1974, two years later than the rest of the UK (McCormick, 2008). Abortion remained illegal until recently, except in certain highly constrained circumstances. It was only in the summer of 2019 that MPs voted to lift the ban on abortions, and this became law in October 2019.

14   The proportion of households comprised of couple families with dependent children in Great Britain declined from 38 per cent in 1961 to 31 per cent in 1981. Over the same period, one-person households increased by 8 per cent, the average household size fell from 3.1 people to 2.7 and the proportion of people living in lone parent households doubled (ONS, 2010). There were brief periods of exception to the general trend in the decline in marriage rates in England and Wales: 2002 to 2004; 2007 and 2008; and between 2010 and 2012 (ONS, 2011, 2019). In England and Wales, the mean age at marriage in

2013 was 36.7 for men and 34.3 for women, while it had been 28.8 for men and 26.1 for women in 1973 (ONS, 2019). As of 2018, in Scotland, marriages had decreased by 30 per cent compared with 1971, although a 2 per cent increase was registered in the number of marriages between 2014 and 2015. The average age at first marriage increased for men and women from 24.3 and 22.4 respectively in 1975 to 34.3 and 32.6 in 2018 (NRS, 2019).

15 Margaret Thatcher used the phrase 'Victorian values', to which she attached positive value, during the 1983 election campaign. John Major continued this theme with the pledge to go 'back to basics' and to return to wholesome traditional family values, although the failure to live up to commitment was later seen to be central to the undoing of his government. See Durham (1991) and Hall (2000).

16 New Labour's welfare state regime has been subject to widespread criticism from social policy analysts. It has been argued that its 'work-centredness' was only instrumentally about social equality and was primarily economically driven (Perrons et al., 2005). Moreover, the move from the male breadwinner to the dual-career model was soon deemed unrealistic due to women's shorter working hours and lower earnings, the very nature of the jobs on offer and the still gendered division of caring and domestic labour (Lewis, 2002, 2003). The focus on responsibility has also been criticized for penalizing those who are most vulnerable and less job ready, often younger parents with younger children, mostly women, who were expected both to find and stay in paid work and to be responsible parents (Williams and Roseneil, 2004). New Labour's reform programme was also criticized for assuming a sex/gender-less, race-less and class-less rational legal subject (Barlow, Duncan and James, 2002), thus underplaying the structural economic and social determinants that influence people's lives and opportunities (Lister, 2006).

17 A similar but more emphatic claim, 'Strong, stable families are the bedrock of our society', was used by the then Secretary of State for Children, Schools and Families Ed Balls to begin his ministerial forward to the 2010 *Support for All: The Family and Relationship Green Paper* (HM Government, 2010: 2).

18 In Scotland this became possible in 2009, and in 2013 in Northern Ireland.

19 Civil partnerships were created specifically for same-sex partners who are assumed to have a sexual relationship, rather than being for carers, siblings or friends. As Stychin points out, the question of what constitutes lesbian and gay sex in the original 2004 Act is 'shrouded in [legal] mystery' (Stychin, 2006a: 907) as the legislation lacks any provision for voidability on the grounds of lack of consummation (a provision that is present in marriage-related policies), or for automatic dissolution on the basis of adultery. This 'suggests that it is only through heterosexual penetration that there can be a clear test of what constitutes sexual behaviour anyway, making the determination of same-sex adultery problematic. Consequently, in the context of lesbian and gay civil partnerships, we are very much in a "grey area" in determining when the parties are in a sexual relationship (with each other), and when they have committed adultery, and what the significance of adultery is for the partnership' (Stychin, 2006a: 907). Barker (2006: 254) argues that this aspect of the law has 'homophobic, or at the very least heterosexist, origins in that the "real" sex act enshrined in the law remains a heterosexual (penetrative) one'. Interestingly, in the plans to introduce opposite-sex civil partnerships, as outlined in the July 2019 government document *Implementing Opposite-Sex Civil Partnerships: Next Steps*, the same parameters set out for same-sex couples are meant to be implemented for 'opposite-sex' couples. Thus, 'adultery should not be a specific "fact" for the purpose of dissolution of an opposite-sex civil partnership' (Government Equalities Office 2019: 8), and non-consummation should not be grounds on which an opposite-sex partnership is voidable.

20 The Adoption and Children Act (2002) already allowed same-sex couples to apply for joint adoption and second parent adoption.

21 Same-sex parenting rights have been more robustly recognized, and for longer, under the more liberal, market-oriented UK assisted conception regime than in Norway or Portugal. Lesbians (single and coupled) have long been able to access assisted conception in private clinics, as long as clinics 'take account' of 'the welfare of any child who may be born as a result of the treatment (including the need of that child for a father)' (Human Fertilisation and Embryology Act, 1990). This is not to say that lesbians have found it easy to access assisted conception; the cost is high in private clinics, and studies suggest lesbians have encountered discrimination when seeking NHS treatment (Langdridge and Blyth, 2001).

22 As Edwards and Gillies (2016) point out, the importance of policy working to secure strong and stable couple relationships does not apply to migrants, who were subject to increased restrictions on family reunification and family visit visas under the Coalition government. Restrictions imposed by immigration policies have also assumed importance in the context of possible Brexit-related developments and the implications that the end of European Freedom of Movement for the UK might have on so-called 'Brexit families' (see Kilkey, 2017).

23 In August 2011, London and other large English cities experienced 'the worst bout of unrest in a generation', triggered by the police shooting and killing a young black man whilst trying to arrest him (Lewis et al., 2011: 1).

24 Marriage and civil partnership ceremonies must legally include some pre-set declaratory words on the lack of any lawful impediment to join the couple in matrimony/civil partnership and the contracting words that the spouses/partners utter to call upon their witnesses when taking each other to be their lawful wedded wife/husband/civil partner. Local authorities often offer different ceremony options, many of which include the declaration by the Superintendent Registrar that 'marriage, according to the law of this country is the union of two people, voluntarily entered into for life, to the exclusion of all others' (see, e.g., Oxfordshire.gov.uk, 2019; Thurrock.gov.uk, 2019; Wokingham.gov.uk, 2019). This is an emphatic reminder about the lifelong and monogamous expectation of how marriage should be. In addition, couples are encouraged to include personalized vows.

6

The Bulgarian intimate citizenship regime

Introduction

Of the four intimate citizenship regimes discussed in this book, Bulgaria stands out as the most conservative. It has historically operated in a highly regulatory manner, incorporating constraining, heteronormative and gendered assumptions about the form and nature of legitimate intimate relationships. At the time of writing there is virtually no recognition in law or policy of the couple-form outside heterosexual marriage, and the couple-norm is instantiated across numerous areas of law and policy, from adoption and assisted contraception, to inheritance, family name and even presence at birth,[1] rendering emotional and sexual bonds outside marital and kinship relations invisible and legally unrecognized.

Contemporary Bulgaria can be described as a post-communist European welfare regime (Fenger, 2005), combining characteristics of 'conservative/corporatist' and 'social democratic' and welfare regimes in its Janus-faced promotion of both the heterosexual family and equality.[2] On the one hand, it has a history of state protection of motherhood and pronatalism. This dates from the beginning of the twentieth century (Therborn, 2004; Ivanov, 2008) and was intensified under communism (1945–89), when married couples were strongly favoured (Roseneil and Stoilova, 2011). On the other hand, the communist regime also introduced a constitutional commitment to gender equality and ensured high levels of female employment (Koeva and Bould, 2007). The post-communist era saw some significant liberalization in law and policy, including a shift towards greater reproductive freedom and protection from violence and discrimination, but the intimate practices of ordinary people have departed more radically from the normative couple-form than legal and policy definitions. There have been significant declines in marriage and fertility rates and increases in divorce and births outside marriage, with the number of children born outside wedlock consistently surpassing the share of births in marriage since 2006 (EC, 2017b).

Independent social movement activism around issues of gender and sexuality started to develop only in the 1990s after the collapse of communism (Daskalova, 1999; Pisankaneva, 2009; Roseneil and Stoilova, 2011). Campaigners began to challenge the institutionalization of the normative couple-form in the early 2000s, in the context of Bulgarian preparations for accession to the European Union (EU) in 2007. Whilst a range of EU-led legal changes addressing discrimination against lesbians and gay men were implemented, their societal impact has been stalled by the lack of wider national public and policy engagement with issues of family and sexual diversity. Therefore, it is not surprising that the push from women's and lesbian and gay organizations for a more inclusive intimate citizenship regime which would legally recognize non-marital cohabitation and same-sex relationships has, thus far, been unsuccessful, with very little achieved beyond what was required by the EU.

Bulgarian society has remained predominantly conservative and patriarchal, notwithstanding the official policies of the communist regime. A Eurobarometer study in 2017 suggested that people in Bulgaria are particularly inclined to believe in traditional gender roles and are amongst the least likely in the EU to support gender equality. Bulgaria has one of the highest proportions of people who agree that the most important role for women is to take care of their home and family (81 per cent) and for men to earn money (81 per cent). Many Bulgarians also agree that women are more likely to make decisions based on emotions (83 per cent) and think that it is unacceptable for men to cry (32 per cent). Similarly, despite the greater visibility of lesbian and gay people in larger cities in recent years, there is continued stigmatization and marginalization of same-sex couples in everyday life (Filipova and Pisankaneva, 2017). This often means that rights and obligations formally established in law and policy are not granted in practice. Overall, there have been relatively few changes to the shape of the couple-norm over time and an inconsistent direction of development – with positive changes linked to less restrictive regulations often being followed by the (re)introduction of more constraints to the freedom of intimate life, as we demonstrate below.

The Bulgarian intimate citizenship regime has remained exclusionary of non-normative practices, leaving large numbers of people outside the 'charmed circle' (Rubin, 1993 [1984]) of heterosexual procreating coupledom.

The regulation of the couple-form before communism

A legal distinction between legitimate and illegitimate intimacies has long been drawn in Bulgaria. The death penalty was introduced for the crime of sexual acts between men at the turn of the tenth century (Roseneil and Stoilova, 2011),[3] with punishment reduced to 'confinement to a dark cell for six months' in 1896. The civil regulation of intimate life by the state came much later. The first attempt was made in 1936 and aimed to introduce civil marriage and to define grounds for divorce (based on irretrievable marriage breakdown).[4] The bill failed to pass due to the strong objections of the Orthodox Church (Todorova, 2002), which sought to preserve the religious authority to legislate for marriage and divorce, along with Muslim, Jewish and other religious authorities (Doncheva, 2002). Notwithstanding its absence from family law, the Bulgarian state was, from the early twentieth century, developing policies – both positive and punitive – that sought to stimulate marriage and promote procreation as a response to declining birth rates. Childbirth was encouraged through entitlements to paid leave from 1905 onwards (Ivanov, 2008) and through child benefits which were made available to married couples from 1941. More punitively, abortion was banned in 1929 (Public Health Law, 1929) and taxes for people who were unmarried or childless were introduced in 1935 (Ivanov, 2008). Marriage was also supported through various forms of tax relief from 1943.

The first time the Bulgarian state succeeded in legislating on marriage and divorce was in 1945 when the Decree on Marriage was introduced (State Gazette, 1945), replacing the religious canons that had previously regulated matrimony and introducing divorce by mutual consent.[5] After this, religious marriage was no longer necessary or legally binding and was allowed to take place only after a civil marriage. The Penal Code made the conduct of a religious ceremony without civil marriage a criminal offence (Doncheva, 2002). This legislation formally secularized couple and family relations and established a universal judicial regime for all Bulgarian citizens, regardless of their religious beliefs (Todorova, 2002: 13; Doncheva, 2002). The assertion of control by the state over what had previously been the domain of the church set the tone for the discouragement of religious practice and the diminution of the influence of religion on the everyday lives of individuals that came to characterize the communist era. Ever since civil marriage was introduced, it has remained the only legally recognized union between two non-blood-related adults and the only arrangement from which rights and obligations arise. Marriage provides numerous entitlements including, for instance, the right to inheritance, to pension or survivor's benefit, to a common 'family name', to joint adoption, to access reproductive technologies, to information or decision-making about a partner's health and to refuse to testify against each other.

Although there was not extensive civil society mobilization around issues of intimate citizenship in the period prior to communism, there were campaigns both for state support for the traditional family, by, for example, the Union for Large Families (Ivanov, 2008), and for changes in law and policy by the women's movement. Feminists in Bulgaria, as in many other countries, sought equality within marriage and divorce on demand, the right for women not to have to take the nationality of their husbands, to end the tradition of women changing their names after marriage and for equality for children born to unmarried mothers. They also argued against prostitution and sexual exploitation, and for the protection of children and minorities (Daskalova, 2005).

The communist intimate citizenship regime

The transnational communist ideology that became the official creed of the Eastern Bloc after the Second World War proclaimed its commitment to women's equality in all spheres of life and its struggle against the traditional values of the 'bourgeois monogamous family'. Coupling was seen as based on love, shared political values and freedom to choose and change partners, while children were raised with community help (Vodenicharov, 2002: 104). In the People's Republic of Bulgaria, which existed from 1946 to 1990, this ideology led to an initial period of liberalization in intimate life, with women taking up work in great numbers. In 1947 the Constitution declared marriage to be gender-equal and secular (Therborn, 2004).

However, the regime quickly changed course and introduced a wave of regressive changes in the late 1940s and early 1950s. As in other European intimate citizenship regimes, the 1950s in Bulgaria

Figure 6.1 'Equal rights. Equal in construction': front cover of *Today's Woman* magazine, February 1945. This image speaks of the emphasis in post-Second World War Bulgaria on equality between women and men as workers. Source: *Today's Woman* magazine, reprinted with permission.

was a decade of conservatism in law and policy. Freedoms that had been gained were quickly lost, as the communist regime revived the pronatalism of an earlier era and brought in new restrictions on intimacy and sexuality. This period was characterized by intense mass propaganda of communist ideas and a totalitarian political system in which the Communist Party controlled all spheres of public life and intervened significantly in matters of personal life (Delev et al., 2006). A comprehensive system of political surveillance over individual intimate lives was gradually established, based on a very narrow notion of legitimate form of intimate life, and with punitive effect on those who were living outside the couple-norm.

After revoking 'sexual impotence' and 'infertility' as grounds for divorce in 1949 (Persons and Family Act, 1949), divorce by mutual consent was retracted in 1952 and a compulsory conciliation session was inserted into divorce procedures for the first time (Law on People and Family, 1952 cited in Todorova, 2002). With the aim of stimulating marriage and procreation, pornography and abortion were banned in 1951 (Penal Code, 1951), and the Decree for Stimulation of Birth Rates (1951) introduced a new tax that was known as the 'Bachelor Tax'. Penalizing both married and unmarried women aged between 21 and 45 and men aged between 21 and 50 who did not have children, it remained in force until 1990. Childless adults were required to pay 5 per cent of taxable income at the age of 21, rising to 15 per cent at 35 (Ministry of Labour and Social Policy, 2006). The motivation for these pronatalist policies, as outlined by the Prime Minister and Head of State at the time Todor Zhivkov, was:

> Administrative measures should be considered in order to overcome parental egoism and unwillingness to give birth and raise children. Those who do not want to have any children have to take part in supporting other people's children. (Zhivkov, 1967 cited in Kalinova and Baeva, 2006: 221, our translation)

These new laws were accompanied by a strong media campaign against the irresponsible disruption of marriage and the publication of stories about abandoned wives who refused to divorce for the sake of their children (Popova, 2004). Follow-up measures to reinforce the promotion of the married couple-form included new provisions in the 1956 Penal Code that introduced punishment in the form of imprisonment, fines and public reprobation for a spouse who left their family and who was living with another person, or who otherwise demonstrated infidelity. As the case of Diana, one of our interviewees in Part III, demonstrates, there were prosecutions under this regulation. 'Comrade Courts' were established in 1961 – local public forums at which Communist Party activists and members of the community discussed and evaluated individuals' intimate lives, particularly cases of extramarital sex, domestic violence and alcoholism, and offered advice on how to preserve marriages (Popova, 2004; Brunnbauer, 2008). 'Comrade Courts' applied moralistic surveillance and aimed to enforce compliance by making public any acts perceived as wrongdoing, instilling shame in those on the receiving end (Brunnbauer, 2008). Procreation within wedlock was further promoted by the legalization of abortion upon request for the first time in 1956, although in 1963, just seven years later, restrictions were introduced again.

None of these measures had the full desired effect: the marriage rate saw a slight but short-lived rise from 8.8 per 1,000 population in 1951 to 9.6 in 1953, before it started falling the next year, and birth rates continued to fall throughout the 1950s and into the 1960s. But early marriage and childbearing were almost universal (Philipov and Kohler, 2001; Frejka et al., 2008), and, as Frejka et al. (2008) point out, there was a limited range of available options for self-realization outside the family.

Under communism 'only reproductive sexual acts between spouses were considered legitimate sexual practices' (Popova, 2004: 1, our translation) and sexual pleasure as an end in itself was disapproved of, even within marriage. The attempt to confine sexuality to the marital relationship was further pursued through the arrest and imprisonment of prostitutes (Meshkova and Sharlanov, 1994; Popova, 2004, 2009) and of men who engaged in same-sex sexual acts (Pisankaneva, 2002; Popova, 2009). Indeed, in 1951 the punishment for homosexuality – considered a crime against public morality – was increased from six months' to three years' imprisonment. The Penal Code criminalized both acts of 'sexual intercourse' and acts of 'sexual pleasure' between people of the same sex, the latter encompassing, for the first time and unusually, sexual acts between women (Bulgarian Helsinki Committee, 2001). This might be understood in the context of the strong social and legal pressure to procreate, to which acts of 'sexual pleasure' would not contribute. In addition, the communist ideology of egalitarianism (Vodenicharov, 2002) and its conceptualization of women as strong and active agents might also have made it possible to imagine women engaging independently of men in sexual activities and giving and receiving sexual pleasure (Roseneil and Stoilova, 2011).[6] However, whilst there was a state campaign against male 'intellectual homosexuals', many of whom were sent to corrective labour camps, no women were sentenced for same-sex sexual acts (Gruev, 2006; Pisankaneva, 2002). In 1968, shortly after the UK and before Norway, homosexuality was decriminalized (Roseneil and Stoilova, 2011; Pisankaneva, 2003). However, this did not mean full equality for lesbians and gay men: the age of consent remained higher (18 years old) than for heterosexual acts (14 years old) until 1986, homosexual intent was regarded as an aggregating factor in sex crimes, and the public display of same-sex relationships could still result in arrest and sentencing to community service in corrective labour camps

(Pisankaneva, 2003).[7] This legal and cultural climate meant that many lesbians and gay men felt compelled to enter heterosexual marriages and to lead double lives (Pisankaneva, 2009).

During this period, there was no independent civil society or social movement activism that could challenge the communist intimate citizenship regime. Following the adoption of a new Constitution in December 1947, civil rights and personal freedoms were limited so that they could not be used against the state (Delev et al., 2006), and a single mass political organization – the Fatherland Front (Отечествен Фронт) – was established, placing civic organizing under the strict control of the state. All civic participation during the communist era had to promote the new morality and social order (Deyanova, 2004). Organized women engaged with issues such as partnership, child-bearing and care, creating around them a discourse of 'right' and 'wrong', with the 'Comrade Courts' serving as a key site through which local activists exercised their moralizing surveillance over the intimate aspects of their neighbours' lives. Thus, while the communist regime was not particularly successful at boosting marriage and childbirth (Brunnbauer and Tylor, 2012), it found many ways to extend state intervention in intimate life and to promote and defend the married procreative heterosexual couple-form.[8]

Post-communist liberalization and its limits

The collapse of communism in 1989 saw a general decline in state intervention in intimate life and a rapid liberalization of the Bulgarian intimate citizenship regime. Within the first few years most of the punitive measures introduced under communism were revoked: abortion on demand became available again, the 'Bachelor Tax' was abolished and the right of each person to a 'family life' unhindered by the state was recognized in the new Constitution of 1991, which set out to grant 'inviolable privacy' to Bulgarian citizens, marking a break with the community policing era of the Comrade Courts. The age of consent was the one area in which the transition initially meant regressive change: the age of consent for homosexual acts, which had been equalized at 14 in 1986, was raised to 16, reintroducing inequality between heterosexuals and homosexuals.

However, the decision to seek accession to the European Union required a number of important changes in law and policy to the benefit of lesbians and gay men. In this context, the newly established Bulgarian Gay Organisation Gemini organized a campaign and collected letters of support from the non-governmental sector and public figures (Queer Bulgaria, 2004) for lesbian and gay equality which provided local pressure from below, as well as from supranational organizations 'above'. This resulted in the (re-)equalization of the age of consent in 2002 and the revocation of two paragraphs of the Penal Code that penalized 'homosexual acts in public places' and 'homosexual acts performed in a scandalous manner or in a manner that may incite others to follow a path of perversion or homosexual prostitution'. The full decriminalization of homosexuality was achieved in 2006 when public reprobation for homosexual acts was also abolished. In addition, in 2004, the Protection against Discrimination Act (PADA) was introduced to meet the demands of the EU Employment Equality Directive of 2000, which banned discrimination based on religion and belief, age, disability and sexual orientation, in employment and occupation, vocational training, and membership of employer and employee organizations. In fact, PADA went beyond this to address equal treatment and equal opportunities 'in principle in every part of the social sphere' (Kukova, 2008: 3), offering protection in the areas of employment, education and training, and provision of goods and services.[9] A year later the Law on Protection from Domestic Violence (2005) sought to free a wide range of intimate relationships from interpersonal violence – including physical, mental or sexual violence. The recognition that violence takes place between people who are or have been related by marriage, co-parenting, kinship or cohabitation marked a major development in the Bulgarian intimate citizenship regime. Together these were important changes in the regulation of the couple-form, signalling a liberalization and equalization of intimate citizenship, in line with emerging European norms of gender and sexual equality.

This progressive change has, however, been halted by Bulgaria's refusal to ratify the Istanbul Convention. Fuelled by fears that the country would have to introduce a 'third sex' and marriage equality, and as part of a wider 'anti-gender' backlash politics in eastern Europe (Kuhar and Paternotte, 2017), there was strong political and public opposition (ILGA Europe, 2019). The 2018 ruling of the Constitutional Court found against the underpinning 'gender ideology' of the Convention and ruled that:

The Constitution and the whole Bulgarian legislation are based on the understanding of the binary existence of the human race [...]

The Convention would require the Republic of Bulgaria to create procedures granting legal recognition of a gender different from the biological sex, which is against the Constitution.

This ruling has already been used by the courts to refuse gender reassignment to trans people (Bulgarian Helsinki Committee, 2019), and the campaign against the ratification of the Convention stimulated a wave of homophobia, coining the term 'gender' as a new insult for LGBT people (Bulgarian Helsinki Committee, 2019; ILGA Europe, 2019, Behrensen and Stanoeva, 2019). In addition, the Criminal Code (2019) failed to introduce recognition of sexual orientation, gender identity or gender expression as aggravating factors in cases of violence or hatred. For example, homophobic and transphobic motives do not result in more severe punishments for murder or inflicting injury in the same way as racist or xenophobic motives do (Bulgarian Helsinki Committee, 2019). Hence, in comparative terms, the contemporary Bulgarian intimate citizenship regime remains conservative and strongly heteronormative.

In parallel, and in line with broad shifts in intimate life practices across Europe, there has emerged a new focus on the couple-form as a relationship based on negotiation and sharing, alongside increased policy concern with the rights and interests of the child (Family Code, 2009; Protection of the Child Act, 2000). A round of revisions to the Family Code between 2006 and 2009 saw the introduction of prenuptial agreements, mediation and further liberalization of divorce regulations, removing, for instance, the need to find a guilty party, even in divorces which are not based on mutual consent. Equality between children born within and outside marriage, and for adopted children, was also legislated in the 2009 Family Code. These alterations to the Family Code were seen by the government as a necessary response to the changing realities of married and family life (Council of Ministers, 2008a: 61) and a recognition of 'basic civil rights, mobility, and freedom of personal life' (Council of Ministers, 2008a: 61). On the other hand, against a background of rapidly declining birth rates and intense political concern about demographic dynamics (Stoilova, 2008), the emphasis on supporting the heterosexual procreative couple-form has continued. The post-communist state explicitly declared its protection of marriage, family life, children and motherhood in two of its key legislative documents – the Constitution (1991, Art. 14) and the Family Code (2019, Art. 2). The government also refused to change family law in ways that would recognize the rights of unmarried cohabiting couples, rejecting the recommendation of an expert parliamentary commission which concluded that the existing legal framework did not correspond to 'the stage of social development and to the new responsibilities that families are facing in raising children' (Council of Ministers, 2008a: 61).

Similar determination to maintain the unique position of the heterosexual married couple-form can be seen in the continued refusal to recognize same-sex relationships. Since the start of the new millennium, lesbian and gay relationships have been increasingly visible in the mainstream media in Bulgaria, and there has been vociferous campaigning by lesbian and gay groups, including the successful pursuit of a number of court cases against homophobia (Stoilova, 2009a). Same-sex marriage, partnership and adoption were widely debated in 2008–9 whilst the Family Code was being revised, and the first Gay Pride event in Bulgaria was organized around the theme 'Me and My Family', with demands for legal recognition at its heart. But both the Constitution (1991, Art. 46: 1) and the Family Code (2019, Art. 5) continue to define marriage as a voluntary union between a man and a woman. The Protection against Discrimination Commission intervened to suggest that the right to recognition of cohabitation should be extended to same-sex couples, but ultimately no recognition of cohabitation (heterosexual or same-sex) was achieved. The former Chair of Parliament Ognyan Gerjikov exemplified the reactionary tenor of the debate, in his reference to the traditions of the Bulgarian nation:

> With all my respect for the different, I cannot accept that gay marriages should be made legal in Bulgaria. We are a patriarchal society and this would detonate public opinion. So, may those who find it necessary to be together in a same-sex [relationship] do that without wanting official recognition of the state for this.
> (Roseneil and Stoilova, 2011: 181, our translation from a broadcast on Nova Television, 2009).

A qualitative study of the experiences of lesbians and gay men in Bulgaria (Filipova and Pisankaneva, 2017) reported that they continue to face discrimination and marginalization as a result of the lack of basic intimate citizenship rights, particularly those concerning separation from or the death of a partner, joint adoption, second parent adoption,[10] and access to information or decision-making related to a partner's health. 'Institutionalised discrimination is something frequent and even expected' (Filipova and Pisankaneva, 2017: 45), and lesbians and gay men seek legal loopholes or private service providers in order to get access to basic services or ordinary human rights, such as the ability to be present when their partner gives birth.

However, the wider context and direction of travel at the European level is rather different. In 2018 the European Court of Justice ruled in the case of *Coman et al. v Romania* that the definition of spouse in European law is neutral with regard to sex and hence that same-sex marriages (of EU citizens) must be recognized for the purpose of freedom of movement in all EU countries, even those that have not legalized same-sex marriage.[11] As a result of the judgment, in July 2019 a married lesbian couple, one of whom is an EU citizen, won the right to settle in Bulgaria as a couple with the ruling of the Supreme Administrative Court that Bulgaria must recognize their foreign marriage. Whilst this in itself does not require the legalization of same-sex marriage in Bulgaria, which remains a matter of national determination, it does further indicate the changing European legal and normative context, making it difficult for EU member states to resist even if they have not equalized marriage. However, the rights of Bulgarian nationals remain restricted, as evidenced in the refusal in 2018 of the Sofia Administrative Court to recognize the union of two women Bulgarian nationals who had married in the UK. The Court ruled that their marriage is against the Bulgarian Constitution and Family Code. Against this backdrop, campaigning by lesbian and gay activists continues, as does the public debate about changing practices of intimacy and the demand for legal recognition of unmarried and same-sex couples.

The landscape of coupledom in contemporary Bulgaria

Despite marriage retaining its unassailable position as the 'gold standard' intimate relationship in the Bulgarian intimate citizenship regime, its popularity as a lived practice has been in dramatic decline. In 2011 the marriage rate reached its lowest point in the history of contemporary Bulgaria, with only 2.9 marriages per 1,000 people, rising again to 4 per 1,000 in 2017 (Eurostat, 2019). This was a large decrease from 6.9 per 1,000 at the end of the communist era in 1990, and 8.8 per 1,000 in 1960 (Eurostat, 2019). Although Bulgaria still has one of the lowest average ages of first marriage in the EU, people get married considerably later in life than during communism; the mean age of first marriage for women has risen from 21.4 years in 1990 to 26.9 in 2010 and 27.5 in 2014 (UNECE, 2019). Divorce rates have increased since the early 1960s, with a rate of 1.2 divorces per 1,000 in 1970, peaking at 2.2 in 2007 and then falling back to 1.5 in 2017, a rate similar to the one at the time of transition from communism (Eurostat, 2019).

As part of the general trend away from early and lifelong marriage, there has been a large increase in solo-living, from 18.2 per cent of households in 1980 to 30.8 per cent in 2010 (UNECE, 2019). There has been a steady decline in the proportion of households composed of couples with children – from 36 per cent in 1980 to 25 per cent in 2011 (UNECE, 2019). Moreover, the proportion of unmarried heterosexual couples with children has more than doubled, from 2 per cent in 2001 to 4.2 per cent in 2011 (UNECE, 2019). The total proportion of couple households has also fallen, from 58 per cent in 1980 to 45 per cent in 2011 (UNECE, 2019).

Alongside these changes, fertility rates have plummeted, from 2.31 children per woman in 1960 to 1.56 in 2017, with a low of 1.26 in 2000 (Eurostat, 2019). The average age at which women give birth for the first time has risen over recent decades, from 21.9 years in 1980, to 23.3 years in 2000 and 27.1 in 2017; yet it remains the lowest of our four countries (UNECE, 2019). Perhaps the most striking change has been in births outside marriage, which have risen from 8 per cent in 1960 to 58.9 per cent in 2017, the highest amongst our four countries, with the biggest jump in the 1990s (Eurostat, 2019). In sum, these statistics highlight the gap that exists between the diversity of intimate lifestyles that Bulgarians are living and an intimate citizenship regime that continues to privilege the procreative married couple-form above all else.

Notes

1 The general practice of state hospitals is to allow only the father to be present with the mother at childbirth, although private hospitals are less restrictive (Filipova and Pisankaneva, 2017).

2 There is a debate about the use of the terms 'C/communism'/'post-C/communism' and 'socialism'/'post-socialism'. Bulgaria was ruled by the Bulgarian Communist Party and was proclaimed to be a 'socialist state' in the Constitution of the People's Republic from 1971. We have chosen to use the terms 'communism'/'communist', reflecting the name of the ruling party, rather than the more disputable characterization of the country as 'socialist'.

3 Under King Simeon (893–927), the death penalty was introduced for those found guilty, except for the 'passive' party if he was under the age of 20 (Bulgarian Helsinki Committee, 2001).

4 Proposed 'Bill on the Conclusion and Termination of Marriage' (Todorova, 2002).

5 Divorce by mutual consent was repealed in 1952 and restored in 1968 (Todorova, 2002).

6   Our argument here has parallels with Löfström's (1998) discussion of why homosexual acts between women were criminalized in the 1889 Finnish Penal Code.

7   A number of other Soviet Bloc countries had already decriminalized sexual acts between men. For example, in Czechoslovakia, where decriminalization was enacted in 1961, it was the medical profession, particularly 'the flourishing field of sexology' (Long, 1999: 247) that led the pressure for change, and Hungary decriminalized in the same year. Bulgaria seems to have followed this liberalization process. There were a number of sexology clinics and a research institute under communism (Okoliyski and Velichkov, 2004).

8   It was not only unconventional intimate lives that were targeted under communism; Muslim communities were pursued particularly harshly by a range of policies, from the 1950s until the collapse of communism, including the prohibition of circumcision, of speaking the Turkish language in public, traditional clothing and Turkish music, and the forceful replacement of Muslim-Arabic names with Slavic ones (Stoilova, 2008).

9   PADA is regarded as revolutionary for the Bulgarian judicial system (Kukova, 2008) in including all aspects of discrimination, direct and indirect, shifting the burden of proof in favour of the victim, and allowing legal non-profit entities to initiate court cases and to act as plaintiffs on behalf of the victims.

10 That is, a same-sex step-parent's acquisition of parental responsibility.

11 See https://europeanlawblog.eu/2018/06/19/free-movement-of-same-sex-spouses-within-the-eu-the-ecjs-coman-judgment/ (accessed 5 August 2019).

7
The Norwegian intimate citizenship regime

Introduction

The late nineteenth and early twentieth centuries were a period of rapid social change in Norway. Until then Norway had had a small, relatively poor and largely rural population and was second only to Ireland in levels of emigration.[1] But industrialization brought people into towns and cities, and the new urban population started to organize politically. There was a growth in civil society organizations and a push for democratization, with votes for all men (not receiving poor relief) achieved in 1898 and votes for women in 1913. Votes for all adults, including those receiving poor relief, were granted in 1919. During the twentieth century, a strong alliance between the growing labour movement and the Labour Party (Arbeiderpartiet) served to establish Norway's characteristic social democracy, with a high degree of consensus about the importance of welfare built into the fabric of national politics. For two vital decades, between 1945 and 1965, the Labour Party was in government. Since then, the country has alternated between Labour, Conservative (Høyre) and coalition governments, but between 1935 and 2019 there were only 22 years when the Prime Minister was not from Labour Party (Tvedt and Bull, 2016).

Social scientists have argued that the Nordic welfare state rests on 'a passion for equality' (Graubard, 1986) and a commitment to egalitarian and universalist values (Siim, 1993). Esping-Andersen conceptualized this as the social democratic Nordic welfare state model, in which there is a fundamental 'universal solidarity in favour of the welfare state. All benefit, all are dependent; and all will presumably feel obliged to pay' (Esping-Andersen, 1990: 28). Other researchers have further argued that institutional trust – in government, authorities and the institutions of the welfare state – is particularly high in the Nordic welfare states (see Delhey and Newton, 2005; Edlund, 2006; Ellingsæter and Pedersen, 2016). This trust can be traced historically (Bergh and Bjørnskov, 2011) and can be seen both as a condition for, and latterly as a result of, the well-functioning welfare state (Listhaug and Ringdal, 2008). It also meant that progressive social movements – the labour, women's and, later, lesbian and gay movements – wished, and have been able, to work closely with state bodies, sharing an 'extensive will to reform' (Mühleisen, Røthing and Svendsen, 2012) in the project of securing an equal, harmonious and stable coupled family life for all.

As well as resting on the Norwegian social democratic welfare state, the development of a 'gender-equal', de-patriarchalized intimate citizenship regime in Norway was also dependent on the liberal individualism of the legal system and on the prevalence of Lutheran Protestantism which recognized the state's power to legislate on family matters and 'did not do battle for patriarchal marriage as a legal institution' (Therborn, 2004: 82). From the early decades of the twentieth century, progressive family law and a focus on gender equality were seen as means to a stable and productive society in Norway. Liberal divorce laws and the granting of rights to children born out of wedlock set the tone for the emergence of the contemporary intimate citizenship regime. At the same time, the 'Nordic model of marriage' (Melby et al., 2006b) consolidated the heterosexual nuclear family and the ideology of the housewife and homemaking, constructing 'progressive maternalism' (Hagemann, 2007) as a central trope of Norwegian policy and culture.

The origins of 'gender-equal' intimate citizenship

Gender equality [*likestilling*] is widely regarded as at the core of the contemporary Norwegian welfare state (Hernes, 1987; Ellingsæter and Leira, 2006; Halsaa, Roseneil and Sümer, 2012), and we similarly propose that it is at the heart of the Norwegian intimate citizenship regime. Helga Hernes (1987) suggests that the inclusion and empowerment of women within 'women-friendly' Nordic welfare states have deep historical roots, and Kari Melby and colleagues substantiate this argument with their historical research on the 'Nordic model of marriage', showing how gender equality was central to Nordic family policy from the early twentieth century (Melby et al., 2006a and b).

Formal gender equality in marriage and no-fault divorce were introduced in 1909, in line with the outcome of the Scandinavian Law Commission, which had been set the task by national governments of proposing changes to family law (Therborn, 2004). These new laws defined marriage as a modern, secular institution, a pact between two independent and free individuals (Melby et al., 2006a, 2006b; Melby, Ravn and Wetterberg, 2008). The reforms 'granted wives equality in marriage, revoking male supervision and giving housework and childcare equal status as providing activity. Thus, women gained equal rights, but also the responsibility of providing for their families' (Haavet, 2006: 191). Melby and colleagues (2006a) argue that the Nordic marriage model, which was implemented between 1909 and 1929, is an early example of the state feminism that later came to be seen as characteristic of Norway and the Nordic countries. In the context of the rapid social change of the early twentieth century there was widespread concern that both the stability and the morality of society were endangered. The rise in divorce and in unmarried cohabitation – often referred to as 'Stockholm-marriage'[2] – in the numbers of single women and people emigrating, alongside a decline in the birth rate, were regarded by politicians, and discussed in the press, as serious problems for the nation. Reforms to family law were seen as an important tool for governments seeking to create societal order and stability. Politicians recognized that traditional patriarchal marriage might be less attractive to modern women, and legislating for gender equality in marriage was partly an attempt to increase its appeal to women and hence to strengthen marriage as an institution, at a time when feminism was making a significant impact on public consciousness (Hernes, 1987; Melby et al., 2006a: 16, 202). Melby and colleagues argue that the overarching goals of the marriage reforms were gender equality, societal stability, prosperity and a 'healthy' population (Melby et al., 2006a: 14). In other words, from the early twentieth century the creation of a gender-equal married couple-form was seen as crucial to society as a whole.

At the same time as gender equality was stressed, and to some extent secured, through the new marriage acts, the Nordic marriage model also consolidated the nuclear family and the ideology of the housewife. During the twentieth century, Norway was the Nordic country with the highest percentage of stay-at-home mothers and had a particularly low level of involvement of women in the labour market (Leira, 1992; Hagemann, 2007). Gro Hagemann (2007) argues that a specifically Norwegian 'progressive maternalism', with roots in agrarian democratic attitudes and non-clerical Lutheran movements, has played an important role in Norwegian policy. In the early twentieth century this maternalism became a significant component of the socialist and social democratic women's movements (Hagemann, 2007). The family unit, the upbringing of children and the conditions of marriage have been the focus of both right-wing and left-wing movements and parties in Norway.

One of the consequences of this is that 'the care-needing child' can be seen as the main focus of Norwegian family policy (Haavet, 2006: 191), with Norway in the 'avant-garde' of children's rights, according to Therborn (2004). The focus on children was also seen in the progressive treatment of children born to unmarried mothers and of lone mothers themselves. The 1915 Castbergian Children's Act effectively abolished the concept of illegitimacy and granted to children born outside marriage the right to their father's name and to paternal inheritance (Therborn, 2004; Haavet, 2006). The Act made it a public responsibility to settle and collect child support from fathers, although public prepayment of financial support was not introduced until 1957 (Haavet, 2006). The law also established a responsibility on local authorities to act as financial provider by granting 'a small municipal benefit to the mother from two weeks before, and up to six months after giving birth, providing she kept her baby' (Haavet, 2006: 198). These policies rested on the belief that it was a benefit to society that poor single mothers should be enabled to care for their own children.[3] More widely, the state was willing to provide economic support for all new mothers, so that they could focus on childcare rather than on paid work (Haavet, 2006), and in some cases the desire to protect children has meant restrictions on the choices of mothers (Peterson, 2015).

The early years of the first wave women's movement in Norway had a strong focus on the rights of women as members of society. The struggle for political citizenship – for suffrage – was at the forefront, along with that for economic citizenship – the need for women to be able to support themselves and live independent lives. Major achievements included the opening up of access for women to university in 1884 and to a range of professions and public offices. These causes were particularly important for single middle-class women (Hellesund, 2003; Melby et al., 2006a; Moksnes, 1984), and Tone Hellesund (2003) has argued that their needs were mobilized in the argument for granting rights to all women. After the vote was won in 1913, the focus soon shifted towards the needs of the wife, mother and housewife (Melby, 1995; Moksnes, 1984). The Norwegian Housewives' Association significantly outstripped the feminist organizations in membership during these years (Melby, 1995; Slettvåg, 1980), and single independent life was less and less seen as an honourable and viable alternative for women (Hellesund, 2003). Margarete Bonnevie, one of the most prominent and influential feminists of the pre- and post-Second World War period, published the book *Ekteskap og arbeide* (Marriage and Work) in 1932. This book exemplified Norwegian progressive maternalism in its focus on women's right to combine work and family. In this position, which we can see as underpinning the Norwegian intimate citizenship regime, it is normative for women both to be married mothers and to participate in paid work and wider society.[4] Hellesund (2003) suggests that Bonnevie's focus on married women and motherhood was a confrontation with the earlier 'spinster-generation' of feminists and was part of a move to prove that feminists of the new generation were 'real women' – married and heterosexual, with their own biological children.

As far as homosexuality was concerned, there was early evidence of the progressive liberalism that came to characterize twentieth-century Norway. The seventeenth-century law that punished 'fornication against nature' with 'stake and fire' was revised by the 1842 Penal Code to punishment by hard labour.[5] By 1902, §213 of the Penal Code, which explicitly criminalized sexual relations between men, stated that they were only to be prosecuted if they caused public damage 'when general conditions so demand' (Herzog, 2011: 78; Halsos, 1999; Jordåen, 2003). As a result, relatively few cases of homosexuality were taken to court during the twentieth century, and the 'problem' of homosexuality shifted location to the realm of psychiatry. As in the United Kingdom over 20 years later (see p. 47), suggestions that sex between women should be included in the new law were rejected.

Intimate citizenship in the era of the housewife

The decades following the Second World War were the peak of what has been called the era of the housewife in Norwegian history (Melby, 1995, 2005). During this period the proportion of married women and the number of housewives rose to an all-time high (Blom, 2005: 350; Melby, 2005: 263; Sarromaa, 2011: 21). The age of marriage reached an all-time low around 1970, and the focus on the nuclear family was prominent in politics as well as popular culture (Danielsen, 2002; Hagemann and Roll-Hansen, 2005; Hellesund, 2003; Sarromaa, 2011). Social reformer Katti Anker Møller had proposed in 1919 that women should be compensated for having children, and this proposal was supported by the women's section of the Labour Party (Arbeiderpartiets Kvindeforbund). Over time the idea of a maternal wage was discussed and worked through, and in 1947 a family allowance was introduced. This universal benefit was paid per child directly to the mother (Haavet, 2006) and remains in place at the time of writing.

Despite the young heterosexual nuclear family being at the centre of political and cultural attention, the principle of universalism in welfare provision that characterized the post-war decades served to improve the security and well-being of all those living outside the couple-form. In 1957 a universal old-age pension was introduced, along with, at different times, specific financial support for widows, divorcees, single mothers and the disabled, and from 1977 the sickness benefit system provided full pay from the first day of an illness, reducing dependency on families and partners (Bjørnson, 1994: 15).

The era of the housewife also saw the formation of two important intimate citizenship organizations that campaigned for the rights of those living outside the heterosexual couple-form. In 1950 a Norwegian branch of the Danish organization for homosexuals, Forbundet av 1948 [The Association of 1948], was founded, and three years later it became an independent organization, The Norwegian Association of 1948 [Det Norske forbundet av 1948, DNF-48]. DNF-48's first pamphlet argued against the law that criminalized male homosexuality and against the idea that homosexuality was a disease. The concept *homofil* (homophile) was introduced to underline that homosexuality had more to do with love between people than with sex (DNF-48, 1951).[6] In 1953 the Committee on the Penal Code suggested removing §213 of the Code, but proposed an age of consent of 18 (as opposed to 16 for heterosexual sex) and sought to introduce a prohibition on 'homosexual propaganda', in order to counter public fears that decriminalization would lead to the spread of homosexuality. DNF-48 took the position that the proposed changes were worse than the existing (mostly 'sleeping') paragraph, and pressure for decriminalization was put on hold. It was only in the late 1960s that the issue was taken up again by the movement, and in 1972 the removal of §213 was supported by an overwhelming majority in parliament (Jordåen, 2003).

In 1957 Ensliges Landsforbund [the National Organization for Single People] was established. The organization's campaigns focused on the discrimination against single people that was built into the Norwegian welfare state, with particular attention paid to housing. National housing policy made it almost impossible for single people to access decent housing. Ensliges Landsforbund also took up issues of

Figure 7.1 Norwegian Labour Party election poster, 1961: 'nye gode ar' ('New good years'). The poster places a close, loving heterosexual couple and their child in a field of melting snow, just outside a modern, orderly town. Standing together as a unit, they are watching the returning geese that herald the arrival of spring. The poster expresses the optimism and familialism of social democratic Norway after the Second World War. Source: ARBARK: AAB-119701. Artist: Borghild Rud.

**Alfhild Brevig
og Agnes Husbyn**

**STERKEST
-ALENE?**

Gyldendal Norsk Forlag

Figure 7.2 *Sterkest-Alene?* ['Strongest Alone?']: book cover, 1979. Alfhild Brevig and Agnes Husbyn, authors of this ground-breaking book, were the prominent leaders of Ensliges Landsforbund [the National Organization of Singles]. They published three books between 1969 and 1985, arguing for fairer economic and material conditions for single people and for the recognition of single life as an honourable alternative to coupledom. This book posed, and answered, a provocative question: 'Do we as humans have a *duty* to live in a group, whether it is in a marriage, a large family or a different intimate arrangement? The answer has to be *no*, but society and the church still act as if humans *do have* such a duty.' Source: author.

economic citizenship, arguing that single people have to pay relatively more in taxes and more in official charges for water and sewage, with the result that they effectively subsidize couples and families (Brevig and Husbyn, 1979; Brevig, 1985). The organization continued to lobby for better conditions for single people, demanding, for instance, tax deductions to compensate for the extra costs of living alone, until it closed in 2019 due to a decline in membership. It is notable that there has not been a comparable organization in the UK, Bulgaria or Portugal, notwithstanding that the couple-norm and the disadvantaging of single people are equally strong, if not stronger, in each of our other case study countries.

Further equalization of intimate citizenship

During the 1970s the level of education among the Norwegian population increased dramatically, particularly for women. The divorce rate also began to rise, and divorce started to be more socially acceptable. Of couples who married in 1945, about 10 per cent were divorced 30 years later, whereas for couples married in 1965, the proportion was 26 per cent (Noack and Mamelund, 1997). The earlier, well-established pattern of couple formation, in which there was first the wedding, then living together and then children, started to break down as people began to cohabit and then have children and only later get married (Vollset, 2011: 10). In 1972, two significant liberalizing changes were enacted in the Norwegian intimate citizenship regime through changes to the Penal Code: heterosexual unmarried cohabitation and sex between men were both legalized.

Prior to the legislation of 1972, it was illegal for an unmarried heterosexual couple to live together 'as married people' and doing so could be punished with fines or imprisonment. Although this legislation had been dormant for many decades, and although the section of the Penal Code outlawing male homosexuality was seldom used, polls showed that both laws were in line with public opinion. Liberal attitudes towards heterosexual unmarried cohabitation did not really take hold until the late 1980s. In 1973, 87 per cent of the population believed that marriage was the best way to organize a relationship between a man and a woman, and in 1977, 71 per cent were still against 'paperless marriages' (i.e. cohabitation) (Alstad, 1993 [1969]: 370–1). This picture changed through the 1980s, and in 1997, 56 per cent regarded unmarried cohabitation as just as acceptable as marriage.

An additional 30 per cent said that cohabitation was acceptable where no children were involved (NOU, 1999: 88). In 25 years, practices and attitudes towards unmarried cohabitation had changed dramatically, to the extent that sociologist Liv Syltevik (2010) argues that it has become a normative part of the life course in Norway, regarded as the right and proper thing do to at the start of a relationship. Many cohabitants meet mild assumptions that they will eventually marry, 'but there is no question of being excluded or sanctioned' (Syltevik, 2010: 458). However, Syltevik acknowledges that 'love and long-term commitment still play a hegemonic role' and that 'cohabitation does not represent a break with the ideal of the long-lasting relationship between two partners' (2010: 458).

Liberal attitudes towards homosexuality were also slow to appear, but decriminalization in the 1970s presaged the development of increasing tolerance and moves towards social inclusion. In a poll in 1947, Norwegians rated sex between persons of the same sex the third most serious crime, after murder and rape. The hierarchy continued downwards with drunk-driving, burglary, forgery and 'hunting outside the hunting season' (Alstad, 1969: 79). A poll in 1973 showed that 55 per cent saw homosexuality as a disease, 27 per cent were unsure and 18 per cent did not think it was a disease (Alstad, 1993 [1969]: 666). In 1974, DNF-48 had started campaigning for people with 'homosexual inclinations' to be added to the list of those protected from discriminatory refusal to supply goods or services (Penal Code, §349a) and from threatening and hateful utterances (§135a), and in a survey in 1978, 69 per cent expressed the opinion that homosexuals should have the same rights as others in their working lives, with 54 per cent believing that homosexuals should be allowed to be teachers and priests (Alstad, 1993 [1969]: 670). In 1981 the Penal Code was revised to include protection on the basis of 'homosexual inclination, lifestyle, or orientation' (Hennum, 2001). This meant that Norway was the first country in the world to legislate against discrimination on the grounds of sexual orientation (Löfström, 1998). In 1994, one year after the Act Relating to Registered Partnership came into force (see below), 40 per cent stated that they were negative towards the idea that people in lesbian/gay relationships should be able to formalize their relationship on the same terms as heterosexual couples. However, in 2005, two surveys showed increasing acceptance of same-sex relationship recognition, with 60 per cent and 63 per cent saying that homosexuals should be able to marry on the same terms as heterosexuals (Anderssen and Slåtten, 2008: 19). Public opinion about non-normative intimacies in Norway thus seems to have followed changes in the law, rather than motivating them, and the pressure groups and political parties that secured change in intimate citizenship law and policy can be seen to have played a crucial role in leading cultural change. And whilst negative attitudes towards homosexuality were dominant in the population until recently, it is now suggested that liberal, inclusive attitudes towards same-sex couples and relationships are seen as integral to Norwegian national identity (Gressgård and Jacobsen, 2008; Røthing and Svendsen, 2010).

The Norwegian women's and lesbian and gay movements have expressed a range of positions over time on issues of intimate citizenship. During the 1970s there were many different ideological positions regarding marriage and the couple-form within the Norwegian women's movement. While some rejected coupledom, monogamy and/or heterosexuality, the majority line in the Norwegian women's movement was to focus on reforming the relationship between men and women (Roseneil et al., 2013; Hellesund, 2013). The lesbian and gay liberation movement of the 1970s, however, took an explicit stand against couple-normativity, and the organiza-tion DNF-48 was explicitly against marriage and privileges for couples (Andersen, 2009). The national meeting of 1973 stated:

> The value of the individual is not dependent on the ability, will or opportunity to be coupled with another human being. DNF-48 cannot accept any form of discrimination towards single people – economic or on a human level. (Andersen, 2009: 126, our translation)

During the 1980s, however, the movement gained increasing power and influence within the formal political system and took on a more reformist agenda. Since the late 1980s, like many other western lesbian and gay movements (Chauncey, 2004; Rydström, 2008, 2011), the Norwegian lesbian and gay movement has had a strong focus on the right to marriage and to have children (Andersen, 2009), and, over the course of 30 years of campaigning, it achieved its ambition to achieve formal equality in the sphere of intimate citizenship.

The first stage in this was the 1993 Act on Registered Partnership. This provided equivalent rights and responsibilities to marriage for 'homophile persons of the same sex/gender' in relation to tax, social security and unemployment benefits, pensions and survivor benefits, carers' allowances and inheritance rights, except that registered partners could not adopt, access assisted conception or register their

Figure 7.3 Photo of the first registered partnership between two lesbians in Bergen, Norway, 1993. The new law allowed the registration of the partnership of 'two homophile persons of same sex'. The law preceded significant transformation in public opinion, as the photo illustrates. The photo won the 1993 Best Norwegian News Photo Prize. Photo by Rune Sævig, Bergensavisen.

partnership in the Church of Norway. However, in June 2008 a new gender-neutral Marriage Act was passed, removing all reference to sexual orientation from marriage law and allowing 'two persons of opposite or same-sex to marry'. This equalized parenting rights for same-sex couples, allowing joint adoption, second parent adoption (i.e. same-sex step-parents' acquisition of parental responsibility) and, for lesbians, access to assisted conception, with parental rights for the non-biological 'co-mother' (*medmor*). Formal equality in intimate citizenship was thereby established for lesbians and gay men.

The turn of the lesbian and gay movement toward relationship recognition and the demand for marriage reflect the extent to which 'respectable' coupledom, family life and domesticity are still regarded as key elements in constructing 'the good life' in Norway. While unmarried cohabiting and same-sex variants of the couple-form have become part of the Norwegian national model of family, marriage still retains a powerful place in the intimate cultural imaginary. It is no longer necessary for a couple to be married to be socially recognized and legitimate: the welfare state and intimate citizenship law and policy make it easy both not to marry and to leave a marriage. But societal expectations propel people towards co-resident coupledom and to a certain degree towards marriage, and they continue to lay down what a couple relationship should look like. Sociologist Arnfinn Andersen (2009) argues that the couple-norm and the 'heteronormal' have been strengthened during recent decades and that the struggle for a gender-neutral Marriage Act was a key part of this.

The expectations of what coupledom should entail can be seen particularly clearly in state discourse about marriage. Nordic marriage legislation has largely avoided references to emotions or morality and has not engaged in defining what a marriage should be or contain (Melby et al., 2006a). The current Norwegian Marriage Act does not state any 'criteria for cohabitation, consummation of the marriage or any other requirements concerning practices, motives or emotions for a marriage to be formally legal' (Eggebø, 2012: 26; Myhrer, 2006; Eggebø, 2013a). Yet the formula used as part of the civil marriage service articulates the contemporary Norwegian intimate citizenship regime's construction of marriage quite poignantly:

> To marry is a pledge to love and be faithful to one another. Vowing to love each other for the rest of your life is the hardest promise we can make to another person, and it requires your sincere desire to strive to achieve these standards, now and in

the years to come. That is the promise you are making to one another today. When entering into marriage you become one, but you also remain two independent and equal individuals. There is no contradiction between love and unity on the one hand, and freedom and self-reliance on the other. Love also means showing respect for one another. (Vedtak om borgerlig vigselsformular 2009 – our translation)

We can see here how romantic love and lifelong fidelity and commitment are central to the contemporary Norwegian couple-norm, alongside gender equality and individual autonomy. These are also expectations and values that shape the intimate imaginary expressed by our Norwegian interviewees when talking about their personal lives, as we shall see in Chapter 12.

Furthermore, in many of the counties of Norway, the local state began, in 2005, offering first-time parents (married or unmarried, heterosexual or same-sex) free 'couple courses' (Danielsen, Ludvigsen and Mühleisen, 2012). In line with the long-established progressive maternalism of the Norwegian welfare state, these courses, delivered by municipal health centres, are intended to create more stable, long-lasting couple relationships and thus better parents for children. They take for granted that the couple-form is based on romantic love, sex and monogamy, whilst also emphasizing that each of these requires consistent effort and hard work (Celello, 2009; Danielsen and Mühleisen, 2009a, 2009b; see also Illouz, 1998). The courses aim to provide the tools couples need to perform this demanding work.

The landscape of coupledom in contemporary Norway

The majority of the adult population in Norway today is in a couple relationship, but the statistics also show how intimate relationship practices have changed significantly over the past five decades. Compared to the other three countries in our study, Norwegians now have the highest age at first marriage and also the highest marriage rate. Both Bulgaria and Portugal have lower fertility rates than Norway. In 2018 the majority of the adult population was in a couple relationship – 42.2 per cent of persons over 18 years old were married and 17.9 per cent were cohabiting outside marriage – but there was a very substantial minority – 39.9 per cent – who were not living in a couple (SSB, 2020a, table 06096). In the age group mostly represented in our study, 30–44 years, 41.8 per cent were married, 27.7 per cent were cohabiting outside marriage and 30.5 per cent were not living in a couple (SSB, 2020c, table 06095). In terms of household living arrangements, in 2011, 41.0 per cent of households were people living alone, up from 27.9 per cent in 1980, although since 2011 the trend has been down, with 38.5 per cent of households composed of one person in 2017 (UNECE, 2019). Households composed of couples with children had fallen from 31.9 per cent in 1980 to 20.3 per cent in 2017, and households of couples (married, unmarried, with children and without) had fallen from 52 per cent in 1980 to 44.3 per cent in 2017 (UNECE, 2019).

Marriage rates have declined from 7.58 per 1,000 population in 1970 to 4.4 per 1,000 in 2017, but are the highest amongst our four countries (Eurostat, 2019). Age at first marriage has increased significantly, from 24.9 in 1980 to 31.9 in 2015 for women, and 27.4 in 1980 and 33.8 in 2015 for men (UNECE, 2019), and is also the highest of the four countries. Divorce rates have also increased significantly, from 0.9 per 1,000 population in 1970 to a peak of 2.4 in 1990, steadying around 2.2 in the early 2000s and 2 per 1,000 in 2017 (Eurostat, 2019). In 2017 Statistics Norway estimated that 40 per cent of all marriages will end in divorce (SSB, 2018, table 05707). All this means that serial monogamy has to a large extent replaced lifelong monogamy. This pattern is even more striking for same-sex couples. From 1993 to 2010, between 0.5 and 1 per cent of marriages/registered partnerships in Norway were between same-sex couples (Wiik, Seierstad and Noack, 2012: 18). The divorce risk for female couples was 2.28 times that for heterosexual couples, and for male couples it was 1.38 times the divorce risk for heterosexual married couples. Although having children did not reduce the risk of divorce for same-sex couples relative to heterosexual couples, having one or more children did significantly reduce the divorce risk for female couples, whereas male couples with children were more likely to divorce than those without children (Wiik, Seierstad and Noack, 2012: 18–19).[7] In 2017, 333 same-sex couples were married, 64 per cent of them women. In the same year 94 same-sex couples were separated and 91 same-sex couples divorced (SSB, 2019).

In line with the decline in marriage, births outside marriage have soared, from 3.7 per cent of births in 1960 to 55.7 per cent in 2017 (Eurostat, 2019). However, fertility rates have dropped very significantly in Norway, as in the other countries in our study – from 2.5 children per woman in 1970 to 1.62 in 2017 (Eurostat, 2019). However, they remain higher than in Portugal and Bulgaria, and amongst women born in 1970 only 13 per cent of Norwegian women did not have children by the age of 45, reflecting the long-standing support for mothers, families and children provided by the 'woman-friendly' progressive maternalism of the Norwegian welfare state (Hamre, 2018).[8]

Notes

1 In 1900 the population was 2,217,971 (Østby, 1999), and in May 2020 it was 5,372,355 (SSB.no, Befolkning, 2020b).
2 In the Nordic countries the term 'Stockholm-marriage' was used in this period to describe cohabitation outside marriage. Stockholm marriages were popularly associated with the freer and more sinful life of the big city. The concept has connotations of middle-class progressiveness, but the practice of cohabitation became particularly widespread among the working class who could not afford to get married (Matovic, 1984).
3 Historians suggest that Norwegian legislation regarding children born outside marriage differed from the Swedish and Danish legislation in that it 'stressed mothers' opportunities to take care of their children more than women's gainful employment' (Blom, 2015: 318).
4 Bonnevie's argument must be read in the context of the economic crisis and the rise in unemployment in the 1920s, leading to married women being pushed out of the labour market. In 1925 the main labour union (LO) and the Labour Party stated that only one member of a married couple should be allowed to have paid work (Lønnå, 1996).
5 In the nineteenth century, only three cases of fornication against nature were taken to the Supreme Court, two of which were cases of woman–woman sex, despite the legal definition referring to ejaculation and anal intercourse. While conviction took place in one, the latter case was acquitted, and this set legal precedent (Aarset, 2000).
6 In Norway 'homofil' is still used as the main term for gay men and often also as the term for lesbians.
7 No studies have yet analysed the reasons for the higher divorce rate among Norwegian same-sex couples.
8 For instance, parental benefit is 49 weeks at full pay or 59 weeks at 80 per cent, with a maternal quota and a paternal quota of 15 weeks each (since 2018) (The Working Environment Act, §12 and The National Insurance Act, §14–19); one hour paid nursing time a day until the child is one year old (and unlimited unpaid nursing time) (The Working Environment Act, §12–18); and the right to heavily subsidized, high-quality day care from the time the child is one year old (The Kindergarten Act).

8

The Portuguese intimate citizenship regime

Introduction

The contemporary Portuguese intimate citizenship regime has, perhaps more than any of the other three that we discuss in this book, made a radical break with the country's recent past. For nearly half of the twentieth century (1926–74), the people of Portugal lived under the longest dictatorship in western Europe. The Catholic ultra-conservativism that underpinned the Estado Novo of Antonio de Oliveira Salazar continued in a less potent form as a thread running through the development of Portugal's characteristically 'southern European' welfare state in the decades that followed the Carnation Revolution. But more recently women's and LGBTQI+ movements have successfully mobilized to enact a rapid liberalization of intimate citizenship law and policy in Portugal, supported by left-wing political parties and the human rights and equality politics of the European Union.

The Catholic patriarchalism of Salazar's dictatorship

The philosophy of 'God, Nation and Family' was at the heart of the Portuguese corporatist dictatorship of the middle decades of the twentieth century. One of the most well-known propaganda images of the Salazar era – illustrating the family model encouraged by the regime – showed a man coming home from work, where his wife and two children (a teenage boy and his baby sister) are making the final arrangements for a family meal. The house displays clear signs of

Figure 8.1 Propaganda poster, 1938, 'Salazar's Lesson. God, Nation and Family – the trilogy of national education'. This is one of a series of seven propaganda posters distributed by the Salazar regime to Portuguese primary schools in 1938. From *Cartazes de Propaganda do Estado Novo 1933–49*, Biblioteca Nacional, Portugal.

Christianity, rural life, tidiness and humbleness – attributes that Salazar cherished – in contrast to urbanism and modernity, which he considered disordered, dangerous and immoral (Pimentel, 2001). Above the image, written in a scroll reminiscent of a religious manuscript or legal document, it says: 'Salazar's Lesson'; and at the bottom of the image 'God, Nation and Family – the trilogy of national education'.[1]

The dictatorship upheld and promoted rigidly dichotomous gender roles, both in law and in mainstream culture. The attachment of men to the world of work and of women to the private sphere were enshrined in law as was the control of women's bodies, all laid down as intrinsic to Portuguese nationhood. Article 5 of the 1933 Constitution of the Portuguese Republic stated that all citizens were equal under the law except when it came to women, due to 'the differences resulting from their nature and for the well-being of the family'. The Civil Code determined that men were 'the head of the family to whom women and children owe obedience' (Portuguese Civil Code, 1966 [1934]). They were expected to be the sole breadwinners and were therefore to be respected as leaders. Women were legally responsible for 'securing cleanliness, order and joy at home' (Portuguese Civil

Code, 1966 [1934]). Domesticity was imposed on women as a moral value: women should be at home, nurturing, tidying, cleaning – making sure everything would be spotless and welcoming to match the male breadwinner's expectations (Pimentel, 2011). The corporatist impetus of the regime led it to establish women's organizations that would develop the kind of women it desired; the Mothers' League for National Education, founded in 1936, and the Feminine Portuguese Youth, founded in 1937, reinforced the connection between sexuality, repro-duction and motherhood for women, with the former instituting a prize for married women who had at least five legitimate, baptized children (Santos, 2013). In 1937 public nursery schools were closed down, as Salazar believed there was no need for them since the primary role of women was to take care of their children (Cardona, 1997; Tavares, 2010). During the 1940s, the Manual on Civic and Moral Education, which was compulsory reading in Portuguese schools, stated that a woman 'must make the home attractive and cosy, and show her husband deference and submission as the chief of family' (Silva and Conceição, 1943:14). There were laws preventing married women from travelling abroad or opening a bank account without their husbands' written permission, and husbands were legally authorized to open and read their wives' correspondence.[2] Women were culturally infantilized and legally dispossessed of both property and agency. They lacked all basic citizenship rights and were expected to remain thankful for their (compulsory) role in the domestic sphere (Pimentel, 2011).

The Portuguese dictatorship was fundamentally entangled with the Catholic Church from the outset, and in 1940 the Concordata was signed between the Portuguese state and the Vatican, reinforcing religious rule in everyday life. The Church played the role of moral guardian and institutional agent of legitimacy of the political regime, whilst also indulging in benefits provided by the regime in return. As sociologist Duarte Vilar notes, 'the Lisbon Patriarch was a personal friend of the dictator Antonio Salazar, and all the acts of the regime were publicly supported by the religious hierarchy' (1994: 215). Catholicism had particular influence in the realm of intimate citizenship, with pronatalist doctrine determining that sex was solely for the purpose of reproduction and the strengthening of the family (Pais, 1996). In this vein, Salazar explicitly declared that women achieve happiness through abnegation, not pleasure (Tavares, 2010: 90), 'family planning' was stigmatized, and in 1929 the sale of contra-ceptives was banned (Prata, 2015). This meant that the transforma-tive impact of the introduction of the contraceptive pill elsewhere in

Figure 8.2 Poster for the Portuguese presidential election campaign, 'To vote with Salazar. And guarantee peace and bread', 1949. The poster shows the model, tight-knit Catholic heterosexual couple with their child to whom the guarantee of safety and security was being offered by the Salazar's Catholic ultra-conservative Estado Novo party. In this campaign, the anti-fascist candidate Jose Norton de Matos stood against António Carmona, who was supported by Salazar. Image: public domain.

Europe in the 1960s was not experienced by women in Portugal at the same time. Moreover, after the 1940 Concordata divorce was no longer available to those who were married by the Catholic Church.[3] The law became even more restrictive with the 1967 Civil Code, in which divorce in civil marriage was subject to a three-year waiting period and required the approval of a judge, thus removing the possibility of divorce through mutual consent.

In pursuance of its patriarchal Catholic ideology, the regime actively shielded traditional family and gender relations from any possible disruptive influence or change (Pimentel, 2001). Media censorship played a vital role in this, enacted by highly vigilant political authorities. One example of this was that words that represented potential challenges to the intimate citizenship regime – such as 'divorce', 'menopause', 'contraceptive pill' and 'homosexuality' – were literally erased from the public sphere; they were no longer used in the media (Pimentel, 2007; Principe, 1979). More broadly, potential cultural subversion and political opposition, particularly by communists, were suppressed by the secret police, and there was little possibility for the open display of dissent, ambiguity or unconventionality in matters of gender and sexuality (Pimentel, 2007). Women's organizations that had been established before the dictatorship, during the 'first wave' of Portuguese feminism, came under attack, and some collapsed whilst others were shut down. For instance, the National Council of Portuguese Women, which had been created in 1914 by women who had been active in the Republican movement that had secured the abolition of the monarchy in 1910, had a broad set of aims concerning women's emancipation, the transformation of traditional roles and the promotion of equal responsibilities between women and men. The National Council was terminated by the political regime after it organized an exhibition of books written by women from all over the world in 1947. In 1949, the former president of the organization, Maria Lamas, was arrested several times and accused of working against the regime, which objected to her international visibility and her repeated excursions into rural Portugal to report on the conditions under which women were living.

As far as homosexuality was concerned, Portuguese law had historically been unspecific about same-sex sexual acts, with the first Penal Code of 1852 addressing 'threats to decency' (Aguiar, 1926) and, in its revision of 1886, 'addictions against nature' (Moita, 2001). The first law used specifically to target those engaging in same-sex sexual acts was the 1912 Law on Begging and Mendicity, which referred to vagrancy and 'false' beggars, such as prostitutes and others who practised 'addictions against nature' (Bastos, 1997). Under Salazar there were regular police raids on places where same-sex sexual encounters took place, and men were arrested and either incarcerated and tortured in *Mitras*, special sites established for the purpose in 1936, or confined in institutions of forced labour (Bastos, 1997). There were also raids on private houses, with both lesbians and gay men imprisoned and tortured, and the *arrebentas* (demolishers) extorted money from those who could pay to avoid being charged (Almeida, 2010; Bastos, 1997). Later in the dictatorship, the Penal Code of 1966 introduced a new offence, with a maximum two-year sentence, that targeted 'whomsoever frequently makes an indecent assault on someone of the same sex' (Article 253).

In 1960, colonial wars broke out in Angola, Guinea-Bissau and Mozambique, rendering the regime more and more fragile. In 1968 Salazar had an accident and was seriously injured – dying two years later – but his authoritarian regime was maintained by Marcello Caetano, who replaced him. Caetano had a softer style of leadership and some of the most oppressive characteristics of the regime were repealed. One such example was the implementation in 1969 of Law

Decree no. 49317, which allowed married women to travel abroad without their husbands' written permission. But when, in 1972, three women – Maria Isabel Barreno, Maria Teresa Horta and Maria Velho da Costa – published the book *New Portuguese Letters*, there was a forceful reaction by the political authorities. It was the first time that women in Portugal had published writing about their own sexual embodiment and pleasure, conveying the message that women were sexual actors in their own right. The book was labelled immoral and pornographic and was banned in 1973. The authors were arrested and charged with 'abuse of the freedom of the press' and 'outrage to public decency', and a new law was drafted to ensure their prosecution (Kramer, 1975). This proto-feminist publication was an important catalyst for feminist action, and the trial of 'the Three Marias' garnered widespread international support and led to the formation of the Women's Liberation Movement in Portugal (Movimento de Libertação das Mulheres – MLM). On 25 April 1974, whilst the Marias were still in court and against the backdrop of discontent amongst the military about the colonial wars, a military coup took place against Caetano, which rapidly morphed into a popular uprising. What came to be called 'The Carnation Revolution' overthrew the dictatorship and replaced it with a provisional government which aimed to establish democracy in the country.

Post-dictatorship democratization and modernization

Following the end of the dictatorship, Portugal underwent an extensive process of juridical and political modernization, with a significant de-patriarchalizing impact on the country's intimate citizenship regime. First and foremost, gender equality was enshrined in the Constitution and incorporated, albeit rather slowly, into the Penal and Civil Codes. The laws of the dictatorship era that subordinated women to men and that imposed the duty of domestic work were abolished. Women gained legal access to all jobs and full suffrage. The rights of a husband to read his wife's correspondence and to deny her authorization to travel abroad were rescinded, and the notion of the 'head of family' disappeared from the Civil Code.[4] In 1975 divorce was legalized, opening up the possibility of both litigious divorce, on the grounds of 'violation of conjugal obligations' or 'rupture of the life in common', and mutually consensual divorce, and the Concordata was revised to grant Catholics access to civil divorce.

Feminist groups, once again able to organize and speak out publicly without censorship or the threat of arrest, began to address a range of intimate citizenship issues, including free contraception, sexual harassment and the right to abortion (Magalhães, 1998; Tavares, 2000, 2010).[5] The early years following the revolution witnessed some progress: abortion under restricted circumstances, family planning available through the national health system and the new Divorce Law. But it soon became clear that culture was moving at a slower pace than law and policy. The first feminist demonstration of the new era of Portuguese democracy took place on 13 January 1975 (Tavares, 2010).[6] Organized by the recently created MLM, it consisted of a public dramatization of stereotypes of womanhood – women dressed as housewives, brides, femmes fatales, domestic workers, and so forth – to protest against the discrimination still faced by women a year after the revolution. Demonstrators planned to light a fire and burn the 'symbols of women's inequality' – the Civil Code, the Penal Code and the Labour Code, books showing biased and discriminatory images of women and toys reinforcing stereotypes. The MLM prepared banners saying 'Democracy yes, Phallocracy no'. The event obtained much media attention and many men rushed to the Eduardo VII Park to verbally and physically abuse the demonstrators, screaming at the participants: 'Women should be at home, cooking' and 'Women – only in bed' (Barbosa, 1981). The fact that the only demonstrator who was not attacked was a woman wearing a wedding dress illustrates the symbolic importance ascribed to marriage.[7] The underlying message of this attack on women was that even in the new democracy, it was only through the legally sanctioned couple-form that women could aspire to securing dignity and the right to inhabit the public space of the street without being insulted or physically attacked.

Like Bulgaria, the decriminalization of same-sex sexual acts in Portugal was enacted during Portugal's process of preparation for accession to the European Economic Community. The European legal and policy climate in this area was clearly changing in the early 1980s, in the wake of *Dudgeon v UK* (1981),[8] and the Council of Europe's Recommendation 924 which 'urged' member states to decriminalize homosexual acts between consenting adults and to equalize the age of consent. Decriminalization, through revisions to the Penal Code in 1982, was accompanied, as it was in the UK and Bulgaria, by the introduction of an unequal age of consent of 16, as opposed to 14 for heterosexual sex, and also by a new crime of 'homosexuality with minors'. Revisions to the Penal Code in 1995 redefined crimes relating to sexuality as 'crimes against sexual freedom and self-determination', instead of as crimes 'against the values and interests of social life', suggesting that the individual right to sexual freedom and self-determination now outweighed the collective moral values of society in the eyes of the lawmakers. The crime of 'homosexuality with minors' was thereby abolished, and a new crime of 'induced misconduct of minors by adults of the same sex' was introduced. Given that the sexual abuse of children, 'teenagers and subordinates' was already illegal, this new crime continued with the punishment of the sexual orientation of the abuser, rather than simply the act of abuse. Both the 1982 and 1995 changes to the Penal Code, therefore, contained provisions that countered progress towards full equality.

Equalization and ongoing regulation in the 2000s

Whilst patterns of intimate life were undergoing transformation by the 1980s, it was not until the 2000s that the most significant legal changes in the Portuguese intimate citizenship regime occurred. These changes took place against the backdrop of a vibrant landscape of social movement activism, with energetic campaigns around intimate citizenship issues by both the women's movement and a new LGBT movement (Santos, 2013). In 2001, the hallowed status of marriage was challenged by two momentous legal changes: legal recognition of de facto unions for both heterosexual and same-sex couples was introduced, and, even more radically, the same rights were opened up to cohabitants of any number and regardless of ties of kinship or sexual/romantic love. The 'shared economy' law (Law no. 6/2001), which broke new legislative ground, was designed to offer protection of the 'situation of people sharing a table and house for over two years and who have established a living experience together [vivência em comum] of reciprocal help and shared resources'. Thus both unmarried couples and household companions – whatever their sexual orientation or relationship – became able to access protection and benefits, including rights to the common home,[9] and to the married couples' tax regime and leave, holiday and absence entitlements.[10] A few years later, in 2007, abortion was decriminalized – a major achievement for the women's movement, which had been fighting for this for over 30 years (Santos and Pieri, 2019). In 2008 a new divorce law was passed, in which the concepts of 'guilt' and 'litigious divorce' were removed,[11] and alongside this the patriarchal notion of 'paternal power' was replaced by the concept of 'parental regulation'.

There was also further equalization of law and policy in relation to same-sex sexuality. In 2004 Portugal became the first European country, and the fourth worldwide,[12] to include in its Constitution the prohibition of discrimination based on sexual orientation.[13] The new LGBT movement had been campaigning vigorously against the unequal age of consent since a scandal about the sexual abuse of boys in a state institution had erupted in 2002, in which journalists used the words 'homosexual' and 'paedophile' interchangeably, and the new consti-tutional provisions provided vital ammunition, as did EU reports and European Parliament resolutions on the age of consent. Finally, in 2007, after two judgments by the Constitutional Court in which the unequal age of consent was found to be unconstitutional, the revised Penal Code equalized the age of consent for same-sex and heterosexual sex. Then, in 2010, Portugal became the eighth country in the world to legalize same-sex civil marriage (Santos, 2013). The achievement of fully equal same-sex partnership rights was celebrated by both the feminist and lesbian and gay movements, as it had been a central plank of their respective agendas for several years.[14] Other liberalizing and equalizing changes to intimate citizenship law and policy during the 2000s included the addition of anti-discrimination clauses to the Labour Code (2003), increased penalties for hate crimes and same-sex domestic violence (2007), gender identity provisions (2011 and 2018), changes to the law on adoption and assisted reproduction (2016) and the ban on unnecessary surgery on intersex infants (2018).

Despite the scale and range of transformations in the Portuguese intimate citizenship regime of recent decades, law and policy continue to exercise powerful normative regulation of the couple-form. The marriage law – which in 2010 granted formal recognition to spouses regardless of gender – still demands a number of duties of spouses: respect (to avoid damaging the honour of the other spouse, their reputation, public image, self-respect, self-esteem, sensitivity or personal susceptibility); fidelity (to have exclusive and sincere dedication to the other spouse); cohabitation (to inhabit the marital home); cooperation (to provide help and support); and assistance (to provide maintenance and to contribute to the costs of everyday family life). However, the legal text is ambiguous and subject to differing inter-pretations. For example, sexual contact between spouses is regarded as a marital duty in many legal textbooks, under the duties of fidelity and cohabitation. Cohabitation is interpreted as 'sharing bed, table and house' (Pinheiro, 2004: 73), that is, not only sharing the same house but also the same bed, and having sexual intercourse – what is known in Portuguese legal texts as the 'spousal debit'. Some legal experts argue that this spousal debit is 'the supreme sexual duty' (Varela, 1999: 345) and 'the most natural and immediate duty among those that result from marriage' (Pais de Amaral, 1997: 82). Indeed, in 2004 the Portuguese Supreme Court of Justice decided that the absence of sexual intercourse between spouses was grounds for reducing the prison sentence previously given to a husband who had killed his wife from 20 to 16 years. The judges found that the victim's refusal to have sex with her husband was a violation of her marital duties.

The five legal marital duties of respect, fidelity, cohabitation, cooperation and assistance have not been subject to contestation, even by the feminist movement, which highlights the strength of the expectation↔injunctions that constitute the couple-norm in Portugal. The marital duties of fidelity and cohabitation have implications for the way that consensual non-monogamous and/or non-cohabiting relationships are perceived and experienced, as multiple sexual partners and separate living arrangements may be considered to violate the marriage contract (Santos, Gusmano and Pérez Navarro, 2019). In relation to fidelity, 'adultery' is the word that, however unspoken in current legal texts, seems morally to haunt the lawmaker and hence is still present in the way the law frames fidelity as a duty. In fact, adultery was historically grounds for divorce and was removed from the Civil Code divorce provisions only in 1975.[15] Nonetheless, adultery is still mentioned twice in the Civil Code. Firstly, the duty of fidelity applies until the moment the marriage is declared dissolved, that is, even when spouses are legally separated (but not yet divorced) it remains in place, and adultery is cited as a reason for excusing the faithful spouse from the two-year waiting period between judicial separation and divorce.[16] Secondly, any disposition in a will in favour of a person with whom a deceased married person committed adultery is considered invalid.[17] The legal injunction to cohabitation and fidelity is also seen in the focus on the 'family residence home' and in the idea of 'deserting the family home'. Cohabitation was, in fact, introduced as a marital duty in 1910 (Decree no. 1, Article 38, no. 2), and in contemporary Portugal married couples must still identify a specific address for the family home, even if they own/partially live in more than one (Pinheiro, 2004: 277).

The ongoing couple-normativity of policy is also in evidence in the tax system, which treats a married couple as a single unit rather than taxing individuals. Article 59 of the IRS Code establishes that married people must submit a joint tax return. The same does not apply to parties in a de facto union, who may decide whether they want to submit a joint tax return or if they prefer individual taxation.[18] The privileging of the married couple-form was also in evidence in the law on assisted reproduction approved in 2006, which banned single women from accessing IVF and other fertility treatments under the national health system. This asymmetry between married and single women regarding access to assisted reproduction was tackled only in 2017, through Law no. 58/2017, which introduced equal reproductive rights for women regardless of their marital status (Santos, 2018).

The landscape of coupledom in contemporary Portugal

Significant change in intimate life practices in Portugal started to become apparent during the 1980s, alongside wider processes of democratization and modernization in the post-dictatorship era, particularly improvements in literacy, health care, labour rights and access to information and technology, and in the context of the increasing visibility and political efficacy of women's and LGBT organizations (Tavares, 2000, 2010; Roseneil et al., 2013; Santos, 2013). One of the most potent examples of this is a significant decline in the marriage rate – from 9.4 per 1,000 population in 1970, close to the end of the dictatorship (the highest amongst our four countries), to 3.3 per 1,000 in 2017 (lower than the UK and Norway) (Eurostat, 2019). However, coupledom remains the norm, with 53.5 per cent of the Portuguese population either legally married (46.6 per cent) or living in a legally recognized de facto union (6.9 per cent), and compared with cohabiting coupledom, solo-living is still highly residual – only 8.2 per cent of the overall population (Instituto Nacional de Estatística, 2012). Amongst women, age at first marriage has increased significantly in recent years, from 23.3 in 1980, to 25.7 in 2000 and 31.0 in 2015 (UNECE, 2019). Divorce rates have soared since the possibility became available, from 0.1 divorces per 1,000 population in 1970 to 0.6 in 1980, five years after legalization, and 2.1 per 1,000 in 2017 (Eurostat, 2019). There has also been a dramatic decline in fertility rates, from an average of 3.16 children per woman in 1970 to 1.38 in 2017 (Eurostat, 2019). The mean age of women at birth of the first child has risen steadily – from 23.6 years in 1980 to 26.5 years in 2000 to 28.9 years in 2010, and 30.2 years in 2015 (UNECE, 2019) – and births outside marriage have increased radically from 7.3 per cent in 1970 to 54.9 per cent in 2017 (Eurostat, 2019).

In terms of household living arrangements, one-person households have increased from 13.8 per cent of households in 1990 to 21.4 per cent in 2011 (UNECE, 2019). The proportion of households comprising a couple with children has declined from 49.9 per cent in 1990 to 37.9 per cent in 2011, and of married couples with children from 42.3 per cent in 1990 to 33.2 per cent in 2011 (UNECE, 2019). The total proportion of couple households has fallen from 72.2 per cent in 1990 to 63.6 per cent in 2011 (UNECE, 2019).

Conclusion

Over the past half-century, the intimate citizenship regimes in each of the four countries have undergone enormous change. Differently paced and nuanced across the four countries, there have been broad shifts towards de-patriarchalized, more gender-equal and increasingly de-familialized and individualized welfare provision, and the legal and policy frameworks that regulate intimate relationships and sexuality have been liberalized and increasingly equalized. There has been a process of disinvestment in marriage by the state and significant moves towards the normalization of same-sex sexualities in law and policy, a process we refer to as homonormalization.

Alongside these changes, patterns of intimate life have also seen radical transformation. The rise in divorce, the decline in marriage and in procreation to below replacement levels, and the pluralization of ways of living outside marriage, to include solo-living, cohabitation and living-apart relationships as common practices, have been conceptualized as constituting a 'second demographic transition' (Lesthaeghe, 2010, 2014) in order to capture their macro-structural significance in the longue durée of human history.[19] Yet despite the magnitude of these changes, living as part of a couple, and even as part of a married couple, is assumed, expected and actively promoted by the state in a range of ways, and this way of life continues to be statistically 'normal'. In the censuses of 2011, 63.6 per cent of households in Portugal, 56.6 per cent of households in the UK, 45 per cent of households in Bulgaria and 44.4 per cent of households in Norway were comprised of a couple (married or cohabiting outside marriage, with or without children) (UNECE, 2019).[20] Although solo-living has grown very significantly, it remains considerably less common than living with a partner, at 41 per cent of households in Norway, 30.8 per cent in Bulgaria, 29 per cent in the UK and 21.4 per cent in Portugal in 2011 (UNECE, 2019).

In Part III, we explore what the social weight of these realities of contemporary intimate citizenship mean for the everyday experiences of people whose lives do not conform to the cohabiting couple-norm.

Notes

1   'A Lição de Salazar. Deus, Pátria, Família: A Trilogia da Educação Nacional', in Cartazes de Propaganda do Estado Novo 1933–1949, Biblioteca Nacional, Portugal.
2   It only became illegal to read the female spouse's correspondence after the dictatorship was over in 1976 (Law Decree no. 474/76, 16 June).
3   The Civil Code of 1867 did not allow divorce, as marriage was defined as a permanent contract, but divorce by mutual agreement had been introduced in Portugal in 1910.
4   Ferreira (1998) points out that these changes took place without any systematic action demanding them, as part of the post-dictatorship process of democratization and modernization.
5   For a discussion of the history and impacts of the women's movement in Portugal, see Roseneil et al. (2008, 2011, 2012).
6   See article in *Diário de Notícias*, 28/01/2006, authored by Maria João Caetano, 'O dia em que as mulheres portuguesas saíram à rua' ('The day Portuguese women went outside'), https://www.dn.pt/arquivo/2006/interior/o-dia-em-que-as-mulheres-portuguesas-sairam-a-rua-635052.html (accessed 17 September 2020).
7   This is reported by Maria João Caetano in https://www.dn.pt/arquivo/2006/interior/o-dia-em-que-as-mulheres-portuguesas-sairam-a-rua-635052.html (accessed 17 September 2020).
8   *Dudgeon v UK* (1981) was the first European Court of Human Rights case to find that the criminalization of consenting sexual relations between adults in private was contrary to Article 8 of the European Charter of Human Rights.
9   They are entitled to stay in the house they have lived in for over two years, if the owner dies, for a period up to five years. They are also given the first option to buy the house, unless the owner had direct relatives who lived with them for over a year or who can prove they have an absolute need for the house (Law no. 6/2001, Article 5).
10 This means that in case of death, the surviving party of a registered de facto union or a shared economy is entitled to five days' leave of absence from work (Article 227 of the Labour Code). They can also submit a joint tax return (Articles 14, 59 and 69 of the IRS Code).
11 The new law allowed a spouse to be granted a divorce without the consent of the other spouse in cases where there has been a de facto separation for over a year, where the mental capacity of the other spouse has been changed for over a year, endangering the life they share, where there has been absence without any form of contact for over a year and for any other reasons that, regardless of guilt, show definite disruption of marriage.
12 The first three were South Africa (1996), Fiji (1997) and Ecuador (1998). Other European countries had already outlawed discrimination based on sexual orientation, but not in their Constitution.
13 The Principle of Equality (Article 13) of the Constitution of 2004 states that 'every citizen shall possess the same social dignity and shall be equal before the law' and places sexual orientation among the grounds on which 'no one shall be privileged, favoured, prejudiced, deprived of any right or exempted from any duty' (Article 13, Sec. 2). The LGBT movement made extensive use of EU law and rhetoric in arguing that the Constitution should be changed to comply with Article 13 of the Amsterdam Treaty.
14 On the campaigns and impact of the LGBT movement in Portugal, see Santos (2013).
15 See 1967 Civil Code, Articles 1778 and 1792.
16 See Civil Code, Article 1795-D, n. 3.

17　See Civil Code, Article 2196. This topic is developed in Coelho and Oliveira (2008: 74).
18　See Decree no. 198/2001, Article 14.
19　The 'first demographic transition' involved the shift from late and non-universal marriage to marriage at younger age becoming almost universal. The second demographic transition was first seen in north-western Europe, the United States, Canada, Australia and New Zealand, then spread to central, eastern and southern Europe and is increasingly evident in Latin America, and to some extent in Japan and Taiwan (Lesthaeghe, 2014).
20　Statistical data breaking this down into same-sex and different-sex couples is not available.

PART III

Case studies in living with and against the couple-norm

9

Interviewees and methodology

In this part of the book we present case studies of the couple-norm in action in people's lives. These 16 case studies are drawn from a corpus of 67 interviews with 'ordinary people' who were leading intimate lives that are unconventional according to the normative standards of the intimate citizenship regimes of the four countries in which they reside.[1] By this we mean that at the time of the interview they were all living outside the cohabiting heterosexual couple-form – they were one or more of the following: single;[2] lesbian/gay/bisexual/ in a same-sex relationship; living in shared housing with non-relatives;[3] in a living-apart relationship.[4] The 41 women and 26 men were aged between their late twenties and mid-fifties, and so were at the point in their lives when not being 'settled' in a cohabiting couple relationship is a minority, counter-normative practice.[5] They were largely 'Generation Xers' who had grown up and were leading their adult lives in the wake of the women's and lesbian and gay movements, and they were all residents of the capital cities of their countries when we interviewed them. They were mixed in both ethnic and class terms. We interviewed members both of the majority ethnic group and of two groups that are minoritized/racialized in each of the countries.[6] We sought out people with a range of class/socio-economic backgrounds, education and occupations, recognizing the variability in the distribution of each of these characteristics between ethnic groups and countries.[7] As a team of white academics, who were living our intimate lives in a range of ways but who were not members of the minoritized/racialized groups that we were researching, recruiting interviewees who were 'minorities amongst minorities' was challenging. The process involved extensive engagement with communities, organizations and groups – real and virtual – in the four cities, slowly building trust, particularly where 'gate-keepers' felt that their communities were over-researched, as was the case in some Sami and Roma groups.[8] We do not claim our sample to be representative of any of the groups of which it is comprised, but seeking to understand socio-biographical complexity and particularity, rather than representativeness, was our aim.

Methodology

We conducted and analysed the interviews using the *biographical-narrative interpretive method* (BNIM) (Breckner and Rupp, 2002; Wengraf, 2009). BNIM is a qualitative psychosocial methodology that focuses on life stories and draws on the German tradition of depth hermeneutics and the long history of sociological research on biographical experience.[9] We chose this approach because of its orientation to the exploration of life histories, lived situations and personal meanings in their socio-historical context, and its attention to the complexity and specificity of 'historically situated subjectivity' (Wengraf, 2009). It enables, and indeed requires, the researcher to focus on both that which is individual and singular in biography and personal meaning and on wider socio-cultural processes and historical and national contexts. It works with an understanding that narratives are expressive both of the conscious concerns of interviewees and of unconscious personal and socio-cultural assumptions and processes. The interview method elicits narratives of past experience rather than self-conscious statements of current belief and discourse about present and past experience. In this, it allows the interviewee to 'wander in and out of recovered memories, in particular those that are seemingly trivial' (Bollas, 1995: 138).

BNIM interviews hinge on a single question designed to elicit a free-form narrative from the interviewee. The question we asked each of our interviewees was, 'Can you tell me the story of your life and personal relationships – all the events and experiences that have been important to you personally, how it has been for you? Please begin wherever you like.'[10] The interviewee was then offered the floor to tell their story in their own way, without interruption or further guidance from the interviewer. The method required us as interviewers to abstain from interrupting and to offer the interviewee a sense of open-ended space within which to speak. During the interviewee's response to the question, we would take notes about the topics discussed by the interviewee, paying particular attention to the sequence in which topics were raised and to the language and terminology used by the interviewee. Then, after the interviewee had exhausted what they had to say and had been prompted for more, we asked direct questions about the events and experiences that had been recounted, seeking more detail about what had happened and how it had felt at the time, in order to draw out 'experience-near' narratives of particular incidents.[11] These questions followed the sequence of topics raised by the interviewee in their initial answer, and they sought to use the same words and phrases as the interviewee. Given our interest in intimate citizenship, we were particularly keen to probe for more detail on issues concerning intimate life, but we only pursued topics already raised by the interviewee. The method, therefore, differed from a conventional semi-structured interview where a pre-set list of questions or themes guides the interview. The interviewees decided for themselves what to speak about, and we only asked for more detail about events and experiences that they themselves first discussed.

We found that this approach produced rich, complex narratives and that it worked well with people from a wide range of backgrounds. Contrary to the concerns some of us had before embarking on the interviews, it was not just a method suited to those 'late modern reflexive subjects' (Giddens, 1991) who are well versed in telling their life stories and speaking about themselves to attentive listeners. The interviewees spoke at considerable length about their lives and the vast majority were keen to talk in detail about their experiences and relationships. Most of the interviews took between two and three hours, with a small number lasting about an hour and several over four hours. We ended each interview with the completion of a standardized questionnaire that elicited socio-biographical data, and in some cases we followed up with a further meeting or a phone call to fill in missing details that seemed important in understanding the person's life story. As soon as possible after the interview, we made a set of reflective field notes about their experience of the interview encounter, which became an important part of the data archive for the study and provided a way of processing the emotional and ethical encounter of the interview.[12]

The first stage of the analysis that we carried out of the interview data thus gathered involved a twin-track process: an analysis of the 'lived life' of the interviewee, the biographical data, followed by an analysis of their 'told story', the narrative data.[13] We chose 20 interviews, five from each country,[14] to subject to an intensive process of data analysis, which meant translating and anonymizing them in full,[15] and then engaging in an in-depth process of group work involving all of us, as well as a number of other researchers who were not part of our research team. For each of these 20 cases we held two interpretation workshops, following the analytic techniques proposed by the biographical-narrative interpretive method (Wengraf, 2009), which involves free-associative group discussion of the data, presented 'chunk-by-chunk'. The first interpretation workshop for each case was dedicated to the exploration of the interviewee's lived life and the second to their told story.[16] The remaining cases were subject to a similar but 'lighter touch' process of analysis by the researcher who had conducted the interview, without the workshops, and after this we wrote up fully anonymized case studies of all 67 interviews.[17]

The second stage of analysis involved working inductively across the whole set of individual case studies, moving from the detail of each case to broader themes, looking for patterns in the biographies and narratives of our interviewees, with a particular focus on key moments and processes of intimate citizenship, occasions when interviewees talked about being included or excluded, recognized or misrecognized, and particularly about feeling unequal, marginalized, pressurized, cajoled and stigmatized in relation to their intimate lives. This stage involved further workshops dedicated to seeking to understand our interviewees' experiences and narratives of intimate citizenship, focusing in turn on sub-groups within the sample.[18] It was through this two-stage process of working with our data, and particularly through our group discussions, that our attention was drawn, over and over again, to the intimate citizenship norms that were shaping our interviewees' lives and stories. Above all, we found ourselves repeatedly identifying the couple-norm at work.

Case studies

The case studies that we present here are chosen as exemplifications of the wide range of ways in which the couple-norm operates in people's lives. No case study straightforwardly 'represents' the group(s) of which its subject is a member, and we cannot generalize from any single case to a wider population. Exemplifications are at once both more and less than their potentially generalizable features. Each interview was a unique intersubjective encounter between two singular individuals – the interviewee and the interviewer – and was inevitably shaped in subtle ways by the biographical history, social characteristics and personality of the interviewer, and how these were experienced by the interviewee. It matters who we are as interviewers and interpreters of the data: our subjectivities, identities and attachments – gendered, political, theoretical, sexual, national, ethnic – are salient in more ways than we can ever fully bring to consciousness. But we believe that our extensive collective process of working with the data, and the involvement of people from outside our research team in the first stage of analysis – people who were not steeped in our research questions and framed by our theoretical orientations – served to challenge and open up many of the unavoidable, unconscious personal and cultural assumptions, blind spots, collusions and prejudices of the researcher who carried out the interview and led on the analysis of each case. This means that there is, we suggest, a robustness to our analysis that allows our findings to speak beyond the particularity of each individual case. And, taken together, the 16 diverse case studies presented here enable us to understand the potency of the couple-norm in contemporary Europe.

Notes

1 In saying that we interviewed 'ordinary people' we mean that we actively sought to limit to a handful the number of spokespersons/key actors in women's and lesbian and gay movements and non-governmental organizations (NGOs) in our sample. The rationale for this was that the project was originally conceptualized as seeking to understand the impact of movements for gender and sexual equality and change on both intimate citizenship law and policy and on the intimate lives of ordinary women and men whose lives might be expected to have been most affected by the cultural shifts set in train by these movements, without having been directly and significantly involved in them. We did, however, draw on the assistance of social movement and NGO networks and actors to recruit some of our interviewees. We did not interview friends or prior acquaintances, and we made strenuous efforts to reach out beyond our own existing networks.

2 By 'single' we mean 'currently unpartnered', rather than unmarried or not currently married. Our 'single' interviewees included people who had never been partnered and those who were divorced, separated or widowed.

3 By 'non-relatives' we mean people to whom the interviewee is not biologically related.

4 See Methodological appendix, Chapter 16, for more information about the sample.

5 None of the interviewees identified themselves to us as trans or non-binary at the time of interview.

6 The minoritized/racialized groups included in our sample were: in the United Kingdom, Pakistani and Turkish; in Bulgaria, Roma and Turkish; in Norway, Pakistani and Sami; in Portugal, Cape Verdean and Roma. Not all of these groups are featured in the 16 case studies in the book. In describing individual interviewees in the case studies that follow we have sought to use terminology that is appropriate in each national context. Hence in the UK we speak about 'white British' and 'British Pakistani' interviewees; in Bulgaria, 'majority-Bulgarian', 'Bulgarian-Roma' and 'Bulgarian-Turkish' interviewees; in Norway, 'majority-Norwegian' and 'Norwegian-Pakistani' interviewees; and in Portugal, 'majority-group Portuguese' and 'Portuguese-Roma' interviewees.

7 See the Methodological appendix, Chapter 16, for more detail.

8 For detailed discussion of how we recruited our interviewees and the challenges therein, particularly in finding 'minorities amongst minorities', see Crowhurst et al. (2013).

9   On the German depth hermeneutics tradition, which was developed by sociologist and psychoanalyst Alfred Lorenzer (1974, 1986), see Krüger (2017), Bereswill, Morgenroth and Redman (2010), Redman, Bereswill and Morgenroth (2010), and Salling-Olesen and Weber (2012). A biographical approach to sociological research began with the work of Thomas and Znaniecki (1996 [1918]), *The Polish Peasant in America and Europe*. See also Plummer (1983, 2001), Stanley (1992), Rosenthal (1993), and Chamberlayne, Rustin and Wengraf (2002).

10 The interviews were recorded using electronic voice recorders.

11 Wengraf (2009) calls this technique 'pushing for PINs' – 'particular incident narratives'.

12 Drawing on Emerson, Fretz and Shaw (1995), our field notes aimed to be contemporaneous, detailed, free associative and written as if there was no recording of the interview, exhaustively, ethnographically and personally.

13 The distinction, fundamental to the biographical-narrative interpretive method, between the 'lived life' and the 'told story' draws on the work of Rosenthal (1993). We use the term 'biographical-narrative' and 'life story' interchangeably in the book.

14 The choice of cases was made after extensive discussion within the team in order to achieve a corpus of intensively analysed cases that ranged across the categories of non-conventionality and the different racialized/ethnic groups.

15 Transcription and translation was carried out by the interviewers themselves, as native speakers of the languages of the interviewees. Great care was taken with transcription and translation, and considerable discussion took place between us as a team about how to translate particular words and phrases into English, and about capturing pauses, hesitations and intonation. When we quote from the interviews we indicate a pause or hesitation as …, and we indicate words that we have omitted from the quotation as […]. Every interview was carefully anonymized as part of the process of transcription, and the robustness of anonymization was checked repeatedly during the analytic and writing process.

16 These 20 interviews were analysed according to the full BNIM protocols. See Methodological Appendix for more information about the process of analysis.

17 The case studies (both 'intensively analysed' and 'lighter touch') were written up using a template (see Methodological appendix, Chapter 16, pp. 245–6).

18 For instance, we had workshops that focused on the following groups across the four countries: the single interviewees; those in same-sex relationships; those in non-cohabiting relationships; those living in shared housing; Roma interviewees; Turkish interviewees; Pakistani interviewees; and others.

10
Living with and against the couple-norm in London

This chapter explores the biographical-narratives of four people living in London, focusing on the ways in which they encountered and negotiated different facets of the couple-norm in the course of their lives. We start with Vanessa, a white British heterosexual woman in her late forties, who embraced the cultural and sexual 'revolutions' of the 1960s and 1970s, defying her parents' expectations that she would lead a more strictly conventional intimate life. Faced with the expectation↔injunction of homogamous coupledom and cultural distaste for age-gap relationships in which a woman is older than her male partner, she broke up with her much younger, ethnically different partner, but she subsequently came to feel content and cared for in the alternative family arrangement that she created with her female best friend.

In sharp contrast to Vanessa's dismissal of her parents' 'old-fashioned' beliefs, Richard, a white British heterosexual man, also in his late forties, embraced the notion that marriage should be for life. He was still deeply sad, many years after his divorce, about having failed to follow in his parents' footsteps in maintaining the permanent conjugal coupledom that they valued so highly. In a living-apart relationship at the time of the interview, he was ambivalent about not cohabiting with his partner: it offered him freedom and emotional independence but less intimacy than he desired.

Ismail, a British Pakistani heterosexual man in his mid-thirties, was in an ongoing and wearying conflict with himself as he sought a way of reconciling what he identified as the very different Pakistani and British expectation↔injunctions about coupledom. He had breached the expectation↔injunction that the couple should be alike, a rupture with the couple-norm that produced intense emotional strain and that seemed to him to cause his relationships to break down. At the time of the interview he had been living what he called a 'bachelor's life' for more than a year. His mother was pressuring him to have an arranged marriage, and he was continuing to resist.

Finally, Imran, a British Pakistani gay man in his early thirties, had struggled from a young age with the conventional couple-form, witnessing the gendered arrangements of his parents' marriage and the ways in which they oppressed his mother. Driven by a powerful desire to be authentic and true to himself, he was committed to living life on his own terms, and in doing so he defied, not without difficulties and sacrifice, the intimate citizenship norms that he felt constrained his individuality and his intimate life choices. At the time he was interviewed he was in a living-apart relationship with a man from a different ethnic, religious and national background, and he felt content with and self-assured about how his intimate life was unfolding.

Vanessa: journeying from 'old-fashioned' family to 'post-coupledom'

Vanessa was born into a white British working-class family in 1960s London. As in many families, there was a history of unconventionality within a seemingly respectable traditional nuclear family. Both her mother and grandmother had defied the rigid normative prescriptions about lifelong marriage and commitment that characterized the mid-twentieth-century intimate citizenship regime. Her grandmother was unmarried when her mother was born, and her parents had each been married before they got together with each other. The stigma of illegitimacy and divorce was never overcome, and Vanessa's story of her childhood and youth was articulated around the unresolved shame and angst in her mother's life and the burden that the family's troubled intimate citizenship history had placed on her parents. She stressed that their struggles in negotiating the challenges of their unconventional intimate life had had a profound reactive influence on the way they brought her up: they were strictly conformist in their expectations of her, requiring a conventionality that they had not been able to achieve and more or less consciously seeking to prevent Vanessa from going through the same trials and tribulations that they had experienced.

Vanessa explained that her parents had both divorced before the change in the law of 1969, which meant that they each had to go through the difficult task of proving fault in their previous marriages:

When they died I found all these divorce papers. My father had had to go in a hotel and pretend to commit adultery and had these photographs taken, and actually it made me realize the big difference in social attitudes towards divorce and stuff, and morality, and 'cos they'd really been miserable for that, and I think my mum was [late thirties] when she had me. I was her second child. She had another one during the Second World War when she was very young,[1] and her husband had been in a prisoner of war camp and came back completely changed. He'd [...] come back like a physical and mental wreck. They divorced. She was only then in her early twenties and she started seeing my father who was like eight or nine years younger than her, so they'd been quite keen to, I suppose, be able to marry, be able to have a family.

The stigma associated with divorce in the late 1960s made her mother highly conscious of the boundaries between acceptable and unacceptable behaviour in the realm of intimate life. But her mother's awareness of intimate normativities predated her own transgressions, and had been learnt as an illegitimate child:

My mum, funnily enough, she was illegitimate. I think my grandfather was actually a member of the aristocracy who knocked up my grandmother when she was a maid, and so my mum was incredibly touchy about being divorced, about anything to do with morality, because she'd been stigmatized lots as a child, and so I was the only child, the apple of their eye.

Her mother's sensitivity about morality and intimate life also manifested itself in her relationships with other members of the family. For instance, she displayed a lack of sympathy and aloofness towards Vanessa's paternal aunt, who had defied conventional conjugal coupledom by having two children out of wedlock, which contrasted sharply with her attempts to regain respectability in waiting to marry again before having Vanessa.

My dad had a sister, [...] and his sister had two children who were illegitimate and they were taken away from her by Dr Barnardo's and sent to Australia,[2] and she never saw them again until they were middle-age men [...]. And she used to write to them every week, and the people at the charity destroyed their letters, because she was an unfit mother. Very sad.

Her aunt, Vanessa expanded, later had a large family, but 'I didn't know them very well, because my mother was very snobbish about her [...], she was very funny about stuff like that'.

Later in the interview, Vanessa explained that her parents' relationship was highly volatile, and that they used to row frequently:

> [T]hat doesn't make you think that matrimony is a great institution, although they stayed together till they died and looked after each other, [...] so as marriage goes, it was probably a success. But me, as a spectator, I thought it was awful, and I was damn sure that, if I was going to have a marriage, it wouldn't have been like that.

Vanessa's choice of the formal term 'matrimony' to describe her parents' marriage, with its implicit conjuring of the phrase 'holy matrimony' that is used in Christian wedding services, and her ensuing comment about it being a success simply for having lasted, emphasizes the distinction she makes between their 'old-fashioned' approach to relationships and her own liberal views. Her parents' traditional marriage was meant to be lifelong, no matter the quality of the relationship, and this was exactly what she did not want for herself. She rejected the prescriptions of the couple-norm that had made her parents' lives a misery and challenged their longing for conventionality, even whilst understanding it, empathetically, within their socio-biographical histories. She explained that she had grown up at a time of great social transformation in intimate and sexual politics and practices which removed the constraints and stigma that came with 'old-fashioned morality'. Yet she was not without ambivalence about the outcome of these changes, saying, 'I don't know if it has actually made for much better in society, better in some ways, worse in others'. She continued:

> I was a product of the '60s and the '70s. So I was growing up, you know, with all these post-, you know, post-pill, post-abortion, post-, you know, I mean all the things that happened in the '50s, late '50s, early '60s, different legislation on divorce, on the family, on, you know, women's fertility issues. Of course, you know, we were already used to taking that kind of stuff for granted by the time I was a teenager, so there was a real difference between the generations that is not so pronounced perhaps now, you know, because if you've got children that they've grown up

with some of that similar expectations to you, whereas there's a terrific jump between my kind of post-war, you know, how my parents grew up with rationing, all this very restrictive moralities and restricted economics, whereas we were in a sort of boom period when we all want to go off to pop concerts. You know, we've got available contraception and you could use it, it was a completely different thing.

Here Vanessa rationalized and contextualized the difference between her life and values and those of her parents. She repeatedly used the term 'post' to situate her different values and intimate life choices both culturally and temporally: she belonged to a new generation whose values and practices of intimacy were antithetical to the restrictions and limitations experienced by her parents.

Vanessa said that she had 'made a point of losing my virginity as early as I could, when I was 14, which in retrospect was a mistake in terms of the quality of the experience'. Two years later she started a seven-year relationship with Tom, who was a few years older than she was. He had briefly been married, but soon realized that his wife was having an affair with his best man. Vanessa's parents were 'scandalized by this [relationship], we had all sorts of argy bargy [quarrelling]'. Her parents eventually grew to like Tom, but things changed completely when they found out that they were having sex.

> I had this boyfriend since I was 15, 16. When she [mother] realized we were sleeping together, she caused immense trouble. […] She went mad, and she knew that my father was old-fashioned and told him and caused an immense argument, so my father, you know, he went berserk. He actually put me into hospital, he beat me up, went to try and attack my boyfriend, they were fighting in the street and everything. Then they were not paying my [university] grant anymore, so you know I had to work in a bar. […] So, I mean, that was very much her take on things.

The relationship with Tom gradually made Vanessa feel stifled: it was 'far too restrictive, and I didn't want my life to be sorted as it was'. She described her feelings of resentment towards him, especially when she was out, socializing in radical, artistic circles, while he was at home watching TV, which 'was all he wanted to do'. These differences led to the end of the relationship.

Vanessa finished her degree and embarked on a life as an artist. In her twenties she had a number of disappointing and unfulfilling relationships:

> I think it was a bit of a shock to me that I wouldn't just meet somebody else who adored me and we'd be steady and settled together, but who was a bit more exciting [than her previous boyfriend]. I had a couple of more exciting relationships, but you know – two-timing, cheating, not prepared to settle down.

After that she started a new 'long but unsuitable' relationship with a man of the same age as she was, who turned out to be 'a nasty piece of work, really, abusive'. It took her many years 'to get rid of him'. After that she 'took a break' from relationships for several years, explaining that she felt traumatized by these experiences:

> You know those types of guy, they don't treat you properly. They don't really want you. But god help you, you get rid of them! [...] So for some time I didn't want any hassle.

In the meantime, when she was in her late twenties, her father had had an accident and subsequently suffered brain damage as a result of medical negligence. Her life changed dramatically from one day to the next, and thereafter she spent many years visiting her father in hospitals and care homes and pursuing legal action against the hospital: 'I had to keep fighting the whole time.' Her father eventually died, and, following a 'long and awful illness', her mother also died, after which Vanessa said that she was 'spaced out' for a long time. She was supported in coping with these bereavements by her long-standing best friend Kalisa.

By then in her early forties, Vanessa made a decision to dedicate the rest of her life to focusing on herself and her artistic work: 'Now it is going to be me, me, me; hairdressers, and massage and going out.' With her inheritance from her parents, she renovated her house and went on holidays. During this time, to her surprise, she met a man, Tarek, and they started a relationship. Vanessa thought that she had 'missed the boat, sort of, and then I went like, wow! And I had the first serious relationship for ages.' She had started teaching at a local college, and he was one of her students. Many people, including her friends and his family, disapproved of their relationship, for a number of reasons: Tarek was her student and much younger than she was;

he was from a different cultural and religious background; and he had children from a previous relationship. Whilst the age gap 'didn't bother him', his family's disapproval did: his 'family did absolutely everything to break us up [...]. They were very manipulative and sneaky and he was very worried that they would take his children away.' Vanessa also put herself 'through hell' worrying that they were too different and that he was too young: 'It did wonders for me though. I lost two stones. My figure was great!' Vanessa said she felt 'girly again' and happy, after the difficult years she had been through with her parents. 'I hadn't really thought that we were going to spend the rest of our lives together, maybe I thought we might have some good years.' But social pressure, particularly on Tarek, and her own worries about the future of the relationship in this context eventually led them to break up.

At the time of the interview Vanessa and Tarek were still seeing each other occasionally as friends, and she had been single for several years. She remained very close to her best friend Kalisa, and their relationship was increasingly taking centre stage in her intimate life and imagined future. She had recently made Kalisa the executor of her will, and they were considering entering a civil partnership for inheritance purposes: 'We are like sisters, I suppose [...]. We are quite lucky because we organize our lives to look after each other, we travel together and do stuff.'[3]

Vanessa told the story of her life as deeply entwined with and shaped by that of her parents: first as a reaction to their conservative morality, then as their carer, and finally as 'liberated' from any responsibility towards them. Her narration of the constraints in their lives, caused by their social and legal exclusion from full intimate citizenship, was at times inflected with humour but also lucidly acknowledged the profound impact that their failure to conform to the expectation↔injunction of lifelong marriage had had both on them and on Vanessa's own upbringing. She, on the other hand, saw herself as having grown up during a period of great change in sexual and intimate life, a time that was 'post' the misery of 'old-fashioned' morality. Already challenging the latter in her teens, she rejected the expectation↔injunction that associated sexual activity with conjugal coupledom. She found her first sexual experience disappointing, but the point had been made. She later broke up with her first long-term boyfriend, who wanted to have a 'normal' couple relationship, which she found boring, particular in comparison with the social and artistic life she was leading at the time. When her ageing parents got sick, and as she cared for them over many years, she tried to find a stable couple relationship in which to 'settle down', as would be expected of a woman in her thirties, but none of them was ever right, and she felt herself abused and mistreated. Years of committed caring for her parents left her exhausted and disbelieving that she could ever have another significant relationship with a man. Meeting and falling in love with Tarek was a surprise, as were the challenges to social expectations that it entailed. By now Vanessa had given up on the belief that coupling should be 'for ever', and she was prepared to enjoy the relationship until it lasted, but the many social differences between Tarek and Vanessa put them under so much pressure that their relationship ended.

However, through most of her adult life Vanessa had nurtured another relationship, which proved to be the strongest and most enduring – that with Kalisa. The friendship between the two women – one white British, the other black British Caribbean – escaped social scrutiny and stigmatization, as it was not recognized by others as a form of coupledom. But a radical idea had occurred to Vanessa: she suggested that they might formalize their relationship via a civil partnership, which would allow them to benefit from the same protection and recognition as 'proper' same-sex couples. With this unconventional proposition, Vanessa was embracing a vision of 'post-coupledom' that she saw herself as pursuing from a young age, and that radically differentiated her from her parents.

Richard: accepting unconventional coupledom as compromise

Richard was born in the early 1960s to a middle-class white British family that he described as 'traditional'. Early in the interview, in a significant speech act that framed his intimate life story, he mentioned that his 'mum and dad are still together, still married', emphasizing the importance of their long-term and stable marriage in making sense of his contrasting experiences of coupledom. His father, who had been in the army, was a strict disciplinarian, and both Richard and his sister were sent to boarding schools at a young age. In his twenties, whilst at university and then after graduation, Richard had two long-term relationships, and in his early thirties he had other girlfriends, 'but they were no big love affairs, or living-togethers, or anything like that. And that situation continued until I met what was to be my wife and is now my ex-wife.'

Richard's account of meeting his ex-wife, Elaine, was a classic romance narrative. It was, he said:

> love at first sight for both of us. [...] After about two years of living with each other – we'd been together for three years by that stage – I asked her to marry me. I must admit that I knew I was going to ask her when I first met her, and she knew what her answer was going to be when she first met me.

Elaine accepted Richard's proposal, and he then followed the gendered ritual of asking her father for her 'hand in marriage'. He saw this request for patriarchal approval as a 'traditional gesture' that 'her parents liked', but it might also be seen as the first indication of what was to become his own ambivalent implication in his intimate relationship as a 'family matter'. Elaine was the first woman whom he had wanted to marry, he said. He was keen to point out, perhaps aware that he was talking to a sociologist, that this decision was not influenced by 'societal pressure': marrying her was what he had wanted, he stated. A year after he had proposed, Richard and Elaine were married.

But 'what had been a good relationship before marriage became complicated afterwards, and we only lasted another two years of married life and then we separated'. One of the reasons that Richard gave for this turn of events was that they both had been very close to their respective families, but after their marriage this closeness felt too intense and stifling. Elaine's mother kept calling her and visiting them. On one occasion they had to cut short a trip that they had been looking forward to for a long time because Elaine's family needed her back home, and Richard was resentful of this interruption and the repeated intrusions into their life together.

> For some reason things just changed. Some people say, if you are happy, why bother getting married? And I understand that. [...] Suddenly I felt a lot more pressure, a lot more demands from her family. Her mum seemed to be constantly coming around, and she wouldn't ask me to do things, she wouldn't ask me directly, she'd ask my wife [...]. Resentment started to develop, and because I resented her family, she started to resent my family.

Richard felt that they were no longer an independent couple: marriage had endorsed them as a couple, but it had also established their relationship as a family matter. They were now part of the larger extended family that Richard experienced as increasingly impinging upon what had previously been their intimate, exclusive union. They both knew that 'things were bad', and despite their efforts to 'save the marriage', they 'couldn't get things back together again'. Committed to the notion that married-couple life requires hard work, Richard and Elaine tried to 'save' their relationship, including living separately for some time and starting couple therapy. However, it only took two therapy sessions for them to acknowledge that their relationship was not working out. They agreed to separate, and Richard moved out of the flat and went to stay with friends.

> She stayed in the marital home. Six months later she said she wanted a divorce. Six months later I had a decree nisi.[4] I didn't contest it. It was very nasty though, for various reasons. She went for unreasonable behaviour, so it was ... her lawyer told her to ... typical. [...] The lawyers hated each other too [laughs] [...] and so it ended very, very, very, very badly. [...] The whole relationship then changed and became one total, total conflict. I mean the fact that you have to deal with a lawyer, and not your partner, is hard enough, and getting all the letters [...]. What was once a loving relationship is now reduced to legalistic terms.

Here Richard stressed again his sense of having lost the intimacy and exclusivity of his 'once loving relationship' with Elaine to another layer of interfering others – not family members now, but, at the moment of final rupture of their union, the legal bureaucratic apparatus of divorce and those working in it.

The tragic demise of their two-year marriage was formalized by the receipt of the decree nisi by post, a moment that he mentioned several other times in the interview.

> She went for unreasonable behaviour, and I remember receiving this document and showing it to my friends and they found it ever so funny. [...] Most of it was made up crap.

He remembered the date he received it, and the impact it had on him:

> Funny how these things, dates, are planted in your mind. Landmarks of one's life, as they say. And I don't know about yourself, or if you have friends who've been divorced, but it can be a turbulent time. [...] For a year [after the divorce], waking

up every morning, divorce, divorce, it hits you, big stigma in society, still is, getting less and less, it has to. In this country, three in five marriages end in divorce. [...] People are less committed to staying in a relationship. You look at my mum and dad's generation, they would never divorce, they would never get pregnant out of wedlock [...]. It shouldn't have the stigma that it does, and I am sure that it is actually losing the stigma. However, from a personal point of view, you still feel it [...]. It's a big thing, especially coming from a family like mine, where, how long have my mum and dad been married now? My god, it must be getting on 50 years [...] It's nice they still hold hands [...]. They would never have got divorced, and as I said, my mum felt more betrayed by Elaine than I did. I felt that I was the one who should have all the pain. She was my wife. My mum felt, how could she? How could she? In fact she probably hates her more than ... I don't hate her [...]. So, as a divorced person, you do have to get used to that. You think about it every day, every day, eventually it phased, I did seek some professional help, a bit of counselling, a bit of talkie-talkie, a bit of cognitive, CBT, no drugs. Unlike my wife. She had to. She was quite bad.

As he repeated here, and many times over the course of the interview, his divorce was 'a very painful experience', and not just for him and his ex-wife: 'Divorce affects the rest of the family, and my mum and dad were very disappointed with Elaine when we got divorced.' Despite all his expressed unhappiness about interfering relatives, Richard had developed a good relationship with Elaine's father, becoming closer to him than he was to his own father, and he missed his father-in-law after the divorce. His marriage had become a 'family affair', for better or worse, and so was its demise. This compounded Richard's emotional turmoil: he had to deal with his own pain about the loss of his relationship with both Elaine and her father, and with the disappointment and anger of his parents. Moreover, the example of their successful marriage was experienced by Richard as a constant reminder of his own failure to abide by the expectation↔injunction, which he had thoroughly internalized, that conjugal coupledom should be for life. For Richard, the fact that 'they would never have got divorced' highlighted the ideal standard of their relationship, which exemplified the honourable commitment of marriage that he had failed to emulate.

After his divorce Richard bought a flat in another part of London and tried to make a fresh start. He started dating other women, but he felt emotionally confused and incapable of establishing an intimate connection with anyone else; he 'wasn't ready yet'. Some months late he met his current partner, Lee, a South-East Asian woman with whom, at the time of the interview, he had been in a living-apart relationship for almost ten years.

> I really felt as if I'd found a kindred spirit, someone who didn't take life so seriously. Again it was an instant attraction, instant, instant attraction, and although we were from very different cultural backgrounds, we had qualities in each other that attracted us. She was looking for a man who was educated, more academic, intellectual, if you like, [...] and by that time I'd already started my love affair with South East Asia [...], so my exposure to different cultures sort of overcame that barrier there was between us. I think that for some English people there may have been, but not for me.

Lee was also divorced and had a child, and she was as keen as Richard to 'take everything quite easily, take things quite slowly, be quite laid back, and not put too many demands or pressures on each other'. Not living together was part of this tacit agreement, although Richard admitted to being ambivalent about it. He explained that he treasured the freedom it gave him, the sense autonomy, of 'being an individual', and that he felt more emotionally protected should their relationship end:

> If we did break up tomorrow, I would not fall to pieces, whereas if we were living together, your partner leaves and you are either left there or you have to move somewhere else. Think about my divorce split-up, which was a very, very dreadful experience. [...] I think am better prepared for that now, because I am better prepared for living on my own – 'cos I do.

However, his ambivalence about 'where we are now' and about his fear of intimacy and the loss of identity emerged in the following comment, in which he seemed to regard himself as, at heart, a 'couple person':

> That's the dual nature of, if you like, the non-traditional relation-ship, of not living together, one kind of non-traditional relation-ship. So that's where we are now. [...] There is that kind of fear

amongst partners of getting married, of being that close, that they lose their identity. Myself, I never worried about it, […] I would put all those individual personal needs to one side and put the needs of the couple first, that is very much the way that I am […]. Some people are very different, they would not compromise, they will not compromise their own individuality, their own individual needs and so that can be a sort of conflict. So that's where we are now.

In the course of his adult life, Richard had rarely been single, and most of his relationships had been long-term. Lee described him as a 'we person', and Richard explained that his character and personality were conducive to being in a couple and 'putting the needs of the couple first'. He made a distinction between individual and coupled personhood, the latter entailing a loss of individuality and sense of self, leading to a cherished fusion into a new entity, the couple, with its unique needs, demands and expectations, all distinct from those of its two individual members. This was at odds with his partner's wishes, and their living-apart relationship meant that they had both maintained their individuality. Richard talked about this set-up as a 'non-traditional relationship' – not the permanent and successful marriage of his parents, but a compromise formation that he resignedly embraced for its guarantee of some level of emotional protection in case of a break-up. Maintaining a guarded level of intimacy was a conscious strategy that he knew he needed to pursue after the pain of his divorce. Fifteen years later, Richard still suffered from the wounds of this painful separation. As a 'we person' he had committed entirely to his ex-wife and his dream of their 'fulfilled coupledom'. However, the marriage that Richard had wanted to sanction his beautiful relationship had actually, he came to believe, functioned as a corrupting force. The expectation that, once married, the couple becomes a 'family affair' had deprived Richard and Elaine of their intimacy, and even the very end of their marriage, the divorce proceedings, had been de-personalized and ruthlessly formulaic. Aware of the increasing number of divorces in the country, although making reference to incorrect statistics, he acknowledged that as a 'divorced person' he was one among many, and that divorce was becoming increasingly normalized. However, being unable to maintain the permanent conjugal coupledom he had striven for was lived as a failure, and he carried the stigma and disappointment of this with him still.

Ismail: negotiating conflicting versions of the couple-norm

Born in London in the early 1970s, Ismail was a second-generation British Pakistani heterosexual man, with a successful career as a lawyer. His parents had been teachers in Pakistan and came to London shortly after their arranged marriage. Ismail grew up in what he referred to as a 'traditional' household: his father had multiple low-skilled jobs and was rarely at home during the day, and his mother, a housewife, spent most of her time at home, taking care of the house and of Ismail and his younger sister.[5] His parents never got along, and either argued or ignored each other, eventually divorcing when he was in his late twenties.

A key thread running through Ismail's story was the difficulty of living between British and Pakistani cultures and values, each of which, he explained, formed part of his 'double identity'. He felt the tensions between them most strongly in his intimate life, because of divergent expectations↔injunctions about how people should behave as couples. He had been aware of the differences between British and Pakistani conventions about marriage and married life since he was a child. He knew that a 'normal Pakistani marriage' would be translated into British culture as an 'arranged marriage', whereas a 'normal English marriage'[6] would be translated into Pakistani culture as a 'love marriage'.

> I think that my parents were ... in a kind of loveless marriage in the beginning anyway. I mean, I remember I used to go to my friends' houses and see what kind of like, 'cos we had this term called 'love marriage', which we call 'normal marriage', you would classify normal marriages, or you know, and I remember going to my friends' houses and stuff, my English friends and they'd have like, their parents would have inverted commas 'love marriages' and to see the genuine affection for each other, and so, 'cos I never really saw my parents show each other affection, ever ... was slightly bizarre ... And they [my parents] were sort of like grumpy flatmates a lot of the time.

The early realization that there existed two different ways of being a couple, one 'grumpy and loveless', which he associated with arranged marriage and Pakistani-ness, and the other 'loving and affectionate', which he associated with love marriage and Englishness, was to exert a powerful influence on Ismail's adult relationships. His movement in the passage above between 'we' as Pakistani ('we had this term called "love marriage"') and 'we' as English ('we call "normal marriage"') points to the tension he still seemed to feel about his identity at the time of the interview. Nonetheless, he became committed to the notion that coupledom should be based on romantic love and sexual and emotional intimacy, and he refused to have his marriage arranged by his parents.

At university Ismail became very religious and was active in the student Islamic society. But during this time he also embarked on his first romantic relationship, which was with a Hindu fellow student, and he found that their relationship met with the disapproval of both their Muslim and Hindu circles:

> I would say that my first, the first girl I went out with, [...] oh, it's not really going out with, the first kind of relationship I had, I suppose, was at university with a girl who was, used to live in the same halls as me, but she was Hindu, so that caused some problems, because you know having a relationship with someone who is not a Muslim is, you know, pretty frowned upon by the people around you and family and things like that. But it didn't last very long. But yeah, it just kind of felt very much like, everything, you know, everything is against you from the start.

A few years later, out of university and working as a lawyer, and becoming less religious, his second relationship was with Karen, an older white British woman he met at work. This relationship soon presented similar problems: 'She was from a very different background from me. She was from like a working-class family, a rural working-class family.' Ismail and Karen were together for four years, and at the beginning Ismail was deeply involved in their relationship. He was, he said, 'naïve and idealistic' about it. However, things started deteriorating when it became clear that he was never going to tell his family about the relationship.

> I think I had a difficulty in accepting the fact that we might have a future. I think, because of our different backgrounds, and I mean the big thing was 'cos I never introduced her to my family, even after four years, although she ... I knew her family very well.

He knew that by being with a non-Muslim, working-class, white British woman, who was also older than he was, he was disregarding his parents' expectation that he would marry a woman from his own background. Unable to face the disappointment that this relationship would have caused to his parents, he eventually decided to break up with Karen.

> Because I mean it is very difficult for us, because it's so frowned upon having a relationship who is either not Pakistani or not Muslim. And I think, I think the biggest thing is you're worried about the disappointment that your parents will feel, because they will feel disappointed, there's, there's, there's no way of getting over that really, and, and especially I think in our culture you spend so much of your time trying to please your parents that even if you are in your thirties there's still a part of you that wants to please them and make them happy, and still now I am sure I'd behave the same way.

A few years of casual dating later, in his early thirties, Ismail met Eleanor, a white British woman with whom he started his second long-term relationship. She was from a 'very different background, she was from a very affluent family and very middle class, and very educated'. About a year after they got together, and after they had bought a flat and started living together, 'we came upon the same problems [due to] my inability, I suppose, to commit, and to talk about this with my family, and go along a normal route'. The 'normal route', Ismail suggested here, was being acknowledged as a couple by their respective families, rather than maintaining a secret relationship known only to the couple themselves. Ismail explained, haltingly, that he spent several months 'soul searching' about this and eventually decided to

> come clean with my family, 'cos I thought that this is, we'll get married, this is, you know, I've done enough procrastination and, and you know, I just have to, ahm, bite the bullet. And so I told my mum and she wasn't very happy, really, she wasn't very happy. I mean she pretended to be happy because she was, you know, she is my mum and she wants me to be happy and things. But I could tell she wasn't happy at all. And I had to tell … it took me about three, four months before I convinced her that it was ok. And, my sister was the same. … She was upset at first, but then kind of got over it and then, and they met.

He found introducing his girlfriend to his mother without having plans to marry her straight away very difficult, because it was another blatant breach of Pakistani culture: 'It was a very strange situation because you know, you just don't [...] introduce a girlfriend to your parents unless you want to marry her.' Cohabiting before marriage was also inappropriate, and Ismail concealed their living arrangements from his family until his mother and sister found some of Eleanor's clothes when visiting him.

> They found some stuff of hers, like overnight stuff, and they were like, my mum was actually horrified that she would actually stay over [laughs]. She was actually mortified. And I, I mean, I think she cried actually [laughs]. I think she cried. Which made me feel very [laughs] ... but she kind of, I think, she gradually accepted it, but every time that she would come she would always try to convince me out of it, wonder when I'd come to my senses.

Ismail also soon realized that even if his mother was going to make an effort to like Eleanor, in her heart she would never be happy with his choice. She expected his partner to become like a daughter to her, and this was not possible if she was not from a Pakistani background.

> My mum was dead set against the idea [of me having a non-Pakistani girlfriend]. She had an idealistic view of some nice Muslim Pakistani girl who would like be her best friend and her daughter-in-law at the same time. I think she had this idealistic idea, this kind of impression, and I think that the thought of it was disappointing.

Ismail found himself caught between his own desires and doing what he thought his family and culture wanted of him. Having fulfilled their professional aspirations, his loyalty to and respect for his parents made him anxious at the prospect of disappointing them with his intimate life decisions. He toyed with the idea of rejecting their expectations outright: 'I mean, you know, I always thought about the possibility of just saying, you know, well screw them, I'm just going to do what I like.' But he was never so confrontational, and it was only after lengthy consideration, and under pressure from Eleanor, that he finally introduced Eleanor to his father:

> because she basically said that she was going to leave unless I did it. So I did it, sort of not completely sure whether it was a good idea or a bad idea, but we did it anyway. And my Dad, bless him,

he was so good. He was like, 'Oh I don't really care that much' [laughs]. So it was a big hoo-ha over nothing really.

The anxiety about his parents' disapproval, and the strain of deciding to 'come clean' with his family, had a significant impact on Ismail and Eleanor's relationship: 'All that just kind of puts cracks in the relationship that even though you kind of do it, it's almost you know, it's almost broken by the time you get there.' However, aware that he had let his mother down with his choice of girlfriend and by cohabiting with her, Ismail felt that it was time for him to fulfil his mother's expectation that he should marry the woman he was living with. He thought that agreeing finally to introduce Eleanor to his parents, which accorded with her wishes, would be rewarded by her willingness to make an equally important compromise – to marry him. Eleanor, however, refused to do so, and Ismail felt that what he had done for her and their relationship had not been recognized and valued. Indeed, he felt humiliated, finding himself in the 'awkward' and somewhat emasculating position of being a man wanting to get married more than his girlfriend:

> 'Cos I mean she was a bit younger than me, she was like [late twenties] and I think she felt maybe that she was too young to commit, and all this sort of stuff. I mean, for men it is harder to understand women at their best of times, but to suddenly to be the one who was kind of driving this, to kind of get married and move in together, and then suddenly say, 'It's a bit too much for me', after all I've gone through, all that. I mean, it was the only time I'd ever told my parents about any of my relationships. So, that was quite hard to take, and so things deteriorated from that point of view and then, then kind of one day she said she was moving out, and I didn't really agree with it but she decided to, and then two weeks later we split up.

Running through Ismail's story was the potent emotional struggle that he experienced about different versions of the couple-norm. He rejected what he saw as the example of the loveless arranged marriage of his parents and pursued instead what he identified as the normal 'English' version of the couple-form. He fell in love without regard to ethnic, religious or class background. He cohabited with his long-term girlfriends without being married to them, and these relationships were fully acknowledged by his partners' wider kin. But it was different with his family, and the one-sidedness of these arrangements was a stark reminder that he was not fully embracing this normal 'English' version of the couple-form. Indeed, he found that being 'normal' with his long-term partners always felt like a troubling and painful choice, because it entailed the dismissal of his parents' expectations for him and the rejection of their 'normality' – having a partner from the same background, 'sharing' her with the rest of his family, not cohabiting before marriage and entering a relationship with the intention of getting married. Ultimately, however, a complete separation of these two versions of being a 'normal' couple, and the choice of one over the other, was not possible, and attempting to integrate his life led to the end of his relationships. At the time of the interview Ismail was still struggling to reconcile family expectations and his own desires and lifestyle: he was indulging in, as he put it, the 'devious behaviour' of a bachelor's life while at the same time being under pressure from his mother to settle down and have an arranged marriage.

Imran: being authentic and defying conventions

Imran was a second-generation British Pakistani man in his mid-thirties. He was born and grew up in the north of England, with his father, a market trader, his mother, a housewife, and brothers and sisters, 'all quite squashed' in a small house in a poor part of town. He had strong bonds with most of his siblings and 'got on very well' with his mother, whom he admired and respected and with whom he felt a close affinity. In contrast, he was angry and resentful towards his father, particularly because he treated his mother 'as if she were nothing. [...] He had a patriarchal notion of the family. He wasn't misogynistic, but had a very patriarchal notion of roles in the family, the man earning, and the wife staying at home.' His parents had frequent arguments, which often involved his father hitting his mother.

A few years after Imran had left home his parents separated, although they never let people beyond their immediate family know. This upset Imran, especially when his parents continued to pretend to be together on 'public' occasions, such as at extended family and religious events. At his sister's wedding, for example:

> My mum had to pretend that she and him were together, because they are not really together anymore. She has to carry on this masquerade, because in my culture it's considered, your value is

lowered if your parents split up, because it suggests that you're from a broken family or there is immorality or whatever in the household. So it's quite peculiar, that cultural burden on how to live your life and that masquerading, pretending. And I always say to my mum, fuck what everyone thinks, they will work things out. Do you think that they don't know that you are separated from my father?

As someone self-consciously committed to the value of authenticity, to being true to himself, whatever the possible consequences of breaking with convention, Imran saw his mother's pretence about her marriage as subjection to what he referred to as a 'cultural burden', one that he did not want her to endure. The association of marriage and stable coupledom with good parenting and healthy family life is deeply embedded in British culture, policy and politics, as we argued in Chapter 5, but Imran saw his mother's attachment to the ideal of lifelong marriage as formed by *their* culture, as a stifling manifestation of the norms of what he called 'this fucking community'. His use of the notion of 'masquerade' points to his dislike of artifice, pretence and 'covering up' one's true self for the sake of convention.

In his early teens, Imran reached a point when he could not tolerate living at home any longer, and his anger was still evident recounting this in the interview: 'I didn't want to be like my family, in a shit hole, in a shit town, in a shit school'. After attempting suicide, he contacted social services and asked for help, and he was taken into care. His mother did not understand what was happening and why he had done this. His father was very upset and worried about the reaction of the community, and he told Imran that he would be a 'complete failure [and] amount to nothing'. His father blamed Imran's mother for his son's behaviour, but Imran emphasised that '*he* was the failure, *he* was the one never around'. Commenting on these harrowing events and his decision to separate from his family, Imran reflected on his childhood as 'quite intense. It's not all happy, happy gay life.'

After leaving care, Imran lived on his own and found a job. A few years later he returned to study, went to university, graduated and eventually moved to London. There he found employment in the media, and then in advocacy and campaigning. Openly gay, and actively involved in the LGBT community as well as in local politics, at the time of the interview, he had been in a living-apart relationship with his Spanish partner for almost a year.

A powerful emphasis on his own self-professed unconventionality and on the many challenges to social and cultural norms that are, and long have been, part of his life was the leitmotiv of Imran's narrative. Reflecting on his sexuality, he spoke about the commonly held view that gay Muslims are particularly subject to homophobia, from both within and outside the Muslim community, as well as experiencing Islamophobia. He acknowledged that for him being gay and Muslim was not easy – 'that was always a challenge, I suppose' – but he argued strongly that it does not have to be an impossible life. He added that being able to move away from home, putting distance between himself and his family, had helped in exploring his sexuality as a Muslim man without feeling the need to conceal his sexual identity from anyone. He said, 'I am quite comfortable in my identity. I never hid the fact that I am gay.' After his relationship with his parents was rekindled, he did not keep his sexuality hidden from them, but it was an aspect of his life that was not talked about:

> We don't really talk about it at home. My mum knows, but we don't really talk about it. I think she's slightly embarrassed about it. But you know I don't get any pressure to get married or anything by my parents […]. It's just part of who I am.

He also argued that having a public presence in the world meant that he needed to be transparent about who he was and about his intimate life:

> I think because I am in politics, I've always been out about myself, you know. I am not going to pretend to be straight or not be gay because of what I may incur in some bigot who may be happy for me to pretend to be straight or hide my gay identity. I think: I am gay. It is who I am. I am not going to pretend that I'm not gay. And you know, if you start hiding who you are, and try to mask who you are, it eventually comes out. It becomes very, very explosive. It becomes more damaging.

Imran's commitment to being open and honest with others and true to himself had attracted him to his partner, Santiago, whose profile on a dating website Imran had found authentic and decent – 'it wasn't pervy' – and he had been drawn to him from their first meeting. Having a different cultural and religious background from his boyfriend had not always been easy, but Imran felt that the confrontations they have had because of their different backgrounds have unfolded in the context of mutual understanding and respect for their differences:

> So, you know, there are, there are clashes. There are. You know, we are not the best fit in some ways, you know, in a bizarre way. But we have a healthy respect for one another and one another's heritage. And ahm, you know, we've come to an understanding, and I don't think that actually, I don't think we've actually had a row you know, in over a year, which is quite amusing.

Imran had been welcomed by Santiago's family and felt that he was getting progressively more and more acquainted with Santiago's 'background, his identity, his community'.

Imran lived in a shared household with other 'professionals', while Santiago had his own house. Their busy lives meant that they often did not see each other for a few days, but when they were both in London Imran would stay at Santiago's:

> [W]e'll compulsorily spend three days together. [...] So you know, we joke about, I practically move in, even my sister says, 'well, you've practically moved in' and when she'll call, she goes 'where are you? Oh you are at Santiago's?' And I say yes, and she says 'oh, don't you ever think about going home?'

Imran's sister, to whom he was close despite the rift with his family as a child, was supportive of his relationship. But she was also putting pressure on him to find a Pakistani Muslim man to marry. Imran laughed at the fact that his sister did not question the unconventionality of his sexual orientation but was more concerned about him conforming to her idea of the couple-norm: as a Muslim man, he should find a Muslim partner and formalize his relationship by getting married. That her gay brother should be coupled and that he should get married was taken as a given; the matter of concern to Imran's sister was that he should marry someone 'like him' in ethnic and religious background. In this extract from the interview, Imran described his sister's perspective and his own response:

> Bizarrely I've never gone out, I've never been out with, another Muslim, which is very, very odd for me, you know, and often I get accused of being a bigot, which I am not. You know, I like my community, but I've never dated a Pakistani or a Muslim, ...

which strikes me as very, very odd. My sister can't understand. It's truly bizarre. My sister is, you know, very broad minded, but she keeps saying things like 'you know you can't carry on like this'. 'Like what?' She says, 'keep going out with everybody, you have to settle down, ahm, you have to find somebody and get married', and she has no problem with me marrying a man, but she she's actually convinced that I need to marry, marry a man, or have a civil partnership and formalize a relationship and establish a permanent relationship, and ideally with a Muslim man, so that, you know, I find a gay Muslim, ahm, you know, which I always think it is really amusing, to live, you know, it's not quite what you would expect in terms of people's attitudes towards, ahm you know, faith and sexuality or race and sexuality or ethnicity and sexuality.

While challenging the Islamophobic association of Muslim people with homophobic beliefs, Imran's encounter with his liberal-minded sister's injunction to find a suitable partner to marry shows how the idea persists that a fulfilled adult life entails forming a stable couple, settling down and getting married. Imran's sister did not show any concern about her brother's homosexuality, but she did care about whether or not his partner shared their cultural and religious background. Imran did not experience his sister's pressure to find and marry a Muslim man as oppressive. On the contrary, he later commented on her inter- vention as 'very sweet' and a sign of her affection for him. He was clear that it would not actually influence his intimate life choices. At the same time, the narration of his sister's views made him ponder the fact that he had not been out with any Muslim men. He rejected the accusation of bigotry and restated his commitment to 'his community', but did not offer any explanation of his preference for non-Muslim men, acknowl- edging only that it was 'very, very odd'.

As someone with a number of intersecting identities – 'British Asian', Muslim and gay – Imran presented himself in the interview as an uncompromising and singular individual. His biographical-narrative was one of self-conscious defiance and determination in overcoming the many obstacles that he had faced, in order to affirm his sense of himself and his autonomy from family, cultural and societal pressures. Being aware of, and having challenged, convention from a young age, he built a life for and by himself, with an awareness of the welfare system and the social policies that might support him in making independent life choices. He did not romanticize his journey, acknowledging that it had not all been a 'happy, happy gay life'. Nevertheless, he used his own experience of being able to forge a path for himself, harrowing and challenging as this had been, to make a point about the possibility of doing just that, even when living at the intersection of multiple minoritized identities. From a young age he was upset by the patriarchal nature of his parents' relationship, and he was outraged by their yielding to community expectations that they should still be together when they had in reality separated. He recognized that revealing their break-up would have reflected negatively on the whole family, including him and his siblings, but he still viewed his parents' decision as cowardly. His decision to leave home by being taken into care as a teenager, which he saw as being about seeking to free himself from the constraints of family and community, and his openness about his sexuality with both his family and in the public realm within which he operated, were central to his sense of himself as a self-reliant and singular individual. In his partner Santiago, he felt he had found another authentic person, alongside whom he was able to live in his own way. Neither of them was afraid of challenging the other's views and exploring the differences in their backgrounds; indeed, they cherished their differences as a cross-cultural couple.

Concluding remarks

Until well into the second half of the twentieth century, intimate citizenship law and policy in the United Kingdom lagged behind social and cultural change, continuing to promote a model of intimate life that was often in tension with, or direct opposition to, the intimate lives that many people were leading. As the intimate citizenship regime started to recognize, protect and support a greater diversity of intimate practices, unprecedented opportunities opened up for people to lead their intimate lives as they desired, with less interference from the state and reprobation from their fellow citizens and close networks.

Yet in these four case studies we see examples of people experiencing, and pushing back against, the constraints that continue to be powerfully exerted by the couple-norm in late liberal London, despite the liberalization and formal equalization of intimate citizenship in law and policy. Vanessa saw her mother as having been deeply affected by being born to unmarried parents, and she felt the intergenerational reverberations of stigma and shame in her own intimate life even though the legal concept of illegitimacy had long been abolished.

Richard had been deeply affected by his divorce, which he experienced both as a personal failure and as socially stigmatizing. Cohabitation before marriage, now commonly accepted as a way of life, was regarded as problematic by Ismail's mother, who was mortified to find out that her son was living with his girlfriend. Imran's defiance of the hetero-norm, and his account of his sister's nonchalant attitude to his homosexuality, are revealing of the changing landscape of heteronormativity in the UK, but the strong expectation↔injunction that he should form a long-term conjugal couple relationship with a man from a similar background to his own remained. Indeed, for Imran, Richard and Ismail the possibility, or actual act, of marriage or civil partnership was a way in which parents and siblings could be reassured that they had 'settled down' as respectable, responsible adults. This is revealing of the significance that is still attributed to the legal formalization of couple relationships and to the making of a public commitment to a lifelong pair bond.

Each of these case studies also reveals some of the gendered expectations↔injunctions and roles that shape and influence heterosexual couple relationships in contemporary Britain, highlighting intersections between the gender-norm and the couple-norm. Ismail felt humiliated as a man wanting to get married, when his girlfriend was much less keen. Richard, in proposing to his future wife, asked for the permission of her father, in the tradition that sees marriage as the exchange of women. In a more critical vein, Imran objected deeply to his father's treatment of his mother, and Vanessa made some poignant comments about women's tendency to get used to being mistreated and even abused by their male partners, and about the difficulty of finding the strength and will to end abusive relationships.

The expectation↔injunction that couples should be alike across key axes of social difference is one of the most conspicuous facets of the couple-norm in the cases explored here. The number of mixed-heritage couples has been increasing over time, suggesting that some of the historical stigma against non-homogamy has relented.[7] Nevertheless, being in a mixed-heritage couple remains a choice that entails more negotiation and social disapprobation than is the case for couples who are 'alike'. Imran and Richard, who acknowledged the effort that is required by couples from different backgrounds to understand each other's cultures, experienced difference in their intimate couple relationships as enriching and valuable. Indeed, Imran found his sister's challenge about why he was not with a Muslim man endearing and interesting, rather than seeing it as threatening to his relationship. Ismail and Vanessa, on the other hand, understood the difficulties associated with being in a mixed-heritage couple as the insurmountable cause of the breakdown of their respective relationships.

Notes

1 Later in the interview Vanessa explained that in reading her mother's correspondence after she had died, she found out that her mother's first husband had custody of her 'half brother', whom Vanessa has never met.

2 As explained in note 5 of Chapter 5, well into the 1960s many illegitimate children were sent to British colonies with the involvement of various religious and philanthropic organizations, of which Dr Barnardo's (now Barnardo's) was one.

3 In the UK there is no formal recognition of, nor are there specific rights (e.g. related to inheritance, ownership of possessions and tax benefits) ascribed to, friends. However, as explained in Chapter 5, whilst civil partnerships are not intended for friends such as Vanessa and Kalisa, there is no legal prohibition on two people who are not in an intimate/sexual couple relationship, same-sex or heterosexual, from entering a civil partnership.

4 A decree nisi is a court order that states that the court does not object to the divorce.

5 According to the 2011 Census, Pakistanis are the second-largest minority ethnic group in the UK, at 1.3 per cent of the population. A gendered domestic division of labour and large family size often limit British Pakistani women's involvement in paid work, arranged marriages continue to be common and divorce rates are lower than amongst the rest of the population. But Qureshi et al. (2012) claim that the stereotype of the stable, 'traditional' British Pakistani family is changing rapidly, and that the increasing number of Pakistani single parents, which has doubled in the past two decades, is an indicator of marital instability and separations. On Pakistani family and intimate life in the UK, see Brah and Shaw (1992), Dale at al. (2002), Dale (2008) and Charsley (2013).

6 Ismail moved between 'English' and 'British' in the interview without clearly distinguishing between the two, as is common in England.

7 The 2011 Census data reveal that in England and Wales nearly one in ten people living as part of a couple were in a mixed-heritage, that is, an inter-ethnic relationship. This number has increased from 7 per cent in 2001 (ONS, 2014).

11
Living with and against the couple-norm in Sofia

This next chapter presents case studies of four people in Sofia whose biographical-narratives exemplify some of the ways in which the couple-norm frames and constrains the living of unconventional intimacies in contemporary Bulgaria. The case studies explore how experiences of the couple-norm unfold over the course of an individual's life and are affected by processes of social and political change, highlighting some of the specificities in the Bulgarian intimate citizenship regime discussed in Chapter 6. Diana's story offers a powerful lens on the changing legal regulation of coupledom over time and the impact of the end of the communist regime on experiences of intimate citizenship. The interview with Bahar draws attention to the ways in which the couple-norm operates through the expectation↔injunctions of friends and family, and how these are experienced and internalized. Kasim's story echoes those of Londoners Ismail and Imran, in the power of the cultural expectation↔injunction of homogamy and that members of a couple should share the same ethnic background. And finally, Maggie's story illustrates both the changes that are taking place in relation to the recognition and visibility of same-sex couples, and also just how far there is to go before full intimate citizenship is achieved for lesbians and gay men in Bulgaria.

Diana: living precariously outside marriage under two regimes

Diana was a Bulgarian-Roma heterosexual woman in her forties, who was unemployed and living with three of her five children in Sofia at the time of the interview. Previously married and divorced, she had been cohabiting with her partner for over 20 years until his recent death. Diana's story straddles the transition from communism to the current post-communist market system, illustrating the oppressive regulative power of the couple-norm across two political regimes in Bulgaria. She experienced both the punitive communist intimate citizenship regime and the continuing penalization of those living outside the conjugal couple-form after 1989.

One of seven children of marginally employed parents, Diana's family of origin struggled financially. At the age of 12, Diana was picked up by the juvenile justice system and sent to a 'labour education school', as most of her siblings had been. Under communism, this was not a rare experience for children whose parents were considered by the state to be failing, especially Roma children.[1] Diana repeatedly ran away from the residential school during her four-year-long stay. During her first escape, still aged 12, she had a sexual encounter with an older Roma boy, enacting thereby what in Bulgarian Roma culture is considered to be a marriage.[2] She lived in hiding with the boy for a month before she was found by social workers and taken back to the school. She finally left the school legally, at the age of 16, when her boyfriend obtained written permission from her parents for a civil wedding.

Married life, however, proved to be difficult as her husband drank heavily and was violent. After having two children in her early twenties, she separated from her husband and went to live with her parents. Soon afterwards she met another man and set up home with him and her two young children. She became pregnant again not long afterwards, and when her daughter was born she was still in the process of divorcing her husband. After this she settled into a calmer relationship with her second partner, whom she never formally married, and they had two more children together.

Diana spoke about these life events in a factual, emotionally detached and laconic manner, focusing her narrative on the hardships in her life, describing herself as a 'rag doll' and repeatedly suggesting that what had happened was her inevitable destiny as a Roma woman. She regarded her life as having followed Roma culture and tradition and she often commented during the interview on how it was not dissimilar from other Roma women's lives, including that of her daughter. There was no sense in her narration that she experienced her life as self-determined or involving progress towards a better future: it was a story of a life driven by destiny. Within this biographical-narrative context, the couple-norm, and its constituent and expectation↔injunctions, can be seen in operation at a number of key moments.

The first of these was her civil marriage at the age of 16 and her subsequent release from the labour education school. Diana would have been discharged from the school on achieving legal adulthood at 18, which is the age at which people can marry in Bulgaria. However, Diana took advantage of a provision in the Family Code allowing people aged 16 or 17 to marry under 'special circumstances'. The adult status granted by state-sanctioned marriage at the age of 16 became her ticket out of the punitive school. At the same time, her Roma marriage at the age of 12 was disregarded by the state authorities. Research suggests that 20 per cent of Bulgarian Roma women enter a traditional (unregistered) marital union by the age of 14, and 40 per cent of Roma people are in such a union at the age of 16 (Pamporov, 2006). However, the Bulgarian state and majority-Bulgarian culture consider these unions deviant and young Roma couples can be prosecuted. Diana explained the different status of the two 'marriages':

> When I escaped [from the labour education school], I thought, 'I'll get married, so they won't take me back'. But I didn't know that, in law, you have to be 18 years old, for them to set you free. And when I got married, for like 20 or 30 days, I was hiding. [...] I was running away all the time, going to him. And one day, I don't know how he found out that we could get married. I turned 16 and he brought a document and they released me. And we got married.

Entering a legally recognized conjugal couple relationship meant that the state regarded her as no longer needing its protection, and she was able to leave the school.

The expectation↔injunction that couples should be married played an even more significant role in Diana's life after she separated from her husband and moved in with her second partner. On the basis of a provision in the Penal Code (1956, Art. 288) the state initiated a court case against Diana and her partner for living together whilst Diana was still married to another person. Diana, who was pregnant at the time, faced a fine, imprisonment of up to three years and public reprobation for 'abandoning' her spouse and living with somebody else. This legislation had been part of the wave of conservative, pronatalist changes introduced in the 1950s (see Chapter 6, pp. 65–8) that were aimed at reducing what the communist regime saw as the 'irresponsible disruption' of marriage and that sought to stimulate higher birth rates (Popova, 2004; Vodenicharov, 2002). Fortunately for Diana, the regime change in 1989 led to the repeal of this legislation and the court case was dropped. This is how Diana explained what happened:

> They even wanted to convict us, but there was an amnesty and the court case was dropped. Before that if you were caught in a 'combination' [unmarried cohabitation], and they caught us, me and him, and there was a case, but they couldn't convict us. [...] I gave birth to my daughter in 1990 and the amnesty caught us and nothing happened. The judge started talking and he came to me, tapped me on the shoulder and said, 'You should be grateful that the amnesty caught you. Otherwise, you would be giving birth in prison.'

Whilst Diana was rather unclear about the law and the 'overnight' changes after the regime collapsed in 1989, she clearly felt that she was lucky to have been spared prison, and her repeated use of the word 'caught' in this passage highlights the continuity in her experience of being captured by the state, in childhood and adulthood, and of being subject to the legal system's seemingly arbitrary powers to disrupt and intervene in her life.

The expectation↔injunction of marriage that is such a central part of the Bulgarian intimate citizenship regime can also be seen impacting on Diana's life over the long term, as someone who has lived much of her life in a non-marital relationship. She gave birth to a daughter conceived with her new partner whilst still in the process of divorcing her husband, and as a result, the man she was divorcing was legally considered the father of the child. She did not go to court to challenge this and failed to get the registered paternity of her child corrected. As a result, the child did not have the right to her biological father's family name and did not receive any inheritance rights to her father's home or to any benefits after he died. Diana too, after being in a cohabiting relationship with her partner of 20 years, was not entitled to any property rights or to survivor's benefits.

As discussed in Chapter 6 (see p. 72), there were heated public debates about the changes in the Family Code between 2006 and 2009, during which the case was made for the legal recognition of unmarried cohabitation. The proposal to do so passed its first reading in parliament but was rejected during the second reading, amidst arguments about the danger of marriage 'dying out', as more and more people cohabit and have children outside marriage. There was strong resistance to change amongst the legislators, who saw the legal recognition of non-marital relationships as a dangerous downgrading of the value of marriage. In some of the parliamentary speeches the 'gold standard' of heterosexual marriage was defended on the basis that it represented the ideal for national public morality, whatever the reality of people's everyday family practices (Council of Ministers, 2008b). This underlines how the intimate citizenship regime in Bulgaria remains one that is not concerned to recognize and support people's actual relationships but is rather about promoting an ideal of the good intimate citizen.

Thus, Diana's 20-year cohabitation with her partner, whom she referred to as her 'second husband', remained unrecognized by law, which created great insecurity for her and her children, as we see in this passage, in which the disjointed and confused narrative seems to perform the precarity of her current situation and the uncertainty of her future prospects:

> The housing belongs to my [second] husband and I don't know now, because we don't have a civil marriage with him, and I don't know if his brothers, because he had grown-up daughters, he has three grown-up daughters [from a previous partnership], and nothing is in my name, only to the children that are registered as his. And the child that was born during the divorce, Kalina, is registered as my first [husband's], during divorce. I don't know what now … They are saying that they want to get me out of there. Well, what can I tell you? My life is hard, dear.

It was apparent that the unrecognized status of Diana's relationship to the man she considered to be her second husband was at the centre of the hardship that she and her children now faced.

Diana's highly gendered and racialized biographical-narrative shows some of the ways in which an individual's intimate life can be shaped, on the one hand, by institutionalized majority norms and the intimate citizenship regime of a totalitarian regime, and on the other hand by the prospects available to an 'ordinary' Roma woman within a traditional patriarchal culture (World Bank, 2014). It demonstrates how the couple-norm was reinforced through repressive state regulation of and intervention in intimate life under communism, and also reveals how the change of regime removed the most punitive element of this regulation – the threat of imprisonment for her 'deviant' extramarital cohabitation. Nonetheless, the new Bulgarian state has remained concerned to promote and protect marriage and to continue to deprive those living outside its bonds of full intimate citizenship rights.

Bahar: pursuing a career and pressured to couple

With the collapse of communism in 1989, the Bulgarian intimate citizenship regime was partially liberalized, as Diana's story demonstrated. Intimate practices have changed significantly since then, with a sharp decline in marriage and an increase in divorce, the mushrooming of births outside wedlock and growing numbers of unmarried cohabiting couples and single parents.[3] Yet the transformation of norms about intimate life has not been so rapid. Although there has been a significant increase in the number of women raising children on their own, single parenting is still stigmatized (Dragova, 2001; Dinkova, 2001: 17) and intimate life is widely understood as being about procreative coupledom (Roseneil et al., 2008). Marriage remains almost unchallenged in its position as the normative prerequisite for parenting and is also regarded by older generations as the ideal form of relationship (Roseneil et al., 2010). There is a very low reported level of voluntary childlessness (Zhekova, 2001; Todorova and Kotzeva, 2003), and great importance is attached to having a family and children and to strong connections with extended family networks.[4] All of these normative pressures can be seen in the case of Bahar.

Bahar was a Bulgarian-Turkish heterosexual woman in her late thirties. Despite considerable success in her career, she was regarded by many of the people in her social network as unfulfilled because she was single, and she had experienced very considerable pressure to find a partner. Bahar was born into a working-class Turkish family at the beginning of the 1970s. In 1989 she had just finished high school when a diktat seeking the forced assimilation of the Turkish population in Bulgaria was introduced, requiring the changing of Muslim-Arabic names. As part of the wave of emigration that followed this oppressive law, Bahar and her family left Bulgaria and moved to Turkey.[5] This was a turning point in Bahar's biographical-narrative, and she described how her dreams of a good education and a successful career were shattered by these events. However, the political changes of November 1989 and the end of the communist regime opened up the possibility for the Turkish emigrants to return to Bulgaria. After a few months in Turkey, Bahar's family headed back, and Bahar was then able to pick up her studies once more, embarking on a vocational degree and eventually starting work as a teacher.

The process of forced migration and return had meant that Bahar had lost touch with her closest friends, many of whom remained in Turkey. Following this traumatic experience, Bahar invested her energy in her career rather than focusing on her personal life, and in her late twenties she decided to study for a second degree, after which she secured a high-profile professional job. Whilst in this role, she had a year-long relationship with a man she met through work, but at the time of the interview she had recently moved to Sofia to take up a new job, and she was single once more and living in a shared flat.

In the narration of her life, Bahar focused on her ambition for education and career, a story which contrasted with Diana's in its sense of self-determination and goal orientation. She talked about the importance of friendship, about the tensions in her relationship with her mother and especially about being single, which was a central theme running through the interview. She spoke about the great social pressure she was experiencing to find a man, to get married and have children – to 'create a family' – which came from both family and friends. Bahar did not explicitly see this as an issue of gender, which is congruent with the lack of discussion of gender inequality more broadly amongst our Bulgarian women interviewees. They often described social imbalances between, and differential social and cultural expectations of, men and women, but they did not seem to understand these as systematic gender-based inequalities or to identify them as shared experiences with other women (Stoilova, 2008). Nevertheless, we found that the women we interviewed, across all four countries, talked more often about feeling pressured to couple, and about being more emotionally impacted by this, than did the men. Bahar described how her friends and colleagues, especially those who were married, made efforts to match-make for her, and how she resented the way that her singleness was continuously at the centre of their attention:

> My friend, the one that I remained closest with, she is very worried that I'm not married, which irritates me a lot, because she is constantly going on about it [...]. She decided to introduce me to someone in Sofia and everyone is cooperating so that I could enlarge my circles, so that they can get me married [laughs]. The big problem! [laughs].

She described how these interventions were seen by her friends as acts of friendship: they cared about getting her married, they said, 'because you are nice, you are my friend'.

Until recently her mother had never put pressure on her to marry and had always encouraged her to study and to be successful in her work. Lately, however, she too had started to prompt Bahar to find a partner and to have children. In Bahar's words, she was 'constantly hinting' and asking, 'do you have someone?' 'You should have! Come on, act!', 'Give birth to a baby, to a grandchild'. And whilst Bahar was annoyed that her friends interfered in her personal life, she was more understanding of her mother's concerns, suggesting that 'perhaps she is getting worried that years are indeed passing by'.

Sometimes being the only one in her social group who was single was an obstacle to spending time with coupled friends. Bahar talked about not having seen her group of previously 'inseparable' best friends who had escaped to Turkey in 1989 for a long time. She felt prevented from visiting most of them, as they were married and had children, and she thought that she would be an inconvenience. After one of her friends got divorced she decided that this was a good opportunity to visit her and to see all her old friends: 'The fact that she was alone seemed more acceptable', she explained. They had a 'fantastic holiday' but it was not long before the marriage talk started again:

> 'Come on, when are we going to get you married?' So she joined the group of other friends, of not-that-close friends, who want to get me married. It's only my best friend, she has never said to me, 'When are we going to get you married?' She is a real friend and we can say anything to each other.

Apart from this one friend, it seemed that everyone in Bahar's social circle was on a mission to get her married. The match-making even involved a marriage proposal made by a friend who asked her to marry his cousin – an intervention that perhaps can be seen as a contemporary version of an 'arranged marriage', organized by friends rather than parents. Even though Bahar liked the 'chosen husband' and they were good friends, at the time she had not considered the proposal because it was made through a third person: 'That moment somehow predetermined the situation', she explained. However, years later she was still thinking about it, wondering whether she had made the right decision, reflecting on it as an opportunity to get married that she had missed. Similarly, her overall narrative of her intimate relationships highlighted a number of 'missed opportunities' and was driven by a sense that things had not gone as expected. Although Bahar objected to her friends' interference in her intimate life and thought that the pressure was unjustified, she also tried to 'diagnose' her own singleness and to find an explanation for it:

For one reason or another, I haven't been able to create a family, which is … now I can admit that it bothers me. I'm trying to find a reason in me [… long pause] but I don't know what the reason is … it's not to be unsuccessful but … As a matter of fact in my environment most of my female friends are uncommitted.

Having friends who were single, or 'uncommitted' – which is the popular expression in Bulgaria for being single – did not seem to remove the pressure to be coupled. Bahar pointed out that marriage and children were 'expected of me […] like everyone'. She explained that although she had always wanted to achieve a lot professionally, she had also wanted to create a 'very good', 'strong' and 'nice' family. And in this confusing passage she expressed her uncertainty about why this had not happened yet:

I don't know why it didn't work out. I even think, even if I am a strong person, sometimes I am afraid, I'm afraid of certain things. I can't decide myself what is for now, if I'm like this in my relationships with people.

Bahar's discomfort with being single arose simultaneously from the intense social pressure of her family and her immediate circle of friends, and from internalizing the wider societal couple-norm. While she clearly disliked the pressure from others to be coupled, she also experienced a powerful desire to be in a couple and a feeling of failure that she had not managed to achieve this yet. Her narrative also illustrated how normative expectations about 'proper' coupledom entailed both marriage and having children, highlighting the strong procreative-norm which accompanies expectation↔injunctions about being in a couple. When speaking about her own desires, Bahar also focused on wanting to have children, to have a 'family', not only on being coupled.

Bahar's case illustrates the expectation↔injunctions placed on individuals to be coupled, enacted by peer groups and families but also by individuals' internalized notions of the normality, and their sense of the desirability, of coupled intimacy, despite the liberalization of law and policy around intimate citizenship in the post-communist era. However, in contrast to Diana, it shows how education and the capacity to earn an independent income as a woman can mitigate the material insecurities – if not the psychic ones – that can face those who are living outside the couple-form.

Kasim: facing the impossibility of a mixed-heritage relationship

Like all our Bulgarian interviewees, Kasim's biographical-narrative is clearly marked by the socio-political changes that took place with the collapse of communism, but his story also draws attention to the importance of issues of ethnic belonging in understanding the potency and operation of the couple-norm. Like Bahar, Kasim spoke about social expectations to be coupled, although, as a man, he experienced much less pressure to marry than she did, and the dominant theme of his story was the rejection by his parents of his mixed-heritage relationship with a majority-Bulgarian woman.

Born in the mid-1970s in a village in northern Bulgaria with a large Turkish population, Kasim was the second son of a working-class Bulgarian-Turkish family. He spoke very fondly of his 'carefree' childhood and described being the 'leading figure' amongst his friends, and a very good football player, who was invited to join a professional team. He juxtaposed this with the period that followed, which was a time of 'anarchy' and 'chaos' created by the forceful change of Muslim-Arabic names in 1989 and the consequent mass emigration of Turks which depopulated his village. This meant that when the time came for him to go to secondary school in another town, and to live away from his family for the first time, he went without his friends from primary school. He was, he said, lonely and scared:

> When I started going to secondary school, there were only 11 families left in the village. None of my friends from school, boys or girls, were there. They had all scattered. And I was alone. With these friends, we were studying in the same class, playing together, playing football, going on holidays. Suddenly, in one month there was nobody. [...] And there was a period – you are still small but also grown up, in eighth grade. After that I couldn't, I don't know ... maybe I couldn't adapt. Maybe I needed more time but ... and you are scared. I enrolled with a Bulgarian name and they restored them [the original Turkish names] at the end of 1989. [...] And there was some uneasiness. It was an unknown environment. You lost many friends, [you are surrounded by] unknown people.

Interviewed over 20 years later, Kasim structured his narrative around this momentous period of change, oppression and loss. He spoke about how he often wondered what his life would have been like if the forced migration and regime change had not coincided with major transitions for him personally – moving to secondary school in a different town and living away from his family. This disorienting, dislocating experience might be seen as introducing a 'biographical blockage' (Hungerbühler, Tejero and Torrabadella, 2002) that made forming close relationships harder in later life, and that also set him apart from his family and community of origin.

The following years involved several more moves. On finishing secondary school and completing his military service, Kasim received a scholarship from a Bulgarian-Turkish organization to attend university in Turkey. He loved the multicultural environment of the university and the opportunity to re-establish relationships with some of his old friends who were living in Turkey. After graduation, he went back to his home village but quickly realized that it offered him few professional opportunities, and so he moved to the capital, Sofia, and started working as a chemist, gradually establishing himself in his career over the following ten years.

In his late twenties Kasim began a relationship with a majority-Bulgarian woman, Raina, who was from Sofia. After a year they moved in together and 'lived as a family' for two years, before they decided to get married. At this point 'these differences [related to] ethnic belonging became somehow very problematic – not for us, but for our families', Kasim explained. He was worried about how his parents would react to a mixed-heritage relationship as they were 'people who have only lived in one place, isolated from things, in a closed circle'. He believed that mixed-heritage marriages were rare, and that people expected marriage to be between people from the same ethnic background:

> When you have a son or a daughter at the age of marriage they [my parents] started asking too. And once I … I expected some reaction, more or less, but not that much because people … they get married somewhere in the region, Turkish to Turkish, Bulgarian to Bulgarian. There were odd cases [of mixed marriages] and now there are more, but I said, she was Bulgarian. And they started, 'What? You can't!' Some things have not developed enough, the way of thinking, the mentality … […] the time when they were brought up [has an impact].

Because he expected a negative reaction from his parents, Kasim postponed telling them about Raina for two years, until the couple started making plans to get married. When he finally did tell them, their reaction was much worse than he had anticipated:

> I don't know if it was my fault, but I had to take her to the village. I went [to my parents] and they said, 'No, you can't'. They are elderly people, and I understand them, but they couldn't understand me. [They said that] there would be problems. I say, 'What's the problem? In what kind of world do we live in now?'
> 'No, no!'
> They didn't accept her. We continued living together but she got tired of it. And you know when you are anxious, the smallest thing starts it off, and as they say, the small stones turn the cart over. There was more and more conflict.

Kasim felt that Raina held him responsible for his parents' reaction, which started to create conflict between them:

> It was around Christmas and New Year. I hadn't been [to my parents' house] for what ... a year? I was thinking, 'What's the point of going?' I rang them and said that she would come with me and my mum said, 'No, your dad won't let you in'. I thought that I should go because they are elderly people. You don't know what will happen ... And there was nobody else, you can't leave an old person who raised you, gave you money. So, I thought I should go for two or three days. And I went and stayed for a few days. I was supposed to come back for New Year. And she rang me and said, 'Why didn't you take me too?' and I said, 'I'll come back, you have to understand what the situation is'. 'I'm gathering my things.' 'Wait for me.' There were things, it's not appropriate to discuss them, but we reached, [accusations] your [parents] are like this, and yours are like that, offensive words, quarrels. When you have had enough of it, you start doing the same.

Kasim seemed split between loyalty to his parents and love for his partner and, although he was determined to continue with the relationship and not to give in to their objections, the emotional pressure asserted by his parents' lack of acceptance affected the couple, and they eventually broke up. Kasim had sympathy for his parents' point of view and understood it in the context of their upbringing and the life of their community, but he was also deeply disappointed that they had not been able to offer him the same respect and understanding. Since the relationship ended, Kasim had been single and had dedicated himself to his work and career, leaving, he said, 'no time for personal life'.

The issue of coupledom and ethnic belonging arose in many of our interviews with both minoritized and majority participants in each of the four countries. We have already seen how Vanessa and Imran in the United Kingdom and Kasim in Bulgaria described the hostility and disapprobation they experienced towards their mixed-heritage relationships, and how pressure from people who mattered became impossible to resist. Bahar also talked about her reluctance to date men from a different ethnic background, explaining the centrality of ethnic belonging in her upbringing and its importance to how members of her community thought about coupledom. In contrast to Kasim, who had wanted to continue his mixed-heritage relationship against the wishes of his parents, Bahar was more accepting of the cultural traditions of her family and community. In both cases, however, the expectation that couples should be ethnically alike was a powerful driver of their intimate citizenship experience. This principle of partner similarity does not apply to all aspects of the couple-form; when it comes to the sex/gender of partners, difference is normatively preferred to sameness, as the next case demonstrates.

Maggie: struggling with exclusion and invisibility

The story of Maggie, a majority-Bulgarian lesbian in her early thirties, speaks of another dimension of the regulation of intimate citizenship in Bulgaria: the experience of those living outside heterosexual coupledom. Maggie's biographical-narrative traced some of the socio-cultural and legal changes of recent decades that have opened up more space for same-sex relationships than had existed under communism, yet it also underlines the ongoing difficulties that result from the lack of recognition of the lives and loves of non-heterosexuals in contemporary Bulgaria.

Maggie's life had been one of frequent movement, as she 'jumped' between places and settings. She had regularly moved home, changed jobs and found new friends and intimate partners as she sought out new experiences. Born in the mid-1970s, Maggie's parents divorced when she was young, and for a time afterwards she and her mother moved in with her grandparents. Both of her parents remarried and had more children, and from the age of 9 Maggie lived with her mother and stepfather. When she was 16 she had her first romantic relationship, with a male friend, and about a year later she had sex for the first time, a one-off encounter with a man she had met while travelling. She was in her late teens when she had her first relationship with a woman, which lasted for about a year and was followed by another same-sex relationship, with Anna, which continued for five years. Soon after the start of the relationship with Anna, Maggie, now in her early twenties, moved to Varna, a large Bulgarian city by the sea and a popular holiday resort, to study. The following years were precarious for her both financially and in terms of housing, and she moved house numerous times in Varna and occasionally back and forth to her home town.

Whilst she was living in Varna, Maggie became part of the emerging lesbian and gay community there and regularly went to a newly established gay club, which was a novelty in post-communist Bulgaria. Sharing a flat with a gay male friend, they presented themselves to their parents as a heterosexual couple and announced that they were to marry. About a year later Anna moved to Varna and Maggie and Anna started living together for the first time, enjoying their freedom and independence, as well as the recognition of their relationship that they received from their friends. Going back to their home town to study two years later, and each living again with their parents, none of whom knew that they were a couple, put great strain on their relationship, and it eventually broke down. Maggie remained single for some time, as she recovered emotionally from the break-up.

In her late twenties, having started a new relationship, Maggie decided the time had come to be open with her parents. She came out to them, but following a homophobic comment by her mother they fell out, and Maggie moved out to live with her new girlfriend. After finishing her studies and splitting up with her girlfriend, Maggie worked briefly in Varna again before moving to Sofia, where she was living and working as a sales assistant at the time of the interview. In her early thirties, Maggie met Petia, an out lesbian, through an online chat forum and started a relationship with her. At the time of the interview, they had been together for over two years and Maggie had introduced Petia to her mother.

Maggie organized the detailed narrative of her life that she offered in the interview into two distinct periods, explaining that she had 'two stories' – before and after Varna – and thereby identifying her first move to Varna as the turning point in her life. In a context in which there was very little public visibility of same-sex relationships or of lesbian and gay social movement activism, Maggie struggled to accept, understand and positively engage with her same-sex sexual desires until she became part of the newly emerging lesbian and gay community in Varna in the mid-1990s:

> At one point this community expanded a lot, the gay community, and suddenly some lesbians crawled out from somewhere, many. Of course, it was the boom in Varna at that time, it was called the gay capital of Bulgaria. There was Spartacus [a gay club], transvestites, gays, lesbians, and whatever comes to your mind, everything in one place, and you could do anything. Perhaps in this community I finally felt like a human being, that I'm normal, I'm not some sort of a freak. [...] [T]here were people who accepted me. I could be myself. They accepted me for who I was, for who I loved. That's why my second story starts there, you see – from the point when you find your place, when you receive support. Regardless of what people say, one needs the support of the people around them.

The need to come out, the discomfort caused by hiding and concealing both herself and her relationships, and the lack of a safe and private space for intimacy were themes that she often came back to during the interview. Maggie's narrative can be recognized as a 'modern coming out story', as identified by Ken Plummer (1995), plotting the transformation of negative experiences of social exclusion and isolation into a positive identity, and hinging on the move to the more open, freer culture and supportive community of Varna.

Even though Maggie reached a point of self-acceptance in her early twenties, the process of coming out had continued, and in her early thirties Maggie was still concealing her sexuality at work and from some family members, which, she was clear, alienated her from them and brought her closer to the friends who knew and cared about her. The lack of support from her family was exemplified by the difficulty her mother had in accepting her sexuality:

> Of course, even up 'til now my mum pretends that she doesn't know [that I'm a lesbian], I mean, she knows very well, but in one way or another she is trying to deny this. [...] Even recently, before I went there with my girlfriend for the first time. I called her to tell her that I was going back home but that I wouldn't be alone. 'You didn't get married, did you?' 'How many times have we discussed this?' 'Yes, but ...'. I don't know if that is her dream, or what, but I did what I could and from here on it's her problem.

Maggie expressed her frustration about the lack of understanding of same-sex sexuality in Bulgarian society in general, suggesting that people do not know much about it. She argued that 'sexuality definitely makes a difference', not because of the difference of same-sex relationships themselves but because of social perceptions of such relationships: 'the differences are because of the people around you, not because of the relationship within the couple.' She felt the lack of social and legal acceptance as a particularly serious problem because she was considering having a child with her partner. In addition to the expense and the difficulty of obtaining IVF treatment, as lesbian couples and single women are not entitled to free treatment,[6] she was concerned about how life would be for her prospective child, both in a homophobic school environment and potentially facing hostility from their own relatives:

> And even after that, when the child grows up, it will be very difficult at school, even though, hopefully, by then things might be better, and people might start accepting these things more and not to bully him or her with 'your mother is a lesbian', 'you have two mothers', or things like that. Children will always find something to grab onto, to offend each other, they are generally very cruel. I don't know. A crazy relative can always come and say that it's not normal for a child to be raised in such an environment.

In the context of these concerns, Maggie did not feel she could have a child at the moment: same-sex relationships were not compatible with current social understandings of appropriate parenthood. Yet she was experiencing pressure from family members to have a child, as a woman of her age should, and she was hopeful that things would change in the future. Indeed, the cultural shifts that she was noticing in younger gay people, who were more open about their relationships than she had ever managed to be, gave her grounds for optimism. Comparing herself with her partner, who is ten years younger, Maggie said:

> When we were still getting to know each other, if I may put it like that, we used to go to the park and so on and it was very difficult for me to get her to learn not to hug me or hold my hand in the street, or when we are sitting in the park and she wants to kiss me. They [younger gay people] are doing it more now. They don't care that much. [...] I have the feeling that suddenly there are many people like this. [...] They are not hiding.

A similar distinction between a new and an older generation of gay people was evident in Maggie's more general comments about the fight for lesbian and gay rights in Bulgaria and current gay activism:

> What I notice among the younger ones is that, it's as if there are more of them, or they don't care and don't hide, but it's more obvious. But something like, some sort of legislation being adopted for marriages and other miracles like that, I can't imagine that at all. And I can't imagine it, not because our society is backward but because our community is unorganized, the community is not unified, you see. [...] In ten or 20 years we might hear about a project for marriage of homosexual people. And it's rather likely that this will happen some time from now. Right now, there is just nobody to do it.

For Maggie, the ability to freely express one's sexual identity and to be open about the love, affection and attraction felt for one's partner was a matter of time and generational difference. She felt much less able to do this than younger women and adopted a rather conservative position in relation to public displays of affection. Expressing a strong dislike of lesbians and gay men 'demonstrating [their sexuality] too much' and 'showing off', she implicitly subscribed to the widespread normalizing strategy of distinguishing between the 'good gay' who does not 'flaunt their sexuality' and the 'bad gay' who does.[7] She wanted to 'live silently and quietly with somebody' and for sexual orientation to be 'something like what sort of music you like'.

Yet, despite this avowed preference, her actual experience was of the impossibility of a fulfilling intimate life without recognition of her relationship and her sexuality. She explained in the interview that the secrecy that surrounded her two previous relationships, and the fact that neither her own nor her partners' parents had known about them, was harmful to the relationships and even caused the break-up with Anna:

> At this point things between us were not going well for the simple reason that she is at home, I'm at home, and [it was like] the most horrible nightmare that we did not have in Varna, because we lived together and we were among people like this, the nightmare of hiding and feeling like a criminal. You don't have any freedom, and spare time, and generally time to relax with this person you are with. And things were not going well, and we broke up as a result.

At the same time she described her 'great relief' that the mother of her current partner knew about their relationship and accepted it, which not only made things easier but also allowed them the necessary freedom and physical space for their relationship:

> Before she moved out I used to go there [to her mum's] very often. I used to sleep there. There was this personal space. The door was never locked, but she used to knock before she entered, never got in before hearing 'yes'. [...] If it's time for dinner, 'Will Maggie stay?' Maggie this, Maggie that. The plans, she could make them with her mum, do you understand? Not to hide, not to separate your life, your family becomes a part of all that, as much as possible. I think that's normal. If you have problems you go and tell your mum, you discuss things and you feel much better. And I feel much calmer because I'm not hiding, I'm not doing performances. Everything is normal.

Whilst clearly evoking the widespread western modern coming-out story, as identified by Plummer (1995), Maggie's biographical-narrative also made explicit references to the specificity of the socio-cultural context of the transition period from communism in Bulgaria. Born and raised during a period of social silence about same-sex sexuality, and when the public display of such acts – between women as well as men – were legally punishable, Maggie struggled to accept her sexuality and seemed to 'prefer' closeted same-sex intimacies. Yet she was also aware of the toll that secrecy and the lack of recognition of same-sex sexuality had taken on her relationships, particularly in the context of the lack of personal space and privacy that was consequent on having to live for extended periods of adulthood in the parental home.

Whilst for Diana, Bahar and Kasim, the future held out the possibility of fulfilling normative expectations of coupledom, for Maggie hopes rested on the realization of the signs of social change that she glimpsed amongst a younger generation of lesbians and gay men. Yet she remained ambivalent about, and uncomfortable with, the more open, public space-claiming behaviour of younger lesbians and gay men, as she grappled with the experiential knowledge she had of the importance of public recognition of same-sex couples to the ability to live a fulfilling intimate life.

Concluding remarks

Amongst the countries in our study, Bulgaria stands out as having the most conservative intimate citizenship regime, with the most powerfully restrictive operation of the couple-norm, which continues to recognize and confer rights on only the married heterosexual couple. More and more people are living outside this conventional arrangement – in same-sex relationships, remaining single, choosing to marry later in life or to cohabit without being married, having children outside wedlock or raising them on their own. Yet the married heterosexual couple-form is still foundational to intimate citizenship in Bulgaria, powerfully constructing deviations as 'unconventional' and unrecognizable.

The Bulgarian case studies illustrate many of the ways in which adults are expected to conform to the different facets of the couple-norm, demonstrating the social, and sometimes legal, pressure that is exerted on those who fail to do so. There was little evidence in these case studies, or in the wider body of interviews that we carried out in Bulgaria, that the ruptures and breaks with the couple-norm of which our 'unconventional' interviewees spoke were chosen and positively embraced. On the contrary, their stories articulated a desire to live a 'normal' life, with the recognition and acceptance of others, and for some, a wish that they might be able to conform to the expectation↔injunctions that they faced – to fit into society as it is. Beyond the personal experiences of misrecognition recounted by our interviewees, there was little political awareness or critique of the multifarious yet persistent ways in which dominant norms about coupledom have the capacity to constrain and impact upon individuals' lives and subjectivities.

By highlighting key encounters with law, policy and culture, and longer-term experiences of the couple-norm across individuals' lives, the cases also show some of the changes that have taken place in the couple-norm in Bulgaria over recent decades. With the end of the communist regime, intimate lives became subject to less interference and policing by the state, and possibilities for living outside the married heterosexual couple-form have increased. The case studies also illuminate the diversity of ways in which individuals negotiate and 'work around' the expectation↔injunctions of normative coupledom against the backdrop of interventions by families, friends and communities who are committed to upholding the couple-norm. They point to the complex ways in which culture, gender, sexuality, and ethnicity intersect in defining how the couple-form should be lived, as well as the capacities of each individual to oppose and challenge such norms.

Notes

1 According to Nwankwo (2011) there were 11 labour education schools, in communist Bulgaria, with between 50 and 80 per cent of the children confined there being Roma.
2 Coontz (2004: 974) points out that 'many societies have had a very casual attitude toward what deserves recognition as a marriage. The "tradition" that marriage has to be licensed by the state or sanctified by the church is more recent that most people assume.'
3 See Keremidchieva (1998), Yachkova (2002), Dimitrova (2006), Kotzeva et al. (2005) and Stoilova (2008).
4 See Todorova (2000), Staykova (2004), Stoilova (2008), Philipov and Kohler (2001), Dimitrova (2006).
5 In just a few months in 1989 over 300,000 Bulgarian Turks fled Bulgaria in an attempt to avoid the forced change of names. In August 1989 Turkey closed its border and refused to accept any more migrants. Some of the Turkish population who were planning to emigrate had to return to their homes in Bulgaria, while others who were already in Turkey decided to come back to Bulgaria after the news of the political changes in November 1989 (Buksenstuz, 2000: 83). This process of forced migration, mockingly labelled by the communist authorities 'The Big Excursion', is described as 'unprecedented in the history of transnational migration' (Hopken, 1989 cited in Buksentstuz, 2000: 83).
6 Arguably, it is not illegal for lesbian couples to obtain IVF treatment in private clinics in Bulgaria, but the law is not explicit about lesbian couples: 'assisted reproduction is done only when the condition of the man or the woman does not allow the fulfilment of their reproductive function in a natural way' (Health Law, 2005, Art. 129). Moreover, there is no possibility of a same-sex partner acquiring parental status in Bulgaria: only the woman who has given birth to the child is legally considered a parent, not her partner.
7 See Rubin (1993 [1984]), Warner (1993), Seidman (2002) and Carabine (2004).

12
Living with and against the couple-norm in Oslo

The next four cases studies, chosen from amongst our interviewees in Oslo, explore how individuals negotiate the couple-norm in contemporary Norway. Shirin, a Norwegian-Pakistani heterosexual woman in her mid-thirties, was living alone with her two adolescent children and struggling with the legacy of her divorce which happened more than ten years prior to the interview. Like Shirin, and also like Richard in London, breaking up with his wife was the dominant theme for majority-Norwegian Bjørn. His separation from his wife had been recent and was the backdrop to a highly reflective interview about coupledom, intimate life and their vicissitudes. Both Shirin and Bjørn were mourning their lost marriages and saw their divorces as having cost them normality. In contrast, and somewhat paradoxically, Paul, a majority-Norwegian gay man in his mid-forties who was married, spoke extensively about how he no longer had any longing for normality in his personal life. He felt free to make unconventional intimate life choices, but he also talked about the limits that he believes exist on being open about these choices: some practices are just too controversial and taboo to make public. The fourth Oslo interview was with Astrid, a majority-Norwegian woman in her mid-thirties, who was married to her female partner. Unlike Bjørn and Shirin, who craved it, Astrid seemed to fear normality, feeling that she was saved from it by the fact that her spouse is a woman.

In our discussion of our Norwegian interviewees we focus on the pleasures and pains of intimate life as they recounted them, and on their more or less explicit beliefs about how they should live their intimate lives. Their stories offer a lens on the specificity of the couple-norm and its place in the intimate citizenship regime of contemporary Norway.

Shirin: surviving the aftermath of an arranged marriage

Shirin was born in the mid-1970s in Pakistan. Her father was the first of the family to migrate to Norway, and she, her mother and siblings followed when she was still very young. In Norway her father worked as a waiter and her mother stayed at home, caring for the children. The main focus of Shirin's biographical-narrative was the breakdown of her three-year-long marriage. Her husband had moved out 12 years earlier, and she had not recovered from the tragedy the divorce entailed for her. At the time of the interview she was working full time as a cashier in a shop, and she was living in her own apartment with her two adolescent children.

Shirin's intimate life was framed by the collectivist familial norms of intimacy shared by many Norwegian-Pakistanis, within which marriage is a matter of course and not marrying is largely not experienced as an option.[1] In her late teens, Shirin was taken out of high school and sent to Pakistan to marry the man her family had chosen for her. After the wedding the young couple moved back to Norway. Shirin was surprised when problems started to emerge in the marriage, because she had tried, she said, to 'be nice and kind, to listen to him, and be like a proper housemother and housewife'. Shortly before Shirin had their second child, three years after their wedding, her husband moved out and demanded a divorce. Three years is the length of time needed for a foreign spouse to gain a residence permit in Norway, and Shirin felt that her husband and his family had used her to gain his residence permit.

Shirin experienced the breakdown of her marriage as a major catastrophe, and she felt in no way prepared to handle a life on her own with two small children.

> Since then I have been alone with two small kids. It was like 'wham' to me. What is happening? How will I manage? I had never worked, and after I married I had only stayed at home. I did not want to leave my husband. It was his choice. It was terribly hard to accept, but when he just left, I had to get back on my feet. Even if I have a large family, everyone is preoccupied with their own lives, they have their own families. So how much support can you count on? I don't make any demands on them. But what I think is a pity is when women who have arranged marriages, when things like this happen to them, I think their parents should take responsibility [...]. When your partner just leaves you, your

Shirin: surviving the aftermath of an arranged marriage

Shirin was born in the mid-1970s in Pakistan. Her father was the first of the family to migrate to Norway, and she, her mother and siblings followed when she was still very young. In Norway her father worked as a waiter and her mother stayed at home, caring for the children. The main focus of Shirin's biographical-narrative was the breakdown of her three-year-long marriage. Her husband had moved out 12 years earlier, and she had not recovered from the tragedy the divorce entailed for her. At the time of the interview she was working full time as a cashier in a shop, and she was living in her own apartment with her two adolescent children.

Shirin's intimate life was framed by the collectivist familial norms of intimacy shared by many Norwegian-Pakistanis, within which marriage is a matter of course and not marrying is largely not experienced as an option.[1] In her late teens, Shirin was taken out of high school and sent to Pakistan to marry the man her family had chosen for her. After the wedding the young couple moved back to Norway. Shirin was surprised when problems started to emerge in the marriage, because she had tried, she said, to 'be nice and kind, to listen to him, and be like a proper housemother and housewife'. Shortly before Shirin had their second child, three years after their wedding, her husband moved out and demanded a divorce. Three years is the length of time needed for a foreign spouse to gain a residence permit in Norway, and Shirin felt that her husband and his family had used her to gain his residence permit.

Shirin experienced the breakdown of her marriage as a major catastrophe, and she felt in no way prepared to handle a life on her own with two small children.

> Since then I have been alone with two small kids. It was like 'wham' to me. What is happening? How will I manage? I had never worked, and after I married I had only stayed at home. I did not want to leave my husband. It was his choice. It was terribly hard to accept, but when he just left, I had to get back on my feet. Even if I have a large family, everyone is preoccupied with their own lives, they have their own families. So how much support can you count on? I don't make any demands on them. But what I think is a pity is when women who have arranged marriages, when things like this happen to them, I think their parents should take responsibility [...]. When your partner just leaves you, your

Concluding remarks

Amongst the countries in our study, Bulgaria stands out as having the most conservative intimate citizenship regime, with the most powerfully restrictive operation of the couple-norm, which continues to recognize and confer rights on only the married heterosexual couple. More and more people are living outside this conventional arrangement – in same-sex relationships, remaining single, choosing to marry later in life or to cohabit without being married, having children outside wedlock or raising them on their own. Yet the married heterosexual couple-form is still foundational to intimate citizenship in Bulgaria, powerfully constructing deviations as 'unconventional' and unrecognizable.

The Bulgarian case studies illustrate many of the ways in which adults are expected to conform to the different facets of the couple-norm, demonstrating the social, and sometimes legal, pressure that is exerted on those who fail to do so. There was little evidence in these case studies, or in the wider body of interviews that we carried out in Bulgaria, that the ruptures and breaks with the couple-norm of which our 'unconventional' interviewees spoke were chosen and positively embraced. On the contrary, their stories articulated a desire to live a 'normal' life, with the recognition and acceptance of others, and for some, a wish that they might be able to conform to the expectation↔injunctions that they faced – to fit into society as it is. Beyond the personal experiences of misrecognition recounted by our interviewees, there was little political awareness or critique of the multifarious yet persistent ways in which dominant norms about coupledom have the capacity to constrain and impact upon individuals' lives and subjectivities.

By highlighting key encounters with law, policy and culture, and longer-term experiences of the couple-norm across individuals' lives, the cases also show some of the changes that have taken place in the couple-norm in Bulgaria over recent decades. With the end of the communist regime, intimate lives became subject to less interference and policing by the state, and possibilities for living outside the married heterosexual couple-form have increased. The case studies also illuminate the diversity of ways in which individuals negotiate and 'work around' the expectation↔injunctions of normative coupledom against the backdrop of interventions by families, friends and communities who are committed to upholding the couple-norm. They point to the complex ways in which culture, gender, sexuality, and ethnicity intersect in defining how the couple-form should be lived, as well as the capacities of each individual to oppose and challenge such norms.

Notes

1 According to Nwankwo (2011) there were 11 labour education schools, in communist Bulgaria, with between 50 and 80 per cent of the children confined there being Roma.
2 Coontz (2004: 974) points out that 'many societies have had a very casual attitude toward what deserves recognition as a marriage. The "tradition" that marriage has to be licensed by the state or sanctified by the church is more recent that most people assume.'
3 See Keremidchieva (1998), Yachkova (2002), Dimitrova (2006), Kotzeva et al. (2005) and Stoilova (2008).
4 See Todorova (2000), Staykova (2004), Stoilova (2008), Philipov and Kohler (2001), Dimitrova (2006).
5 In just a few months in 1989 over 300,000 Bulgarian Turks fled Bulgaria in an attempt to avoid the forced change of names. In August 1989 Turkey closed its border and refused to accept any more migrants. Some of the Turkish population who were planning to emigrate had to return to their homes in Bulgaria, while others who were already in Turkey decided to come back to Bulgaria after the news of the political changes in November 1989 (Buksenstuz, 2000: 83). This process of forced migration, mockingly labelled by the communist authorities 'The Big Excursion', is described as 'unprecedented in the history of transnational migration' (Hopken, 1989 cited in Buksentstuz, 2000: 83).
6 Arguably, it is not illegal for lesbian couples to obtain IVF treatment in private clinics in Bulgaria, but the law is not explicit about lesbian couples: 'assisted reproduction is done only when the condition of the man or the woman does not allow the fulfilment of their reproductive function in a natural way' (Health Law, 2005, Art. 129). Moreover, there is no possibility of a same-sex partner acquiring parental status in Bulgaria: only the woman who has given birth to the child is legally considered a parent, not her partner.
7 See Rubin (1993 [1984]), Warner (1993), Seidman (2002) and Carabine (2004).

12
Living with and against the couple-norm in Oslo

The next four cases studies, chosen from amongst our i[...] Oslo, explore how individuals negotiate the couple-nor[...] porary Norway. Shirin, a Norwegian-Pakistani heterosex[...] her mid-thirties, was living alone with her two adolescen[...] struggling with the legacy of her divorce which happen[...] ten years prior to the interview. Like Shirin, and also [...] London, breaking up with his wife was the dominant them[...] Norwegian Bjørn. His separation from his wife had been [...] the backdrop to a highly reflective interview about coupl[...] life and their vicissitudes. Both Shirin and Bjørn were [...] lost marriages and saw their divorces as having cost the[...] contrast, and somewhat paradoxically, Paul, a majority-[...] man in his mid-forties who was married, spoke extensi[...] he no longer had any longing for normality in his perso[...] free to make unconventional intimate life choices, but [...] about the limits that he believes exist on being open abou[...] some practices are just too controversial and taboo to m[...] fourth Oslo interview was with Astrid, a majority-Norwe[...] her mid-thirties, who was married to her female partne[...] and Shirin, who craved it, Astrid seemed to fear norma[...] she was saved from it by the fact that her spouse is a wo[...]

In our discussion of our Norwegian interviewe[...] the pleasures and pains of intimate life as they re[...] and on their more or less explicit beliefs about how [...] their intimate lives. Their stories offer a lens on th[...] the couple-norm and its place in the intimate citizer[...] contemporary Norway.

family should support you. But I have managed on my own, and it was not easy.

From assuming that she would live a normal life as a married woman in a lifelong marriage, staying at home and looking after her children as she had been brought up to expect, Shirin's life was turned upside down. She had to take on tasks and responsibilities that she never imagined herself having to deal with, and as a divorced woman she felt ashamed and ostracized within the Pakistani community. She also felt excluded from her family, and she found it hard to find an alternative network of friends to offer support and help with childcare.

Whilst Shirin did not turn wholly against arranged marriage, she admitted to feeling bitter about her own experience. She had been prevented by her family from pursuing a relationship that she desired when she was younger, but she had gone along with the marriage her parents wanted for her, and she had tried to make it work:

Most important to me was that I went to school with a boy, and I was in love with him, and my family didn't like it [...] And that's why they took me to Pakistan and got me married away there [...]. After I married I forgot my boyfriend, thought about my husband, was faithful to him and started over. But it did not turn out well. Deep down I am very bitter. Because I loved one person, but my parents would not let me marry him. They chose someone and he left me. And now I am left here alone with two children. And I didn't want to end up like this.

She had not chosen her fate, and she was angry about the lack of 'follow-up' by her family and community of origin when the marriage did not go according to plan. She felt that since her family had taken responsibility for the arrangement of the wedding, they should also take responsibility for how the marriage turned out. This resonates with Norwegian sociologist Anja Bredal's research in which she found that young Norwegian-Pakistanis see arranged marriages within a 'logic of responsibility' (2006: 255): if a young person decides to take charge of her own marriage and to marry whomever she wants, she must also take full responsibility for how the marriage turns out, but if the parents arrange the marriage, they are obligated to support and help out the marriage. But as Bredal's (2006: 253–5) research suggests, and as Shirin painfully experienced, these expectations are not always shared by parents or followed through. Shirin had accepted the familial orientation to her couple relationship and had adapted to her parents' wishes for her, and their, future, despite being in love with someone else. But the mutual help and support that she expected from her family was not forthcoming when her husband left her and the marriage failed. She felt that her parents were being uncaring and unsupportive. She spoke of her emotional distress, both about the end of her marriage and about not being embraced within the family and community after her divorce, describing how she felt left to sit 'alone and cry' with her two boys. Through the divorce Shirin lost the dream of a practical, grounded married-couple life with a man with whom she could share responsibilities, and she lost her dream of romantic love. In addition to this she felt excluded from her family and the wider Pakistani community and, no longer belonging to a proper family unit, she felt marked by shame.

In her narrative, Shirin referred to conflicting but co-existing ideals of love and marriage: on the one hand, a practical or 'realist love', based on the sharing of everyday tasks and responsibilities; and on the other hand, an ideal of love and marriage based on romance and passion.[2] Shirin was prepared for a practical marriage, having always expected to have an arranged marriage. But she had also hoped this would include (romantic) love and a lifelong partnership.

> To me, marriage was ... [laughs] ... an honest man, a happy family, to spend your life together and have fun, to help each other ... I wanted a man who trusted me, and who had given more time [to the children and me] ... who loved me more than heaven and earth. And who just cared about me and my children. But I ended up with the opposite kind of person.

Whilst she was not in love when she married, it was important to her that she should fall in love:

> When I married him, I actually came to care about him. I tried to fall in love with him, and in the end I managed to. And I tried to do exactly what he wanted, so in a way you could say that I became a lot like my mother – to make your husband happy and be like ... a servant, really.

Her husband did not appreciate her efforts and spent little time at home. Shirin kept trying to please him and to address the problems in their relationship. For instance, they had separate bedrooms, and very little sex or romance, which Shirin did not find acceptable. She tried to change things:

> And then one day I asked him, 'why can't we sleep together? We are husband and wife, right?' And he thought that was very rude of me … that I was being rude. I just went, 'excuse me, but I'm talking to my husband, and I'm allowed to talk to him. If I want sex, then that is all right. I'm supposed to be able to get that. From you!' And he just said, 'No. You're a Pakistani girl, and you shouldn't talk like that.' And we could have sex when it suited him. And he never wanted to. I don't know why that is. He was a very cold person. You could well say that we had sex twice, and that was the two times I got pregnant. No romantic life at all. He was not romantic at all, while I on the other hand, was. And I really tried to make it work. I bought him gifts, and he never said thank you. He didn't even remember my birthday, not a single time, and never Valentine's Day, or any of that. But I always remembered, and I bought him little presents and tried to make him happy. When he was sleeping I would make him breakfast on a tray, with a little present and a piece of cake, and 'here you go'. And he would just go, 'psh, I don't want anything'. That's how he always was. And it broke my heart, every time.

Shirin expected both sex and romance to be a part of her marriage, but all her efforts failed: 'He was never in love with me.' Nor did her husband fulfil his obligations to care practically for her and their children. She complained about how he sent most of their money back to his family in Pakistan and spent most of his time outside their home. She was left at home, alone and lonely, and when she was pregnant with her second child he left her permanently. Having grown up relating to both Norwegian and Pakistani ideals of coupledom, it was clear to Shirin, in retrospect, that her relationship with her husband did not meet any of them. Nonetheless, her commitment to the marriage was such that she wanted to hold on to it and make it work.

Alongside this story of the disappointment inherent in her failed marriage, Shirin also focused on the disappointment she felt in relation to her parents. She talked about how hard the involuntary break with the couple-norm that had been forced upon her had been, and about how her parents had failed to support her through this; they were bad parents to her. She had been raised to depend on husband and family, and not to be independent, and she had been abandoned by both. She related this experience to the conflict that she felt between two very different cultures, as a woman with roots in traditional Pakistani culture who was living in Norway, where gender relations and norms of love and sexuality were very different from her parents' Pakistan.

> For us girls from two cultures, it is very hard. I am half Pakistani, half Norwegian. There are no Pakistani girls living alone in our community, but I do. What does that make me? Norwegian or Pakistani? But I am not allowed to have a cohabitant because I am a Pakistani, but I am allowed to live alone. I don't get it. Sometimes something is allowed, and other times it isn't. When is it allowed? When it suits others, not when it suits you.

Shirin was critical of what she saw as the strong focus in Pakistani culture on family obedience and on shame, and she criticized her parents for not following up on what she saw as the other part of the intergenerational contract: care for her well-being and responsibility for her life after the (unsuccessful) marriage they had arranged. Although Shirin had not broken ties with her family, at the time of the interview she felt unloved and uncared for by her parents. Yet she could not give up on what she saw as an unrealistic hope: that her parents, one day, would start to love her and show her that they loved her.

Whilst Shirin had made some friends at work, she saw a new marriage as the best way to find companionship and support and to escape her current loneliness. However, she recognized that this was problematic, because her parents had strict rules about whom they would allow her to marry, and they were trying to push her towards reconciliation with her ex-husband. Despite her anger towards her parents for neglecting her and her children after the divorce, and whilst blaming them for choosing the wrong husband for her, she still found it impossible to oppose their wishes:

> For example ... when I started working, I met this guy who liked me, and I thought 'yes, why not? Why not get married again? The children are growing up, and soon they will have their own life. Then I will be lonely, and that is boring.' So I'm like, 'ok, I'll try'. And I told him the whole story – that I have a family, I'm divorced, I have two children. And it was all right with him. He was a very kind, loyal and nice man. Despite all these things, he still wanted to spend his life with me. And then I talked to my

family about it, and they just said, 'No, we are against it. You can get married if you like, and we will not try to stop you, but then we will cut off all ties to you.' So now I have a choice between the two of them, and I can't make it. Even though I know that this man is ... He has helped me and has been very kind to me. We have known each other for a long time ... We had a relationship for something like three years. And still I don't dare to make the decision. I didn't dare. I was just like, 'no, I don't want to lose my family'. The family that was never there for me. The family that never cares about me. Like I said, if I'm sick, I can't expect any help from them. But still, I prefer them to him. He has actually been there for me, but still I don't dare, and that's ... I don't know why I ... I can't.

Shirin found it hard to understand her own persistent loyalty to her parents, her attachment to the family that had not supported her properly and her inability to follow her own desires. She was critical of her mother for never daring to make any decisions on her own and always waiting for her husband's opinions. But in the interview she expressed her anxiety that she had become as indecisive and dependent as her mother, and she described trying to be more resolute in front of her children. She did not want them to become like her mother. She had been brought up to obey her parents and her future husband; she had tried to follow the rules, but given the way her life had turned out, she wondered if she should not have chosen a different, and more individualist, route:

I have tried to be a good daughter-in-law, but I was never accepted. I have tried to be a good wife, but I was never accepted. I tried to be [laughs] a good daughter – I listened to my parents – but I never got back what I wanted. So, every now and then, I regret everything. I should have listened to my heart, and done everything the way it suited me, instead of just trying to please them. Then, perhaps my life would have been different now.

Still now, I don't want to hurt them. I love my parents and I love my family. I don't want to do anything stupid that I'll regret afterwards. When I do things like that I'm only hurting myself, because the truth is that I never get anything back from my parents anyway. They don't see that ... how much I need them or how much I love them. It's the same to them whether I'm there or not. They don't care about me at all. [...] That hurts. Because it's not the way that I think at all. I want a family around me. I want a man who loves me … who means something to me, and to whom I mean something.

She would, she made clear in the interview, be happy to submit to a husband. She would gladly be a stay-at-home mother, with her husband taking charge and holding responsibility for the family. But, at the same time, she would like to be able to make her own choices, and she was enjoying some aspects of her forced independence. This was a psychologically tortured place to be, and she expressed considerable distress in the interview about her predicament.

Shirin's story of her intimate life was one about her involuntary passage to non-conventionality, and about her struggle to find ways to come to terms with, and handle, this failure. She saw this as partly her parents' failure – to find her a good husband – but she knew that she was the one who had to carry the burden of failure in her life, and this made her angry and sad. Shirin's story was also one of being caught between different intimate expectation↔injunctions and ideals: about love (between practical and arranged love and romantic love), about parenting (between Pakistani and majority-Norwegian ideals) and about what a woman's life should be like (submission to family authority or individual autonomy and self-responsibility).

Shirin's case exemplifies a version of the couple-norm in which adults are expected to be married, and where the couple is seen as a family matter. It highlights tensions regarding the role that romantic love and rationality should play in a marriage, a tension expressed and negotiated in both Norwegian-Pakistani culture and majority-Norwegian culture.[3] While Shirin thought that she wanted nothing more than to live in a happy, lifelong marriage arranged by her family, circumstances forced her to reflect upon the different expectations about love, marriage and parenthood that exist in the world around her. While she, for the most part, saw this forced reflexivity as a burden consequent on an enormous loss, there were also hints of hope and new possibilities in her story. She acknowledged that in many ways she had adjusted to being single and admitted that she enjoyed being able to make decisions about her own daily life. Her strongest desire, however, was to find a new husband:

I want a loving man by my side, and perhaps … perhaps a daughter, too. If I can have that … (laughs). And a happy life. That is what I want.

Despite the disappointment and traumatic experience of her marriage, yearning and hope for lasting coupledom remained.

Bjørn: grappling with the catastrophic failure of divorce

Bjørn was a majority-Norwegian heterosexual man in his mid-forties. He worked as a high school teacher and at the time of the interview he had recently separated from his wife of 12 years. He and his wife had met just after he had finished his studies. They started living together straight away, married within a year and had a child within two years. They had shared a passion for the outdoors, and their early years together were filled with significant events and joint projects: their wedding, the birth of children, moving several times, buying a house and carrying out renovations.

The story of Bjørn's 'failed marriage' was the central theme of the interview, as it was for Shirin. He described the divorce as a 'catastrophe'. There had been troubles in the marriage for many years, which they attempted to address through various forms of therapy, mostly on his initiative, and they talked about splitting up. Approximately five months before the interview, Bjørn learnt that his wife had been having an affair with another man. This immediately led to them separating, and Bjørn was still in an emotionally raw state at the time of the interview. He had recently bought a new house close to his ex-wife, who stayed in the family home, and they planned to share the children 50/50.

Although Bjørn and his wife had openly spoken about problems in the marriage and had discussed the possibility of separating, he was shocked and deeply hurt by the break-up. He was clear that one of the reasons for his hurt was the sexual betrayal he had experienced. Bjørn had wanted a more active sex life with his wife, but he said that he had very often been rejected, and that they had sex very infrequently:

> I behaved like a modern man who not only demanded and did his thing, but yes, tried different things to make it work. But I met quite a bit of resistance. And then of course ... that makes the fall harder. ... And what happens when she ... gets so absorbed by another man, and it is very explicitly sexual the communication they had, then it's very odd because I thought I lived with an asexual being. And it did something to the self-confidence.

Sex is regarded as a crucial element of being a couple in contemporary Norway, but it is an expectation that has to be carefully negotiated, particularly since the norm of gender equality and the belief in women's right to a fulfilling sexual life also have become dominant (Danielsen & Mühleisen, 2009a). As a 'modern man', Bjørn had learnt that he had to be considerate and not to put his own sexual needs before the needs or desire of his female partner. He tried to 'work on' the sex in the relationship, as couples are expected to do, but felt that he got little positive response from his wife.[4] He pointed out that, although he had been tempted, he had never been unfaithful to his wife. He felt that infidelity was an option that was not open to him because it would destroy his family. The rejection and humiliation he felt as a result of his wife wanting sex with another man when she did not want it with him was part of his explanation of the devastation he felt about their separation. His wife broke with expectation↔injunctions that are intrinsic to the couple-norm, both by not wanting to have sex within the relationship and then by choosing to have sex outside the relationship.

On an even more fundamental level, Bjørn saw his divorce as a major failure. He stated clearly that he saw what he called 'intact families' as the ideal and divorce as problematic and shameful. He also considered lifelong monogamy to be a shared cultural value in Norwegian society. Just as Shirin seemed to have taken marriage, and a lasting marriage, for granted, so did Bjørn. He had assumed that he would get married at the right age and that he would stay with his wife for the rest of his life.[5]

> The hardest part of my divorce is that I no longer ... that I didn't manage to stand by what has been my ideal, and which still is the societal norm, which is the intact family [...]. I have had to prepare myself for not being a part of an intact family, and come to terms with the shame, the social shame I experienced by not being a part of an intact family [...] When I married, the ideal for my family was, of course, that I should be old together, and die in the marriage with my wife. I don't really know to what extent I had reflected on this – that was just the way it is. I had never imagined that I would get divorced. And I have told colleagues and friends that I would put up with a lot before I would let my children become children of divorce, in a kind of understanding that to be a child of divorced parents is a disaster, and that it is pushing them to be drug addicts or anything bad.[6]

While Bjørn took coupledom and parenthood for granted when he was young, his own turbulent marriage produced reflexivity around what it means to be a couple and about the norms that pertain to intimate relationships. He had read a lot of self-help literature, and he initiated different forms of couple counselling in order to save his marriage. While the shame of the divorce in Shirin's case seemed to be connected to her failing to be a good woman – given that a good woman is necessarily married – Bjørn's shame partly seemed to be connected to him not being able to be a proper man.

> For me, not to manage this family project is a matter of shame. I don't know. ... To not succeed. Failure. Relationship failure. Like the major project of a life, marriage, it didn't work out for me. And it is almost like losing a competition. It can be shameful. But not to manage what you set out to, that's something. ... I think that is why I talk about shame. And others make it, so why can't I make it?

According to his ideals of masculinity, a man should accomplish what he sets out to do. A man takes action when problems occur. He finds solutions. A man fulfils his woman sexually, and a man takes care of his family to the best of his ability. He succeeds at the challenges he takes on, especially when that challenge is 'the major project of a life'.

These traditional components of masculinity are complemented in Bjørn's case by an expectation, inflected by the emphasis on gender equality in the Norwegian intimate citizenship regime, that he should also take emotional responsibility within the couple, not leaving the emotion-work solely to the woman. Of the Norwegian interviewees, Bjørn was the one who talked most explicitly and extensively about shame. He had worked long and hard to keep his family 'intact', to adhere to the couple-norm, and he felt profound shame when this project failed.

In contrast to Shirin, however, who also felt ashamed and dejected at the failure of her marriage, Bjørn already saw life after divorce as full of opportunities. He confessed that he had become 'addicted' to several dating sites on the internet, and he seemed to assume that he would form a new couple relationship soon. Although his ideal was the cohabiting or married couple, he was preparing himself for the fact that a future girlfriend would probably also have children, which would make cohabitation problematic, because he assumed that all divorced parents want to live close to their ex and to their children's schools.[7]

At the same time as being emotionally devastated by the end of his marriage, there was a sense in Bjørn's narrative that divorce was inevitable. Without explicitly saying so, it seemed that he saw his wife's infidelity as the final straw that broke a marriage that was heading ineluctably towards divorce. Their marriage had been unhappy for a long time, and Bjørn had made many attempts to try to 'fix it' without much success. He had also, he admitted, had passing thoughts about the possibility of 'cheating' or starting a new relationship himself. In his narrative he did not present divorce as a big surprise, but because the marriage had ended as it did, his wife now got most of the blame for the break-up. His wife's clear culpability elicited much sympathy for him from family, friends, colleagues and acquaintances, and given the extent to which he felt that a broken marriage was a failure, he was expressly relieved that he was not the main one to blame. This suggests that his feelings of shame and sense of responsibility were somewhat counterbalanced by an ability to apportion blame and to find relief in attributing it to his wife.

Bjørn's story illustrates a number of key facets of the couple-norm in contemporary Norway: the expectation↔injunctions that a couple should marry and stay together for life, that couple relationships take dedicated emotional work, care and active effort, by the man as well as the woman, that sex is central to a couple relationship and that sex outside the relationship constitutes an irrevocable fracture. It also speaks to the specificity of contemporary Norwegian middle-class masculinity and how this relates to the practice of coupledom, a masculinity which is double-edged: sensitive to and respectful of the woman's wishes, but at the same time responsible for exploring blockages in the relationship and mending her sexual appetite to bring it into line with his own.

Paul: challenging expectations of monogamous romantic love

Paul, a majority-Norwegian gay man, was a successful engineer in his mid-forties. He was living in a partnership that he described as happy with his spouse of 15 years.[8] In his youth Paul had struggled with his sexuality, keeping his emerging gay identity to himself and thinking that he did not want to live a 'gay life'. He felt that homosexuality would make him an outcast, a 'social loser', and he made sure he excelled in all other areas to compensate for the burden of outsiderness that he would carry through life. Throughout his adolescence the 'social fall' that he believed he would suffer if his sexuality was more widely known was his main concern: 'I never had any guilt about being gay. I just felt it was a social defeat, plain and simple. It ruined the facade, and I wanted my facade to look good.'

After he finally came out to those around him, aged about 25, he had some wild and rather turbulent years, with a lot of falling in and out of love and many short relationships. He did not see this as a good period of his life:

> I have very few positive experiences of falling in love. I have never experienced a crush that ends in anything but disaster. So the higher I got [emotionally], the more I would prepare for that horrible backlash that I knew would come eventually.

In middle age, Paul now lived what in many ways was a conventional life, given the transformation in the Norwegian intimate citizenship regime to include those in same-sex relationships within the 'charmed circle' (Rubin, 1993 [1984]) of respectable, state-sanctioned coupledom. His career was flourishing and he was happily married. He and his husband had responsibility for children. He had, he explained, always wanted a stable and secure life, and he had achieved exactly what he wanted. Yet, alongside this normative success, his intimate life actively broke with two important expectations that are central to the couple-norm in contemporary Norway: romantic love and monogamy.

His explanation of his rejection of romantic love was grounded in his experience of 'falling in love' as highly problematic. As someone for whom rationality and self-control were central to his sense of self, the first time he fell in love felt like being sick:

> It was purely unpleasant. I just wanted to get through it and be finished with it, because it is terribly exhausting. And I couldn't use it for anything positive. You just had to live through it, like 'flu. It has to pass by itself, but it takes far too long time.

This was confirmed by later experiences: falling in love was an exclusively negative condition that ruined both his peace of mind and his self-image. His relationship with his husband was as good as it was exactly because they never had been 'crazily in love'. When he told the story of how he met his husband he said that it was never a 'passionate, romantic affair, with flowers and chocolate and all that':

> So no, I was never heedlessly in love with him, but I felt good with him. I felt safe when I was with him, because he was such a safe person. [...] He is a teacher, a nice dresser, and he isn't provocative in any sense of the word. He can talk and make conversation. So that summer we were going on a holiday together for three weeks, we drove all over Norway. And when we had completed that holiday I remember telling myself: 'you know, this has gone very well. We have been spending all our time together for three weeks, and I have been comfortable all the time. There have been no problems. This is the man of my life.' And after that I have never considered it any further. Then I had what I needed; this was the man I wanted to live with.
>
> And we never have those big philosophical discussions where we bare our souls to each other and evaluate our relationship and our feelings for each other. I can remember that a friend was very critical of us because we didn't penetrate the deeper layers. But I told him that neither of us ever needed it. We never had that phase ... or, we never had a relationship where we put everything out there: 'Now I feel this and that, and what do you feel now?' We have been companions and best friends, and we are very different people with very different personalities. But it has never been like my other relationships, where I have always felt the need to talk about love, life, death and the ocean. We never did that. And at the beginning I wondered if maybe we shouldn't do that: is there something wrong with this relationship, because we really should do that. But I didn't really miss it.

In late modernity, the couple – a 'pure relationship' (Giddens, 1992) – is normatively expected to be based on both romantic love and emotional intimacy, the communion of souls, 'disclosing intimacy' (Jamieson, 1998).[9] But for Paul it was comfort, security and care, rather than romance and intense emotional exchange, that mattered – echoing Jamieson, whose rejoinder to Giddens's thesis on the transformation of intimacy emphasizes that in successful (heterosexual) relationships 'acts of practical love and care have been more important than a constant dynamic of mutual exploration of each other's selves' (Jamieson, 1999: 477).

Yet Paul's story is more complex than this picture of marital safety and comfort might suggest. Paul sees his relationship, and its lack of intensity and passion, as unconventional, and as representing a taboo way of thinking about love and relationships in contemporary Norway – so taboo that he was aware that he and his husband could not talk about their relationship in this way publicly. To enter a relationship without being passionately in love broke with the couple-norm in such a threatening way that it was not even to be articulated out loud.[10]

Bredal analyses the way in which ideals of 'sense' and 'sensibility' are negotiated among her Norwegian-Pakistani and other South Asian interviewees in Norway. Like Paul, some of her interviewees also talked about how rational considerations should come before feelings, and they took pride in the fact that they managed to use their brains rather than being swept away by their emotions (Bredal, 2006: 236ff). While 'sense' is the respectable approach to marriage amongst many Norwegian-Pakistanis, 'sensibility' is the acceptable approach to coupledom in the majority-Norwegian middle-class culture to which Paul belongs; 'falling in love' is the only legitimate starting point of a relationship (see Danielsen and Mühleisen, 2009a; Eggebø, 2012, 2013a).

Alongside rationality, fulfilment of sexual desire is a central value for Paul. He has an active sex life with many sexual partners in addition to his husband. His husband knows of, and sometimes shares, both Paul's practice of non-monogamy and his sexual partners. Paul underlined that he never fell in love with any of these other men, but that many of them turned into close friends and came to be important in his and his husband's social life as a couple. Paul's separation of sex and being/falling in love can be seen to be in accordance with a community ethical norm amongst many gay men of his generation. This tends to regard fidelity 'in terms of emotional commitment rather than sexual behaviour' (Weeks, Heaphy and Donovan, 2001: 122) and sits alongside the widespread practice in lesbian and gay communities of incorporating ex-lovers into friendship networks.[11]

Paul hid his non-monogamy from most of his friends and family.[12] He and his husband only discussed this aspect of their relationship with other gay male couples who also enjoyed 'non-committal', 'free sex'. Paul clearly saw his gay 'promiscuity' as a break with normative coupledom, and he was highly critical of the homonormalizing process to which he saw the struggle for lesbian and gay rights and same-sex marriage contributing:

> I actually find that Norwegians, including gays, are basically very puritanical with regard to non-committal sex for those in a relationship. So I think a part of the struggle, and everything that is happening around the Act of Partnership, the normalization of us lesbians and gays, that makes it politically correct, and the ultimate goal for gays is to live in monogamous relationships as similar to heterosexual relationships as possible. And now it's damn well that we should have kids as well. And that's the ultimate happiness, to go to America, have a surrogate mother and one or two children. So, instead of cultivating the opportunity for free sex and promiscuity, and taking advantage of what is inside us as men, gays have become socialized to be as much like the others as possible. They know how different we are, and then I will argue that we have lost something that gays experience as positive – the sex, the promiscuity – which is seen as positive by a lot of gays. We had to let that go.

Paul expressed his belief that most men have a naturally strong sexual drive, and that gay men should not constrain their sexual conduct in accordance with societal norms. In this he was echoing a long history of gay men seeing, and campaigning for, sex as a liberatory, creative and transformative practice.[13] As the gay activist Dennis Altman expressed it in an article first published in 1982:

> Too much of the rhetoric of gay leaders has ignored the reality: most gay men do not behave sexually, and do not want to behave sexually, according to the dominant norms of this society. Increasingly I have come to see this as a virtue, and one we should be prepared to defend. Gay men are developing new forms of sexual relationships that make it possible to reconcile our needs for commitment and stability with the desire for sexual adventure and experimentation (Altman, 1997 [1982]: 530).
>
> For if the gay movement stands for anything beyond civil rights it stands for a breaking down of the sexual repressions and fears that fuel so much of the violence and paranoia of modern life (Altman, 1997 [1982]: 534).

For these activists, as for Paul, sexual liberation and sexual self-expression create an ethic of their own. To suppress one's sexuality, to subject it to conventional moralities, would be unethical within this value system. While this radical sexual politics was quite visible – although highly controversial – in Norwegian lesbian and gay politics in the 1970s and 1980s, the movement shifted its focus to partnership and family in the 1990s. While Paul appreciated his blossoming career and his success in creating a stable and happy home life with the man he loved, he also strongly valued his extramarital sexual life. For him, non-monogamy was the best route to stable, happy, long-term coupledom, and he articulated his belief that gay men have been able to establish relationships characterized by stability, love and lifelong commitment, whilst also allowing the freedom to pursue sexual encounters outside the relationship and to 'take advantage of what lies in the man'. Many of his gay friends who have been together for ten to 20 years have the same kind of agreements, and he regarded them as well-functioning relationships, involving strong friendship and companionship.

> While the lesbians, they are serially monogamous … they get dramatic; that is my view, anyway. Monogamy is very important to them. But they stop having sex. So they become friends instead. And one of them will go out and fall in love, and then she is thrown straight out. Because it seems to me that they are unable to have a good relationship at home and at the same time have something on the side […]. They say that men can have only one thought in their head at any one time, while women can have more than one thought. But in this instance I think that men can have several sexual relations going at the same time, and also have a stable emotional relation. While, with women, everything needs to be clean and tidy. There is only one bed at the time, and they don't want to hear about anything else.

Ideas about gender and gender roles are strongly present in Paul's story. He sees men and women as significantly different, and he generally prefers the ways of men. Although Paul here is articulating a narrative about the differences between lesbians and gay men in their couple relationships that is well known in the United Kingdom and the United States (Gordon, 2006; Weeks, Heaphy and Donovan, 2001: 138–48), publicly voiced narratives in Norway have tended not to focus on gendered differences between the two groups, and Paul's argument is not often spoken in the Norwegian public sphere.

Paul had never been particularly interested in children, and he had tended to find them rather bothersome. It was more by chance than design, then, that he and his husband started to take increasing responsibility for the children of two lesbian acquaintances, and that they now have an arrangement in which they regularly care for the children. Paul spoke about really enjoying his relationships with these children. Moreover, Paul and his partner were spending more and more time with the mothers of the children. But Paul described trying to resist 'becoming one big happy family'. He wanted, he explained, to have a relationship with the children on his own terms, and not to be forced into a pre-established pattern of parental roles and family life. He wanted to be a part of the children's lives, but he also wanted to keep his active extramarital sex life, and no family role should interfere with that.

In contrast to Shirin and Bjørn, Paul was not sorry, regretful or ashamed that he was breaking with conventional expectations about coupledom. He saw himself as having freely chosen his transgressions of several facets of the couple-norm, and he felt that he was in a privileged position to be able to make such choices. Through his break with the hetero-norm, Paul seemed to feel free to redefine the couple-norm in a way that he felt was better suited to his (and maybe, he thought, all men's) practical, emotional and sexual needs. Long-term commitment and love were separated from the demand for romantic love, as well as from the expectation↔injunction of monogamy. For Paul, the rejection of key elements of the couple-norm (as with the hetero-norm) was not associated with loss, but with exciting new opportunities. He had not always felt this way, and he remembered clearly how in his younger years he had seen homosexuality as an impossibly severe rupture with societal norms, and as incompatible with the successful and respectable life for which he wished. But now, in middle age, he appreciated the choice and freedom he experienced in his intimate life. He felt that he had the best of all worlds: a loving, stable, long-term relationship, a parental role, and sexual excitement and transgression outside the couple that was fully sanctioned by his husband. Yet, despite his satisfaction with how well things had turned out, Paul felt that he had to keep secret from most people in his life both his non-monogamy and the absence of romantic love as a base for his partnership. While he could talk about non-monogamy with some of his gay friends, the lack of initial romantic love and intensity with his husband was taboo and perhaps even shameful. The couple-norm, and its constituent expectation↔injunctions, take their toll even on a cosmopolitan, well-educated man like Paul, who in many ways feels that he has freed himself from conventional norms of intimacy.

Astrid: happily committing to contemporary coupledom

As a majority-Norwegian woman in her late thirties who described herself as bisexual, Astrid was living with her partner of ten years, Anne, and their cat. She was close to her family, and Astrid and Anne were devoted aunts to their nieces and nephews, who loved their 'cool' aunts. Astrid had grown up in an affluent suburb and her strong friendship network included friends from her teenage years, as well as many new friends made in the artistic world in which she works. Astrid is deeply dedicated to her creative career, devoting a great deal of time and energy to her work. She commented that she sometimes felt that she was spending too much time with colleagues – not because she did not like doing so, but because she felt she should conform to a norm about proper work–life balance. After surviving a crisis in their relationship, Astrid and Anne were, at the time of the interview, trying to have a baby.

Whereas for Paul coming out as gay had been a long and traumatic process, it was much simpler for Astrid. She had only had relationships with men until she met Anne in her late twenties, and in her biographical-narrative the shift from heterosexuality to homosexuality was completely unproblematic. Her choice was applauded by her old group of friends from childhood; they were happy to have Astrid as the 'token homo' of the group. Whilst becoming part of a same-sex couple could be seen as at odds with the hetero-norm, Astrid had not experienced it as problematic. Although there are complex and often singular contexts around the process of coming out, there are also several culturally relevant differences in Paul's and Astrid's stories. Whilst Paul was about 15 when he recognized his same-sex desires, Astrid was 29. Research suggests that 'coming out' at a young age poses bigger challenges (Hegna and Wichstrøm, 2007; Hegna, 2007), and Paul and Astrid were also in different places geographically. While Paul was living in the farming village in which he had grown up and where his family had lived for generations, Astrid was brought up in an affluent suburb close to a big city, and when she met Anne she was living in Oslo. There is also a significant difference in historical time. While Paul admitted his homosexuality to himself in the late 1970s, Astrid started her first relationship with a woman in the late 1990s. Enormous changes had taken place in the Norwegian intimate citizenship regime during those 20 years, and homosexuality had become radically more visible and socially acceptable.

Although Astrid did not perceive living in a same-sex couple as counter-normative, in her search for clear guidance about what we wanted her to talk about in the interview she asked if we wanted her to focus on the fact that she did not 'live a completely A4 life'.[14] 'A4', the standard European format for a sheet of paper, is often used in Norwegian to describe something ordinary, something that fits squarely within the standard size and shape of things. Due to her relationship with a woman, Astrid felt that she was living a life outside the standard format, and she regarded a 'non-straight' life as a good thing. Choosing a female partner was, for Astrid, a way of making a positive break with a suffocating ordinariness:

> Yes, I could have ended up in a kind of A4. I had, you know, a sort of lover, a boyfriend, when I was younger, so we could have easily ended up together. But luckily we did not. [...] The A4 life I could have ended up living would have been with this boyfriend of my youth, and we could just have stayed together and married when we were 24 and bought a semi-detached house and children and car and ... And I would surely have ended up with a completely different career than I have now. And I do not think I would have been as happy. [...] I would probably have ended up working in a store or something. But it's like you ... or what I've been afraid of, what I think of as an A4 life, that it would bore me to death. But of course, it's not certain that those who live that way think it is. And nowadays my life is actually not all that different either. I have a house and a lover, a cat, car and job. It's not all that different.

In the interview, Astrid suggested a fear of disappearing in the crowd, of drowning in ordinariness. For her, the consequence of having a female partner was a welcome unordinariness (see Hellesund, 2011; Hellesund et al., 2019). Yet she also acknowledged that her coupled life was not so different from the normality she rejected.

Astrid talked about her family, colleagues, friends and a few former lovers, painting a picture of a sociable, easy-going and well-liked sister, daughter, friend, colleague and lover. Astrid and Anne had, however, recently recovered from a crisis in their relationship:

> We had a really rough period a couple of years ago, when I fell in love with someone else. It was very mutual. But then I decided to

stay. But it hasn't been easy for any of us, because I carry around a broken heart over something that will never happen, and my girlfriend has to live with the fact that I grieve over another person. It took a year before it was okay again. But now at least we are very sure that we shall be together, and in a very different way than we were before. So I think that's how you do if, if one had been married and had a child, or just bought a new house or something, I probably wouldn't have allowed myself to fall that much in love. But if you're in a period in your relationship where things have been the same for several years, so ... But it ended well. But it was pretty heavy.

Instead of this 'rough period' leading to a questioning of the expectation of monogamy, or to a feeling of failure for having desires outside the couple, this experience seemed to have confirmed for Astrid a contemporary, late modern ideal of coupledom in which reflexivity, communication and hard work are seen as necessary and healthy ingredients in a relationship (Illouz, 1998; Danielsen and Mühleisen, 2009a, 2009b). On the basis of this experience, Astrid argued that couples need both change and continuous joint projects to maintain the attention and interest of both parties. Historically the self-building of homes played a significant part in the lives and bonding of gender-conservative families, particularly from the 1950s to the 1980s (Gullestad, 1984), and sociologist Helene Aarseth (2008) argues that construction and do-it-yourself projects continue to have a similar place in the relationships of highly educated, equality-oriented heterosexual couples in contemporary Norway. Aarseth (2007) also points out how joint domestic projects help the new creative middle class, to which Astrid belongs, avoid what they dread in a relationship: routine, ordinariness and staleness.

Astrid and Anne were trying to have a baby at the time of the interview, and it was clear that the stable, monogamous, procreative couple-form constituted an important ideal for Astrid. During the part of the interview in which she talked about children, she explained:

I think [having children] is a lot about having a project together that lasts longer than ..., like, lasts forever. I have a theory that that is why gay men don't last that long together, because there are limits to how many houses you can redecorate and how many summer houses you can have and things like that. And finally it is not enough anymore, and it is too problematic [for gay men] to have a child. And finally there are no shared projects any more, and the relationship ends. But I don't know if this is true. In this regard I guess it is easier for women.

Astrid went on to explain her approach to relationships:

> It is no pipe dream to be alone. I have been alone before, and in the long run it is not so much fun. And then it is a dream to. ... that you get to know another person so incredibly well, and that you still like each other after many years, and still have a strong desire to be together and spend time together. There is something good about such a relationship. I don't know if ... Of course you can have that several times, with a lot of different people, but ... I think many people my age who have small children give up too easily. As soon as things get kind of tiring, not so fun anymore, then they leave each other, and then. ... So that's kind of sad. But among my friends from high school, those who met when they were young, none of them have divorced yet. Even though I have always seen that as incredibly boring, getting together with someone at 16, and then you don't experience anything more. So in that regard I think it is healthy not to end up with your high school sweetheart.

Astrid saw the traumatic time when she was in love with someone else as having had a 'happy ending' because she decided to stay in her long-term relationship. Yet at the same time she found the idea of couples who got together in their teens and who were still together as adults as 'incredibly boring'. Even though monogamy and coupledom were profoundly important to her, it was vital that they were built on a firm foundation of individual past experiences. For Astrid, the ideal situation was to find your partner when you are in your late twenties. By that time you have experienced some things in life, but you are still young enough to have children together. Living in a same-sex couple provided an element of non-conventionality that Astrid valued deeply, and that she felt saved her both from boredom and from being boring. Living in a same-sex couple in Norway at the end of the first decade of the twenty-first century was uncomplicated and fully acceptable, but still unconventional enough to prevent her from disappearing into the grey, anonymous masses.

Astrid's conjuring of an image of childless gay male couples without truly shared projects served as a contrast to the life that she and Anne were trying to create, in the same way that the image of lesbians as serial monogamists without the ability to maintain sexual passion or to open up their relationships operated as a counterpoint to Paul's autobiographical story. The mirroring between Astrid's argument that gay men break up more often than lesbians because they don't have children, and Paul's argument that lesbians break up more often than gay men because they stop having sex and are unable to handle non-monogamy, is striking. Gender stereotypes about biological drives for sex and procreation were perhaps serving a function in the intimate imaginary of each, to validate their own chosen route and to disparage and disavow an alternative, potentially equally desirable pathway. Indeed, the more complex, gender-norm-crossing reality of their lived lives was that Paul and his partner were deeply committed to the children for whom they cared, and Astrid had only recently been exploring non-monogamy. Interestingly, having had a relationship outside her long-term couple, Astrid was the only one of these four Norwegian interviewees who did not speak explicitly about sex in her interview. Whether she was avoiding a troubling issue in her relationship or not talking about something that was relatively unimportant or unproblematic to her is impossible to know.[15]

But it is clear from the interview that for Astrid, the coupled life that she was living matched her expressed values and there was an easy fit between her values, her lifestyle and those of her social network and community. She saw herself as leading an ordinary life, with the slight unconventionality of living with another woman serving as a welcome difference that supported and meshed well with her creative career and self-image. Looking forward to starting a family with her partner, she was avoiding the boredom of the A4 life, whilst fitting happily into a society in which the couple-norm and procreative-norm continue to hold sway.

Concluding remarks

For over a hundred years Norwegian legislators have been seeking to formulate inclusive family law and policy. From changing marriage and divorce laws in order to make marriage more attractive to modern women and destigmatizing births outside marriage in the early twentieth century, through the legalization of heterosexual cohabitation in the 1970s, to the gender-neutral Marriage Act of the early twenty-first century, governments have sought both to adapt to changing times and to include new groups in old concepts of family and belonging. But, despite long-standing liberal divorce laws and little formal pressure towards marriage, there is still a cultural expectation in Norway, amongst both majority and minoritized groups, that coupledom should be validated by marriage. While discussions and critique of monogamous coupledom in general, and the nuclear family in particular, were present within both the feminist movement and the lesbian and gay movement in the 1970s, this critique has disappeared since the late 1980s. But whilst the ideological critique of the nuclear family fell silent, it was during the same decades that intimate practices were radically diversifying, as divorce and unmarried cohabitation rates rose, and serial monogamy, as well as the visibility of lesbians and gay men, increased.

We can see many of these features of the Norwegian intimate citizenship regime reflected in the stories of our Oslo interviewees. The expectation that successful adulthood involves marriage or at least a stable, long-term couple relationship was shared by all four interviewees, across differences of sexuality, and whether or not a long-term couple relationship had been maintained. They each expressed a strong desire for long-term, preferably lifelong, relationships with their partners. For Shirin and Bjørn this seemed to have been taken for granted and was mostly referred to through the devastation of their divorces, which prevented them from achieving this, and which therefore signalled their failure at the primary project of intimate life. Both Paul and Astrid, perhaps having been forced to reflect more on this aspect of the couple-norm because of their positioning outside the hetero-norm, had explicitly thought about the issue of long-term relationships and decided that that was what they wanted for themselves.

Only Paul, the gay man, believed that a couple could be non-monogamous. Both Astrid and Bjørn had experienced breaches to the sexual sanctity of their couple relationship (although from different positions – as 'agent' and 'victim'), but neither questioned the basic tenet of the couple-norm that monogamy constituted fidelity, nor considered any other solution than that one of the relationships would have to end. Bjørn's wife tried to hide her affair from him, and he ended the marriage as soon as he found out. Astrid, on the other hand, had told Anne about her affair, and they were able to talk about it whilst the affair was going on. For neither Bjørn nor Astrid, however, was non-monogamy seen as a viable choice. In contrast, Paul did not regard sexual exclusivity as a prerequisite for a happy, solid and ethical marriage. Rather he regarded sexual excitement outside the relationship as making possible the long-term coupledom that provides him with security and stability. However, Paul also recognized that his lifestyle strongly conflicts with the expectations that constitute the Norwegian couple-norm.

While there is no law requiring romantic love within marriage, there is a strong expectation in majority-Norwegian culture that it is the foundation of, and a prerequisite for, coupledom. This pressure towards romantic love is not present in the same way in the Norwegian-Pakistani community, although it is not absent from the emotional lives of members of the community. Thus, whilst Astrid and Bjørn never questioned romantic love as the foundation of the couple, neither Shirin nor Paul built their relationships on romantic love, albeit for different reasons. Although Shirin had experienced a romantic love relationship in her teens, she was always prepared to have an arranged marriage. While she did not know her husband until after she married him, she underlined in the interview that she did fall in love with him over time. Not having romantic love as a foundation for marriage was not necessarily problematic for Shirin, but falling in love after the wedding was important to her story. Moreover, having failed at an arranged marriage, she now wanted the freedom to try a love marriage, or at least a husband she chose herself. Meanwhile, Paul resisted the expectation of romantic love, as he resisted the injunction to monogamy, and felt that the absence of romantic love (which for him meant a high level of passion and intensity) was the most controversial aspect of his life. Whilst he felt free to talk about his non-monogamous lifestyle with gay friends, deciding to be with his partner without being in love with him felt so unacceptable that it was not something he ever talked about. Our interviewees related to both the realist and the romantic love narratives, but for all of them a romantic element seemed a crucial part of a valid self-narrative that could be presented to the world.

The couple-norm is closely entangled with the procreative-norm, and children were prominent in all four life stories. Bjørn and Shirin seemed to have taken for granted that they should, and would, become parents. Astrid also felt that becoming a parent was important, and she saw children as a logical step in a committed relationship. For Paul the issue was different: he had never displayed any interest in children until he and his husband 'accidentally' took on a kind of parental role in relation to the children of some friends. Astrid was the only one of these Norwegian interviewees who did not have caring responsibility for children, but she and her partner hoped to be parents in the near future, and she saw having children as the one 'project' that was big enough to hold a couple together. Only recently have significant numbers of lesbian and gay couples started to produce children within their relationships with the help of sperm donors and surrogate mothers.[16] Most lesbian and gay couples have thus been positioned differently from heterosexuals with regard to this aspect of the couple-norm. Whilst Astrid's assumptions about the higher stability of lesbian as opposed to gay male couples do not find support in the statistics,[17] her belief about children reducing the risk of divorce does.[18]

Bjørn's and Astrid's narratives about coupledom correspond neatly with the values expressed in the official Norwegian marriage vows and in the ethos of the state-provided couples' courses mentioned in Chapter 7. Romantic love, sexual fidelity and a commitment to working on the relationship were taken for granted as the basis of their relationships. They also both subscribed to the contemporary Norwegian emphasis on equality, individuality and independence within a couple, and negotiating on the basis of these values in their relationships. For Shirin, as a young woman, majority-Norwegian values of gender equality and personal independence had been less salient than a Norwegian-Pakistani collectivist, familial orientation toward marriage. But as an older divorced woman contemplating future possibilities for her intimate life, Shirin was grappling with the tensions between different cultural expectations and contradictory desires in relation to couple relationships. Paul diverged from dominant Norwegian values about the centrality of romantic love and fidelity, regarding them as unnecessary, a hindrance even, to a successful marriage. But he held firmly to dominant versions of the couple-norm in his attachment to the maintenance of individuality and independence within his marriage.

These case studies have shown how four Norwegians, of different sexualities and backgrounds, are living in relation to the couple-norm and its complex contemporary landscape of sometimes confusing and conflicting constituent expectation↔injunctions. With repressive laws and illiberal policies no longer a feature of the Norwegian intimate citizenship regime, and a national culture that professes its tolerance of diversity, it was the opinions, attitudes, judgements and support of family and friends that our interviewees spoke about most explicitly and that seemed to be shaping their intimate life choices. Feelings of failure, shame and embarrassment that were expressed in three of the four interviews. This highlights how, even in a social democratic, gender-equal and de-patriarchalized intimate citizenship regime that emphasizes individual choice and personal freedom and that offers support and security to those living outside conventional couples and families, the couple-norm, and its constituent expectation↔injunctions, are internalized as fundamental standards by which intimate lives are judged. Whatever the complexity of their own biographical history and present reality of couple relationships, each of the interviewees wanted to be part of a couple, and saw being coupled as essential to a good and happy life. In this regard they have much in common with the young same-sex couples interviewed by Heaphy, Smart and Einarsdottir (2013) in the UK who saw couplehood and marriage as key life events, representing maturity, stability and (ontological) security. They naturalized their desire for a loving partnership, and as a contrast saw adult life outside a couple as a more or less incomplete, or even inauthentic, life (Heaphy, Smart and Einarsdottir, 2013: 88). Single life was described as 'not being much of a life' (2013: 152).

Shirin, Bjørn, Paul and Astrid were all aware of different, and sometimes contradictory, cultural expectation↔injunctions regarding coupledom and recognized that they were themselves relating to these simultaneously. Whereas having a self-chosen partner is normative amongst the majority population, arranged marriages are normative for Norwegian-Pakistanis, and whilst passionate romantic love is a widely held expectation of couples in majority-Norwegian culture, equally strong is the view that realistic, everyday love, based on will and hard work, is the route to a happy, long-term relationship. Offering space for reflection on the complexities of experience over time, the interviews were sites of struggle for several interviewees in finding ways to speak about how their own relationship did not fulfil key facets of the couple-norm. Being liberal about different ways of organizing coupledom, as Norwegian culture largely is, does not make it easy to admit to breaking with central aspects of the norm that are not widely questioned, such as eschewing romantic love, or not having (enough, or good enough) sex. Feelings of failure and shame all work to reproduce the couple-norm.

Notes

1   South Asian cultures (along with many other non-western cultures) are often described as having a collectivist rather than individualistic orientation. See Shaw (2001), Bredal (2006), Modood (1995), Modood et al. (1994) and Triandis (1995).
2   This echoes the work of Illouz (1998).
3   See Bredal (2006) on Norwegian-Pakistani cultures of love and marriage, and see Danielsen and Mühleisen (2009a, 2009b) on majority-Norwegian cultures. Anthropologist Charles Lindholm (2006) argues that the ideal of romantic love is not uniquely a western ideal, but that it appears under specific social conditions. The romantic ideal is currently spreading, and 'cross-cultural studies from Pakistan to China, from Polynesia to Malawi, nowadays are

likely to show that young people say they no longer want their marriages to be arranged; instead they hope for a passionate romantic affair that will sweep them off their feet and eventually unite them with an ideal beloved and an idyllic marriage of soul mates' (Lindholm, 2006: 5–6). At the same time, Bredal (2006), Jamieson (2008) and Illouz (1998) are amongst the many scholars showing that the romantic ideal still has competition from other ideals of love and marriage, both among minority and majority populations.

4   This is in line with the teaching of the couples' courses provided by the Norwegian government, discussed in Chapter 7.

5   Bjørn did not specify what the right age for coupling is, but like most educated middle-class majority-Norwegians he seemed to think that it is appropriate to find one's first permanent partner towards the end of one's student years, which is when Bjørn met his wife.

6   Bjørn used the Norwegian term for children of divorced parents, 'skilsmissebarn' (literally: 'divorce child'), a term that became common in the 1970s and 1980s when the divorce rate started to increase. The term has powerfully sad and negative connotations.

7   Family policy in Norway has focused on the need for divorced parents to share childcare and to cooperate in raising their children, and there is now a strong expectation of both parents staying (ideally equally) involved in their children's lives (see, e.g., Gíslason and Eydal, 2011). Bjørn's assumptions about parenthood after divorce are in line with the policy interventions of successive Norwegian governments over recent decades to strengthen the involvement of fathers in their children's lives and to increase equality between mothers and fathers. Whilst the vast majority of children have their main residence with their mothers after divorce (over 85 per cent in 2002, according to Jensen (2005)), the number of children sharing their time equally between both parents is rapidly increasing (7 per cent in 2002, and almost 25 per cent in 2010) (Jensen, 2005; Midling, 2012).

8   Paul and his partner were registered under the 1993 Act Relating to Registered Partnership (see Chapter 7). Paul described himself as being married and his partner as his husband.

9   See also Coontz (2005), Danielsen and Mühleisen (2009a, 2009b), Jamieson (2008).

10   In Eva Illouz's study of the relationship between romantic fiction and romantic autobiographies, she shows how 'slow-paced' love stories focusing on choice and have a less clearly codified meaning than 'fast-paced' stories focusing on passion and attraction. Asking 50 interviewees to interpret the same 'slow-paced' love story, she found that their responses varied from seeing it as a 'cold hearted and calculated enterprise' to 'mature love' (Illouz, 1998: 165). Paul talks about not being 'madly in love' with his husband, and he sees the absence of this passionate, intense love as a taboo. To be 'madly in love' is what is most easily recognized as a typical love story both by Paul and by the interviewees in Illouz's study. However, Illouz's study suggests, perhaps, that the story of Paul's marriage speaks to a different narrative of romantic love, a story of mature love, of a love that will last, a kind of love that is healthy, comfortable and realistic. At the same time as Illouz's interviewees characterized the fast-paced story as unrealistic and as a media construction, they also said that they liked this story the best. They saw it as the most interesting, passionate and fun.

11   See Bringle (1995), Bryant and Demian (1994), Heaphy, Donovan and Weeks (2004) and LaSala (2001) on non-monogamy amongst gay men and lesbians. See Altman (1997 [1982]), Weston (1991), Nardi (1992, 1999), Roseneil (2000c), Weeks, Heaphy and Donovan (2001) and Roseneil and Budgeon (2004) on ex-lovers and friendship in lesbian and gay communities.

12   Silence about his arrangement is something Paul shares with most practitioners of non-monogamy (Jamieson, 2008: 50–1).

13   See Altman (1997 [1982]), Foucault (1996), Klesse (2008), Shernoff (2005) and Spring (2010).

14   Astrid was the Norwegian interviewee who was most resistant to the BNIM style of the interview. She was very uncomfortable with the open-ended initial question which asked her to tell the story of her life and personal relationships, and she repeatedly asked for more specific instructions about what to talk about.

15   Several studies suggest that long-term lesbian couples have less sex than both gay male and heterosexual couples (Peplau, Fingerhut and Beals, 2004: 301; Gordon, 2006; van Rosmalen-Nooijens, Vergeer and Lagro-Janssen, 2008). It is argued that like heterosexual women, lesbians tend to have a relational or partner-centred orientation to sexuality (Peplau and Garnets, 2000). Liahna Gordon expands on this and argues that many lesbians

seems to conform to white, middle-class sexual stereotypes, in which women are seen as less sexually driven than men. When they are sexual, it is also understood that it is more emotional and less physical than it is for men (Gordon, 2006: 178). Following the notion that sex is primarily about emotional intimacy and connection, dominant norms among many white middle-class lesbians seem to be, according to Gordon (2006: 179), that sex should only occur within relationships and that couples should be monogamous. Blair and Pukall (2014), however, found that lesbian couples spend longer having sex than heterosexual and male same-sex partners (i.e. that lesbians' sexual encounters last longer), and Garcia et al. (2014) and Frederick et al. (2018) found that lesbians experience orgasm more frequently when having sex with a familiar partner than heterosexual or bisexual women.

16 Surrogacy is illegal in Norway, so people (gay or straight) seeking surrogacy have to go abroad.

17 Statistics show that in Norway, male same-sex couples have a 38 per cent higher risk of divorce than heterosexual couples, while female same-sex couples have more than twice the divorce risk of heterosexual married couples. The divorce risk for female same-sex couples is 71 per cent higher than the risk for male couples (Wiik, Seierstad and Noack, 2012: 18). See also Balsam, Rothblum and Wickham (2017).

18 Wiik, Seierstad and Noack (2012) found that having one or more children significantly reduced the divorce risk among female couples. Male couples with common children were, on the other hand, more prone to divorce than male couples without children (2012: 19). They do, however, also warn readers that male couples with shared children are of marginal statistical significance – only 49 couples in Norway between 1993 and 2011, or 2.7 per cent of male couples (2012: 19). In the same period there were 661 children registered to female couples, and one in five female couples had children (2012: 18).

13
Living with and against the couple-norm in Lisbon

The final four cases are selected from amongst the interviews that we conducted in Lisbon. They illustrate the living out of the tensions between choice and constraint in intimate life within a postcolonial, post-dictatorship southern European context, in which family and religion continue to play a significant role in shaping expectations about coupledom. Luisa, a Portuguese-Roma woman in her late forties who volunteered in a women's organization, told us the story of her life and personal relationships as a single, never-partnered, financially independent woman within a community in which patriarchal marriage is foundational. Daniel, a recently divorced majority-group Portuguese heterosexual man in his early forties, offered us a narrative of love, loss and coming to terms with uncoupling after a long-term relationship, against a backdrop of depression and emotional instability. Joana, a majority-group Portuguese bisexual woman in her thirties, described her experience of grappling with the hetero-norm alongside the couple-norm, whilst at the same time being strongly invested in mothering her young son. Finally, Vera, a majority-group Portuguese woman in her late thirties who identifies as heterosexual and as having relationships with men who are significantly older than her, presented a story about the conscious rejection of key facets of the contemporary Portuguese intimate citizenship regime, particularly the expectations of sameness of partners, of cohabitation and of procreation that are central to the couple-norm. Together these four case studies speak about the possibilities and difficulties of living outside the couple-norm in contemporary Portugal – as a single woman, a divorced man, a bisexual single mother, and a woman in a living-apart relationship.

Luisa: staying single to evade patriarchal control

Luisa had been born into a Roma family in southern Portugal during the dictatorship. Her father was a market trader and her mother was a housewife who occasionally worked on the family stall, selling clothes. Luisa had stopped attending school when she was 11, several years before the statutory school leaving age, and she spent her time at home, helping to look after the family. When she was 20 the family moved to Lisbon, around the time that the Republican National Guard issued a regulation to government authorities that they should be particularly vigilant of 'nomads'. At the age of 29, Luisa passed her driving test, which was an important symbolic and practical achievement, as it meant personal mobility and increased autonomy. A driving licence enabled her to travel, allowing her to move away from where she was living and opening up new work possibilities. After her father's sudden death when she was in her early thirties, she started working on her own, following in his footsteps, selling clothing and driving from one market to the next. In the late 1990s, she got involved in informal education within the Roma community, mentoring and organizing workshops for children and young women. These workshops started at about the same time that protection against discrimination on the grounds of race, colour, nationality and ethnic origin was introduced in Portuguese law (Law no. 134/99), and Luisa became an activist for Roma women's rights. She also returned to formal education herself and at the time of the interview she had recently completed the obligatory years of schooling that she had missed as a young person, and she was working full-time with Roma women and children. She did not have any children of her own but was emotionally very close to and involved with her teenage niece.

Luisa's life had been led in the context of the long-standing oppression and marginalization of the Roma community within Portuguese society. Although Roma are formally recognized as Portuguese citizens, and equality is proclaimed by the Constitution, a history of laws dating back to the early sixteenth century forbidding the entry of Roma people to the country and enacting the eviction of those who were settled have left profound legacies of social exclusion.[1] Associations of Roma with theft and witchcraft are deeply embedded in majority-Portuguese culture, and discrimination remains entrenched (see Pinto, 2005; Dias et al., 2006).[2] Marginal employment, poverty, low levels of education and poor, insecure housing are common experiences of the Roma community. Not completing secondary school, as Luisa did, is common, and even in 1998 only 55 per cent of Roma pupils completed primary education, and very small numbers have graduated from university.[3] Hostile attitudes to Roma are common amongst a significant minority of the Portuguese population. In a 1998 study (Pais, 1998), 20.1 per cent of respondents agreed with the statement, 'Roma people should be expelled from Portugal as they only generate problems'. In 2012, 27 per cent of Portuguese respondents reported they would feel 'totally uncomfortable if their children had Roma schoolmates' (EC, 2012), and in 2015, 19 per cent of Portuguese respondents to the Eurobarometer Survey on Discrimination said they would feel very uncomfortable if one of their colleagues at work belonged to the Roma community (EC, 2015).

In the context of such widespread hostility and discrimination, Roma in Portugal maintain a strong group identity and tight bonds of family and kin. Traditionally men are the head of the family and it is the women's role to look after their daughters' 'honour'– that is, their virginity – before marriage (Mota, 2002: 508; Mourão, 2011). In the eyes of the Portuguese state, most Roma couples are in de facto unions, whereas they consider themselves to be married according to Roma law (Casa-Nova, 2009), as we also saw in the case of Diana in Bulgaria. In a study in Porto, most Roma marriages took place before the age of 16: 61 per cent of women were married between 12 and 14 years old, and 42 per cent of men were married between 14 and 16 (Pinto, 2000).[4]

Luisa's story illustrates tensions between the expectation↔ injunctions that constitute the couple-norm within majority-Portuguese and Roma communities. When she was growing up, Roma marriage was required in order to be recognized as an adult within the community, and she was expected to get married. Marriage was not (necessarily) the outcome of a romantic encounter, but rather was often arranged by two families early in their children's lives. However, Luisa reported making a clear decision for herself not to get married. She explained that this was because she could not find the sort of relationship that she wanted, which was one in which romantic love was at the centre.

> I constructed my own love story. It would have to be with someone who I cared for, with love, with much love. But at that time, in my ethnicity, there was no such thing. [...] So, if anyone looked at me or said anything to me, I would pretend I had nothing to do with it. I would get away. [...] When I realized, age had already passed me by. [...] I've always avoided gypsy weddings. Because of the

amount of display at gypsy weddings, even today, I find it … Erm,
from a very early age, young girls start going to weddings and
[families are] showing off their daughters, dressing them up …
And that's why they look so stunning when they are single and
then when they get married they get fat, get sloppy … And I used
to say we were like cows going to the market to be sold, and I
didn't want to be sold. My mum used to get angry at me, wanting
me to go to weddings. And if I had to go, I would, but I would stay
still. I wouldn't dance, no, because that meant nothing to me.

From an early age, Luisa seemed to have learnt implicitly about
both the patriarchal gender-norm of differentiation and hierarchy,
and about the couple-norm. In the passage above we can see how she
had developed a critical perspective on the treatment of women and
girls, and of expectations regarding marriage, whilst at the same time
echoing normative perspectives on women's bodily appearance ('they
get fat, sloppy'). She grew up, she explained, being told what she could
and could not do and with an acute awareness that the greatest danger
was to be 'badly spoken of', for people to spread rumours about her
and her family, because that could seriously hinder the possibility of
getting herself a 'good husband', which was a crucial goal for Roma
women of her generation. However, Luisa also developed an understanding that the expectation↔injunctions that she faced as a Roma
girl could be side-stepped given the right arguments. For instance,
her mother used to say that girls should not be able to read or write
because they would write to boyfriends. Her older sisters explained to
her mother that times were changing; they regretted that they could
not read or write and made sure the same would not happen to their
younger sister. Thus, whilst Luisa did not complete the obligatory years
of schooling until much later, the fact that she could read and write –
unlike her sisters and mother – positioned her differently, both within
and outside her family. This was only the first of several instances in
which her life story departed from conventional practice within the
Roma community.

One of the most significant threads in Luisa's story was about
learning to drive and acquiring independent mobility. She was in her
late twenties when she persuaded her mother to allow her to learn to
drive, arguing that a driving licence could provide a means of survival
later on in life. It was unusual for Roma women of her generation to
be able to drive, and she was the first to do this in her family. She
proudly described how she passed her driving test at her first attempt

and was then given a car by her father and her sister, who was, by then, both married and working. But what she felt as an achievement was interpreted differently by people in the local community:

> I got my driving licence and there was a big 'Awww!' … like, 'Why would she want a driving licence if she is the age to get married?'

As she saw it, there was a contradiction between being independent – driving, having a job and being mobile – on the one hand, and conceding to a submissive marriage on the other:

> A relationship with a man – I wasn't thinking of that too much. I stopped doing that. […] After a certain age, am I going to put up with a man? I already had my driving licence. I was already independent … I disregarded that possibility. […] To search for a man to get married to … I mean, how would life be with him? I can't be bothered! I can't be bothered! My life is already so full. A gypsy man giving me orders, me having to obey his rules … Maybe even be beaten on the top of that […] No. No. Not at my age. […] And also, I've got my job. If I was married, my husband would not allow me to work. Then I wouldn't be able to walk around as much … No, I'm not into that, I'm not into that … I want to help people. I want a different life from that. I'm really not into that.

However, Luisa's narrative of her struggle for selfhood and autonomy in a context in which patriarchal marriage was the rule was not without some regret about having remained single. The following excerpt refers to the time when she started driving and working as a seller:

> I wasn't considering getting married then, not anymore. My dreams were over […] When I realized, age had already passed me by […] If I was like my niece, maybe today, with the mentality I've got today, maybe I would have given it a second thought and would have searched more, because they [good husbands] don't come flying out from the sky. We must also do our share. And maybe I would then have been able to find my prince on his white horse! But I didn't make any effort to find the prince on his white horse […] I had ideas which were completely different, and that's why [I didn't marry]. Sometimes I say I regret not having married because I'm no longer a young person and if I had married perhaps

I'd have children, a husband, and people who could renew me. And now, if I die, I don't leave anything behind. And they [her cousins] tell me, 'You didn't get married because you didn't want to. You know how we were, and we were difficult, and we had a different way of thinking about things.'

Despite recognizing the conscious choice she made to avoid marriage, Luisa's narrative was tinged with sadness and a sense of possibilities forgone, particularly having children. Her story was full of contextualizing details about Roma culture and history, offered to the non-Roma interviewer by way of background and explanation, which highlight her awareness of the differences between Roma and non-Roma people in Portuguese society, especially when she was a teenager. Most of her remarks about Roma culture concerned the gender-norms regarding relationships and match-making that she said existed within the Roma community. Whilst recognizing that Roma culture had been changing in recent years, Luisa criticized 'Roma law' (referring to tradition within the Roma community) for being too strict in relation to women's intimate lives.

A girl runs away with a non-Roma man: she is talked about, her parents are deeply sad, they cry. As time passes, her parents will lose their anger, their grief about what she has done. If their daughter is well married, if he is a good person, they will accept it, they won't reject her, they will try to keep her, help her in keeping her husband [...], in having a good life with her husband. [...] But 20 years ago it was completely different. This same girl would be banned from the family, would feel too ashamed to get close to her parents, and would never be seen again. The sister of one of my brothers-in-law ran away with a non-Roma man. They only saw her again when she was dying, because they never wanted to see her again. Then they wore black when she died, and I wonder why. It's not worth it. People need our affection while they are alive, not after they are dead.

Living under such normative conditions, Luisa felt that she had little choice but to remain single; she was born ahead of her time.[5] The aspects of the couple-norm to which she objected were, from her perspective, simply too strong to be resisted from within a Roma marriage. But from outside, as a single woman, she was able to challenge the patriarchal gender-norm, seeking economic independence and an ability to travel freely by herself. In this she was, in many instances, supported by members of her family, including her father, and through her close relationship with her niece, whom she had nurtured and guided since birth, she was passing these alternative possibilities on to the next generation. During the interview, Luisa acknowledged her ambivalence about the choices she made and explained that she would probably do things differently if she were a young woman now: 'If I was like my niece, maybe today, with the mentality I've got today, maybe I would have given it a second thought and would have searched more [for a suitable partner/ husband].' She implied that the loosening of some of the traditional constraints of Roma culture were making it possible to imagine aspiring to a love marriage – a 'prince on his white horse' – for her niece, if not for herself. Whilst marriage remained central to Luisa's intimate imaginary, she was clearly thinking differently about what marriage might mean today from how she understood it when she was younger: an ideal of romantic love was superseding the fear of patriarchal control.

Luisa's life posed a powerful challenge to the expectation↔ injunction that women will marry and have children. In setting herself against patriarchal control, she chose to remain single, defying the traditions of early arranged marriage and lavish weddings within the Roma community. Yet her family supported her in this, and as times changed in the direction in which she was pushing, she remained highly embedded within, and actively engaged with, her community, particularly its women and children. As such Luisa's story offers a vivid example of the entangled relationship between the transformations in cultures of intimate citizenship that take place within communities and the personal choices of individual members who are living with and against the cultures that have formed them.

Daniel: coupling conventionally and uncoupling consciously

Daniel was born in the 1960s to a wealthy conservative Catholic family that was highly invested in education. He was the oldest of three siblings and the first grandchild, which placed a considerable burden of familial expectation on him. At university in the 1980s, he started dating fellow student Tania. After they graduated and started working, they began living together, and a few years later they decided to get married. Sometime afterwards they had their first child and bought a house. With the exception of their premarital cohabitation, during all of this time Daniel was following a common script for men and women of his generation – finding a 'proper' partner at, and of, the appropriate age, getting married, having children, buying a house. Everything seemed to be going according to (the normative) plan.

But there was disruption and distress to come. As they progressed in their careers, both Daniel and Tania were travelling a lot, often together but also separately. Daniel was working longer hours, while Tania was more and more frustrated with her job, and their relationship became strained. Daniel recalled that they stopped having sex, and they experienced the first crisis in their marriage, after which he was unwell for several months. He recovered from this illness without having any formal diagnosis. Their frequent, separate work trips continued, and they lived apart for several months whilst Daniel was working overseas, which he described as a pleasant experience for both of them. However, whilst undertaking post-graduate training, Daniel started having episodes of work-related anxiety, and he received treatment from a psychiatrist who gave him anti-anxiety medication. Around this time, Tania started psychotherapy because she was unhappy with her life. Daniel was taking himself away from the family for longer periods to give himself space to write, away from interruption, and when he finally completed his training he became increasingly tired and hopeless and fell into a serious depression. He considered quitting his job. Tania took the children on holiday without him, and whilst they were away he had a mental breakdown. During the period that followed, in which he was severely depressed, he received emotional support from friends, and financial and practical support from his parents and sister. The decision to separate after being together for over 20 years was reached over the phone whilst Tania was away. Upon Tania's return from holiday, they stopped sharing a bed and announced their decision to the children. Daniel moved in with friends while he looked for a flat close to the family home. After the divorce Daniel got a dog, and at the time of the interview he and Tania were sharing custody of the children, living in the same street, and they remained, he said, close friends.

Daniel's story of the most significant events in his personal life was centred on his relationship with Tania, and he offered great detail – dates, places and his reasoning about how it developed and changed. In one of the longest interviews of the study – six hours – Daniel never mentioned another significant romantic/sexual relationship, nor did he provide details about his childhood and youth before meeting Tania. His relationship with Tania was the focal point of his intimate biography, the most important element in his 'story of his life and personal relationships', exemplifying a life story framed in accordance with the cultural expectation that adults should be committed to lifelong, monogamous, legally sanctioned and procreative relationships. Daniel's account of his experience as a recently divorced parent challenged the agentic role often ascribed to men by the mainstream intimate imaginary in Portuguese culture: the man as the unfaithful, uncommitted and often violent partner. Daniel saw himself as not having chosen his current situation, and he did not flinch from describing his mental strife and instability. He had expected to remain coupled. He had been in love with his partner for the last 20 years, and he spoke of Tania in a respectful, caring way. In this, his story spoke of a new form of masculinity, and of continuing to love and care beyond the formal ending of the couple relationship.

Despite the clear centrality of the relationship with Tania in Daniel's biographical-narrative, this was not consciously related to an expressed belief in the institution of marriage as a mandatory element in intimate life. The way Daniel spoke about the decision to get married indicated instead that marriage was expected by his family, and that he had not wanted to challenge their conventional expectations:

> At a certain point, we decided to get married. [...] It was something that seemed appropriate at the time. We were very much in love with each other; we had had experiences of living together and living separately. [...] My family is very conservative and Catholic, although they did not put direct pressure. [...] I think it was Tania who suggested we got married first. I immediately thought it was a good idea – it would make my parents happy. [...] We did because it was a tradition and it would please both families.

This passage signals the weight of tradition and the influence that seeking to please family members can have in determining the shape of couple relationships. It also provides a powerful example of the connections between time and intimacy, namely the temporal linearity of coupledom according to which, after a while, and provided that people still are romantically involved with each other, it seems 'appropriate' to get married.

After several hours of describing his relationship with Tania in considerable chronological detail, particularly the painful years that led to their divorce, Daniel offered a rather surprising evaluation of his current intimate arrangements, which expressed his contentment with his situation.

> There was nothing bad to come out of this separation. To me, the advantages result from the novelty of the situation. It is very pleasant to have a week on my own, exclusively, when I do what I want. I work the hours I want, go out for dinner if I want. I have absolute freedom. And then a week with my children, when I end up spending more time with them, quality time, much better than before.

Daniel identified the positive outcomes of separation and divorce, celebrating the autonomy, agency and choice associated with living on his own, something which was quite new for him. In fact, having been in a (largely) cohabiting relationship since he was a student, he had never had the opportunity to experience adult life independently. The only exception to this was the time when he and Tania briefly lived apart for professional reasons. Referring back to that period, he said:

> It was such an experience, as a single man, as a researcher dedicated exclusively to enjoying life and doing research. A luxury. When I returned, I remember I felt really well, full of energy, in a good mood, without any anxieties. [...] People could tell from a physical point of view that I was very different and much better [laughs]. This distance was good for my relationship with Tania because we exchanged emails and letters. A sort of distance love relationship, something we had never done before – not like that. That was revitalizing. And it was good to be able to come back longing. It was very good.

Thus, despite cohabiting coupledom having been the central theme of his adult life, Daniel was able to grasp and enjoy the possibility of both being in a non-cohabiting relationship and, more recently, being uncoupled. Alongside the pleasures of being single, he also enjoyed becoming a part-time parent: he was now more invested in spending quality time with his children during the weeks they spent with him than he had been when he was married and living with them full-time.

Also striking was Daniel's clear rejection of the blame/guilt trope that appeared in many of our interviews, and that is culturally expected to accompany divorce. He described a process of uncoupling that was calmly and consciously undertaken:[6]

I feel that during this whole process that led to my illness and separation, nobody did anything wrong. Bad things can happen without anyone being to blame. [...] Everyone had the best intentions. We were not the sort of couple who were fighting, and there was no one else involved. There was no obvious reason, nothing to notice. [...] They [the children] had never seen us fighting, and there were no third persons. There were no obvious reasons. It was difficult to explain, I don't even remember how I explained it to them. I can't remember. I didn't want to say that I was no longer in love, because I guess I was still in love. I mean, I was unable to feel a thing – for a cat or a dog, it didn't matter. But when the conversation was over, Tania gave me a hug. It was the last time that she hugged me. She said I had done really well. Tania had no responsibility at all for my illness. And I had all the responsibility for her unhappiness. That is something I can only regret.

In the passages above Daniel was asserting his refusal of the dynamics of anger and mutual blame that tend to accompany divorce. There was nothing that could be identified as having caused the breakdown of the relationship. Therefore blame, as a hermeneutic resource, was not available in his analytical toolkit for making sense of his divorce. The end of love occurred without notice and is narrated as an incomprehensible but inescapable fate. Whilst stating that there was 'no obvious reason' for the separation, Daniel nevertheless identified a temporal sequence of events: there was his illness first, and the breaking up of his 20-year-long relationship came afterwards. From his narrative it is not clear whether he was consciously tying these two disruptive life events together, or if they were simply mentioned in the same sentence because he was trying to capture his life story through a coherent timeline that unconsciously posed a causal link between them. In fact, his interview was thoroughly and systematically chronological, avoiding jumps, gaps and the tendency, common in almost all the other interviews, to move backwards and forwards in time.

Despite having produced a couple-oriented narrative about his life up until this point, Daniel seemed to have found the time and space to blossom as an individual in the aftermath of divorce, and in the final part of the interview he spoke about his sense of well-being and his ability to enjoy time by himself. In this regard, Daniel's current situation exemplifies the decentring of the sexual/love relationship that Roseneil and Budgeon (2004) identified in their research on people living outside conventional couples, and the importance that practices of self-care and the cultivation of a stronger relationship with the self often take on for those who do not have a cohabiting partner (Roseneil, 2007).

Joana: seeking self and stability as a mother and partner

Joana, a majority-group Portuguese woman who identified as bisexual, was born in the early 1970s. Following the death of her mother, when she was 12, Joana and her older sister were raised by their father. She spoke of this time as turbulent and unhappy because her father regularly brought different women home to spend the night with him. Joana disliked this intensely and, at the age of 16, she decided to leave home, telling her father that she needed more stability than he was providing if she were to be able to pursue her studies as she wished.

In her early twenties, Joana embarked upon her first significant intimate couple relationship, with a man whom she described as 'much older' than she was and with whom she had a child. The relationship was, she said, troubled and unfulfilling because of his traditional ideas about women and sexuality. He expected her to be a stay-at-home mother and to refrain from spending time with her friends. Moreover, she reported that he had no interest in 'foreplay' or in her sexual pleasure. When her son was a year old, she left both her partner and her son and 'entered the gay scene'. A few years later she fell in love with 'a much older woman' and they moved in together, and Joana's son came to live with them. The relationship ended sometime after this, when Joana fell for another 'much younger woman'. Differences of age between her and her partners played an important part in Joana's narrative, with each partner accounted for as either 'much older' or 'much younger' than she was, which implicitly acknowledged that such age gaps were noteworthy in their counter-normativity. When she was interviewed Joana was in her late thirties and was living with her 'much younger' partner and her son. Despite the legal impossibility of same-sex step-parent adoption in Portugal at that time – even after the legalization of same-sex civil marriage in 2010 – in practice Joana and her partner shared parental responsibilities for Joana's biological child.[7]

The way Joana spoke about her first significant relationship, which was with a man, reveals a tension between traditional heterosexual coupledom and the desires and expectations she was developing. She regarded herself as having been 'ignorant about emotions and relationships' and as having been emotionally dependent on him. She described feeling conflicted about 'what was available out there and what was available at home', suggesting that her desires for sex and intimacy were not fulfilled by him. She tried to 'introduce novelty' into their relationship, to which he responded: 'You don't like me, you want to leave. You have a child to raise. So, you must stay home. You can't go out.' The gender-norm and the couple-norm operated in tandem in the relationship, with her partner's patriarchal tendencies so strong that she eventually felt impelled to make a radical change in her life, leaving him and their child to explore her sexuality and the gay scene. Yet whilst her narrative spoke of her experience of straining against convention and yearning for more in her intimate life, Joana provided little detail about the conflicts she felt between the world 'out there' and home, and she did not explain what she meant by 'novelty'. Sexual desire and its un/fulfilment were the threads that ran through her story, but she was only able to hint at them, not discuss them explicitly.

Leaving her male partner and child was a key moment of rupture in Joana's intimate biography. She described it as 'cutting the umbilical cord' and as starting again from scratch, in a clear reference to the asymmetry of their relationship. She was also perhaps unconsciously recognizing the connection between having tied herself to this older partner and the early loss of her mother, the relationship that should have provided her with sustenance until she was ready for adult independence. Propelled by the death of her mother and her father's subsequent destabilizing sexual life, she had left the parental home much earlier than was usual in Portugal, where 'late emancipation' is normal.[8] Partnering then with an older man who curtailed her intimate desires, restricted her sociability and directly reproached her, Joana felt infantilized. But there is double meaning at play here: against the injunction that a mother must be, and remain, coupled, and indeed challenging the powerful cultural expectation that mothers will be the primary carers of their children, Joana also left her child – cutting the umbilical cord – in order to become an independent adult, to live her own life as a woman. In so doing she was simultaneously breaking with the patriarchal gender-norm, the couple-norm, the hetero-norm and the procreative-norm. She began to explore the gay scene in the company of a gay male friend, but she found herself disappointed by the sort of relationships that seemed to be on offer to her, having expected that 'the gay world was something else, secret and tender'. She felt angry and upset to find out it was not necessarily so:

The sporadic encounters, the sexual encounters, the next day you don't even recall the person's name. [...] When you go out at night you don't meet people, you meet bodies. And I wanted to meet people. [...] Me and my friend used to say we were going to the butcher's, meaning gay nightlife. That's what I felt – my soul being scratched. Because I thought I would find different people, who had difficult lives that made them more prepared and with emotional needs [...] And I realized that it wasn't like that after all.

Faced with the absence of the sort of intimate relationship for which she longed, Joana and her friend posted an advert in a newspaper seeking other lesbians and gay men, and they started to receive letters from people in rural Portugal. Through this, and the correspondence in which she engaged with some of the women who responded to the advert, Joana became aware of the discrimination and isolation that lesbians experienced, particularly those living outside the big cities (Santos, 2016). One letter was from a cook who was in her fifties and had never told anyone that she was lesbian. Joana felt really strongly about this letter, wondering what it would be like to be living her life:

What will become of me? What's going on here? What is this? What sort of life is this, of these people? Realizing the isolation of these people was very upsetting to me, the emotional isolation.

Acknowledging the pain and marginalization of the people who had responded to the advert was profoundly disturbing to Joana, and it propelled her to get involved in politics. In the left-wing party that she joined she encountered a new world of politicized lesbians, many of whom had not been part of the gay scene that she had grown to dislike.

Joana's relationships with women opened up new relational possibilities and new ways of seeing herself, particularly in terms of her ability to choose autonomously what she considered to be the best path for herself and her child.

What I learned from the two lesbian relationships I had was that there was always a big understanding and a big cooperation in relation to my child. [...] A joint parental effort. [...] These two relationships helped me to grow up as a person and gave me the sort of stability I thought I could no longer have, after all I had heard [about same-sex relationships].

A commitment to pursuing personal happiness and fulfilment – almost as a moral duty to self – emerged as a dominant theme in Joana's narrative. Echoing Roseneil's (2007) argument about the salience of self-care and 'reparative practices of the self' to those living intimate lives that depart from conventional heterosexual coupledom, Joana's narrative unfolded around the lessons that she had learnt over the years about the 'need' to be true to herself and to attend to her own needs and desires, in order to be able to love and care for others. This is illustrated by the way she spoke about herself and her relationship with her son, and about the years they spent apart: 'I was cementing myself inside, as a person, in order to feel I was able to be with him. [...] This wasn't so much as a moment, but more of a prolonged emotional process.'

A few years later, when she accepted the fact that she had fallen in love with another woman, she thought about the possible implications. She decided she must speak to her son about it: 'I want him to be able to speak to me, to know I am a person who can fall in love, has a life of her own, who has doubts, who gets anxious.' She described the conversation they had, when he was 11:

> 'Listen, I have some doubts about the person we're living with, and in relation to another person, but I think I've made a decision and it's possible we'll need to move home again. But I think you prefer to have a happy mum, rather than a mum who is enduring things.' I didn't want to be with someone and still have doubts about it. So I told him that. [...] And it was so good because he said – when he was 11 years: 'I already know who she is, and I'm happy because we play a lot together, and we paint. And I see you are very happy around her, and we all play together. So I want you to be happy, and you know I support you.' And he was always by my side, almost as a grown-up person. And that moved me so much because that is what I want the most – for him to be a person, above all, a person. And he was truly a person to me. And he said 'I am with you, regardless of the person who you choose to be with'.

This passage casts new light on one of the key elements of the couple-norm: the expectation that the couple is a family matter. Rather than sharing her decision with older family members and depending on parental approval, Joana's main concern was with her son and his approval. This points to the ongoing democratization of the parent–child relationship, as noted by Anthony Giddens (1992). But she was also conscious of her responsibility for providing her son with stability, and she was anxious about introducing another major change into his life. She feared that she might be behaving as her father had done after her mother had died, asking herself, 'what would he think of me and my relationships?'

At the time of the interview, Joana was feeling that she had reached a point in her life when she no longer considered coupledom to be essential to her sense of self. She was aware of the benefits of what she called a 'healthy solitude':

> After spending all of this time feeling that I needed to be in a rela-tionship, thinking that a relationship is my backbone, that I really need it [a relationship], now I think I am in another phase, in which I think maybe I don't need it. I want to try that, to be alone, to see what I can learn from myself and from others. [...] I don't think solitude is negative. What is negative is exclusion. So maybe I am entering a phase of a healthy solitude. [...] Almost independ-ence from that idea that you must have someone beside you. It is not vital to your survival to have someone beside you.

Despite arriving at the possibility of a 'healthy solitude', Joana's life hitherto spoke of a powerful investment in being coupled and in repeatedly seeking a better experience of coupledom. Her decisions to leave unsatisfactory relationships rested on a belief that she had a right to be happy, to have a fulfilling sex life and to exercise agency, and she was not willing to allow traditional cultural expectations about coupledom to interfere with this. Although she did not explicitly talk about movements for gender and sexual equality, Joana's story evolved parallel to the approval of the de facto union law in 2001 and captured many of the tensions and possibilities that exist in times of significant socio-cultural and political change, as she pursued her ideal 'pure', intimate relationship (Giddens, 1992).

Vera: bending the couple-norm

Vera was born in the early 1970s, at the time of the overthrow of the Salazar regime, the first child of a working-class majority-group

Portuguese couple. Like many children of her generation, she was cared for by her grandparents and aunts for several years whilst her parents were working. As a university student, in her late teens, Vera got involved in party politics and developed a strong sense of herself as a political animal, devoted to critiquing the status quo.

In telling the story of her 'life and personal relationships', Vera identified her relationship with Alberto as a determining influence on her subsequent intimate biography. They had met when they were both students, and four years into their relationship, at a point at which it felt stable and long-standing, they decided to live together. At the time, Vera said, moving in together seemed like the logical next step; they accepted unquestioningly the expectation, so central to the couple-norm, that coupledom should, as it develops along its natural course, eventually mean cohabitation. But two years after setting up a home together, the relationship broke down. Vera explained her firm belief that the relationship ended because cohabitation destroys love relationships. After this experience she resolved never again to live with a partner: living-apart became her strategy for shielding intimate relationships from the pressures of sharing a home.

> Love relationships are more protected, more positive, if they share everything people want except for the daily things. [...] The day-to-day really wears out a relationship, I think. It is very eroding, because a lot of what comes into play is not part of the relationship – it's related to people themselves, their idiosyncrasies. It is funny, because it exhausts a love relationship, but it doesn't exhaust a friendship relationship. [...] He [Alberto] was the only person I've lived with, and those almost two years really wore out the relationship in a way that hadn't happened before in six years of relationship, right? And it was then that I understood, and it was after this that I learned the lesson that is very important to me [...]. I've learned that the best way is each one to their own house.

Since her decision to refuse the dominant expectation of cohabitation in future relationships, Vera had had two other significant relationships – both with 'older men': first with Carlos, a relationship which lasted for three years, and subsequently with her partner at the time of the interview, Victor, who was divorced and had children from a previous relationship, and with whom she had had a living-apart relationship for two years. She had discussed the issue of cohabitation with each of them and her commitment to not living together prevailed in both relationships. Thinking back about her relationship with Carlos, and then comparing it with her current relationship with Victor, Vera explained her personal values about coupledom:

> With our busy lives, it was really rather against the nature of a relationship, what I think a relationship is all about. Because we used to open our diaries and say, 'All right, then, this coming week, when can we be together?' I think this just, erm, it is a bit … Because a relationship is today. Let it roll. Today we feel like it, and so we are together. Whereas we scheduled. […] It was a bit like constructing the relationship, which I think should really be more, more emotive, more emotional, rather than scheduled. With Victor, our relationship is more like that. […] I didn't want to move in with him, but I also didn't want to schedule. […] I think from all of these experiences that I had, this is – and it's been a year and a half – what I enjoy the most, because it is the one that is less pushy, that gives me more freedom.

This passage illustrates how Vera has developed her own ideas about coupledom that counter aspects of the couple-norm. In contrast to the value conventionally placed on the linear progress over time from dating to cohabitation and/or marriage (Roseneil, 2006a), Vera's own values were about the preservation of personal freedom and the pursuit of mutual pleasure in the here and now. She rejects intimacy that she perceives as fake, forged (she talked about 'constructing' and 'forging' the relationship) or planned, valorizing instead spontaneous emotion and living in the present.

Vera's narrative expressed a strong sense of selfhood, a personal drive towards finding what made her happy and what she thought was best for her at a particular moment in time. In this regard, her story presented striking similarities to Joana's proclaimed need to be authentic to herself, and her representation of happiness as a moral duty to both herself and her significant others, especially her son. Indeed, both stories constituted a powerful example of the cultural impact of women's (post-)feminist demands for autonomy and self-determination as individuals outside the heterosexual couple-form.

Vera's current life was grounded in a stable, long-term relationship with a gay friend, Bruno. They had bought a flat together and registered their non-sexual, non-romantic domestic partnership as a 'shared economy'.[9] She spoke about loving this living arrangement, which she was well aware subverted conventional expectations around coupledom.

> We share a house, life, erm, we share almost everything [laughs], except these more private love relationships. [...] And I think this is how I like to live, really. [...] The relationship with Bruno is also a personal relationship which is very important to me. It is not a love relationship, but it is one of the main relationships in my life. [...] We've got a long-term joke which is to say that Bruno is my husband! [...] When I say 'my husband' everyone knows I am referring to Bruno, and so [laughs] all of the others who come in the interim are my lovers. [...] If we wanted to transpose this to a normal or normalized family relationship, say, the one that is considered normal by society, Bruno would be indeed my husband because it is him with whom I share almost everything.

Although in Vera's narrative there were no extended self-reflexive accounts about the impacts or implications of age difference in intimate relationships, in practice Vera's experience also challenged the expectation that spouses or partners should be alike in terms of age. In fact, the most significant intimate relationships throughout her life have been with either much younger or much older men. Like Joana, Vera's narrative about significant people in her life was always described in relation to age difference, signalling her awareness of how normative it is to partner with someone of a similar age.

As a person who was living 'gladly apart' (Roseneil, 2006a) from her 'lover' and with her non-sexual 'husband', Vera spoke of her life in a way that seemed resistant to social pressure, presenting herself as empowered and unapologetic in her unconventional choices. Yet her narrative had an argumentative feel to it; she knew that she was living counter-normative intimacies, and she was passionate in their defence, seeming to feel the need to proclaim both their value and the values that underpinned them. Moreover, her account of her intimate life was not without contradictions and difficult encounters with dominant cultural expectations. For instance, a few weeks before the interview Victor suggested to Vera that they should have a child together, and this proposal was troubling Vera and had unsettled her. Being child-free had long been central to her sense of who she was and the life she had chosen, and she had always made sure that this was clear to her partners. She suspected that Victor's suggestion might provoke tension between them, about a topic that was, for her, non-negotiable.

Vera's way of living her intimate life posed profound challenges to many facets of the couple-norm. Playing knowingly, queerly even, with her gay male partner in domesticity to reconfigure the idea and ideal of the conjugal couple, whilst also pursuing a sexual/love relationship with a man with whom she has no intention of living, she was reinventing the couple-form in creative ways that do not comply with the traditions and expectations of the Portuguese intimate citizenship regime. Stressing the advantages of a 'pure relationship' (Giddens, 1992), detached from the moral and social necessity of cohabitation and marriage, and valued only for the pleasure it brought to both parties, like Joana, Vera's life was exemplary of new practices of intimacy that have become possible in the wake of the women's liberation movement.

Concluding remarks

The stories that Luisa, Daniel, Joana and Vera told us about their complicated, challenging relationships to the couple-norm collectively speak of the radically changed landscape of intimate citizenship in Portugal that has emerged in the decades following the Carnation Revolution. The socio-legal modernization and democratization of Portuguese society, accession to the European Economic Community and energetic campaigning by those seeking change in gender and sexual relations have opened up the range of possibilities available to people in their intimate lives (Amâncio et al., 2007; Roseneil et al., 2011, 2012, 2013; Santos, 2013, 2016).

Luisa, the oldest of the four, had grown up under the dictatorship. Opportunities to lead an independent, self-determining life as a Roma woman were scarce, both in terms of the national legal and the group-specific socio-cultural frameworks within which she became an adult. The political regime forbade women to travel abroad or open a bank account without their husband's permission, and women were expected to serve as carers and homemakers, confined largely to the domestic sphere (Pimentel, 2001; Rosas, 1994). Within the Roma community, rules about the appropriate behaviour of women were strict, constraining the exercise of agency and the possibilities of romantic love-based (as opposed to arranged) relationships. Under conditions of legal and socio-cultural oppression such as these, and in the absence of a strong women's movement to provide a powerful counter-script, Luisa's only choice seemed to be to remain outside the couple-form.

It was more possible for Vera and Joana, who grew up under the feminist winds of change that circulated after dictatorship, to subvert the couple-norm and to seek to create new modes of intimate life. For each of them coupledom held the potential to offer what they expected and hoped for from intimate relationships, without losing sight of their autonomous, independent selves. Like Luisa, they did not wish to embrace, or endure, a traditional coupled relationship, which they each perceived as likely to hinder their freedom and self-determination. But unlike Luisa, Joana and Vera were actively engaged in the remaking of coupledom in their current relationships. They deployed recent trans-formations in law and policy to these ends: the shared economy law in the case of Vera, and the de facto union law in the case of Joana. They also consciously rejected traditional elements of the couple-norm, including marriage, cohabitation and age similarity. Vera and Joana were women who have chosen to be coupled on their own terms. Whilst appearing not to reject monogamy or romantic love, they were aware that their current circumstances of coupledom were neither static nor necessarily lifelong, and they implicitly embraced the value that coupledom should be a currently mutually fulfilling state rather than a permanent commitment.

Similar to Vera and Joana, Daniel's story illustrates recent legal and cultural transformations in the Portuguese intimate citizenship regime, particularly in relation to divorce and masculinity. His narrative focused on his marriage of 20 years and its unravelling. Compared with the other men in the study, across all four countries, Daniel was distinctive in his openness about his emotional life and his struggle with difficult feelings and mental ill-health, and in his reflexive introspec-tion about forming and breaking up his couple relationship. Staying friends with his ex-wife, and sharing custody of their children, were facts he alluded to with pride, as important elements of his account of uncoupling consciously and with care.

Across their differences and singularities, the biographical-narratives of Luisa, Daniel, Joana and Vera shared an ambivalence towards the cohabiting couple-form.[10] None rejected coupledom entirely or on principle, but each case points to the profound tensions that inhere in living in relation to many of the dominant expectation↔injunctions, ideals and values that constitute the couple-norm. And each person's story illustrates the creative challenges and responses that result from these tensions, as coupledom, and life outside it, are reinvented.

Each of these 16 case studies offers an analytic distillation of an individual's story of their life and personal relationships through the lens of our concern with the couple-norm. The case studies do not tell the 'whole story', if indeed such a thing were possible, of each person's life; details have been removed, careful changes have been made to ensure anonymity, and the full complexity of the twists and turns of biographies and the nuance of narratives have been deliberately compromised in the process of production. Nonetheless, each case study captures the essence of our understanding of how that person's life has been impacted by the couple-norm. Together, as a collection of case studies of the couple-norm in action, they provide a multifaceted picture of how people live with and against the couple-norm in the context of different intimate citizenship regimes and communities of identity and belonging. Whilst in no way representative of the populations of the United Kingdom, Bulgaria, Norway and Portugal, or even of people in mid-life living outside the conventional couple-form in each of these countries, the case studies offer insight into some of the national specificities, as well as the cross-national similarities, in the operation of the couple-norm in everyday life. As such, they serve as exemplifications of the ubiquity and capaciousness of the couple-norm.

Notes

1 The first law against Roma people in Portugal came into force in 1526 (Mota, 2002; Pinto, 2000).

2 Roma are the group that is most likely to experience discrimination in housing in Portugal. The *Report on Racism and Xenophobia in the Member States of the EU*, published in 2007, reported that 59 per cent of Roma people in Portugal feel that they have been denied the opportunity to buy or rent an apartment or house. During recent decades there have been several episodes of forced evictions, with majority-Portuguese communities demanding that authorities move Roma camps to other places that are not close to schools or other houses. For instance, in 1993 the Municipality of Ponte de Lima declared that any Roma living in the city would have to leave within the next eight days and would not be allowed to stay longer than 48 hours in future. The intervention of the Ombudsman later determined that the Municipality had no legal right to enforce that regulation (Dias et al., 2006).

3 According to the European Monitoring Centre on Racism and Xenophobia, Roma people in Portugal have low levels of participation in preschool education, high levels of school failure and early drop-out rates: 'during 1998, although 91.6 per cent of Roma pupils attended the four years of the first cycle of primary education, only 55.4 per cent managed to complete it compared to a national average of 87.7 per cent. [...] There are no data regarding tertiary education, but a 2000 study points to only two Roma graduates' (Bastos and Bastos, 2000: 6, our translation).

4 Research conducted in 2009 with 55 Roma families in Portugal demonstrated the weight of endogamy (only eight out of 55 Roma couples in the study included a non-Roma spouse) and also highlighted the early age of marriage – largely between 14 and 19 for women and 15 and 21 for men (Casa-Nova, 2009).

5 For a critical discussion of the complex relation between singlehood, gender and time, see Lahad (2017).

6 Daniel's description of his break-up with Tania, and the personal growth associated with it, resonate with the notion of 'conscious uncoupling' popularized by psychotherapist Katherine Woodward Thomas (see 2015) and famously used by actor Gwyneth Paltrow.

7 Step-parent adoption only became legally available to all, whatever the sexual orientation of the parents, in 2016 (Law no. 2/2016).

8 According to Almudena Moreno Mìnguez, who has analysed late 'emancipation' in Spain, this phenomenon stems from familialism, 'defined as solidarity within and dependence on the family, characteristic of Mediterranean countries' (2003: 1), which is related to economic insecurity and high rates of unemployment.

9 See Chapter 8, p. 99, for an explanation of the Portuguese shared economy law.

10 On ambivalence in contemporary intimate life, see Roseneil (2006c).

PART IV

The tenacity of the couple-norm

14
Understanding the tenacity of the couple-norm

Recent decades have seen radical transformation in the intimate citizenship regimes of the four European countries discussed in this book. Despite very different political histories, there has been an historic movement away from repressive laws and illiberal policies governing personal life and sexuality. Broadly similar processes of de-patriarchalization, individualization, liberalization, equalization and pluralization have remade the legal and policy frameworks regulating intimate life, albeit at differing paces and to rather different timetables and extents. Male domination in personal relationships has been attenuated, although certainly not abolished, as women have gained more power in the public sphere, and as de-patriarchalizing legislation has challenged deeply entrenched cultural ideas about sex, gender and parenting. Heterosexual marriage is no longer mandated by law as the only proper framework for family life, and there is increasing tolerance and recognition by states of the diverse ways in which people choose to live and love in three of the four countries – the United Kingdom, Portugal and Norway. Same-sex sexualities and coupledom have moved from being positioned as, at best, unspeakable, and at worst criminal, towards almost complete normalization and assimilation within these three intimate citizenship regimes. Bulgaria's intimate citizenship regime, however, has remained more conservative, with a cyclical movement between periods of liberalization and recognition of same-sex sexualities followed by waves of conservatism, as demonstrated by recent regressive political mobilizations and the explosion of 'anti-gender' rhetoric (Behrensen and Stanoeva, 2019). As in a number of central and eastern European countries, a wave of opposition to gender equality, and of homophobia and anti-trans feeling, has swept through mainstream media and public discourse amidst claims about threats to national identity, morality and religion (Kuhar and Paternotte, 2017; Verloo, 2018; Behrensen and Stanoeva, 2019).

Amidst this changing social and political landscape of intimate life, the committed cohabiting couple-form continues to be the structure of domestic life and care-giving assumed by welfare states, promoted by governments and reproduced by law and policy. And, crucially, the couple-norm sits at the heart of contemporary intimate citizenship regimes not just because it is institutionalized through law and policy, but because of its ubiquity in everyday life. Indeed, as the legal mandating of the heterosexual, married couple-form has diminished, the social enforcement and cultural promotion of the couple-form has become more important in maintaining couple-normativity. Indeed, legal sanctions for breaches of the couple-norm have been largely replaced by informal social sanctions and processes of positive reinforcement.

In contemporary intimate citizenship regimes, the couple-norm is enacted within relationships between people who matter to each other, in primary reference groups and social networks – families, friendship groups and communities of ethnic or local belonging. Sometimes explicitly articulated, but often not, the couple-norm shapes people's intimate life choices, their subjectivities and intimate imaginaries in a myriad of ways. It is, variously, embraced and celebrated, complied with and survived, challenged and evaded, resisted and rejected, struggled with and worked around, as people seek to reconcile their intimate desires with what feels right and socially acceptable. Operating differently across national contexts and between social groups, at different points in people's lives and always in relation to an individual's singular biographical history, it remains remarkably consistent in its centrality to contemporary intimate life.

How then can we understand the tenacity of the couple-norm? What makes its hold over people's lives so powerful? And what might be done to loosen its grip? How might we imagine intimate citizenship beyond the couple-norm? In what follows in this part of the book we address these questions, offering a theoretical summation of the findings of our research and some more speculative thoughts about possible futures in which the tenacious grip of the couple-norm might be loosened.

The capaciousness of the couple-norm

On the basis of our research, we suggest that the potency of the couple-norm resides very significantly in its capaciousness. Around its core construction of coupledom as the normal, natural and superior state of being, it is composed of a number of expectation↔injunctions that work together, in varying intersections, to shape, guide and/ or regulate, more or less rigorously, how people orient themselves in their intimate lives within the broad, overarching demand that they are coupled. These expectation↔injunctions about how coupledom should be lived constitute the specificity of the couple-norm in particular social contexts, yet they remain largely unspoken as direct, explicit instructions, operating tacitly to shape people's lives and often only articulated when they are in danger of being breached. The case studies presented in Part III open up to scrutiny the internal workings of the couple-norm, enabling us to unpack its constituent expectation↔injunctions and hence to understand how it operates. On the basis of the case studies and the wider body of interviews, we identified six expectation↔injunctions: family approval; homogamy; marriage/lifelong commitment; romantic love; sex within the couple; and dedicated work.

The expectation↔injunction of family approval

The persistence and ubiquity of the idea that the couple is rightly a family matter – of concern and interest to parents, siblings and wider kin, not just to the couple itself – was one of the most startling findings of our interviews with people living unconventional intimate lives. The expectation↔injunction of family approval of the couple relationship was articulated in some way in almost every interview we conducted, challenging the straightforward dichotomy that is widely believed to exist between 'autonomous' and 'arranged' 'mate selection systems', in which the partners themselves and the family respectively are the decision-makers.[1] A traditional, collectivist orientation to what is, in contemporary European legal systems and dominant cultures, regarded as an individual's most personal of decisions was a particularly strong thread in the biographical-narratives of interviewees from Pakistani, Turkish and Roma backgrounds, but it was also evident amongst majority-group interviewees.[2]

Where there was direct interference in the couple by family and parents, interviewees often expressed considerable criticism of their family's behaviour and sought to resist it. Richard, for instance, felt that both his own and his wife's families had been too intrusive of the privacy of their relationship and that this had caused irreparable harm, contributing to its demise. Shirin was highly critical of her parents for subjecting her to an arranged marriage and then failing to support her when her husband left her. Ismail and Luisa both actively evaded attempts by their families to arrange marriages for them, and Ismail and Kasim found their parents' disapproval of their choice of partners deeply troubling.

But in many ways, interviewees accepted, endorsed and even encouraged their family's engagement with their relationship and longed for their approval. Embracing a practice rooted in the traditional patriarchal view of marriage as the exchange of women between families, Richard asked his girlfriend's father for permission to marry her. Some years later, and notwithstanding his regret about the interference and intrusiveness of both his own and his wife's family in their relationship, he did not criticize them for being disappointed and angry about the divorce. Indeed, it was clear that he respected and admired his parents' stable marriage, and that it provided the ideal, and unattained, model of adult intimate life against which he judged his personal failure. Daniel had become aware that he had implicitly been seeking his highly traditional Catholic parents' approval in getting married and settling down at an appropriate age, and Imran, whilst amused by his sister's suggestions that he should find a Muslim man to marry, did not object to her desire to intervene. Perhaps the most intense longing for family approval of a relationship was Maggie's, for whom the hetero-norm was at work alongside, and entangled with, the couple-norm. Having spent many years presenting as heterosexually coupled to her family and feeling that her real relationships with women had been greatly harmed by this, Maggie risked coming out to her mother in order to give a new relationship a better chance. Despite a deeply wounding homophobic comment and ongoing, determined non-recognition of the reality of her sexuality by her mother, she persisted in trying to secure the maternal approval that mattered so much to her. The difference that having family recognition and support made was clear to her from the experience of her girlfriend, whose mother was generous and open with her daughter and Maggie. Maggie continued to wish that her same-sex relationship were assimilable within her own family, as well as within wider society.

The need for family approval and the desire to fulfil parental expectations remained a strong urge even amongst interviewees who were critical of their parents and of their parents' own relationship. In Imran's case, his rejection of his father's patriarchal behaviour towards his mother meant that he valued only his mother's and sister's recognition, and whilst he had a strong sense of himself as leading an autonomous, self-directed life, being known as who he was by them mattered greatly to him. Ismail's parents had been very unhappy together and had divorced. This influenced his attitude towards 'Pakistani marriages', of which he was very critical, and he was resisting his mother's attempt to arrange his marriage, but nonetheless, he was still trying to please his parents. Shirin was angry with and disappointed by her parents, but she was not able to break away from them sufficiently to make a new, happier life for herself after her divorce; a cohabiting relationship with a boyfriend was impossible for her parents to tolerate and hence for her to choose.

The expectation↔injunction of homogamy

That partners should be similar to each other in culturally important ways was another expectation↔injunction to emerge from our research and was in evidence across all four countries. The strength of the expectation↔injunction of homogamy became apparent when it was not being met and was often closely entangled with the expectation↔injunction of family approval. In many cases, the profound impact of differences between the interviewee and their partner on their relationship was a significant focus of their story. Mixed-heritage relationships, in which members of the couple came from different cultural, ethnic or religious backgrounds, were particularly problematized, but age-gap relationships also drew comment, disapproval and in some cases hostility.

Ismail's story, for instance, revolved around his negotiations of conflicting versions of the couple-norm, as he felt himself caught between seemingly irreconcilable Pakistani and British ways of living intimacy. Central to this was the impact of the social disapprobation of friends and parents, actual and anticipated, of mixed-heritage partnering on his relationships with Hindu and white British women, and his parents' wish for him to have an arranged marriage with a Muslim woman. As a Bulgarian-Turk, and against the backdrop of the forced migration of the Turkish minority from Bulgaria in the late 1980s, Kasim feared his parents' serious disapproval of his relationship with a majority-Bulgarian woman. Having kept the relationship secret for two years, until they planned to get married, his parents' reaction was even worse than he had anticipated, and their complete rejection of his partner ultimately led to the breakdown of the relationship. There was a similar thread about the travails of mixed-heritage relationships in Vanessa's story, although there it was her younger Muslim partner's parents' disapproval of their differences that contributed to the ending of the relationship. Bahar also felt that mixed-heritage relationships were difficult, but in contrast to the other interviewees she owned the discomfort as her own, as well as seeing it as originating in her family and upbringing, rather than locating it entirely in the attitudes and behaviour of others. In Imran's story the challenges of a mixed-heritage relationship were ones he felt that he and his Spanish partner were tackling successfully together, but the cultural and religious differences between them were an issue for his sister, who wanted him to settle down with and marry a Muslim man.

The expectation↔injunction of similarity of age within the couple did not hold the same central place in interviewees' narratives as did that of shared ethnic, cultural and religious backgrounds, but there were numerous mentions of differences of age between partners, and often these age gaps were accorded considerable determining significance in the unfolding and destiny of the relationship. According to Vanessa, the combination of differences in background and age – with her partner being Muslim and considerably younger than she was – was too much for his parents, and hence for the relationship, to handle. For Ismail, the difficulties of having relationships with white British women were exacerbated by the additional differences of age between him and each of them. In one relationship his partner was older, and in the other she was younger, with both situations creating mismatches in terms of each party's expectations for the relationship. In the cases of both Vera and Joana, having older male partners featured in their life stories as worthy of discussion and seemed to add to their respective sense of themselves as living somewhat on the borders of expected, respectable forms of intimacy.

The expectation↔injunction of marriage and lifelong commitment

The third potent expectation↔injunction evident in the case studies was that of marriage. Despite the long-term de-patriarchalizing and equalizing changes enacted in the legal frameworks regulating marriage and the liberalizing of divorce laws, and notwithstanding the radical decline in marriage rates and the rise in divorce rates over recent decades, the experience of the couple-norm recounted by many of our interviewees related specifically to the expectation↔injunction of legally recognized conjugality and the lifelong commitment that this entails.

Bahar's biographical-narrative was structured around the pressure she felt to find and marry a man in order to have children and build a family, articulating the lynchpin status of marriage and the interconnectedness of the couple-norm, the hetero-norm and the procreative-norm in the culture of intimate citizenship that prevailed within her personal network in the Turkish-Bulgarian community. She emphasized particularly the role that her friends and colleagues played in seeking a marriage partner for her, with her mother only more recently pushing her to settle down. Luisa, in contrast, demonstrated the potency of the expectation↔injunction of marriage in the Portuguese Roma community in the centrality to her story of her adamant and outright refusal of marriage and the patriarchal control it would entail. For Daniel, marriage was just the normal, expected thing to do – the logical next step for a man from a conservative Catholic background to take a few years after graduating from university and having tried out his relationship by cohabiting with his girlfriend.

Others evidenced the expectation↔injunction of marriage, and hence of lifelong commitment to the couple, more obliquely, but no less powerfully, through the strength of their emotional response to the end of their marriages. Richard, who considered himself a couple-oriented person, was deeply sad and regretful about his divorce, whilst Bjørn experienced his as a catastrophic failure. Shirin's abandonment by her husband was the cause of great disappointment and shame, casting her adrift as a stigmatized divorced woman living without a man in the Pakistani community in Oslo.

The impact of the historical legal framing of intimate citizenship around marriage resonated negatively, in different ways, through the stories of both Vanessa and Diana. In Vanessa's case, the intergenerational legacy of stigma associated with illegitimacy and divorce shaped her intimate life through the reactively conventional and strict upbringing her parents gave her and their 'old-fashioned' attitudes to her having sex with her first boyfriend. In Diana's case, the illegality, under the 1956 Bulgarian Penal Code, of living with another man whilst still married to her husband led to the initiation of a court case against her and her partner, and the threat of up to three years in prison, a fine and public reprobation. Moreover, the birth of a child conceived with her new partner before she was divorced from her husband meant exclusion for the child from inheritance when her partner died, and the fact that they had never married left Diana herself living in great precarity, with no rights to property or survivor's benefits after a 20-year relationship.

The ongoing strength of the expectation↔injunction of marriage and lifelong commitment was also evident in the stories of some of those who were self-consciously living unconventional intimate lives and who were creating, or hoping for, a modernized version of the traditional relationship, an alternative long-term, committed couple-form. Paul valued his stable, committed civil-partnered couple relationship with the man he proudly called his husband as the grounding of his life, from which they were both able to adventure sexually. Vera delighted in the playful idea that her committed domestic companionship and life partnership with her gay male friend was a relationship of 'husband' and 'wife', and Vanessa was contemplating entering a civil partnership with her close female friend, with whom she was making lifelong plans. For Maggie, same-sex marriage and the societal recognition it would entail would be a 'miracle', but it was, she thought, regrettably, a long way in the future in Bulgaria. In the meantime, she sought long-term stability with her girlfriend.

The expectation↔injunction of romantic love

'Falling in love' and 'being in love' were common themes across the interviews, notions that served repeatedly to explain, justify and describe particular relationships and life-moments in people's life stories. But the contemporary western expectation↔injunction that the couple should be based, at least initially, on romantic love was most extensively discussed and clearly articulated, perhaps because it is so taken-for-granted, by those who regretted not being able to live accordingly – Shirin and Luisa – and by Paul, who self-consciously rejected romantic love as the grounding of a stable, long-term relationship. For Shirin and Luisa, the allure of romantic love was in conflict with the expectation↔injunctions in their communities of belonging of marriages arranged by parents, on a considered and often avowedly rational basis, rather than driven by personal desire. Their preference for relationships based on romantic love adhere instead with mainstream, majority ideals in Norway and Portugal, and both expressed deep regret about not being able to build a life grounded in a romantic love relationship. In sharp contrast, Paul's distaste for the irrationality of romantic love was a singular instance of counter-normativity, with little resonance in any of the communities of which he was a part. Indeed, he felt so strongly his departure from conventionality in this respect that he would not admit to friends and family that he had never been in love with his husband.

The expectation↔injunction of sex within the couple

The expectation↔injunction that coupledom has at its core a mutually fulfilling sexual relationship that is intimate and exclusive was also in evidence in cases where people felt that this had been missing in their lives.[3] Bjørn and Shirin both found it unacceptable and upsetting that what they regarded as their natural and legitimate sexual desires were not reciprocated by their spouses. Daniel noted the waning and absence of sexual intimacy as his relationship with his wife deteriorated, as if pointing to key evidence for their break-up, and Joana spoke about the unfulfilling, inattentive sex she had with her male partner as part of her explanation of why the relationship did not last. The expectation↔injunction of the sexual exclusivity of the couple emerged in the stories of Bjørn, Astrid and Paul. Both Bjørn and Astrid fully endorsed and took for granted the imperative of monogamy. Bjørn assumed that his devastation at his wife's sexual infidelity, and the ending of their relationship because of it, needed no explanation. Astrid was similarly clear that sexual desire outside her relationship was unacceptable and that she had to make a choice between her long-term partner and another sexual/love interest. Paul, again, was the exception who proved the rule: he was as sceptical about the need for monogamy as he was about romantic love. He made much of how he and his husband relished their unconventional sexual lives: having sex with other men, separately and together, was a core element in their mutually fulfilling and deeply committed relationship. Their sexual non-exclusivity was, he believed, a distinctively gay male way of living that should be celebrated, rather than being brought in line with the heteronormative version of the couple-norm.

The expectation↔injunction of dedicated work

In contradistinction to the expectation↔injunction of romantic love as the basis of coupledom is the expectation↔injunction of dedicated work as a key component of a lasting couple relationship. This more rational approach to the maintenance of coupledom featured in a number of interviews and tended to be discussed in the context of disappointment that the dedicated work undertaken had not produced the desired end: the saving of the relationship. Both Richard and Bjørn, whose marriages ended in divorce, spoke about having gone into therapy in an attempt to repair their relationships. Richard and his wife embarked on couple therapy together, and Bjørn tried a number of different therapies as well as reading self-help books and endeavouring to work on his sexual relationship with his wife. The emotional effort that they put into their marriages was notable for its gender counter-normativity, and their frustration that it did not pay off was clearly in evidence in their interviews. Shirin also expended considerable labour in trying to make her marriage work: she 'managed' to 'fall in love' with the husband her parents had chosen for her, and she tried hard to give him everything he wanted, and even things he did not know he wanted, such as the romantic gesture of breakfast on a tray. Astrid too was explicit about investing in shared work with her partner in pursuit of a lasting relationship. She believed that building a life together rested on practical, daily joint enterprises, which might, she hoped, eventually include raising a child together, the most consequential dedicated work in which a couple might engage.

The interconnectedness of the couple-norm

Our analysis of intimate citizenship law and policy and of the biograph-ical-narratives of our interviewees led us to see intimate citizenship regimes as normative systems, and to identify four core, interrelated norms that are at the heart of contemporary intimate citizenship regimes: the couple-norm, the gender-norm of differentiation and hierarchy, the hetero-norm and the procreative-norm. These norms are analytically distinguishable, and each can be understood in terms of its own history and modes of operation in state action and everyday life, whilst also being closely entangled in lived experience. In focusing in this book on the couple-norm, we have tended to bracket off attention to the other core norms, but their mutual entanglement as part of a normative system means that they work together as more than the sum of their parts.[4] Our understanding of how the couple-norm has evolved historically has therefore, necessarily, attended also to how law and policy relating to gender, sexuality and reproduction have changed; transformation in one norm of intimate citizenship has repercussions for the others. The progressive equalization of conditions for women and lesbians and gay men, for instance, has impacted significantly on the contexts within which couple relationships are formed and lived. As the legal and economic imperatives for women to enter and remain in heterosexual couples are reduced, the couple-norm loosens its grip. Similarly, the abolition of illegitimacy as a legal state reduces the stigma of unmarried parenting and impacts thereby upon the couple-norm. However, working in the opposite direction, the opening up of marriage to people in same-sex relationships serves to remake and extend the couple-norm, as it embraces new constituencies in a process of homonormalization.

In the lives and stories of our interviewees, the couple-norm was often tightly interwoven with the other norms of intimate citizenship, and indeed its tenacity and potency can be seen as residing to a significant extent in this entanglement. Thus, for instance, the pressure that Bahar experienced from friends and family was simultaneously about complying with the couple-norm, the gender-norm, the hetero-norm and the procreative-norm. Shirin was caught up in powerful, gender-normative ideas about the proper behaviour of a woman in her community, central to which was being married, and Bjørn felt that his divorce signalled his failure as a man. Luisa's rejection of coupledom was underpinned by her determination to avoid the patriarchal oppression that she saw marriage as entailing.

But it was the procreative-norm – far more than the other two norms, in which there has been much more radical change – that was most tightly bound up with the couple-norm. The desire to partner and parent with the same person was a persistent theme in many interviews, particularly where this had not (yet) been achieved, and the belief that the two activities go hand in hand was unquestioned by almost everyone, whatever their sexuality. A notable exception to this was Paul, who had been pleasantly 'surprised' to find himself involved in raising the children of two lesbian friends, never having imagined or deliberately sought out children. Notwithstanding the fall in the birth rate of recent decades and the widespread use of assistive reproductive technologies, having children is still regarded as the most natural of activities, forming and living in a family with children as the normal, and very best, if not quite the only way of being an adult. Indeed, the temporal demand exerted by the biological exigencies of procreation served to intensify the pressure of the entangled couple-norm and procreative-norm, particularly for women of childbearing age. As procreation increasingly takes place outside the married heterosexual couple-form, yoking the couple-norm to the procreative-norm serves to strengthen both, but the former is perhaps in greater need of reinforcement than the latter.

The psychosocial workings of the couple-norm

What then does this all add up to as a theorization of the couple-norm? To summarize the findings of our research: the expectation↔injunctions that we have discussed above, which together constitute key elements of the couple-norm, operate conjunctively and in tandem with the other norms of intimate citizenship – the gender-norm, the hetero-norm and the procreative-norm – to fundamentally shape how people live their intimate lives. They vary in intensity – from the lighter pressure of expectation to the compelling demand of injunction – according to local/community-specific social and cultural contexts, within the wider frameworks of national intimate citizenship regimes, and they are not all always actively in play in any individual's life at any particular moment. They are, at times, explicitly and more or less consciously exercised by those in an individual's personal social network – family members, friends, work colleagues and acquaintances – as well as acting more diffusely through the shared beliefs and moral codes about the right and proper way to live as an adult that suffuse the cultures of mainstream society and of communities of ethnic, religious and cultural belonging.

Much of the time, the couple-norm is embraced, even by many of those whose lives do not adhere to its constituent expectation↔injunctions. For significant periods of their lives, people might positively endorse all or some aspects of the couple-norm, often not thinking much about the choices that are being made, but sometimes with a self-reflexive awareness that they are following convention or choosing 'tradition'.[5] People pursue potential partners. They look for, and settle down with, someone who is culturally similar to them, someone suitable, someone who is socially acceptable. They believe in romantic love and its importance as the foundation of a strong relationship. They fall in love. They seek family approval of their intimate life choices. They long to get married and make a public, legal commitment to their partner, with the intention of staying together for the rest of their lives. They desire sex with their partner, regard sex as a crucial component of a good relationship and eschew sex outside the couple. They believe that a lasting relationship needs dedicated work if it is to survive and thrive.

However, people might also experience the couple-norm in general, or specific expectation↔injunctions, as social and cultural pressure that they understand as coming from 'outside'. They can be acutely conscious of this pressure and might be critical of it and those exerting it. They can feel directed, pushed, nagged, cajoled and even forced in the direction of particular couple-normative behaviours. They can feel criticized, socially marginalized and stigmatized for not living according to the expectation↔injunctions of the couple-norm. The actions and interventions of certain individuals, especially family members and known others, are much more readily identified and blamed for this than cultural pressure of a more generalized nature, for which no single person or group is directly responsible. Politicized critiques of oppressive norms of intimate citizenship, informed by the ideas of the women's and LGBT movements, are also increasingly widespread and provide a language with which to think about uncomfortable, unsatisfying, unequal or coercive practices. And so the couple-norm and its expectation↔injunctions are, variously, questioned, evaded and sometimes resisted and rejected. Counter-normative agency rises up to challenge convention and established practice.

But the core of the couple-norm – the construction of coupledom as the normal, natural and superior way of being an adult – is also often experienced as 'internal' pressure, as the wish, desire or longing to find and keep a partner. The *need* to be part of a couple can be strong. The yearning can feel organic, natural, as if it were coming from 'inside', and it can feel more real and more intense than any 'external' reality. Moreover, failure to live up to the couple-norm, and non-conformity with its expectation↔injunctions, can produce profound inner turmoil – feelings of shame, lack and despair. Where a relationship has ended, when a partner has been lost, and with them the socially recognized status of a coupled person, the guilt, grief and regret can be all-consuming. The desire to return, often with great haste, to coupledom can be compelling. There can be a pull to repeat, to find again the safety of the known and recognized place of the couple. Such over-whelming feelings serve as internal sanctions against breaches of the couple-norm and reinforce the sense of the naturalness and superiority of coupledom. This sense does not reside in conscious awareness as a belief. It is so deeply accepted as an experiential reality, as truth, that it is not seen as a belief, as a matter of determination or choice.[6]

Woven into the fabric of subjectivity, the feeling that coupledom is the ideal state of being is often experienced as fundamental to being human. This might be understood as the very essence of a successful norm – fully internalized and existing below conscious awareness, part of what we might call the 'normative unconscious'.[7] To extend this psychosocial conceptualization of the operation of the couple-norm a little further through a psychoanalytic lens, we might suggest that the sense that being single, or not following the expectation↔injunctions of the couple-norm, might be a positive way of living, that it might offer possibilities of autonomy and freedom, adventure and excitement, and time and space for creative experimentation, is repressed, split off from conscious knowledge. In the normative valorization of coupledom, the attractions of life outside the conventionalized couple-form are repudiated. This is how the couple-norm works at a psychic level.

Yet the internalization of norms is never complete and without resistance. As Judith Butler says, in theorizing the ways in which the unconscious thwarts norms of gender and sexuality, 'norms do not exercise a final or fatalistic control, or not always' (Butler, 2004: 15). Psychoanalysis suggests that psychic life is riven with conflict and that subjectivity is far from stable. Vitally for the couple-norm, desire and sexuality, the search for pleasure, are inherently unruly and destabilizing. Repression can never be absolute: 'what is split off from consciousness does not disappear but rather continues to haunt the psyche' (Layton, 2002: 199). The lure of different ways of being, uncoupled and loose, uncommitted and promiscuous, a life of inappropriate liaisons lurks in the shadows, waiting to break through into consciousness or to be enacted when impulse takes over and control is lost. To paraphrase Lacanian feminist Jacqueline Rose (1987: 91), 'there is resistance to the couple [identity] at the very heart of psychic life'.

Moreover, if, drawing on relational psychoanalysis,[8] we conceptualize the human subject ontologically as constituted through our relationships with others, but also as always living within the tension between autonomy and relationality (Roseneil and Ketokivi, 2016), we might understand fundamental relational impulses as working to internalize norms, and autonomous impulses as working to resist 'being bent to the will of the other' (Layton, 2004: 42).[9] With conformity to norms comes the recognition by others that is vital to being human – that is, literally, in infancy, and beyond, life-giving and life-sustaining. We each need the care, love and approval of significant others, the respect and social belonging that are granted by conformity to normative practices. We fear the loss of love and care, of being cast outside family and community. Normative unconscious processes work to maintain our attachments to others and to the normative social order by keeping the sense that there are alternatives and that other ways of living might be fruitful and generative, split off and repressed – out of bounds, unimaginable, unconscionable. But through resistance to norms comes a sense of separateness and difference, the development of the singularity that inheres in being a person. Counter-normative agency, the will to autonomy, is also an innate property of subjectivity, a life force with the power to disrupt and undo.

The human subject is, then, divided-conflicted between adherence to the couple-norm and its constituent expectation↔injunctions and departure from them. The experience for any individual of normative unconscious conflict, the tension between embracing and resisting the couple-norm, can be deeply troubling, unsettling established ways of being and causing psychic pain and relational disruption. But this experience is highly contingent. It is not possible to predict what meaning any individual will make of their situation and how they will orient themselves in relation to the norm: 'the autonomy inherent in human subjectivity is at the heart of this indeterminacy' (Layton, 2004: 42). The particularity of an individual's biography, their personal, affective history of attachment and family relationships, early losses of loved ones, the death or divorce of parents, their place in their community and wider society, how they have been treated in life, the intimate citizenship regime within which they find themselves, all matter hugely, yet they are not determining.[10] Psychoanalysis suggests that 'good enough care', first in earliest infancy from primary care-givers (Winnicott, 1965, 1974; Hollway, 2006), and then through childhood and into adult life, and which includes a robust, responsive welfare state (Froggett, 2002), develops the capacity to be alone, forging a self secure enough to be creative and to play, and facilitating the ability to find a self-determined path through the expectations and injunctions of the social world. But, as our interviewees' stories demonstrate, being able to choose how to navigate the couple-norm and its constituent expectation↔injunctions – whether and when to enter or leave a relationship, with whom to partner, how to be together – is an ongoing struggle, a complex, unstable achievement, dependent upon, but not decided by, supportive legal and policy frameworks and relational histories – contexts that are productive of, or at least conducive to, intimate agency.

Moreover, crucially, and central to the complexity of its psychosocial operation, the couple-norm is not just any norm: it is a norm that is about an intimate, loving, sexual attachment to another person. Whilst the drive for autonomy might feed the impulse to resist the couple-norm, the drive for relationality can be seen, at times, as exercising a powerful pull towards the couple-form that is in excess of the demands of normative sociality – it is about much more than pleasing significant others, following convention and fitting in with social groups.

Psychoanalysis offers us a way of understanding the overwhelming intensity of the desire for a couple relationship – for the intimate/sexual dyad – that can be experienced at particular moments in a person's life, by tracing this felt 'need' back to the vital attachments and dependencies of earliest infancy. Whilst we challenge the implied universalism and normativity of much psychoanalytic theorizing of intimate relationships, which has historically failed to recognize, and has indeed often pathologized, the experiences of those who live generative lives outside the conventional heterosexual couple-form, the identification of an extra-normative relationality as at the heart of the urge to couple speaks to important aspects of human experience. One strand of psychoanalytic thinking stresses the sensuous intimacy and merging offered by the couple-form and their echoes of early embodied experience. As Otto Kernberg says, the 'lifelong yearning for physical closeness and stimulation, for the inter-mingling of body surfaces, is linked to the longing for symbiotic fusion with the parental object, and by the same token, to the earliest forms of identification' (1995: 32–3).[11] In a similar but more critical vein, Adam Phillips's (1996: 38) disquisition on monogamy speaks of the entangled beginnings of human life: 'If you start life as part of someone else's body, your independence is a dismemberment. Being a couple reminds us, persuades us again, that we are also someone else; of a piece with them.' We might also draw on the work of feminist psycho-analyst Bracha L. Ettinger (2006) on 'matrixial trans-subjectivity', the fundamental reality that we are gestated inside the body of another human being, and therefore that our earliest preconscious experiences are of the most profound connectivity, merged symbiotic dependence upon, and containment within, another human being. In work influenced by John Bowlby's (1969) theorization of the universal human tendency to seek closeness to another person and to feel secure in the presence of that person, attachment theorists emphasize the comfort and support provided by the 'safe haven' of the couple relation-ship and the 'secure base' it offers from which partners may venture out to explore and learn in the world (Castellano, Velotti and Zavattini, 2010; Beebe and McCrorie, 2010).

Recognition, social belonging, physical closeness, intimacy, safety, security, familiarity, home: the psychosocial promise of coupledom is broad and deep. Although the reality of actual lived couple relationships often falls far short, providing, in particular, neither the consistent love and bodily pleasures nor the ongoing psychological comfort and safety that are sought, glimpses and moments of such experience in the past, and the unconscious belief in their potentiality, fuel hopeful investments, and repeated reinvestments, in the idea and ideal of the couple: such is the 'cruel optimism' (Berlant, 2011) of the couple-norm.

Notes

1   See Lee and Stone's (1980) cross-cultural study of mate selection systems and the deconstruction of the dichotomy between nuclear family/autonomous systems and extended family/arranged systems.

2   The importance of 'conventional reasons for marrying' – following parental wishes, religious practice and the social conventions of a community – amongst both white and ethnic-minority British adults born in the late 1960s has been established by Maclean and Eekelaar (2005). However, they also found that there was a tendency amongst the white British interviewees to '"distance" themselves from the conventions they were following by characterizing themselves as "traditional"'. They explain this as follows: 'Tradition has a compromise quality to it. Following tradition suggests a lifestyle choice, freely entered, rather than being subject to prescriptions by reason of one's membership of a community that one may not have freely chosen' (2005: 284).

3   There was relatively little discussion of sex in our interviews. We attribute this to our interview method, which involved asking just one question, which did not mention sex, and then only following up with further questions about issues and topics mentioned by the interviewee in their response to this question. Sex therefore tended to be talked about by interviewees when it had become a problem or issue in their lives.

4   In this we agree with Ewald (1990: 153), who emphasizes the correlative quality of norms, arguing, 'just as norms can only exist socially, there can be no such thing as a norm that exists in isolation, for a norm never refers to anything but other norms on which it depends'.

5   Maclean and Eekelaar's research (2005) identifies a distinction between white British interviewees, who were more inclined to see themselves as active agents choosing 'tradition' when they decided to marry, and ethnic-minority interviewees, who were more likely to regard themselves as following the conventions of their religious or cultural group and/or the wishes of their parents.

6   This is what Britton (1998) calls an 'unconscious belief'.

7   See Layton (2002, 2004) for discussions of the normative unconscious and normative unconscious processes. The idea that 'the unconscious is as permeated by cultural norms as is the conscious mind' (Layton, 2002: 218) is controversial within psychoanalysis and is rejected by more classically Freudian and Lacanian theorists (see Layton, 2004).

8   Whilst the origins of a psychoanalytic conceptualization of relationality stretch back to Freud's theory of identification, a distinctive school of 'relational psychoanalysis' developed from the early 1980s in the United States in the work of Greenberg and Mitchell (1983). See also Mitchell and Aron (1999), Aron and Harris (2005) and the formative work of American psychoanalytic feminists (Chodorow, 1978; Benjamin, 1988, 1995, 1998; Dimen, 2003; Layton, 2004).

9   Jessica Benjamin's theorization of intersubjectivity is key here (1988, 1995, 1998).

10 Hence the value of the detailed biographical-narratives we gathered in our research and that we have presented in the case studies in Part III.

11 Otto Kernberg has played an influential role in psychoanalytic thinking and practice concerning relationships and sexuality, in particular establishing the couple-normative idea that 'health' resides in sexual intimacy within the long-term heterosexual couple. However, he also provides a powerful example of the rethinking of sexuality, particularly homosexuality, that has been under way within mainstream psychoanalysis in recent years. His early work (1975), and the book cited here (1995), associate homosexuality with psychopathology, but his thinking has shifted very significantly to what Drescher (2002) calls 'a normal variant paradigm' (Kernberg, 2002).

15
Imagining intimate citizenship beyond the couple-norm

In the course of this book's exploration of the operation of the couple-norm within contemporary European intimate citizenship regimes, we have seen many examples of the discomfort and distress, guilt and shame, exclusion and stigma, pressure and coercion, hardship and precarity that it exerts on ordinary people who are living to some degree outside or in opposition to its expectation↔injunctions. Indeed, there were many more stories of misrecognition, disappointment and struggle in relation to the couple-norm amongst the other 51 people we interviewed whose lives do not feature here as case studies. We believe that we have identified a widespread and common set of experiences that are consequent on couple-normativity, albeit ones are that diverse and contingent.

However, we also wish to emphasize, as we conclude our discussion, that it is the couple-*norm* that produces these effects, rather than *coupledom* per se. Coupledom – and actually existing couple relationships – have been neither our object of study nor the target of our critique: coupledom is not in itself, necessarily, a social ill or a negative influence in people's lives. Indeed, being part of couple can be one of the greatest sources of pleasure, fulfilment and security that life in a competitive, uncertain, fast-changing, sometimes dangerous, often precarious social world can offer. Rather, the social problem that we have identified is that created by the potency of the couple-norm as a regulatory, disciplining and channelling force – a power that comes increasingly into view as other intimate citizenship norms have been diminishing in potency and, paradoxically, as it becomes more possible to live outside the conventional cohabiting, conjugal heterosexual couple-form.

This leaves us with the classic question that haunts all socially engaged researchers: what is to be done? It would be too easy to end with a rhetorical denunciation of couple-normativity, in the hope that our analysis and critique will, in themselves, contribute to the dismantling of the couple-norm. But we have argued that the couple-norm exerts an especially strong, and complex, hold over people, and it will, no doubt, survive our critique.

The hope that we find in our research rests on the reality that whilst there is no social or psychic life outside normativity, norms are in constant motion as they are confronted, negotiated and reworked in everyday life. The movement is mostly imperceptible, but over time change becomes identifiable and can be significant. In living up against the couple-norm, our interviewees were enacting both small everyday challenges and stronger, self-conscious alternatives that gradually, and in aggregate, are remaking the intimate citizenship regimes within which they live. They were, variously, centring their lives around friendship, choosing to remain single, embracing solitude, forging non-cohabiting partnerships, sharing the raising of children outside the couple-form, resisting the romantic imperative, forming relationships with people from different backgrounds and defying monogamy. They were envisaging, and often finding, stability, security, love, intimacy, sex and domesticity in many different ways, outside the conventional couple-form. In living their intimate lives thus, however hard it was for each of them as individuals at the time, they were expanding the possibilities for others, opening up spaces, however marginal, that reduce the pressure to conform and that enable people to feel less stigmatized and more socially recognized.

What would it mean for an intimate citizenship regime to cease to promote coupledom and to work instead actively to attenuate the negative impacts of the couple-norm? How could we collectively develop mechanisms that support and recognize, rather than bear down upon and mistreat, people like those we have interviewed? This should not be inconceivable; after all, governments have committed to, and succeeded in, transforming many of the laws and policies that have historically enacted and reproduced gender inequalities and heteronormativity. But with no social movement dedicated to challenging couple-normativity, and few lobbying groups working in the interests of people living outside the couple-norm, as well as new nationalist and reactionary movements challenging what has been achieved so far, a manifesto and programme of action is required – a vision needs to be developed.

To gesture towards a process for imagining intimate citizenship beyond the couple-norm, discussions could be initiated about how the right to life outside the couple-form might be enshrined in international human rights instruments, such as the Universal Declaration of Human Rights and the European Convention on Human Rights, alongside the recognized fundamental right to family life. Consideration might be given to how freedom of movement in intimate life could be better supported, recognizing that desires and relationships change over time and that the ability to uncouple is often highly constrained culturally, socially and financially. A rethinking of welfare policies could be undertaken, focusing on how to protect and support people in the lives they wish to, or have to, lead outside the conventional couple-form: living alone, sharing a home with a non-sexual partner or with a group of friends, being single, not marrying, forming a non-cohabiting relationship, parenting with more than one other person and having complex, multiple intimate/sexual relationships – and moving between these states. The implications for law and policy concerning housing, taxation, social security, minimum wages, child support, immigration, pensions, health and mental health provision, reproductive rights, care in sickness and old age, and inheritance all require consideration. Through this we might start to build a pluralistic 'single-person friendly' and 'friend-friendly' welfare state (Roseneil, 2004) that supports solo and group living, and that no longer assumes and privileges the cohabiting (hetero)sexual couple-form.

In all of this, we would be developing an intimate imaginary that opens up visions of the good life, of human flourishing, beyond the narrow confines of the conventional couple and family. In sum, we could seek to establish an intimate citizenship regime – encompassing both state and civil society – that supports personal choice and agency in intimate relationships, and that respects and recognizes the dynamic, changing form these take over time. Were such transformations to manifest, the tenacious grip of the couple-norm would be loosened, and everyone, coupled or not, would be a little freer – a little closer to exercising full intimate citizenship.

PART V

Methodological appendix

16
Researching intimate citizenship

The FEMCIT project

The research on which this book is based was conducted as part of the 'Gendered Citizenship in Multicultural Europe: the impact of contemporary women's movements' (FEMCIT) project. FEMCIT was funded by the European Commission's 6th Framework between 2007 and 2011. It aimed to provide a new critical, multidimensional understanding of contemporary gendered citizenship in the context of a multicultural and changing Europe, and to evaluate the impact of contemporary women's movements on gendered citizenship. It focused on six dimensions of citizenship: political, social, economic, ethnic/religious, bodily/sexual and intimate citizenship. The programme of research was organized into 'work packages', each dealing with a different dimension of citizenship.

In the intimate citizenship work package, from which this book draws, our overall objective was to understand the role of women's movements and other movements for gender and sexual equality in transforming intimate citizenship in contemporary Europe. We operationalized this to mean looking both at the laws and policy that frame intimate citizenship and at the everyday experiences that constitute intimate citizenship as it is lived (Roseneil, 2012; Roseneil et al., 2012).

We carried out our research on four countries, chosen according to a 'most different' comparative methodology (Przeworski and Teune, 1970), to give a range of welfare regimes and both long-standing and newer democracies with different histories of civil society/state relations: the United Kingdom – a north-western European 'late liberal' welfare state; Bulgaria – a 'post-communist' state; Norway – a 'social democratic' Nordic welfare state; and Portugal – a 'southern European', Catholic, post-dictatorship state. In each country we addressed three spheres of intimate citizenship: civil society action, state activity and everyday life. This involved carrying out, for each country:

(i) an historical study of the claims and demands of movements for gender and sexual equality and change (specifically, women's movements and lesbian and gay movements) in relation to intimate life and intimate citizenship (focusing particularly on the period from 1968 to 2008) (see Roseneil et al., 2010, 2011);

(ii) a critical analysis of law and policy concerning intimate life (see Roseneil et al., 2008); and

(iii) a biographical-narrative study of everyday experiences of intimate citizenship, focusing on people living outside conventional nuclear families and couples (who might be seen to be at the forefront of the processes of individualization and de-traditionalization in intimate life that have been linked by sociologists (e.g. Giddens, 1991, 1992; Beck and Beck-Gernsheim, 1995, 2002) to the impact of women's and lesbian and gay movements).

Part II of this book draws primarily on (i) and (ii) and Part III on (iii).

Intimate citizenship issues

In the historical study of the claims and demands of movements for gender and sexual equality and change (i), and the critical analysis of law and policy (ii), we structured the research around an investigation of four areas of intimate citizenship, and within these we focused on a number of issues, as follows:

Partnership: marriage; divorce; non-marital heterosexual relationships/cohabitation; same-sex relationship/partnership recognition; selfhood, financial autonomy, independence within relationships; immigration and partnership, family reunion; non-monogamy/polyamory; single people and solo-living; care and partnership;
Reproductive rights and parenting: contraception; abortion; assisted conception/reproductive technologies; motherhood,

fatherhood, parenting; adoption rights; lesbians and reproduction and parenting; childcare;

Sexual politics: women's sexual pleasure; regulation of sexual practice/acts; lesbianism, lesbian rights and recognition; homosexuality and anti-discrimination; prostitution; pornography; sex education;

Gender and sexual violence: domestic/intimate partner violence; rape and sexual assault; child sexual abuse; trafficking; homophobic and transphobic violence.

The biographical-narrative study

Place

We recruited our interviewees from inhabitants of the capital city of each national case study country – London, Sofia, Oslo and Lisbon – as the places which are usually thought to be most subject to social and cultural transformation, and which contain the largest numbers of people living non-conventional intimate lives.[1] We sought to interview people in their own homes, wherever possible, as the place where they were most likely to feel comfortable and relaxed. However, interviews also took place in the interviewees' workplaces, in public spaces (cafes, parks, on a beach), in a hospital room, at non-governmental organization offices, at an interviewee's partner's home, and in the interviewer's office, home or car.

Sample

Size

We interviewed 67 people: 18 in the UK, 17 in Norway, 16 each in Bulgaria and Portugal.

Gender

The final sample comprised 41 women and 26 men. No one identified themselves to us as trans or non-binary at the time of interview. We had aimed to interview eight men and eight women in each national case study site, but it proved more difficult to recruit men to discuss their 'lives and personal relationships'. As a team of white women researchers, it was particularly difficult to engage men from the Roma and Pakistani communities in our project.

Intimate life categories

In terms of their intimate lives, the sample comprised:

- 40 interviewees who were single (currently unpartnered) (11 in Bulgaria and Portugal and nine in Norway and the UK);
- 20 interviewees who were lesbian/gay/in a same-sex relationship (seven in the UK, five in Bulgaria and Norway, and three in Portugal), one Norwegian who refused sexual categories and three UK interviewees who offered their own categories (e.g. 'big queer', 'anarchosexual');
- 21 interviewees who were in a living-apart relationship (seven in the UK, six in Norway, five in Bulgaria and three in Portugal);
- 21 interviewees who were living in shared housing (eight in Norway, seven in the UK, five in Bulgaria and one in Portugal.

Age

The interviewees were aged between 28 and 54, of whom

- three were aged 28–29;
- 19 were aged 30–34;
- 20 were aged 35–39;
- 11 were aged 40–44;
- 11 were aged 45–49;
- three were aged 50–54 years.

Ethnic diversity

We interviewed members of the national majority ethnic group (26 in total) and of two ethnic groups that are minoritized/racialized in each of the countries (41 in total). We chose these ethnic groups for their significant presence (in terms of size, importance in national political debate etc) in each country/capital city. The sample was as follows in terms of membership of/ backgrounds from majority and minoritized/ racialized communities:

- UK: seven national ethnic majority, six Pakistani, five Turkish;
- Bulgaria: six national ethnic majority, five Bulgarian Roma, five Turkish;
- Norway: seven national ethnic majority, five Norwegian-Pakistani, four Sami, one who identified as both Sami and majority;
- Portugal: six national ethnic majority, five Portuguese Roma, five Cape Verdean.

Class/socio-economic/educational diversity

After an extended discussion of the difficulty of operationalizing class/socio-economic categories across our national case study sites, we decided to sample for variability of class/socio-economic status/ educational level/occupation, rather than to focus on particular groups. We recognized that amongst particular groups there might not be great variability of class/socio-economic status (e.g. Roma).

As a proxy for class/socio-economic status, we present information about the highest level of education completed by our interviewees. The sample was significantly skewed towards people who had completed higher education, with 40 of the 67 having done so:

- 26 people had higher degrees (eight in the UK and Bulgaria,[2] and five in Norway and Portugal);
- 14 people had an undergraduate degree (six in the UK, five in Norway and three in Portugal);
- 15 people had completed secondary school (four in Bulgaria, four in Norway, three in Portugal and four in the UK);
- 12 people had been educated to the age of 16 years old or less (four in Bulgaria, three in Norway, five in Portugal and none in the UK); in Bulgaria all four are Roma, in Norway all three are Pakistani and in Portugal all five are Roma.

For further discussion of how we recruited our interviewees and the challenges of this, see Crowhurst et al. (2013).

Biographical-narrative interviewing

Following the biographical-narrative interpretive method (BNIM), we asked one standard open-ended question (a 'single question inducing narrative', SQUIN) of all our interviewees:

'Can you tell me the story of your life and personal relationships – all the events and experiences that have been important to you personally, how it has been for you? There's no rush, we've got as much time as you need for this. I'll listen first; I won't interrupt. I'll just take some notes, in case I have any questions for you after you've finished telling your story.

So, please can you tell me the story of your life and personal relation-ships, all the events and experiences that have been important to you personally?

Please begin wherever you like'

After this the interviewee was allowed to speak, telling their story in their own way, without interruption or guidance from the interviewer. The method requires the interviewer to abstain from interrupting and to offer the interviewee a sense of open-ended space within which to speak. If the interviewee sought guidance about whether they were answering correctly, or giving the interviewer what she wanted, interviewers were asked to reply by assuring the interviewee that whatever they wanted to say was relevant and, if necessary, reminding them of the wording of the SQUIN. During the interviewee's response to the SQUIN, the interviewer would take notes about the topics discussed by the interviewee, paying particular attention to the sequence in which topics were raised and the language used by the interviewee. When the interviewee reached the end of their answer and had been encouraged to add anything else they might want to say (*'Is there anything more you'd like to add, anything else you remember?'*), there was a short break whilst the interviewer reviewed her notes. This first part of the interview was referred to as *subsession 1*.

The second part of the interview, *subsession 2*, then consisted of questions formulated by the interviewer:

'You said/talked about x. ...

Do you remember any more details about how that all happened/how it happened/how it came about/how things changed?

[or] *Do you remember any more about that particular situation/ time/phase/example/day/occasion/happening/event/incident/emotion? How it all happened?*

[or] *Do you have any images or feelings about that, that struck you at the time?*

[or] *Do you have any thoughts about that?'*

The questions followed the sequence of topics raised by the interviewee in their initial answer to the SQUIN and used the interviewee's own words, concepts and terminology, asking for more narrative detail and seeking to elicit narratives of particular incidents ('pushing for PINs' in BNIM terminology – PINs being 'particular incident narratives'). BNIM suggests that the first and last topic raised by the interviewee should always be acknowledged by the interviewer, even if not particularly relevant to her research interests, as a way of demonstrating that the interviewee has been heard.

The assumption underlying this aspect of the interview method is that people make sense of their lives by telling stories and that this probing for narrative detail draws out of the interviewee further information about personal meanings and emotional life. Interviewers were encouraged to pursue questioning about issues of intimate citizenship (with reference to the list of issues identified above) that had arisen in subsession 1, and to seek to elicit more narrative detail about these.

The third and final part of the interview, *subsession 3*, involved non-narrative questions, including points of clarification about interviewees' biographies, and the completion of a standard socio-demographic questionnaire.

Biographical-narrative data analysis

From the 67 interviews, we chose 20 cases for intensive analytic treatment, of which 16 are discussed in this book. We first transcribed each of these interviews in full and translated the Bulgarian, Norwegian and Portuguese interviews into English. Following this the analytic process involved two interpretation workshops for each case (held several weeks apart) to 'kick-start' the analysis: the first workshop focused on the lived life (the biographical data analysis), the second on the told story (the narrative text structure sequentialization). Each workshop used a 'future blind, chunk by chunk' process to hypothesize as freely around the data as possible (for further information about how BNIM workshops operate, see Wengraf, 2009). These workshops involved all of us, as the research team, together with one or two external researchers (social scientists interested in intimate life and/or psychosocial methodologies/ the biographical-narrative interpretive method).

The workshops proved to be highly effective in challenging the individual researcher whose case was being analysed in terms of her national preconceptions, personal prejudices and cultural expectations. The workshops also served to promote collective reflexivity, to develop a cross-national, plural mindset in relation to the data and thinking across cases and countries, and to ensure methodological consistency across the national research sites. In total 40 interpretation workshops were held, each lasting a minimum of three hours.

Biographical data analysis workshops: focusing on the 'lived life'

The first stage of the process of biographical data analysis was the construction of a chronology of 'objective life events' from the interview transcript. This chronology was stripped of the subject's interpretation and focused on the observable/verifiable facts of the subject's life as they laid them out in the interview. This biographical data chronology was then divided into chunks, which could then be presented, one at a time, in the data analysis workshop.

In the workshop the researcher who had conducted the interview that was being analysed would act as scribe, recording the hypotheses generated around each chunk of data. She asked the participants, as freely as possible, without self-censorship or conscious theorizing, to generate, firstly, *experiencing hypotheses* about how the interviewee might have experienced this chunk of 'lived life' and, secondly, *following hypotheses* about what the interviewee might have done next, in response to each data chunk. For each hypothesis offered, *counter-hypotheses* and *tangential hypotheses* were requested, and participants were encouraged to consider emergent *structural hypotheses*, which offered early summations of an emerging interpretation of the lived life of the interviewee.

At the end of the workshop, each workshop participant spent 15 minutes 'free writing' a summary of the interviewee's lived life, drawing together the hypotheses that they felt to be the most convincing.

After the biographical data analysis workshop, the researcher whose case had been the focus of analysis gathered together the lived life case summaries, along with the extensive notes written of the hypotheses generated, to use in developing her own analysis of the interviewee's lived life, with reference to key turning points and phases in the interviewee's life.

Narrative data analysis workshops: focusing on the 'told story'

To prepare for the second workshop, which focused on the interviewee's narrative, the researcher engaged in a detailed process of text structure sequentialization, which means dividing the transcript into chunks defined by changes within the text of the following: speaker, 'text-sort' and topic. Each chunk contained the page and line number from the transcript, the text-sort and the gist of what was said (enough to serve as a reminder of the verbatim transcript that it summarizes).

The text-sorts that we used to analyse the narrative were:

- argumentation
- evaluation
- description
- report
- generic incident narrative
- particular incident narrative.

In the workshop, these chunks were presented by the researcher, one at a time, asking of the participants the following questions (the full range of answers to which the researcher recorded on flipcharts):

- Why is the interviewee presenting this particular topic, and why at this point?
- Why are they using this text-sort to present it?
- Why might they have stopped where they did?
- What might they be experiencing (in respect of the past, in respect of the present interview situation)?
- How might we interpret the significance of this?
- What counter-hypotheses might there be?
- What previous hypotheses might be strengthened by the new chunk of text?
- What might happen next in the story? (*following hypothesis*)
- What might be the overall pattern of the narrative from now on? (*structural hypothesis*)

At the end of the workshop, participants spent 15 minutes writing a summary of their thoughts about the nature of the interviewee's narrative – what was spoken of, how it was spoken of and why. Due consideration to the experiences, events and periods of life that were discussed, and those that were not, was encouraged in these summaries.

After the narrative data analysis workshop, the researcher gathered together these summaries of the told story, and the notes of the discussions and hypotheses generated during the workshop, in order to develop her own analysis of the case, with ongoing recursive attention to the full transcript and to the material generated from the biographical data analysis workshop.

'Lighter touch' cases

The remaining 47 cases were subject to a lighter touch process of analysis, carried out by the researcher alone but following the same structure, with attention first to the biographical data and then to the narrative.

Case studies

The case studies (both 'intensively analysed' and 'lighter touch') were written up using a template that included basic socio-demographic data about the interviewee; summary of their lived life; summary of their told story/narrative, with a focus on key turning points, struggles, conflict and dilemmas in the story, and emotional expression; intimate citizenship moments and issues; commentary on issues of racialization/minoritization and non-conventionality in the lived life and/or told story; and commentary on interview dynamics.

Ethical issues

The interviewees, the majority of whom were members of racialized/minoritized groups, and all of whom were living intimate lives that were in some way non-normative, shared with us their life stories, including a considerable amount of information about their personal relationships. They invested great trust in the research team, and the responsibility to treat their stories with respect and to protect their identities was paramount to us. We were told stories about experiences of physical and sexual violence and abuse, about abductions, abortions, divorce, forced marriages, pro forma marriages, and about sexual and relationship practices which are often deemed unacceptable by interviewees' families, communities or colleagues. We believe that it is of the utmost importance that these stories are able to inform social scientific knowledge about intimate citizenship, whilst the identities of the interviewees are protected.

In order to secure 'informed consent', we gave each interviewee an Information Sheet about the research in their own language, which we talked through with them at considerable length before asking them to sign a Consent Form, also in their own language. We were very clear with interviewees that they could stop the interview at any time, either for a break or to terminate it entirely. No interviewee broke off the interview or decided to terminate early. We ensured that all interviewees were able to contact the researcher after the interview, by phone and email, so that they could add to, update or withdraw information given in the interview, or receive support after the interview. A small number of interviewees made use of our contact details in this way.

Transcripts of interviews and fieldwork notes were fully anonymized and pseudonymized by the interviewer before any data was shared with the rest of the team. Our process of data analysis involved working collectively with interview material, and this was always carried out with anonymized data and with strong attempts to ensure the confidentiality of the identity of the interviewees. We required participants in the data analysis process from outside the immediate research team to agree to respect the confidentiality of the discussions within the workshops. During the data analysis process, we encountered a number of issues relating to the protection of the identity of interviewees, where interviewees had a highly distinctive individual biography and were either members of small, tightly knit communities and so might be recognizable to others or were 'public figures' in some way. In one or two cases we decided to exclude interviewees from our intensively analysed case studies because we could not be sufficiently certain that we could protect their identities whilst holding onto the depth and richness of attention to biography that our group work method requires. In each of the cases discussed in this book, we were able to ensure the protection of identity by withholding identifying features (e.g. year of birth, place of birth, details about family) and changing (within acceptable parameters) key identifying features (e.g. the exact job/field of employment, university attended, etc.). We tackled these problems collectively, as a research team, and kept the issue of confidentiality and anonymity at the forefront of our minds during the data analysis and writing process.

Notes

1 For instance, according to the 2011 census, each of our capital city regions (as with the rest of the EU) had lower proportions of married couple households, and higher proportions of unmarried cohabiting couple, lone mother and same-sex couple households, as well as higher proportions of single-person households than the national average. https://ec.europa.eu/eurostat/statistics-explained/index.php?title=File:Family_nuclei,_national_averages_and_capital_regions,_2011_(%25_share_of_all_family_nuclei)_PITEU17.png#file (accessed 11 August 2019).

Family nuclei types by national average country and capital region, 2011 (% of all family nuclei):

Country	Capital region	Married couples – national average	Married couples – capital region	Cohabiting couples – national average	Cohabiting couples – capital region	Single-mother families – national average	Single-mother families – capital region
Bulgaria	Sofia	71.6	66.2	13.7	15.3	11.8	15.8
Portugal	Lisbon	73.8	64.8	11.3	16.4	12.9	16.2
UK	Inner London	64.7	48.9	16.6	22.2	15.8	24.7
Norway	Oslo	63.9	58.6	14.1	14.7	11.9	13.5

2 BA/BSc degrees have only recently been introduced in Bulgaria; prior to this the terminal first degree was at Master's level. All the Bulgarian samples who have completed higher education have higher degrees.

References

Aarset, A. H. (2000) *Rettslig regulering av homoseksuell praksis: 1687–1902*, Institutt for offentlig retts skriftserie, nb. 2/2000.

Aarseth, H. (2007) 'Between Labour and Love: The Re-Erotization of Home-Making in Egalitarian Couples within a Nordic Context', *NORA – Nordic Journal of Feminist and Gender Research*, vol. 15, nos. 2–3, 133–43.

Aarseth, H. (2008) 'Hjemskapingens moderne magi', Doctoral Thesis, Institutt for sosiologi og samfunnsgeografi, Universitetet i Oslo.

Aarseth, H. (2011) *Moderne familieliv. Den likestilte familiens motivasjonsformer* (Oslo: Cappelen Damm Akademisk).

Abbott, A. (2007) 'Against Narrative: A Preface to Lyrical Sociology', *Sociological Theory*, vol. 25, no. 1, 67–99.

Abbott, M. (2003) *Family Affairs: A History of the Family in Twentieth Century England* (London and New York: Routledge).

Adam, B. D. (2010) 'Relationship Innovation in Male Couples', in M. Barker and D. Langdridge (eds.), *Understanding Non-monogamies* (London and New York: Routledge), pp. 55–70.

Adams, C. (1976) *Single Blessedness: Observations on the Single Status in Married Society* (New York: Basic Books).

Against Equality (2017) http://www.againstequality.org/ (accessed 20 September 2020).

Almeida, S. J. (2010) *Homossexuais no Estado Novo* (Lisbon: Sextante Editora).

Alstad, B. (ed.) (1969) *Politikk og samfunn. Norske meninger, bind 2* (Oslo: Pax Forlag).

Alstad, B. (ed.) (1993 [1969]) *Norge, nordmenn og verden. Norske meninger, bind 1* (Oslo: Sigma Langslet).

Altman, D. (1971) *Homosexual: Oppression and Liberation* (New York: Outerbridge & Dienstfrey).

Altman, D. (1997 [1982]) 'Sex, the New Front Line for Gay Politics', in M. Blasius and S. Phelan (eds.), *We are Everywhere. A Historical Sourcebook of Gay and Lesbian Politics* (London and New York: Routledge), pp. 529–34.

Amâncio, L., M. Tavares, T. Joaquim and T. Sousa de Almeida (eds.) (2007) *O Longo Caminho das Mulheres: Feminismos 80 anos depois* (Lisbon: D. Quixote).

Andersen, A. J. (2009) 'Det norske seksuelle medborgerskapet', in W. Mühleisen and Å. Røthing (eds.), *Norske seksualiteter* (Oslo: Cappelen Akademisk), pp. 121–36.

Anderssen, N. and T. Hellesund (2009) 'Heteronormative Consensus in the Norwegian Same-Sex Adoption Debate?', *Journal of Homosexuality*, vol. 56, no.1, 102–20.

Anderssen, N. and H. Slåtten (2008) *Holdninger til lesbiske kvinner, homofile menn, bifile kvinner og menn og transpersoner (LHBT Personer). En landsomfattende representativ spørreundersøkelse* (Bergen: Universitetet i Bergen).

Angelov, Z. (2018) 'Regulatory Basis of the Boarding School in Bulgaria', *Doctorantski chetenia*, vol. 2, 173–82.

Anthias, F. and N. Yuval-Davis (1983) 'Contextualizing Feminism: Gender, Ethnic and Class Divisions', *Feminist Review*, vol. 15, 62–75.

Archer, M. (2007) *Making our Way through the World: Human Reflexivity and Social Mobility* (Cambridge: Cambridge University Press).

Aron, L. and A. Harris (2005) *Relational Psychoanalysis*, vol. 2: *Innovation and Expansion* (Hillsdale, NJ: The Analytic Press).

Astell, M. (1700) *Some Reflections Upon Marriage, Occasioned by the Duke and Dutchess of Mazarine's Case; Which is Also Considered* (London: John Nutt).

Atay, T. (2010) '"Ethnicity within Ethnicity" among the Turkish-Speaking Immigrants in London', *Insight Turkey*, vol. 12, no. 1, 123–38, http://file.setaistanbul.com/Files/Pdf/insight_turkey_vol_12_no_1_2010_atay.pdf (accessed 8 February 2018).

Badgett, M. V. L. (1997) 'Beyond Biased Samples: Challenging the Myth on the Economic Status of Lesbians and Gay Men', in A. Gluckman and B. Reed (eds.), *Homo Economics: Capitalism, Community, and Lesbian and Gay Life* (London: Routledge), pp. 65–86.

Badgett, M. V. L. (2003) *Money, Myths, and Change: The Economic Lives of Lesbians and Gay Men* (Chicago: University of Chicago Press).

Balsam, K. F., E. D. Rothblum and R. E. Wickham (2017) 'Longitudinal Predictors of Relationship Dissolution among Same-sex and Heterosexual Couples', *Couple and Family Psychology: Research and Practice*, vol. 6, no. 4, 247–57.

Barbosa, M. (1981) 'Women in Portugal', *Women's Studies International Quarterly*, vol. 4, no. 4, 477–80.

Barker, M. and D. Langdridge (2010) *Understanding Non-Monogamies* (London and New York: Routledge).

Barker, N. (2006) 'Sex and the Civil Partnership: The Future of (non) Conjugality?', *Feminist Legal Studies*, vol. 14, no. 2, 241–59.

Barker, N. (2013) *Not the Marrying Kind: A Feminist Critique of Same-Sex Marriage* (Basingstoke: Palgrave Macmillan).

Barlow, A., C. Burgoyne, E. Clery and J. Smithson (2008) *Cohabitation and the Law: Myths, Money and the Media*, British Social Attitudes, 24th Report (London, Thousand Oaks, CA, and New Delhi: SAGE).

Barlow, A., S. Duncan and G. James (2002) 'New Labour, the Rationality Mistake and Family Policy in Britain', in A. Carling, Duncan S. and Edwards R. (eds.), *Analysing Families: Morality and Rationality in Policy and Practice* (London and New York: Routledge), pp. 110–28.

Barreno, M. I., M. T. Horta and M. Velho da Costa (1994) *The Three Marias: New Portuguese Letters* (London: Readers International).

Barrett, M. and M. McIntosh (1982) *The Anti-Social Family* (London: Verso Books).

Barrett, M. and M. McIntosh (1985) 'Ethnocentrism and Socialist-Feminist Theory', *Feminist Review*, vol. 20, no. 1, 23–47.

Bastos, J. G. P. and S. P. Bastos (2000) *Ciganos em Portugal, Hoje* (Lisbon: Centro de Estudos de Migrações e Minorias Étnicas, FCSH).

Bastos, S. P. (1997) *Estado Novo e os Seus Vadios. Contribuição para o estudo das identidades marginais e a sua repressão* (Lisbon: Dom Quixote).

Bauman, Z. (2000) *Liquid Modernity* (Cambridge, Oxford and Malden, MA: Polity Press).

Bawin-Legros, B. (2004) 'Intimacy and the New Sentimental Order', *Current Sociology*, vol. 52, no. 2, 241–50.

Beaujouan, E. and M. Ní Bhrolcháin (2011) *Cohabitation and Marriage in Britain Since the 1970s. Population Trends no. 145* (Southampton: ESRC Centre, Southhampton University), https://link.springer.com/content/pdf/10.1057%2Fpt.2011.16.pdf (accessed 20 September 2020).

Beck, U. (1992) *Risk Society: Towards a New Modernity* (London, Thousand Oaks, CA, and New Delhi: SAGE).

Beck, U. and E. Beck-Gernsheim (1995) *The Normal Chaos of Love* (Cambridge, Oxford and Malden, MA: Polity Press).

Beck, U. and E. Beck-Gernsheim (2002) *Individualization. Institutionalized Individualism and its Social and Political Consequences* (London, Thousand Oaks, CA and New Delhi: SAGE).

Becker, S. O., S. Bentolila, A. Fernandes and A. Ichino (2005) *Youth Emancipation and Perceived Job Insecurity of Parents and Children*, IZA Discussion Paper No. 1836 (Bonn: Institute for the Study of Labor).

Beebe, B. and E. McCrorie (2010) 'The Optimum Midrange: Infant Research, Literature and Romantic Attachment', *Attachment: New Directions on Psychotherapy and Relational Psychoanalysis*, vol. 4, 39–58.

Behrensen, M. and E. Stanoeva (2019) 'Hypochondriac Identities: Gender and Nationalism in Bulgaria and Germany', In M. Behrensen, M. Heimbach-Steins and L. Hennig (eds.), *Gender – Nation – Religion* (Frankfurt and New York: Campus Verlag), pp. 147–88.

Bell, D. and J. Binnie (2000) *The Sexual Citizen: Queer Politics and Beyond* (Cambridge, Oxford and Malden, MA: Polity Press).

Benedict, R. (1946) *The Chrysanthemum and the Sword* (Boston, MA: Houghton Mifflin).

Benjamin, J. (1988) *The Bonds of Love: Psychoanalysis, Feminism and the Problem of Domination* (New York: Pantheon).

Benjamin, J. (1995) *Like Subjects, Love Objects: Essays on Recognition and Sexual Difference* (New Haven, CT: Yale University Press).

Benjamin, J. (1998) *Shadow of the Other: Intersubjectivity and Gender in Psychoanalysis* (London and New York: Routledge).

Bennett, J. M. (2000) '"Lesbian-Like" and the Social History of Lesbianisms', *Journal of the History of Sexuality*, vol. 9, nos. 1–2, 1–24.

Benson, S. (1981) *Ambiguous Ethnicity: Interracial Families in London* (Cambridge, UK: Cambridge University Press).

Bereswill, M., C. Morgenroth and P. Redman (eds.) (2010) 'Alfred Lorenzer and the Depthhermeneutic Method', *Psychoanalysis, Culture & Society*, vol. 15, no. 3, 221–50.

Bergh, A. and C. Bjørnskov (2011) 'Historical Trust Levels Predict the Current Size of the Welfare State', *Kyklos. International Review for Social Sciences*, vol. 64, no. 1, 1–19.

Berlant, L. (2000) (ed.) *Intimacy* (Chicago: University of Chicago Press).

Berlant, L. (2001) 'Love (A Queer Feeling)', in T. Dean and C. Lane (eds.), *Psychoanalysis and Homosexuality* (Chicago: Chicago University Press), pp. 432–51.

Berlant, L. (2011) *Cruel Optimism* (Durham, NC: Duke University Press).

Berlant, L. and M. Warner (1998) 'Sex in Public', *Critical Inquiry*, vol. 24, no. 2, 547–66.

Bersani, L. (1987) 'Is the Rectum a Grave?', in D. Crimp and L. Bersani (eds.), *AIDS: Cultural Analysis/Cultural Activism* (Cambridge, MA: MIT Press), pp. 197–222.

Bhavnani, K. K. and M. Coulson (1986) 'Transforming Socialist-Feminism: The Challenge of Racism', *Feminist Review*, vol. 23, no. 1, 81–92.

Bjørnson, Ø. (1994) *Langsomt ble landet et velferdssamfunn: trygdens historie 1894–1994* (Oslo: Ad notam Gyldendal).

Blair, K. L. and C. F. Pukall (2014) 'Can Less be More? Comparing Duration vs. Frequency of Sexual Encounters in Same-sex and Mixed-sex Relationships', *The Canadian Journal of Human Sexuality*, vol. 23, no. 2, 123–36.

Blom, I. (2005) 'Brudd og kontinuitet. Fra 1950 mot årtusenskiftet', in I. Blom and S. Sogner (eds.), *Med kjønnsperspektiv på norsk historie: fra vikingtid til 2000-årsskiftet* (Oslo: Cappelen Akademisk), pp. 333–90.

Blom, I. (2015) 'Ugifte mødre – fra moralsk avvik til anerkjent familieform; norsk lovgivning i skandinavisk perspektiv fra slutten av 1800-tallet til 1980', *Tidsskrift for velferdsforskning*, vol. 18, no. 4, 318–27.

Bollas, C. (1995) *Cracking Up: The Work of Unconscious Experience* (London: Routledge).

Bonnevie, M. (1932) *Ekteskap og arbeide* (Oslo: Some).

Bourdieu, P. (1991) *Language and Symbolic Power* (Cambridge, MA: Harvard University Press).

Bowlby, J. (1969) *Attachment and Loss*, vol. 1: *Attachment* (New York: Basic Books).

Bradby, H. (1999) 'Negotiating Marriage: Young Punjabi Women's Assessment of their Individual and Family Interests', in R. Barot, H. Bradley and S. Fenton (eds.), *Ethnicity, Gender and Social Change* (Basingstoke: Palgrave Macmillan), pp. 152–66.

Brah, A. and S. Shaw (1992) *Working Choices: South Asian Women and the Labour Market.* (Sheffield, England: Employment Department). http://hdl.voced.edu.au/10707/105803 (accessed 20 September 2020).

Bray, A. (1982) *Homosexuality in Renaissance England* (London: Gay Men's Press).

Breckner, R. and S. Rupp (2002) 'Appendix A: Discovering biographies in changing social worlds: the biographic-interpretive method', in P. Chamberlayne, M. Rustin and T. Wengraf (eds.), *Biography and Social Exclusion in Europe: Experiences and Life Journeys* (Bristol: Policy Press).

Bredal, A. (2006) 'Vi er jo en familie'. Arrangerte ekteskap, autonomi og fellesskap blant unge norsk-asiater (Oslo: Unipax).

Brevig, A. (1985) Du kan vel sove i stua? Om ensliges kamp for sine rettigheter (Oslo: Friundervisningens Forlag).

Brevig, A. and A. Husbyn (1979) Sterkest – Alene? (Oslo: Gyldendal).

Bringle, R. (1995) 'Sexual Jealousy in the Relationships of Homosexual and Heterosexual Men: 1980 and 1994', Personal Relationships, vol. 2, 313–25.

Brittain, Vera (1920) The Superfluous Woman. Available from https://allpoetry.com/Vera-Brittain (accessed 11 September 2020).

Britton, R. (1998) Belief and Imagination: Explorations in Psychoanalysis (Hove: Routledge).

Brunnbauer, U. (2008) 'Making Bulgarians Socialist: The Fatherland Front in Communist Bulgaria (1944–1989)', East European Politics and Societies, vol. 22, no. 1, 44–79.

Brunnbauer, U. and K. Tylor (2012) 'Creating a Socialist Way of Life', in K. Kaser (ed.), Household and Family in the Balkans (Berlin: LIT), pp. 283–312.

Bryant, A. S. and N. Demian (1994) 'Relationship Characteristics of American Gays and Lesbians: Findings from a National Survey', Journal of Gay & Lesbian Social Services, vol. 1, no. 2, 101–17.

Budgeon, S. (2008) 'Couple Culture and the Production of Singleness', Sexualities, vol. 11, no. 3, 301–25.

Buksenstuz, U. (2000) Малцинствената политика в България. Политиката на БКП към евреи, роми, помаци и турци (1944–1989) (Sofia: International Centre for Minority Studies and Intercultural Relations). Bulgarian Constitutional Court (2018) Decision 13 from 27 July 2018. Sofia. Available from: http://constcourt.bg/bg/Acts/GetHtmlContent/f278a156-9d25-412d-a064-6ffd6f997310 (accessed 20 September 2020).

Bulgarian Helsinki Committee (2001) Bulgarian Legislation about Homosexuals, Special Thematic Reports, http://issuu.com/bghelsinki/docs/name1740a4?viewMode=magazine (accessed 20 September 2020).

Bulgarian Helsinki Committee (2019) Human Rights in Bulgaria in 2018 [in Bulgarian] (Sofia: Sibi), http://www.bghelsinki.org/media/uploads/annual_reports/annual-bhc-report-2018-issn-2367-6930-bg.pdf (accessed 20 September 2020).

Butler, J. (1990) Gender Trouble: Feminism and the Subversion of Identity (London and New York: Routledge).

Butler, J. (1991) 'Imitation and Gender Insubordination', in D. Fuss (ed.), Inside/Out: Lesbian Theories, Gay Theories (London and New York: Routledge), pp. 13–31.

Butler, J. (1993) Bodies That Matter: On the Discursive Limits of Sex (London and New York: Routledge).

Butler, J. (1997) The Psychic Life of Power: Theories in Subjection (Stanford, CT: Stanford University Press).

Butler, J. (2004) Undoing Gender (London and New York: Routledge).

Butler, J. E. (ed.) (1869) Woman's Work and Woman's Culture: A Series of Essays (Cambridge, UK: Cambridge University Press).

Byrne, A. and D. Carr (2005) 'Caught in the Cultural Lag: The Stigma of Singlehood', Psychological Inquiry, vol. 16, no. 2, 84–141.

Caballero, C., R. Edwards and D. Smith (2008) 'Cultures of Mixing: Understanding Partnerships Across Ethnicity', Twenty-First Century Society: Journal of the Academy of Social Sciences, vol. 3, no. 1, 49–63.

Cabinet Office (2008) Families in Britain: An Evidence Paper, Department for Children, Schools and Families, https://dera.ioe.ac.uk/9502/1/Families%20Evidence%20Paper%20v0%20 32%20181202.pdf (accessed 20 September 2020).

Calhoun, C. (2000) Feminism, the Family, and the Politics of the Closet (Oxford: Oxford University Press).

Calhoun, C. (2008) 'In Defense of Same-Sex Marriage', in A. Soble and N. P. Power (eds.), The Philosophy of Sex: Contemporary Readings (London: Rowman and Littlefield), pp. 197–212.

Canguilhem, G. (1994) A Vital Rationalist (New York: Zone Books).

Carabine, J. (ed.) (2004) Sexualities: Personal Lives and Social Policy (Milton Keynes: Open University Press).

Carby, H. (1982) 'White Woman Listen! Black Feminism and the Boundaries of Sisterhood', in Centre for Contemporary Cultural Studies (ed.), *The Empire Strikes Back: Race and Racism in 70s Britain* (London: Hutchinson), pp. 212–35.

Cardona, M. J. (1997) *Para a História da Educação de Infância em Portugal. O Discurso Oficial (1834–1990).* Colecção Infância No. 3 (Porto: Porto Editora).

Cargan, L. (2007) *Being Single on Noah's Ark* (Lanham, MD: Rowman & Littlefield).

Carling, A. (2002) 'Family Policy, Social Theory and the State', in A. Carling, S. Duncan and R. Edwards (eds.), *Analysing Families: Morality and Rationality in Policy and Practice* (London and New York: Routledge), pp. 3–20.

Carling, A., S. Duncan and R. Edwards (eds.) (2002) *Analysing Families: Morality and Rationality in Policy and Practice* (London and New York: Routledge).

Carrigan, M. A. (2011a) 'There's More to Life than Sex? Difference and Commonality within the Asexual Community', *Sexualities*, vol. 14, no. 4, 462–78.

Carrigan, M. A. (2011b) '"How Do You Know You Don't Like It if You Haven't Tried It?" Asexual Agency and the Sexual Assumption', in T. G. Morrison (ed.), *Sexual Minority Research in the New Millennium* (New York: Nova Science), pp. 3–20.

Carrigan, M., K. Gupta and T. G. Morrison (2013) 'Asexuality Special Theme Issue Editorial', *Psychology & Sexuality*, vol. 4, no. 2, 111–20.

Carter, J. (2010) 'Why Marry? Young Women Talk about Relationships, Marriage and Love', Doctoral Thesis, Womens Studies, University of York.

Carter, J. and S. Duncan (2018) *Reinventing Couples: Tradition, Agency and Bricolage* (London: Palgrave Macmillan).

Casa-Nova, M. J. (2009) *Etnografia e Produção de Conhecimento. Reflexões Críticas a partir de uma Investigação com Ciganos Portugueses* (Lisbon: ACIDI).

Castellano, R., P. Velotti and G. C. Zavattini (2010) *What Makes Us Stay Together? Attachment and the Outcomes of Couple Relationships* (London: Karnac).

Celello, K. (2009) *Making Marriage Work: A History of Marriage and Divorce in the Twentieth-Century United States* (Chapel Hill: University of North Carolina Press).

Chakrabarty, D. (2008 [2000]) *Provincializing Europe: Postcolonial Thought and Historical Difference* (Princeton, NJ and Oxford: Princeton University Press).

Chamberlayne, P., Tod M. Rustin and T. Wengraf (eds.) (2002) *Biography and Social Exclusion in Europe: Experiences and Life Journeys* (Bristol: Policy Press).

Chandler, J. (1991) *Women without Husbands: An Exploration of the Margins of Marriage* (London: Macmillan).

Chandler, J., M. Williams, M. Maconachie, T. Collett and B. Dodgeon (2004) 'Living Alone: Its Place in Household Formation and Change', *Social Research Online*, vol. 9, no. 3.

Charsley, K. A. H. (2013) *Transnational Pakistani Connections: Marrying 'Back Home'* (London and New York: Routledge).

Chasin, A. (2001) *Selling Out: The Gay and Lesbian Movement Goes to Market* (London: Palgrave Macmillan).

Chasteen, A. L. (1994) '"The World Around Me": The Environment and Single Women', *Sex Roles*, vol. 31, nos. 5–6, 309–28.

Chauncey, G. (2004) *Why Marriage? The History Shaping Today's Debate over Gay Equality* (New York: Basic Books).

Cherlin, A. J. (2004) 'The Deindustrialization of American Marriage', *Journal of Marriage and Family*, vol. 66, no. 4, 848–61.

Cherlin, A. J. (2005) 'American Marriage in the Early Twenty-First Century', *The Future of Children*, vol. 15, no. 2, 33–55.

Cherlin, A. J. (2010) *The Marriage Go-Round: The State of Marriage and the Family in America Today* (New York: Alfred A. Knopf).

Chodorow, N. (1978) *The Reproduction of Mothering. Psychoanalysis and the Sociology of Gender* (Berkeley and Los Angeles: University of California Press).

Clarke, J. (2008) 'Living With/in and Without Neoliberalism', *Focaal. European Journal of Anthropology*, vol. 51, 135–47.

Clarke, J. and A. Cochrane (1993) *Comparing Welfare States: Britain in International Context* (London: SAGE).

Clarke, J., K. Coll, E. Dagnino and C. Neveu (2014) *Disputing Citizenship* (Bristol: Policy Press).

Clayhills, H. (1991) *Kvinnohistorisk uppslagsbok* (Stockholm: Raben & Sjögren).

Cobb, M. (2012) *Single: Arguments for the Uncoupled* (New York and London: New York University Press).

Coelho, A. (1995) *Os Ciganos de Portugal com um Estudo sobre o Calao* (Lisbon: Pub. Dom Quixote).

Coelho, F. P. and G. Oliveira (2008) *Curso de Direito da Família* (Coimbra: Coimbra Editora).

Coelho, L. (2005) 'Participação das mulheres na actividade e conciliação entre vida familiar e vida professional, Paper for the seminar on Núcleo de Estudos sobre Governação e Instituições da Economia', CES, University of Coimbra, March 2005.

Coldey, B. M. (1995) *Child Migration to Catholic Institutions in Australia* (Box Hill: Tamanaraik).

Collett, C. (2017 [1854/5]) *The District Governor's Daughters* (London: Norvik Press).

Collins, J., E. Leib and D. Markel (2008) 'Punishing Family Status', *Boston University Law Review*, vol. 88, 1327–423.

Commonwealth of Australia (2001) *Lost Innocents: Righting the Record – Report on Child Migration*, https://www.aph.gov.au/Parliamentary_Business/Committees/Senate/Community_Affairs/Completed_inquiries/1999-02/child_migrat/report/index (accessed 20 September 2020).

Conrad, R. E. (2010) *Against Equality: Queer Critiques of Gay Marriage* (Lewiston, ME: Against Equality Publishing Collective).

Conservatives (2011) *David Cameron: Leadership for a Better Britain*, https://www.conservative-councillors.com/news/leadership-better-britain (accessed 19 December 2017).

Cook, H. (2005) 'The English Sexual Revolution: Technology and Social Change', *History Workshop Journal*, vol. 59, no. 1, 109–28.

Cook, M. (2014) *Queer Domesticities: Homosexuality and Home Life in Twentieth-Century* (London, Basingstoke and New York: Palgrave).

Coontz, S. (2004) 'The World Historical Transformation of Marriage', *Journal of Marriage and Family*, vol. 66, 974–9.

Coontz, S. (2005) *Marriage, a History: From Obedience to Intimacy or How Love Conquered Marriage* (New York: Viking).

Cooper, D. (1994) *Sexing the City* (London: Rivers Oram).

Cooper, D. (1995) *Power in Struggle: Feminism, Sexuality and the State* (New York: New York University Press).

Costa, E. M. (1995) 'Os ciganos em Portugal: breve história de uma exclusão', in L. Cortesão and F. Pinto (eds.), *O povo cigano: cidadãos na sombra* (Porto: Ed. Afrontamento), pp. 13–20.

Council of Europe (1981) *Recommendation 924*, Discrimination Against Homosexuals, http://assembly.coe.int/nw/xml/XRef/Xref-XML2HTML-en.asp?fileid=14958&lang=en (accessed 20 September 2020).

Council of Ministers (2008a) Проект за Семеен кодекс, Judicial Commission, Session 8, 01.04.2008, Number 802-01-37, http://www.parliament.bg/bills/40/802-01-37.pdf (accessed 20 September 2020).

Council of Ministers (2008b) Стенограми от пленарни заседания, 02.10.2008, http://www.parliament.bg/bg/plenaryst/ns/2/period/2008-10 (accessed 4 January 2018).

Cover, R. (2006) 'Producing Norms: Same-Sex Marriage, Refiguring Kinship and the Cultural Groundswell of Queer Coupledom', *Reconstruction: Studies in Contemporary Culture*, vol. 6, no. 2, 1–14.

CRFR (Centre for Research on Families and Relationships) (2002) 'Divorce in Scotland', Research Briefing number 6, https://era.ed.ac.uk/bitstream/handle/1842/2804/Resbriefing6.pdf?sequence=1 (accessed 20 September 2020).

Crossley, S. (2015) '"Realising the (Troubled) Family", "Crafting the Neoliberal State"', *Families, Relationships and Societies*, vol. 5, no. 2, 263–79.

Crowhurst, I., S. Roseneil, T. Hellesund, A. C. Santos and M. Stoilova (2013) 'Close encounters: researching intimate lives in Europe', *International Journal of Social Research Methodology*, vol. 16, no. 6, 525–33.

Dale, A. (2008) *Migration, Marriage and Employment Among Indian, Pakistani and Bangladeshi Residents in the UK*. Cathie Marsh Centre for Census and Survery Research. CCSR Working Paper 2008-2, http://hummedia.manchester.ac.uk/institutes/cmist/archive-publications/working-papers/2008/2008-02-migration-marriage-and-employment.pdf (accessed 20 September 2020).

Dale, A., E. Fieldhouse, N. Shaheen and V. Kalra (2002) 'The Labour Market Prospects for Pakistani and Bangladeshi Women', *Work, Employment and Society*, vol. 16, no. 1, 2–25.

Daly, M. (2000) *The Gender Division of Welfare: The Impact of the British and German Welfare States* (Cambridge: Cambridge University Press).

Daly, M. (2010) 'Shifts in Family Policy in the UK Under New Labour', *Journal of European Social Policy*, vol. 20, no. 5, 433–43.

Daly, M. (2011) 'What Adult Worker Model? A Critical Look at Recent Social Policy Reform in Europe From a Gender and Family Perspective', *Social Politics*, vol. 18, no. 1, 1–23.

Daly, M. and K. Rake (2003) *Gender and the Welfare State: Care, Work and Welfare in Europe and the USA* (Cambridge and Malden, MA: Polity Press).

Daly, M. and K. Scheiwe (2010) 'Individualisation and Personal Obligations – Social Policy, Family Policy, and Law Reform in Germany and the UK', *International Journal of Law, Policy and the Family*, vol. 24, no. 2, 177–97.

Danielsen, H. (2002) *Husmorhistorier* (Oslo: Spartacus Forlag).

Danielsen, H. K. Ludvigsen and W. Mühleisen (2012) Governing Couple-Sexuality: Publically Funded Couples' Courses in Norway', *Culture, Health and Society*, vol. 14, no. 6, 645–58.

Danielsen, H. and W. Mühleisen (2009a) 'Statens oppskrift på parseksualiteten', in W. Mühleisen and Å. Røthing (eds.), *Norske seksualiteter* (Oslo: Cappelen Damm Akademisk), pp. 79–98.

Danielsen, H. and W. Mühleisen (2009b) 'Statens parkurs Godt Samliv. Idealer og normer for samliv og kommunikasjon', *Tidsskrift for samfunnsforskning*, vol. 50, 3–23.

Daskalova, K. (1999) Феминизъм и равенство в българския XX век', in R. Muharska (ed.), Майки и дъщери. Поколения и посоки в българския феминизъм (Sofia: Polis), pp. 80–105.

Daskalova, K. (2005) 'Kym istoriq na bylgarskite socialni dvijenia v bulgaria: bylgarskite feminismi (1857–1944)', in D. Koleva and M. Grekova (eds.), *Kulturata: Granici I Sredstva* (Sofia: Kl. Ohridski), pp. 301–34.

Daugstad, G. (2006) *Grenseløs kjærlighet? Familieinnvandring og ekteskapsmønstre i det flerkulturelle Norge*, Rapporter 2006/39, Statistisk sentralbyrå.

Davidoff, L., M. Doolittle, J. Fink and K. Holden (1999) *The Family Story: Blood, Contract and Intimacy 1830–1960* (Harlow: Longman).

Davidoff, L. and C. Hall (1987) *Family Fortunes: Men and Women of the English Middle Class 1780–1850* (London and New York: Routledge).

Davis, S. N. (2010) 'Is Justice Contextual? Married Women's Perceptions of Fairness of the Division of Household Labor in 12 Nations', *Journal of Comparative Family Studies*, vol. 41, no. 1, 19–39.

Dawson, M., L. McDonnell and S. Scott (2016) 'Negotiating the boundaries of intimacy: the personal lives of asexual people', *The Sociological Review*, vol. 64, no. 2, 349–65.

de Aguiar, A. A. (1926) 'Evolução da pederastia e do lesbismo na Europa: Contribuição para o estudo da inversão sexual', *Arquivo da Universidade de Lisboa*, vol. 11, 335–620.

Decree on Marriage (1945) *State Gazette*, Vol. 108/12.05.1945.

Deeming, C. (2017) 'The Lost and the New "Liberal World" of Welfare Capitalism: A Critical Assessment of Gøsta Esping-Andersen's The Three Worlds of Welfare Capitalism a Quarter Century Later', *Social Policy & Society*, vol. 16, no. 3, 1–18.

Delev, P., V. Kacunov, E. Kalinova, I. Baeva and B. Dobrev (eds.) (2006) *Istoriq i civilizacia* (Sofia: Trud).

Delhey, J. and K. Newton (2005) 'Predicting Cross-National Levels of Social Trust: Global Pattern or Nordic Exceptionalism?', *European Sociological Review*, vol. 21, no. 4, 311–27.

Delphy, C. and D. Leonard (1992) *Familiar Exploitation: A New Analysis of Marriage in Contemporary Western Societies* (Cambridge, Oxford and Malden, MA: Polity Press).

D'Emilio, J. (1992) *Making Trouble: Essays on Gay History, Politics, and the University* (London and New York: Routledge).

DePaulo, B. M. (2006) *Singled Out: How Singles Are Stereotyped, Stigmatized, and Ignored, and Still Live Happily Ever After* (New York: St Martin's Press).

DePaulo, B. M. (2011) *Singlism: What It Is, Why It Matters, and How to Stop It* (Charleston, SC: DoubleDoor Books).

DePaulo, B. M. and W. L. Morris (2005) 'Singles in Society and in Science', *Psychological Inquiry*, vol. 16, nos. 2–3, 57–83.

Deyanova, L. (2004 [1948]) Символна еуфория, символен терор', in A. Vacheva, Y. Eftimov and G. Chobanov (eds.), *Kultura i Kritika*, vol 4: *Ideologiqta – Nachin na upotreba* (Varna: LiterNet), n.p.

Diário de Notícias, (2006) 'O dia em que as mulheres portuguesas saíram à rua'. Available online at https://www.dn.pt/arquivo/2006/o-dia-em-que-as-mulheres-portuguesas-sairam-a-rua-635052.html (accessed 20 September 2020).

Dias, E. C., I. Alves, N. Valente and S. Aires (2006) *Comunidades Ciganas: Representações e Dinâmicas de Exclusão / Integração* (Lisbon: ACIME).

Diduck, A. and F. Kaganas (2006) *Family Law, Gender and the State* (Oxford: Hart).

Dimen, M. (2003) *Sexuality, Intimacy, Power: Relational Perspectives* (London and New York: Routledge).

Dimitrova, E. K. (2006) 'Second Demographic Transition in Bulgaria: Preconditions, Transformations, Implications', Doctoral Thesis, Centre for Population Studies, Bulgarian Academy of Science, Sofia.

Dinkova, M. (2001) 'Майчинството в България между XX и XXI век', in C. Kiuranov and M. Dinkova (eds.), *Съвременният свят и жената* (Sofia: ACCA-Me).

DNF-48 (1951) 'Hva vi vil'. Available online at Skeivt arkiv, https://skeivtarkiv.no/dnf-48s-forste-brosjyre (accessed 20 September 2020).

Doan, L. (2001) *Fashioning Sapphism: The Origins of Modern English Lesbian Culture* (New York: Columbia University Press).

Dobrowski, A. and J. Jenson (2004) 'Shifting Representations of Citizenship: Canadian Politics of "Women" and "Children"', *Social Politics*, vol. 11, no. 2, 154–80.

Doncheva, V. (2002) *За гражданския и църк?овен брак* [On Civil and Religious Marriage], http://www.djure.net/feature.php?id=14 (accessed 23 August 2012).

Dragova, S. (2001) 'Самотното майчинство – социални и емоционални аспекти на самотата и родителски стилове на възпитание', *Психологични изследвания*, vol. 4, no. 1, 109–14.

Drescher, J. (2002) 'Homosexuality and Psychoanalysis Revisited', *Journal of Gay and Lesbian Mental Health*, vol. 6, no. 1, 1–8.

Duggan, L. (1994) 'Queering the State', *Social Text*, vol. 39, 1–14.

Duggan, L. (2002) 'The New Homonormativity: The Sexual Politics of Neoliberalism', in R. Castronovo and D. Nelson (eds.), *Materializing Democracy: Toward a Revitalized Cultural Politics* (Durham, NC: Duke University Press), pp. 175–94.

Duggan, L. (2003) *The Twilight of Equality: Neoliberalism, Cultural Politics, and the Attack on Democracy* (Boston, MA: Beacon Press).

Duggan, L. (2012) 'Beyond Marriage: Democracy, Equality, and Kinship for a New Century', *The Scholar & Feminist Online*, vol. 10, no. 1 and vol. 10, no. 2 (Fall 2011/ Spring 2012), http://sfonline.barnard.edu/a-new-queer-agenda/beyond-marriage-democracy-equality-and-kinship-for-a-new-century/ (accessed 20 September 2020)

Duncan, S. (1995) 'Theorizing European Gender Systems', *Journal of European Social Policy*, vol. 5, no. 4, 263–84.

Duncan, S. (2011) 'Personal Life, Pragmatism and Bricolage', *Sociological Research Online*, vol. 4, no. 16, 1–12.

Duncan, S., A. Barlow and G. James (2005) 'Why Don't They Marry? Cohabitation, Commitment and DIY Marriage', *Child and Family Law Quarterly*, vol. 17, no. 3, 383–98.

Duncan, S., J. Carter, M. Phillips, S. Roseneil and M. Stoilova (2012) 'Legal Rights for People who "Live Apart Together"?', *Journal of Social Welfare and Family Law*, vol. 34, no. 4, 443–58.

Duncan, S., J. Carter, M. Phillips, S. Roseneil and M. Stoilova (2013) 'Why do People Live Apart Together?', *Families, Relationships and Societies*, vol. 2, no. 3, 323–38.

Duncan, S., M. Phillips, J. Carter, S. Roseneil and M. Stoilova (2014) 'Practices and Perceptions of Living Apart Together', *Family Science*, vol. 5, no. 1, 1–10.

Duncombe, J. and D. Marsden (1993) 'Love and Intimacy: The Gender Division of Emotion and Emotion Work', *Sociology*, vol. 27, no. 2, 221–41.

Duncombe, J. and D. Marsden (1995) '"Workkaholics" and "Whingeing Women": Theorising Intimacy and Emotion Work – The Last Frontier of Gender Inequality?', *Sociological Review*, vol. 43, no. 1, 150–69.

Durham, M. (1991) *Sex and Politics: The Family, Morality and the Thatcher Years* (Basingstoke: Macmillan).

Durham, M. (2001) 'The Conservative Party, New Labour and the Politics of the Family', *Parliamentary Affairs*, vol. 54, 459–74.

Durkheim, E. (2014 [1893]) *The Division of Labour in Society* (New York: The Free Press).

Dustin, M., N. Ferreira and S. Millns (eds.) (2019) *Gender and Queer Perspectives on Brexit* (Cham: Palgrave Macmillan).

DWP (Department for Work and Pensions) (2014) *Family Test: assessing the impact of policies on families*, https://www.gov.uk/government/publications/family-test-assessing-the-impact-of-policies-on-families (accessed 20 September 2020).

Dybendal, K. E. and T. Noack (2010) 'Fra registrert partnerskap til felles ekteskapslov', *SSB magasinet*, https://www.ssb.no/befolkning/artikler-og-publikasjoner/fra-registrert-partner-skap-til-felles-ekteskapslov (accessed 20 September 2020).

EC (European Commission) (2009) *Special Eurobarometer 317: Discrimination in the EU in 2009*, http://ec.europa.eu/commfrontoffice/publicopinion/archives/ebs/ebs_317_en.pdf (accessed 20 September 2020).

EC (European Commission) (2012) *Eurobarometer 393: Discrimination in the EU in 2012*, http://ec.europa.eu/commfrontoffice/publicopinion/archives/ebs/ebs_393_en.pdf (accessed 20 September 2020).

EC (European Commission) (2015) *Eurobarometer Report: Discrimination in the EU, Fact Sheet Portugal*, http://ec.europa.eu/COMMFrontOffice/publicopinion/index.cfm/Survey/getSurveyDetail/instruments/SPECIAL/surveyKy/2077 (accessed 20 September 2020).

EC (European Commission) (2017a) *Eurobarometer: Gender Equality*, http://ec.europa.eu/commfrontoffice/publicopinion/index.cfm/Survey/getSurveyDetail/instruments/SPECIAL/surveyKy/2154 (accessed 1 March 2018).

EC (European Commission) (2017b) *Population and Social Conditions*, http://ec.europa.eu/eurostat/ (accessed 6 December 2017).

Edlund, J. (2006) 'Trust in the Capability of the Welfare State and General Welfare State Support: Sweden 1997–2002', *Acta Sociologica*, vol. 49, no. 4, 395–417.

Edwards, R. and V. Gillies (2016) 'Family Policy: The Mods and Rockers', in H. Bochel and M. Powell (eds.), *The Coalition Government and Social Policy* (Bristol: Policy Press), pp. 243–64.

Eekelaar, J. (2013) 'Then and Now: Family Law's Direction of Travel', *Journal of Social Welfare and Family Law*, vol. 35, no. 4, 415–25.

Eekelaar, J. and M. Maclean (2013) *Family Justice: The Work of Family Judges in Uncertain Times* (Oxford: Hart).

Eggebø, H. (2012) 'The Regulation of Marriage Migration to Norway', Doctoral Thesis, Department of Sociology, Universitetet i Bergen.

Eggebø, H. (2013a) 'A Real Marriage? Applying for Marriage Migration to Norway', *Journal of Ethnic and Migration Studies*, vol. 39, no. 5, 773–89.

Eggebø, H. (2013b) '"With a Heavy Heart": Ethics, Emotions and Rationality in Norwegian Immigration Administration', *Sociology*, vol. 47, no. 2, 301–17.

Elias, N. (1978 [1939]) *The Civilizing Process*, vol, 1: *The History of Manners* (Oxford: Basil Blackwell).

Ellingsæter, A. L. and A. Leira (eds.) (2006) *Policing Parenthood in Scandinavia: Gender Relations in Welfare States* (Bristol: Policy Press).

Ellingsæter, A. L. and E. Pedersen (2016) 'Institutional Trust: Family Policy and Fertility in Norway', *Social Politics: International Studies in Gender, State and Society*, vol. 23, no. 1, 119–41.

Emens, E. F. (2004) 'Monogamy's Law: Compulsory Monogamy and Polyamorous Existence', *New York University Review of Law and Social Change*, vol. 29, no. 2, 277–376.

Emerson, R. M., R. I. Fretz and L. L. Shaw (1995) *Writing Ethnographic Fieldnotes* (Chicago: University of Chicago Press).

Emery, R. E. (2013) *Cultural Sociology of Divorce: An Encyclopedia* (Thousand Oaks, CA, London and New Delhi: SAGE).

Eng, D. L., J. E. Muñoz and J. Halberstam (2005) 'Introduction: What's Queer About Queer Studies Now?', *Social Text*, vol. 84–5, 1–17.

Ensliges Landsforbund (2017) Ensliges Landsforbund homepage, http://www.ensliges.no/ (accessed 17 December 2017).

Eskridge, W. N. (1996) *Case for Same-sex Marriage: From Sexual Liberty to Civilized Commitment* (New York: The Free Press).

Esping-Andersen, G. (1990) *The Three Worlds of Welfare Capitalism* (Cambridge, UK: Polity Press).

Esping-Andersen, G. (1999) *Social Foundations of Postindustrial Economies* (Oxford: Oxford University Press).

Esping-Andersen, G., D. Gallie, A. Hemerijck and J. Myles (2002) *Why We Need a New Welfare State* (Oxford: Oxford University Press).

Ettinger, B. L. (2006) 'Matrixial Trans-subjectivity', *Theory, Culture and Society*, vol. 23, nos. 2–3, 218–22.

Eurostat (2019) Demography and Migration statistics, https://ec.europa.eu/eurostat/web/popu lation-demography-migration-projections/data/main-tables (accessed 11 August 2019).

Evans, D. (1993) *Sexual Citizenship: The Material Construction of Sexualities* (London: Routledge).

Evans, J. and J. Tonge (2018) 'Partisan and Religious Drivers of Moral Conservatism: Same-Sex Marriage and Abortion in Northern Ireland', *Party Politics*, vol. 24, no. 4, 335–46. http://eprints.whiterose.ac.uk/100349/3/PP%20evans_tonge%20preprint.pdf (accessed 20 September 2020).

Evans, M. (2003) *Love: An Unromantic Discussion* (Cambridge: Polity Press).

Ewald, F. (1990) 'Norms, Discipline and the Law', *Representations*, vol. 30, no. 1, 138–61.

Faderman, L. (1985) *Surpassing the Love of Men: Romantic Friendship and Love Between Women From the Renaissance to the Present* (London: Women's Press).

Felski, R. (1999) 'The Invention of Everyday Life', *New Formations*, vol. 39, 15–31.

Fenger, H. (2005) 'Welfare Regimes in Central Eastern Europe: Incorporating Post-Communist Countries in a Welfare Regime Typology', Netherlands Institute of Government Annual Conference, Nijmegen, 11 November 2005.

Ferguson, A. (2007) 'Gay Marriage: An American and Feminist Dilemma', *Hypatia*, vol. 22, no. 1, 39–57.

Ferreira, S. (2005) 'The Past in the Present: Portuguese Social Security Reform', *Social Policy and Society*, vol. 4, no. 3, 331–8.

Ferreira, V. (1998) 'Engendering Portugal: Social Change, State Politics and Women's Social Mobilization', in A. Costa Pinto (ed.), *Modern Portugal* (Palo Alto, CA: Society for the Promotion of Science and Scholarship), pp. 153–92.

Ferreira, V. (2014) 'Employment and Austerity: Changing Welfare and Gender Regimes in Portugal', in M. Karamessini and J. Rubery (eds.), *Women and Austerity: The Economic Crisis and the Future for Gender Equality* (London: Routledge), pp. 207–27.

Ferrera, M. (1996) 'The "Southern Model" of Welfare in Social Europe', *Journal of European Social Policy*, vol. 6, no. 1, 17–37.

Filipova, G. and M. Pisankaneva (2017) *Rainbow Families sin Bulgaria* (Sofia: Bilitis Resource Centre), http://www.bilitis.org/db/images/RainbowFamilies.pdf (accessed 20 December 2017).

Finch, J. and D. Morgan (1991) 'Marriage in the 1990s', in D. Clark (ed.), *Marriage, Domestic Life and Social Change: Writings for Jacqueline Burgoyne (1944–88)* (London and New York: Routledge), pp. 55–82.

Finch, J. and P. Summerfield (1991) 'Social Reconstruction and the Emergence of Companionate Marriage', in D. Clark (ed.), *Marriage, Domestic Life and Social Change* (London and New York: Routledge), pp. 7–32.

Fink, J. (2000) 'Natural Mothers, Putative Fathers, and Innocent Children: The Definition and Regulation of Parental Relationships Outside Marriage, in England, 1945–1959', *Journal of Family History*, vol. 25, no. 2, 178–95.

Finley Scott, J. (1971) *Internalization of Norms: A Sociological Theory of Moral Commitment* (Englewood Cliffs, NJ: Prentice-Hall).

Firestone, S. (1970) *The Dialectic of Sex: The Case for Feminist Revolution* (New York: William Morrow and Co.).

Firestone, S. and A. Koedt (eds.) (1970) *Notes From the Second Year: Women's Liberation* (New York: Firestone and Koedt).

Fjell, T. I. (2008) *Å si nei til meningen med livet?: en kulturvitenskapelig analyse av barnfrihet* (Trondheim: Tapir akademisk forlag).

Flaquer, L. (1999) *La estrella menguante del padre* (Barcelona: Ariel).

Flaquer, L. (2000) *Las políticas familiares en una perspectiva comparada* (Barcelona: Fundación La Caixa).

Foucault, M. (1978) *The History of Sexuality*, vol. 1: *An Introduction* (New York: Pantheon Books).

Foucault, M. (1991 [1977]) *Discipline and Punish: The Birth of the Prison* (London: Penguin).

Foucault, M. (1996) *Foucault Live: Interviews, 1961–84* (New York: Semiotext(e)).

FRA (European Union Agency for Fundamental Rights) (2007) *Report on Racism and Xenophobia in the Member States of the EU*, https://fra.europa.eu/sites/default/files/fra_uploads/11-ar07p2_en.pdf (accessed 20 September 2020).

Fraser, N. (1997) 'Heterosexism, Misrecognition, and Capitalism: A Response to Judith Butler', *Social Text*, nos. 52–3, 279–89.

Frederick, D. A., H. K. St. John, J. R. Garcia and E. A. Lloyd (2018) 'Differences in Orgasm Frequency Among Gay, Lesbian, Bisexual, and Heterosexual Men and Women in a U.S. National Sample', *Archives of Sexual Behavior*, vol. 47, no. 1, 273–88.

Fredman, S. (1997) *Women and the Law* (Oxford: Clarendon Press).

Frejka, T., T. Sobotka, J. M. Hoem and L. Toulemon (2008) 'Summary and General Conclusions: Childbearing Trends and Policies in Europe', *Demographic Research*, vol. 19, no. 2, 5–14.

Friedan, B. (1963) *The Feminine Mystique* (London: W.W. Norton).

Froggett, L. (2002) *Love, Hate and Welfare: Psychosocial Approaches to Policy and Practice* (Bristol: Policy Press).

Frost, G. (2008) *Living in Sin: Cohabiting as Husband and Wife in Nineteenth-Century England* (Manchester: Manchester University Press).

Fuss, D. (1991) *Inside/out: Lesbian Theories, Gay Theories* (London and New York: Routledge).

Gamble, A. (1988) *The Free Economy and the Strong State: The Politics of Thatcherism* (London: Macmillan).

Garber, L. (2001) *Identity Poetics: Race, Class, and the Lesbian-Feminist Roots of Queer Theory* (New York: Columbia University Press).

Garcia, J. R., E. A. Lloyd, K. Wallen and H. E. Fisher (2014) 'Orgasm Occurrence by Sexual Orientation', *Journal of Sexual Medicine*, vol. 11, no. 11, pp. 2645–52.

Gardyn, R. (2001) 'A Market Kept in the Closet', *American Demographics*, vol. 23, no. 11, 37–43.

Gautier, A. (2005) 'Legal Regulation of Marital Relations: A Historical and Comparative Approach', *International Journal of Law Policy and the Family*, vol. 19, no. 1, 47–72.

Giddens, A. (1991) *Modernity and Self-Identity: Self and Society in the Late Modern Age* (Stanford: Stanford University Press).

Giddens, A. (1992) *The Transformation of Intimacy. Sexuality. Love & Eroticism in Modern Societies* (Cambridge, UK: Polity Press).

Gil, D. J. (2002) 'Before Intimacy: Modernity and Emotion in the Early Modern Discourse of Sexuality', *ELH*, vol. 69, no. 4, 861–87.

Gil, D. J. (2006) 'Before Intimacy: Asocial Sexuality in Early Modern England' (Minneapolis and London: University of Minnesota Press).

Gill, A. (1998) *Orphans of the Empire: The Shocking Story of Child Migration to Australia* (Sydney: Random House Australia).

Gillies, V. (2003) *Families and Intimate Relationships: A Review of the Sociological Research*, Working paper 2, Families & Social Capital ESRC Research Group.

Gillies, V. (2008) 'Family and Intimate Relationships: A Review of the Sociological Research', South Bank University, http://www1.lsbu.ac.uk/ahs/downloads/families/familieswp2.pdf (accessed 20 September 2020).

Gillis, J. R. (1985) *For Better, For Worse: British Marriages, 1600 to the Present* (Oxford and Malden, MA: Oxford University Press).

Gillis, J. R. (1996) *World of Their Own Making: Myth, Ritual, and the Quest for Family Values* (Cambridge, MA: Harvard University Press).

Ginsburg, N. (1992) *Divisions of Welfare: A Critical Introduction to Comparative Social Policy* (London: SAGE).

Gíslason, I. V. and G. B. Eydal (eds.) (2011) *Parental Leave, Childcare and Gender Equality in the Nordic Countries* (Copenhagen: Nordic Council of Ministers).

Goffman, E. (1963) *Stigma* (London and New York: Penguin Books).

Goldberg, J. (1992) *Sodometries: Renaissance Texts, Modern Sexualities* (Stanford: Stanford University Press).

González-López, M. J. (2002) 'A Portrait of Western Families New Models of Intimate Relationships and the Timing of Life Events', in A. Carling, S. Duncan and R. Edwards (eds.), *Analysing Families Morality and Rationality in Policy and Practice* (London and New York: Routledge), pp. 21–47.

Gordon, L. E. (2006) 'Bringing the U-Haul: Embracing and Resisting Sexual Stereotypes in a Lesbian Community', *Sexualities*, vol. 9, 171–92.

Gordon, T. (1994) *Single Women: On the Margins?* (Basingstoke: Palgrave Macmillan).

Government Equalities Office (2019) *Implementing Opposite-Sex Civil Partnerships: Next Steps*, https://assets.publishing.service.gov.uk/government/uploads/system/uploads/attachment_data/file/815741/Civil_Partnerships_-_Next_Steps_and_Consultation_on_Conversion.pdf (accessed 20 September 2020).

Gov.uk (2011a) 'Speech on Families and Relationships', https://www.gov.uk/government/speeches/speech-on-families-and-relationships (accessed 20 September 2020).

Gov.uk (2011b) 'PM's Speech on the Fightback after the Riots', https://www.gov.uk/government/speeches/pms-speech-on-the-fightback-after-the-riots (accessed 20 September 2020).

Gov.uk (2015) 'Registration Opens for New Married Couples Tax Break', https://www.gov.uk/government/news/registration-opens-for-new-married-couples-tax-break (accessed 20 September 2020).

Gramsci, A. (1971) *Selections from the Prison Notebooks of Antonio Gramsci* (New York: International).

Graubard, S. R. (ed.) (1986) *Norden: The Passion for Equality* (Oslo: Norwegian University Press).

Greenberg, J. and S. Mitchell (1983) *Object Relations in Psychoanalytic Theory* (Cambridge, MA: Harvard University Press).

Greer, G. (2006 [1970]) *The Female Eunuch* (London and New York: Harper Perennial).

Gressgård, R. and C. Jacobsen (2008) 'Krevende toleranse. Islam og homoseksualitet', *Tidsskrift for kjønnsforskning*, vol. 2, 22–39.

Gross, N., W. Manson and A. McEachern (1958) *Explorations in Role Analysis: Studies of the School Superintendency Role* (New York: John Wiley and Sons).

Gruev, M. (2006) 'Комунизъм и хомосексуализъм в България (1944–1989)', *Anamnesis*, vol.1, http://www.anamnesis.info/broi1/scenes.htm (accessed 3 February 2018).

Guidotto, N. (2006) 'Cashing in on Queers: From Liberation to Commodification', *Canadian Online Journal of Queer Studies in Education*, vol. 1, no. 1.

Gullestad, M. (1984) *Kitchen Table Society: A Case Study of the Family Life and Friendships of Young Working-Class Mothers in Urban Norway* (Oslo: Universitetsforlaget).

Haavet, I. E. (2006) 'Milk, Mothers and Marriage: Family Policy Formation in Norway and its Neighbouring Countries in the Twentieth Century', in N. F. Christiansen, K. Petersen, N. Edling and P. Haave (eds.), *The Nordic Model of Welfare: A Historical Reappraisal* (Copenhagen: Museum Tusculanums Forlag), pp. 189–214.

Hagemann, G. (2007) 'Maternalism and Gender Equality: Tracing a Norwegian Model of Welfare', in G. Hagemann (ed.), *Reciprocity and Redistribution: Work and Welfare Reconsidered* (Pisa: Edizioni Plus), pp. 61–87.

Hagemann, G. and H. Roll-Hansen (eds.) (2005) *Twentieth-century Housewives: Meanings and Implications of Unpaid Work* (Oslo: Unipub).

Hall, D. E. and A. Jagose (eds.) (2012) *The Routledge Queer Studies Reader* (London and New York: Routledge).

Hall, K. (1995) '"There's a Time to Act English and a Time to Act Indian": The Politics of Identity among British-Sikh Teenagers', in S. Stephens (ed.), *Children and the Politics of Culture* (Princeton, NJ: Princeton University Press), pp. 243–64.

Hall, L. (2000) *Sex, Gender and Social Change in Britain since 1880* (Basingstoke: Palgrave Macmillan).

Hall, R. (1928) *The Well of Loneliness* (London: Jonathan Cape).

Hall, R. and P. E. Ogden (1999) 'Living Alone: Evidence From England and Wales and France for the Last two Decades', in S. McRae (ed.), *Changing Britain: Families and Households in the 1990s* (Oxford: Oxford University Press), pp. 265–96.

Hall, R. and P. E. Ogden (2003) 'The Rise of Living Alone in Inner London: Trends Among the Population of Working Age', *Environment and Planning A*, vol. 35, no. 5, 871–88.

Hall, S. (1983) 'The Great Moving Right Show', in S. Hall and M. Jacques (eds.), *The Politics of Thatcherism* (London: Lawrence and Wishart), pp. 19–39.

Hall, T. and H. Williamson (1999) *Citizenship and Community* (Leicester: Youth Work Press).

Halperin, D. M. (1998) 'Forgetting Foucault: Identities, and the History of Sexuality', *Representations*, vol. 63, 93–120.

Halsaa, B. and L. Nyhagen Predelli with C. Thun, K. Perren and A. Sandu (eds.) (2012) *Majority–Minority Relations in Contemporary Women's Movements: Strategic Sisterhood* (Basingstoke and New York: Palgrave Macmillan).

Halsaa, B., S. Roseneil and S. Sümer (2011) *FEMCIT: Gendered Citizenship in Multicultural Europe. The Impact of Contemporary Women's Movements*, FEMCIT Final Report, https://pdfs.semanticscholar.org/e497/c429ccbaf381ac39e165bbb92c048efd2c0d.pdf (accessed 20 September 2020).

Halsaa, B., S. Roseneil and S. Sümer (eds.) (2012) *Remaking Citizenship in Multicultural Europe: Women's Movements, Gender and Diversity* (Basingstoke and New York: Palgrave Macmillan).

Halsos, M. S. (1999) *Alminnelig borgerlig straffelov av 1902. Homoseksualitet i Norge og rettslige sanksjoner mot den fra slutten av 1800-tallet til 1972. Hovedoppgave i historie* (Oslo: Universitetet i Oslo).

Halsos, M. S. (2001) *§213 i alminnelig borgerlig straffelov av 1902: homoseksualitet i Norge og rettslige sanksjoner mot den fra slutten av 1800-tallet til 1972* (Oslo: Institutt for kriminologi og rettssosiologi, Avdeling for kriminologi, Universitetet i Oslo).

Hamilton, C. (1981 [1901]) *Marriage as a Trade* (London: The Women's Press).

Hamre, K. (ed.) (2018) *Women and Men in Norway 2018* (Oslo: Statistics Norway), https://www.ssb.no/en/befolkning/artikler-og-publikasjoner/women-and-men-in-norway-2018 (accessed 20 September 2020).

Hanisch, C. (1970) 'The Personal is Political', in S. Firestone and A. Koedt (eds.), *Notes From the Second Year: Women's Liberation* (New York: Firestone and Koedt), pp. 76–8.

Haskey, J. (2005) 'Living Arrangements in Contemporary Britain: Having a Partner who Usually Lives Elsewhere and Living Apart Together (LAT)', in *Population Trends 122* (London: ONS), pp. 35–45.

Hayton, R. (2015) 'Cameronite Conservatism and the Politics of Marriage Under the UK Coalition Government', *Families, Relationships and Societies*, vol. 4, no. 1, 151–6.

Health Act (2005) *State Gazette*, vol. 70/10.08.2004.

Heaphy, B., C. Donovan and J. Weeks (2004) 'A Different Affair? Openness and Nonmonogamy in Same Sex Relationships', in J. Duncombe, K. Harrison, G. Allan and D. Marsden (eds.), *The State of Affairs: Explorations in Infidelity and Commitment* (Mahwah, NJ: Lawrence Erlbaum), pp. 167–86.

Heaphy, B., C. Smart and A. Einarsdottir (2013) *Same-Sex Marriages: New Generations, New Relationships* (Houndmills: Palgrave Macmillan).

Heath, S. (2004) 'Shared Households, Quasi-Communes and Neo-Tribes', *Current Sociology*, vol. 52, no. 2, 161–79.

Heath, S. (2009) 'Young, Free and Single? The Rise of Independent Living', in A. Furlong (ed.), *Handbook of Youth and Young Adulthood: New Perspectives and Agendas* (London and New York: Routledge), pp. 211–16.

Heath, S., K. Davies, G. Edwards and R. Scicluna (2017) *Shared Housing, Shared Lives: Everyday Experiences Across the Lifecourse* (London and New York: Routledge).

Heckert, J. (2010) 'Love without Borders? Intimacy, Identity and the State of Compulsory Monogamy', in M. Barker and D. Langdridge (eds.), *Understanding Non-Monogamies* (London and New York: Routledge), pp. 255–66.

Hegna, K. (2007) 'Homoseksualitet, homofil identitet og psykisk helse: Risikable følelser eller eksperimentering?', in I. L. Kvalem and L. Wichstrøm (eds.), *Ung i Norge. Psykososiale utfordringer.* (Oslo: Cappelen Damm Akademisk), pp. 51–66.

Hegna, K. and L. Wichstrøm (2007) 'Suicide Attempts among Norwegian Gay, Lesbian and Bisexual Youths: General and Specific Risk Factors', *Acta Sociologica*, vol. 50, no. 1, 21–37.

Heinen, J. (2009) 'Clashes and Ordeals of Women's Citizenship in Central and Eastern Europe', in J. Lukić, J. Regulska and D. Zavirsek (eds.), *Women and Citizenship in Central and East Europe* (London and New York: Routledge), pp. 81–100.

Hellesund, T. (2003) *Kapitler fra singellivets historie* (Oslo: Universitetsforlaget).

Hellesund, T. (2011) 'A4: en tekst om å ville, og ikke ville være vanlig', *Tidsskrift for kulturforskning*, vol. 10, nos. 2–3, 50–61.

Hellesund, T. (2013) 'Intimitet i forvandling: om hvordan den nye norske kvinnebevegelsen satte intimitet på dagsordenen', in H. Danielsen (ed.), *Da det personlige ble politisk: den nye kvinne- og mannsbevegelsen på 1970-tallet* (Oslo: Scandinavian Academic Press), pp. 61–102.

Hellesund, T., S. Roseneil, I. Crowhurst, A. C. Santos and M. Stoilova (2019) 'Narrating and Relating to Ordinariness: Experiences of Unconventional Intimacies in Contemporary Europe', *Ethnologia Scandinavica*, vol. 48, 92–113.

Hennum, R. (2001) 'Lesbiske og homofiles rettsstilling', in K. O. Åmås (ed.), *Norsk homoforskning* (Oslo: Universitetsforlaget), pp. 85–104.

Henriksen, K. (2007) *Fakta om 18 innvandrergrupper i Norge*. Statistisk sentralbyrå (SSB) 2007/29.

Herman, D. (1994) *Rights of Passage: Struggles for Lesbian and Gay Equality* (Toronto: University of Toronto Press).

Hernes, H. M. (1987) *Welfare State and Woman Power* (Oslo: Norwegian University Press).

Herzog, D. (2011) *Sexuality in Europe: A Twentieth Century History* (Cambridge, UK and New York: Cambridge University Press).

Hesford, V. (2009) 'The Politics of Love: Women's Liberation and Feeling Differently', *Feminist Theory*, vol. 10, no. 1, 5–33.

Hines, S. and A. C. Santos (2018) 'Trans* Policy, Politics and Research: The UK and Portugal', *Critical Social Policy*, vol. 38, no. 1, 35–56.

HM Government (2010) *Support for All: The Family and Relationship Green Paper* (London: The Stationery Office).

Hochschild, A. R. (1990) *The Second Shift: Working Parents and the Revolution at Home* (London: Piatkus).

Hochschild, A. R. (2003) *The Commercialisation of Intimate Life* (San Francisco and Los Angeles: University of California Press).

Hochschild, A. R. (2012) *The Outsourced Self: What Happens When We Pay Others to Live Our Lives for Us* (New York: Henry Holt).

Hofstede, G. (1991) *Cultures and Organizations: Software of the Mind* (London: McGraw-Hill).

Holden, K. (2007) *The Shadow of Marriage: Singleness in England 1914–60* (Manchester: Manchester University Press).

Hollway, W. (2006) *The Capacity to Care: Gender and Ethical Subjectivity* (London and New York: Routledge).

Home Office (1998) *Supporting Families* (London: the Stationary Office).

Homocult (1992) *Queer with Class, the First Book of Homocult* (Manchester: MS ED [The Talking Lesbian] Promotions).

Höpken, W. (1992) 'Emigration und Integration von Bulgarien-Türken seit dem Zweiten Weltkrieg. Ein Vergleich der Auswanderungswellen von 1950/51 und 1989', in G. Seewann (ed.), *Minderheitenfragen in Südosteuropa. Beiträge der Internationalen Konferenz* (Munich: R. Oldenbourg Verlag), pp. 359–76.

Horn, C. (2001) 'Sociological Perspectives on the Emergence of Norms', in M. Hechter and K.-D. Opp (eds.), *Social Norms* (New York: Russel Sage Foundation), pp. 3–33.

Horta, M. T. (2007) Interview published 26 April 2007, http://cadernosdejornalismo.uc.pt/00/14-18.pdf (accessed 26 February 2008).

Hungerbühler, W., E. Tejero and L. Torrabadella (2002) 'Suffering the Fall of the Berlin Wall: Blocked Journeys in Spain and Germany', in P. Chamberlayne, M. Rustin and T. Wengraf (eds.), *Biography and Social Exclusion in Europe* (Bristol: Policy Press), pp. 23–40.

ILGA Europe (2019) *Annual Review of the Human Rights Situation of Lesbian, Gay, Bisexual, Trans, and Intersex People in Bulgaria,* https://www.ilga-europe.org/sites/default/files/bulgaria.pdf (accessed 20 September 2020).

Illouz, E. (1997) *Consuming the Romantic Utopia: Love and the Cultural Contradictions of Capitalism* (Berkeley and Los Angeles: University of California Press).

Illouz, E. (1998) 'The Lost Innocence of Love: Romance as a Postmodern Condition', *Theory Culture, Society*, vol. 15, 161–86.

Instituto Nacional de Estatística (2012) *Census 2011 Resultados Definitivos – Portugal* (Lisbon: INE).

Israel, B. (2002) *Bachelor Girl: The Secret History of Single Women in the Twentieth Century* (New York: William Morrow).

Ivanov, A. (2008) *Българските политики за насърчаване на майчинството, брачността и раждаемостта*, National Council for Cooperation on Ethnic and Demographic Issues, Demographic Studies, http://www.nccedi.government.bg/page.php?category=112&id=735 (accessed 30 August 2017).

Jackson, S. (1998) 'Sexual Politics: Feminist Politics, Gay Politics, and the Problem of Heterosexuality', in T. Carver and V. Mottier (eds.), *Politics of Sexuality: Identity, Gender, Citizenship* (London and New York: Routledge), pp. 68–78.

Jackson, S. and S. Scott (2004) 'The Personal Is Still Political: Heterosexuality, Feminism and Monogamy', *Feminism and Psychology*, vol. 14, no. 1, 151–7.

Jamieson, L. (1998) *Intimacy: Personal Relationships in Modern Societies* (Cambridge, Oxford and Malden, MA: Polity Press).

Jamieson, L. (1999) 'Intimacy Transformed? A Critical Look at the "Pure Relationship"', *Sociology*, vol. 33, no. 3, 477–94.

Jamieson, L. (2004) 'Intimacy, Negotiated Nonmonogamy and the Limits of the Couple', in J. Duncombe, K. Harrison, G. Allan and D. Marsden (eds.), *The State of Affairs: Explorations in Infidelity and Commitment*, (London and New York: Routledge). pp. 33–57.

Jamieson, L. (2008) 'Intimacy Transformed? A Critical Look at the "Pure Relationship"', in A. Diduck, *Marriage and Cohabitation. The Family, Law & Society* (Aldershot: Ashgate), pp. 21–38.

Jamieson, L. and R. Simpson (2013) *Living Alone: Globalization, Identity and Belonging* (London and New York: Palgrave Macmillan).

Jamieson, L., F. Wasoff and R. Simpson (2009) 'Solo-Living, Demographic and Family Change: The Need to Know More About Men', *Sociological Research Online*, vol. 14, nos. 2–3.

Jeffreys, S. (1985) *The Spinster and Her Enemies: Feminism and Sexuality, 1880–1930* (London: Pandora Press).

Jensen, A.-M. (2005) 'Barn som bor med far bor også med mor', *Samfunnsspeilet*, vol. 19, no. 2, 30–8.

Jensen, T. and I. Tyler (2012) 'Austerity Parenting: New Economies of Parent-Citizenship', *Studies in the Maternal*, vol. 4, no. 2.

Jenson, J. (2007) 'The European Union's Citizenship Regime: Creating Norms and Building Practices', *Comparative European Politics*, vol. 5, no. 1, 53–69.

Jenson, J. (2009) 'Lost in Translation: The Social Investment Perspective and Gender Equality', *Social Politics*, vol. 16, no. 4, 446–83.

Jenson, J. and S. D. Phillips (1996) 'Regime Shift: New Citizenship Practices in Canada', *International Journal of Canadian Studies*, vol. 4, 111–35.

Jordåen, R. (2003) 'Frå synd til sjukdom. Konstruksjonen av mannleg homoseksualitet i Norge 1886–1950', Master's Thesis, Department of History, University of Bergen.

Kalinova, E. and I. Baeva (2006) *Bulgarian Transitions 1939–2005* (Sofia: Paradigma).

Kaufmann, J.-C. (2011) *The Curious History of Love* (Cambridge and Malden, MA: Polity Press).

Keremidchieva, M. (1998) *Политика за семейството* (Sofia: University Publishing House 'Stopanstvo').

Kernberg, O. (1975) *Borderline Conditions and Pathological Narcissism* (New York: Aronson).

Kernberg, O. (1995) *Love Relations: Normality and Pathology* (New Haven, CT and London: Yale University Press).

Kernberg, O. (2002) 'Unresolved Issues in the Psychoanalytic Theory of Homosexuality and Bisexuality', *Journal of Gay and Lesbian Psychotherapy*, vol. 6, no. 1, 9–27.

Kilkey, M. (2017) 'Conditioning Family-life at the Intersection of Migration and Welfare: The Implications for "Brexit Families"', *Journal of Social Policy*, vol. 46, no. 4, 797–814.

Kilminster, R. (2013) 'Critique and Overcritique in Sociology', *Human Figurations: Long-term Perspectives on the Human Condition*, vol. 2, no. 2. https://quod.lib.umich.edu/h/humfig/11 217607.0002.205?view=text;rgn=main (accessed 20 September 2020).

Kipnis, L. (2003) *Against Love: A Polemic* (New York: Pantheon).

Kirby, J. (2009) 'From Broken Family to the Broken Society', *The Political Quarterly*, vol. 80, no. 2, 243–47.

Kitzinger, C. and S. Wilkinson (2004) 'Social Advocacy for Equal Marriage: The Politics of "Rights" and the Psychology of "Mental Health"', *Analyses of Social Issues and Public Policy*, vol. 4, no. 1, 173–94.

Klesse, C. (2006) 'Polyamory and its "Others": Contesting the Terms of Non-Monogamy', *Sexualities*, vol. 9, no. 5, 565–83.

Klesse, C. (2007a) 'Polyamory or the Promise of Loving More than One Person: A Commentary on Current Research', *Zeitschrift für Sexualforschung*, vol. 20, no. 4, 316–30.

Klesse, C. (2007b) *The Spectre of Promiscuity: Gay Male and Bisexual Non-Monogamies and Polyamories* (Aldershot: Ashgate).

Klesse, C. (2008) *Spectre of Promiscuity: Gay Male and Bisexual Non-Monogamies* (Aldershot: Ashgate).

Klett-Davies, M. (2012) 'A Critical Analysis of Family and Relationships Policies in England and Wales (1997–2011)', *Families, Relationships and Societies*, vol. 1, no. 1, 121–31.

Klinenberg, E. (2012) *Going Solo: The Extraordinary Rise and Surprising Appeal of Living Alone* (New York, Toronto and London: Penguin).

Knijn, T. and A. Komter (eds.) (2004) *Solidarity Between the Sexes and the Generations: Transformations in Europe* (Cheltenham: Edward Elgar).

Koeva, S. and S. Bould (2007) 'Women as Workers and as Carers under Communism and After: The Case of Bulgaria', *International Review of Sociology*, vol. 17, no. 2, 303–18.

Kotzeva, T., M. Sugareva, V. Zhekova and G. Mihova (2005) 'Експертна оценка на демографските процеси в България и насоки ба търсене на ефективно регулиране на неблагоприятните последици', *Naselenie*, vol. 1–2, 55–74.

Kramer, J. (1975) 'The Three Marias', *New York Times*, 2 February 1975, https://www.nytimes.com/1975/02/02/archives/the-three-marias.html (accessed 27 August 2018).

Krüger, S. (2017) 'Dropping Depth Hermeneutics into Psychosocial Studies: A Lorenzerian Perspective', *Journal of Psychosocial Studies*, vol. 10, no.1, 47–66.

Kuhar, R., S. Monro and J. Takács (2018) 'Trans* Citizenship in Post-socialist Societies', *Critical Social Policy*, vol. 38, no. 1, 99–120.

Kuhar, R. and D. Paternotte (eds.) (2017) *Anti-Gender Campaigns in Europe: Mobilizing against Equality* (London: Rowman & Littlefield International).

Kukova, S. (2008) *Legal Study on Homophobia and Discrimination on Grounds of Sexual Orientation in Bulgaria*, European Union Agency for Fundamental Rights (FRA), http://fra.europa.eu/fraWebsite/attachments/FRA-hdgso-NR_BG.pdf (accessed 20 September 2020).

Lahad, K. (2012) 'Singlehood, Waiting, and the Sociology of Time', *Sociological Forum*, vol. 27, no. 1, 163–86.

Lahad, K. (2017) *A Table for One: A Critical Reading of Singlehood, Gender and Time* (Manchester: Manchester University Press).

Land, H. (1979) 'The Boundaries Between the State and the Family', in C. Harris, D. H. J. Morgan and D. Leonard (eds.), *The Sociology of the Family: New Directions for Britain*, Sociological Review Monograph, vol. 28, no. S1, 141–59.

Langdridge, D. and E. Blyth (2001) 'Regulation of Assisted Conception Services in Europe: Implications of the new Reproductive Technologies for "the Family"', *Journal of Social Welfare and Family Law*, vol. 23, no. 1, 45–64.

Langford, J. (1999) *Revolutions of the Heart: Gender, Power and the Delusions of Love* (London and New York: Routledge).

LaSala, M. C. (2001) 'Monogamous or Not: Understanding and Counselling Gay Male Couples', *Families in Society*, vol. 82, no. 6, 605–11.

Layton, L. (2002) 'Cultural Hierarchies, Splitting, and the Heterosexist Unconscious', in S. Fairfield, L. Layton and C. Stack (eds.), *Bringing the Plague: Toward a Postmodern Psychoanalysis* (New York: Other Press), pp. 195–223.

Layton, L. (2004) 'A Fork in the Royal Road: Defining the "Unconscious" and its Stakes for Social Theory', *Psychoanalysis Culture & Society*, vol. 9, no. 1, 33–51.

Lee, G. R. and L. H. Stone (1980) 'Mate-selection Systems and Criteria: Variation According to Family Structure', *Journal of Marriage and the Family*, vol. 42, no. 2, 319–26.

Lehmiller, J. J. and C. R. Agnew (2006) 'Marginalized Relationships: The Impact of Social Disapproval on Romantic Relationship Commitment', *Personality and Social Psychology Bulletin*, vol. 32, 40–51.

Lehmiller, J. J. and C. R. Agnew (2007) 'Perceived Marginalization and the Prediction of Romantic Relationship Stability', *Journal of Marriage and Family*, vol. 69, no. 4, 1036–49.

Lehmiller, J. J. and C. R. Agnew (2008) 'Commitment in Age-gap Heterosexual Romantic Relationships: A Test of Evolutionary and Socio-cultural Predictions', *Psychology of Women Quarterly*, vol. 32, 74–82.

Leira, A. (1992) *Welfare State and Working Mothers: The Scandinavian Experience* (Cambridge, UK: Cambridge University Press).

Lesthaeghe, R. (2010) 'The Unfolding Story of the Second Demographic Transition', *Population and Development Review*, vol. 36, no. 2, 211–51.

Lesthaeghe, R. (2014) 'The Second Demographic Transition: A Concise Overview of its Development', *Proceedings of the National Academy of Sciences*, vol. 111, no. 51, 18112–15.

Levin, I. (2004) 'Living Apart Together: A New Family Form', *Current Sociology*, vol. 52, 223–40.

Levin, I. and J. Trost (1999) 'Living Apart Together', *Community, Work and Family*, vol. 2, no. 3, 279–94.

Lewis, J. (1992) 'Gender and the Development of Welfare Regimes', *Journal of European Social Policy*, vol. 2, no. 3, 159–73.

Lewis, J. (2001a) *The End of Marriage? Individualism and Intimate Relations* (Cheltenham: Edward Elgar).

Lewis, J. (2001b) 'Marriage', in I. Zweiniger-Bargielowska (ed.), *Women in Twentieth Century Britain* (Harlow: Longman), pp. 69–85.

Lewis, J. (2001c) 'Is Marriage the Answer to the Problems of Family Change?', *Political Quarterly*, vol. 72, no. 4, 437–45.

Lewis, J. (2002) 'Political Intervention and Family Policy in Britain', in A. Carling, S. Duncan and R. Edwards (eds.), *Analysing Families* (London and New York: Routledge), pp. 51–56.

Lewis, J. (2003) 'Responsibilities and Rights: Changing the Balance', in N. Ellison and C. Pierson (eds.), *Developments in British Social Policy* (Basingstoke and New York: Palgrave), pp. 75–89.

Lewis, J. and J. Haskey (2006) 'Living-Apart-Together in Britain: Context and Meaning', *International Journal of Law in Context*, vol. 2, no. 1, 37–48.

Lewis, J., T. Knijn, C. Martin and I. Ostner (2008) 'Patterns of Development in Work/Family Reconciliation Policies for Parents in France, Germany, the Netherlands, and the UK in the 2000s', *Social Politics*, vol. 15, no. 3, pp. 261–86.

Lewis, K. G. and S. Moon (1997) 'Always Single and Single Again Women: A Qualitative Study', *Journal of Marital and Family Therapy*, vol. 23, no. 2, 115–34.

Lewis, P., T. Newburn, M. Taylor, C. Mcgillivray, A. Greenhill, Aster, H. Frayman and R. Proctor (2011) *Reading the Riots: Investigating England's Summer of Disorder* (London: The London School of Economics and Political Science and *The Guardian*).

Lindholm, C. (2006) 'Romantic Love and Anthropology', *Etnofoor*, vol. 19, no. 1, 5–21.

Lister, R. (1989) *The Female Citizen* (Liverpool: Liverpool University Press).

Lister, R. (1994) '"She Has Other Duties": Women, Citizenship and Social Security', in S. Baldwin and J. Falkingham (eds.), *Social Security and Social Change: New Challenges to the Beveridge Model* (Hemel Hempstead: Harvester Wheatsheaf), pp. 31–44.

Lister, R. (1997) *Citizenship: Feminist Perspectives* (Basingstoke and New York: Palgrave Macmillan).

Lister, R. (2003) 'Investing in the Citizen-workers of the Future: Transformations in Citizenship and the State under New Labour', *Social Policy and Administration*, vol. 37, no. 5, 427–43.

Lister, R. (2006) 'Ladder of Opportunity or Engine of Inequality', *Political Quarterly*, vol. 77, no. S1, 232–6.

Lister, R. (2007) 'Inclusive Citizenship: Realizing the Potential', *Citizenship Studies*, vol. 11, no. 1, 49–61.

Lister, R. and F. Bennett (2010) 'The New "Champion of Progressive Ideals?" Cameron's Conservative Party: Poverty, Family Policy and Welfare Reform', *Renewal*, vol. 18, nos. 1–2, 84–109.

Lister, R., F. Williams, A. Anttonen, J. Bussemaker, U. Gerhard, J. Heinen, S. Johansson, A. Leira, B. Siim, C., with A. Gavanas (2007) *Gendering Citizenship in Western Europe* (Bristol: The Policy Press).

Listhaug, O. and K. Ringdal (2008) 'Trust in Political Institutions', in H. Ervasti, T. Fridberg, M. Hjerm, and K. Ringdal (eds.), *Nordic Social Attitudes in a European Perspective* (Cheltenham: Edward Elgar), pp. 131–51.

Löfström, J. (1998) 'A Pre-modern Legacy: The Easy Criminalisation of Homosexual Acts Between Women in the Finnish Penal Code of 1889', in J. Löfström (ed.), *Scandinavian Homosexualities: Essays on Gay and Lesbian Studies* (New York: Howarth Press), pp. 53–80.

Long, S. (1999) Gay and Lesbian Movements in Eastern Europe: Romania, Hungary and the Czech Republic. In Adam, B.D., Duyvendak, J.W., Krouwel, A. (eds.) *The Global Emergence of Gay and Lesbian Politics: National Imprints of a Worldwide Movement*. Philadelphia: Temple University Press.

Lønnå, E. (1996) *Stolthet og kvinnekamp. Norsk Kvinnesaksforenings historie fra 1913* (Oslo: Gyldendal Norsk Forlag).

Lorde, A. (2012 [1984]) *Sister Outsider: Essays and Speeches* (Berkeley, CA: Crossing Press).

Lorenzer, A. (1974) *Die Wahrheit der psychoanalytischen Erkenntnis. Ein historischmaterialistischer Entwurf* (Frankfurt/M.: Suhrkamp).

Lorenzer, A. (1986) 'Tiefenhermeneutische Kulturanalyse', in A. Lorenzer (ed.), *KulturAnalysen: Psychoanalytische Studien zur Kultur* (Frankfurt/M.: Fischer), pp. 11–98.

Lowe, N. V. (1988) 'The Family Law Reform Act 1987: Useful Reform but an Unhappy Compromise?', *The Denning Law Journal*, vol. 3, no. 1, pp. 77–88.

Lowe, N. V. and G. Douglas (2007) *Bromley's Family Law* (Oxford and New York: Oxford University Press).

Luhmann, N. (1986) 'The Autopoiesis of Social Systems', in F. Geyer and J. van der Zouwen (eds.), *Sociocybernetic Paradoxes* (London: SAGE), pp. 172–92.

Lyndon Shanley, M. (1993) *Feminism, Marriage, and the Law in Victorian England, 1850–1895* (Princeton, NJ: Princeton University Press).

McCandless, J. and S. Sheldon (2010) 'The Human Fertilisation and Embryology Act (2008) and the Tenacity of the Sexual Family Form', *The Modern Law Review*, vol. 73, no. 2, 175–207.

McCormick, L. (2008) 'The Scarlet Woman in Person: The Establishment of a Family Planning Service in Northern Ireland, 1950–1974', *Social History of Medicine*, vol. 21, no. 2, 345–60.

McIntosh, M. (1968) 'The Homosexual Role', *Social Problems*, vol. 16, no. 2, 182–92.

McLaughlin, E. and C. Glendinning (1994) 'Principles and Practice of Social Security Payments for Care', *International Social Security Review*, vol. 47, nos. 3–4, 137–55.

Maclean, M. (2002) 'The Green Paper *Supporting Families*, 1998', in A. Carling, S. Duncan and R. Edwards (eds.), *Analysing Families: Morality and Rationality in Policy and Practice* (London and New York: Routledge), pp. 64–8.

Maclean, M. and J. Eekelaar (2005) 'The Significance of Marriage: Contrasts between White British and Ethnic Minority Groups in England', *Law and Policy*, vol. 27, no. 3, 379–98.

Maclean, M. and J. Eekelaar (2013) *Managing Family Justice in Diverse Societies* (Oxford: Hart).

Macvarish, J. (2006) 'What Is "The Problem" of Singleness', *Sociological Research Online*, vol. 11, no. 3, 1–8.

Magalhães, M. J. (1998) *Movimento Feminista e Educação. Portugal, decadas de 70 e 80* (Lisbon: Celta Editora).

Mahoney, J. (2000) 'Path Dependence in Historical Sociology', *Theory and Society*, vol. 29, no. 4, 507–48.

Mann, K. and S. Roseneil (1999) 'Poor Choices? Gender, Agency and the Underclass Other', in G. Jagger and C. Wright (eds.), *Changing Family Values* (London and New York: Routledge), pp. 98–118.

Mansfield, P. and J. Collard (1988) *The Beginning the Rest of Your Life* (London: Palgrave Macmillan).

Marks, L. (2001) *Sexual Chemistry: A History of the Contraceptive Pill* (New Haven: Yale University Press).

Marshall, T. H. (1950) *Citizenship and Social Class: And Other Essays* (Cambridge, UK and New York: Cambridge University Press).

Martin, B. (1996) *Femininity Played Straight: The Significance of Being Lesbian* (London and New York: Routledge).

Mathieu, S. (2016) 'From the Defamilialization to the "Demotherization" of Care Work', *Social Politics*, vol. 23, no. 4, 576–91.

Matovic, M. R. (1984) *Stockholmsäktenskap: familjebildning och partnerval i Stockholm 1850–1890* (Stockholm: Liber).

Mätzke, M. and I. Ostner (2010) 'Introduction: Change and Continuity in Recent Family Policies', *Journal of European Social Policy*, vol. 20, no. 5, 387–98.

Melby, K. (1995) 'Kvinnelighetens strategier: Norges husmorforbund 1915–1940 og Norges lærerinneforbund 1912–1940', PhD Thesis, Universitetet i Trondheim.

Melby, K. (2005) 'Husmortid 1900–1950', in I. Blom and S. Sogner (eds.), *Med kjønnsperspektiv på norsk historie: fra vikingtid til 2000-årsskiftet* (Oslo: Cappelen Damm Akademisk), pp. 255–331.

Melby, K., A. Pylkkänen, B. Rosenbeck and C. C. Wetterberg (2006a) *Inte ett ord om kärlek: äktenskap och politik i Norden ca. 1850–1930* (Göteborg: Makadam förlag).

Melby, K., A. Pylkkänen, B. Rosenbeck and C. C. Wetterberg (2006b) 'The Nordic Model of Marriage', *Women's History Review*, vol. 15, no. 4, 651–61.

Melby, K., A.-B. Ravn and C. C. Wetterberg (eds.) (2008) *Gender Equality and Welfare Politics in Scandinavia: The Limits of Political Ambition?* (Bristol: The Policy Press).

Meshkova, P. and D. Sharlanov (1994) *Българската гилотина: тайните механизми на народния съд* (Sofia: Agencia Demokracia).

Midling, A. S. (2012) 'Skilsmissebarn savner tid alene', *Forskning*, https://forskning.no/samliv-sosiale-relasjoner-barn-og-ungdom/skilsmissebarn-savner-tid-alene/726485 (accessed 20 September 2020).

Mihajlova, D. (2006) *Законът за защита срещу дискриминацията като инструмент за защита на жертвите на неравно третиране, основано на признака сексуална ориентация*, National Anti-Discrimination Campaign, European Institute, http://diversity.europe.bg/page.php?cat egory=309&id=1739&page=3 (accessed 20 September 2020).

Millar, J. (2003) 'Squaring the Circle? Means Testing and Individualisation in the UK and Australia', *Social Politics and Society*, vol. 3, 67–74.

Miller, D. (2007) 'What Is a Relationship? Kinship as Negotiated Experience', *Ethnos. Journal of Anthropology*, vol. 72, no. 4, 535–54.

Millett, K. (2000 [1970]) *Sexual Politics* (New York: Doubleday).

Ministry of Labour and Social Policy (2006) *National Strategy for Demographic Development of the Republic of Bulgaria 2006–2020*, http://www.mlsp.government.bg/bg/docs/demography/STRATEGY-%20FINAL.pdf (accessed 23 August 2012).

Minkenberg, M. (2003) 'The Policy Impact of Church–State Relations: Family Policy and Abortion in Britain, France, and Germany', *West European Politics*, vol. 26, no. 1, 195–217.

Mitchell, J. (1966) 'Women: The Longest Revolution', *New Left Review*, vol. 40, no. 1, 11–37.

Mitchell, S. A. and L. Aron (eds.) (1999) *Relational Psychoanalysis: The Emergence of a Tradition* (Hillsdale, NJ: The Analytic Press).

Modood. T. (1995)'The Limits of America: Rethinking Equality in the Changing Contexts of British Race Relations' in Ward, B. and Badger, T. (eds.) *The Making of Martin Luther King and the Civil Rights Movement* (London: Macmillan), pp. 181–93.

Modood, T., Beishon, S. and Virdee, S. (1994) *Changing Ethnic Identities*. Series: PSI research report (794). Policy Studies Institute: London.

Moita, G. (2001) 'Discursos sobre Homossexualidade no Contexto Clinico', Doctoral Thesis, Instituto de Ciências Biomédicas, University of Porto.

Moksnes, A. (1984) *Likestilling eller særstilling? Norsk kvinnesaksforening 1884–1913* (Oslo: Gyldendal).

Møller, K. A. (1919) *Kvindernes fødselspolitik* (Kristiania: Det norske arbeiderpartis forlag).

Monro, S. and J. Van der Ros (2018) 'Trans* and Gender Variant Citizenship and the State in Norway', *Critical Social Policy*, vol. 38, no. 1, 57–78.

Moran, R. F. (2004) 'How Second-Wave Feminism Forgot the Single Woman', *Hofstra Law Review*, vol. 33, no. 1, 223–98.

Moreno Mìnguez, A. (2003) 'The Late Emancipation of Spanish Youth: Keys For Understanding', *Electronic Journal of Sociology*, http://www.sociology.org/content/vol7.1/minguez.html (accessed 20 September 2020).

Morgan, D. (1991) 'Ideologies of Marriage and Family Life', in D. Clark (ed.), *Marriage, Domestic Life and Social Change* (London and New York: Routledge), pp. 114–38.

Mota, G. (ed.) (2002) *Minorias Étnicas e Religiosas em Portugal. História e Actualidade* (Coimbra: Instituto de História Económica e Social, Universidade de Coimbra).

Mourão, J. S. (2011) 'O Casamento Cigano. Estudo sócio-jurídico das normas ciganas sobre as uniões conjugais', MA Dissertation, University Fernando Pessoa, Porto, http://bdigital.ufp.pt/bitstream/10284/2236/1/DM.pdf (accessed 20 December 2017).

Mühleisen, W., Å. Røthing and S. H. B. Svendsen (2009) 'Grenser for seksualitet. Norske seksual-itetsforståelser i familie- og innvandringspolitikk', *Tidsskrift for kjønnsforskning*, vol. 33, 253–75.

Mühleisen, W., Å. Røthing and S. H. B. Svendsen (2012) 'Norwegian Sexualities: Assimilation and Exclusion in Norwegian Immigration Policy', *Sexualities*, vol. 15, no. 2, pp. 139–55.

Munson, M. and J. Stelboum (eds.) (1999) *The Lesbian Polyamory Reader: Open Relationships, Non-Monogamy, and Casual Sex* (New York: Haworth Press).

Myhrer, T.-G. (2006) 'Er proformaekteskap menneskesmugling?', *Tidsskrift for strafferett*, vol. 2, 101–22.

Nardi, P. M. (1992) 'That's What Friends Are For: Friends as Family in the Gay and Lesbian Community', in K. Plummer (ed.), *Modern Homosexualities: Fragments of Lesbian and Gay Experience* (London and New York: Routledge), pp. 108–20.

Nardi, P. M. (1999) *Gay Men's Friendships: Invincible Communities* (Chicago: Chicago University Press).

Neves, S. (2008) *Amor, Poder e Violências na Intimidade: Os caminhos entrecruzados do pessoal e do político* (Coimbra: Quarteto).

Noack, T. (2005) 'Skilsmisser i registrerte partnerskap og ekteskap. Partnere skiller seg oftest', *Samfunnsspeilet*, vol. 6, http://www.ssb.no/samfunnsspeilet/utg/9703/3.html (accessed 17 September 2016).

Noack, T., H. Fekjæra and A. Seierstad (2002) 'Skilsmisser blant lesbiske og homofile partnere – hvem er mest stabile?', *Samfunnsspeilet*, vol. 3, http://www.ssb.no/samfunnsspeilet/utg/9703/3.html (accessed 3 December 2017).

Noack, T. and S.-E. Mamelund (1997) 'Skilsmisser før og nå: Som man måler får man svar', *Samfunnsspeilet*, vol. 3, http://www.ssb.no/samfunnsspeilet/utg/9703/3.html (accessed 3 December 2017).

Norges Domstoler (2012) Domstol.no. *Vigsel. Teksten i vigselsformularet*. Norwegian version at: http://www.domstol.no/datemplates/article.aspx?id=3049&epslanguage=NO (accessed 30 August 2012).

NOU (1999) 25. *Samboerne og samfunnet* (Oslo: Statens forvaltningstjeneste).

Nova Television (2009) *Всичко за майката*, Темата на Нова, Broadcast 27 March 2009.

NRS (National Records of Scotland) (2018) *Vital Events Reference Table 2018*, https://www.nrscotland.gov.uk/statistics-and-data/statistics/statistics-by-theme/vital-events/general-publications/vital-events-reference-tables/2018/section-3-births (accessed 15 September 2019).

NRS (National Records of Scotland) (2019) *Scotland's Population 2018*, https://www.nrscotland.gov.uk/files//statistics/nrs-visual/rgar-2018/rgar-2018-infographic-booklet.pdf (accessed 15 September 2019).

NSI (National Statistical Institute) (2005) *Population and Demographic Processes* (Sofia: NSI).

NSI (National Statistical Institute) (2011) *Census Data*, http://www.nsi.bg/census2011/index.php (accessed 20 December 2017).

Number10.gov.uk (2012) 'Prime Minister's Speech at Lesbian, Gay, Bisexual and Transgender Reception', http://www.ukpol.co.uk/2016/01/22/david-cameron-2012-speech-at-lgbt-reception/ (accessed 16 September 2016).

Nwankwo, P. O. (2011) *Criminology and Criminal Justice Systems of the World: A Comparative Perspective* (Bloomington, IN: Trafford), pp. 284–312.

Oakley, A. (1974) *Woman's Work: The Housewife, Past and Present* (New York: Vintage Books).

O'Connor, J. (1993) 'Gender, Class and Citizenship in the Comparative Analysis of Welfare State Regimes: Theoretical and Methodological Issues', *British Journal of Sociology*, vol. 44, no. 3, 501–18.

Okoliyski, M. and P. Velichkov (2004) 'Bulgaria', in R. Francoeur and R. Noonan (eds.), *International Encyclopaedia of Sexuality* (London: Continuum).

ONS (Office for National Statistics) (2005) *Inter-Ethnic Marriage*, Census 2001, http://archive.is/BbQrt (accessed 20 December 2017).

ONS (Office for National Statistics) (2010) *Divorces in England and Wales*, http://www.ons.gov.uk/ons/rel/vsob1/divorces-in-england-and-wales/index.html (accessed 18 December 2017).

ONS (Office for National Statistics) (2011) *Marriages in England and Wales (Provisional), 2011*, http://www.ons.gov.uk/ons/rel/vsob1/marriages-in-england-and-wales--provisional-/2011/index.html (accessed 20 December 2017).

ONS (Office for National Statistics) (2012) *Families and Households, 2001 to 2011*, http://www.ons.gov.uk/ons/dcp171778_251357.pdf (accessed 20 December 2017).

ONS (Office for National Statistics) (2013a) *Live Births in England and Wales by Characteristics of Mother 1, 2012*, http://www.ons.gov.uk/ons/rel/vsob1/characteristics-of-Mother-1--england-and-wales/2012/sb-characteristics-of-mother-1--2012.html (accessed 20 December 2017).

ONS (Office for National Statistics) (2013b) *Divorces in England and Wales*, http://www.ons.gov.uk/peoplepopulationandcommunity/birthsdeathsandmarriages/divorce/bulletins/divorcesinenglandandwales/2013 (accessed 20 December 2017).

ONS (Office for National Statistics) (2014) *What Does the 2011 Census Tell Us About Inter-ethnic Relationships?*, http://webarchive.nationalarchives.gov.uk/20160105160709/http://www.ons.gov.uk/ons/dcp171776_369571.pdf (accessed 20 December 2017).

ONS (Office for National Statistics) (2015) *Births in England and Wales: 2015*, http://www.ons.gov.uk/peoplepopulationandcommunity/birthsdeathsandmarriages/livebirths/bulletins/birthsummarytablesenglandandwales/2015#the-percentage-of-births-outside-marriage-or-civil-partnership-continues-to-rise (accessed 20 December 2017).

ONS (Office for National Statistics) (2017) *Families and Households: 2017*, https://www.ons.gov.uk/peoplepopulationandcommunity/birthsdeathsandmarriages/families/bulletins/familiesandhouseholds/2017 (accessed 15 September 2019).

ONS (Office for National Statistics) (2018) *Births in England and Wales: 2018*, https://www.ons.gov.uk/peoplepopulationandcommunity/birthsdeathsandmarriages/livebirths/bulletins/birthsummarytablesenglandandwales/2018 (accessed 15 September 2019).

ONS (Office for National Statistics) (2019) *Marriages in England and Wales: 2016*, https://www.ons.gov.uk/peoplepopulationandcommunity/birthsdeathsandmarriages/marriagecohabitationandcivilpartnerships/bulletins/marriagesinenglandandwalesprovisional/2016 (accessed 6 July 2020).

Orloff, A. S. (1993) 'Gender and the Social Rights of Citizenship: The Comparative Analysis of Gender Relations and Welfare States', *American Sociological Review*, vol. 58, no. 3, 303–38.

Orloff, A. S. (1996) 'Gender in the Welfare State', *Annual Review of Sociology*, vol. 22, no. 1, 51–78.

Orloff, A. S. (2009) 'Gendering the Comparative Analysis of Welfare States', *Sociological Theory*, vol. 27, no. 3, 317–43.

Østby, L. (1999) *Statistikk mot år 2000: 1900–1901. Befolkningen ved inngangen til århundret*, https://www.ssb.no/befolkning/artikler-og-publikasjoner/befolkningen-ved-inngangen-til-aarhundretI (accessed 6 January 2018).

Ostner, I. (2004) '"Individualisation": The Origins of the Concept and its Impact on German Social Policies', *Social Policy and Society*, vol. 3, no. 1, 47–56.

Oxfordshire.gov.uk (2019) *Oxfordshire: The Place to Marry*, https://www.oxfordshire.gov.uk/sites/default/files/file/birth-death-marriage/ThePlaceToCelebrate.pdf (accessed 15 September 2019).

Pais, J. M. (1996) 'Austeridade e moralismo dos padrões estéticos', in A. Reis (ed.), *Portugal Contemporâneo* (Lisbon: Alfa), pp. 349–75.

Pais, J. M. (ed.) (1998) *Gerações e Valores na Sociedade Portuguesa Contemporânea* (Lisbon: ICS).

Pais de Amaral, J. (1997) *Do Casamento ao Divórcio* (Chamusca: Cosmos).

Pamporov, A. (2006) *Everyday Life of Bulgarian Roma* (Sofia: International Centre for Minority Studies and Intercultural Relations).

Pankhurst, C. (2001) 'The Great Scourge and How to End It' (1913), in J. Marcus (ed.), *Suffrage and the Pankhursts*, Women's Source Library Volume VIII (London: Routledge).

Parmar, P. (1982) 'Gender, Race and Class: Asian Women in Resistance', in Centre for Contemporary Cultural Studies (ed.), *The Empire Strikes Back: Race and Racism in 70s Britain* (London: Hutchinson), pp. 235–74.

Parsons, T. (1951) *The Social System* (London: Routledge & Kegan Paul).

Pascall, G. (1999) 'UK Family Policy in the 1990s: The Case of New Labour and Lone Parents', *International Journal of Law, Policy and the Family*, vol. 13, no. 3, 258–73.

Pascall, G. and J. Lewis (2004) 'Emerging Gender Regimes and Policies for Gender Equality in a Wider Europe', *Journal of Social Policy*, vol. 33, no. 3, 373–94.

Pateman, C. (1989) *The Disorder of Women: Democracy, Feminism, and Political Theory* (Redwood City, CA: Stanford University Press).

Patton, C. (1993) 'Tremble, Hetero Swine!', in M. Warner (ed.), *Fear of a Queer Planet: Queer Politics and Social Theory* (Minneapolis and London: University of Minnesota Press), pp. 143–77.

Patton, C. (1995) 'Refiguring Social Space', in L. Nicholson and S. Seidman (eds.), *Social Postmodernism: Beyond Identity Politics* (Cambridge and New York: Cambridge University Press), pp. 216–49.

Patton, C. (1998) '"On Me, Not in Me": Locating Affect in Nationalism after AIDS', *Theory, Culture & Society*, vol. 15, nos. 3–4, 355–77.

Patton, C. (1999) "'On Me, Not in Me": Locating Affect in Nationalism after AIDS', in M. Featherstone (ed.), *Love & Eroticism* (London and Thousand Oaks, CA: SAGE), pp. 355–74.

Penal Code (1951) *State Gazette*, vol. 13/13.02.1951.

Penal Code (1956) *State Gazette*, vol. 16/24.02.1956.

Peplau, L. A., A. Fingerhut and K. P. Beals (2004) 'Sexuality in the Relationships of Lesbians and Gay Men', in J. H. Harvey, A. Wenzel, and S. Sprecher (eds.), *The Handbook of Sexuality in Close Relationships* (Mahwah, NJ: Lawrence Erlbaum Associates), pp. 349–69.

Peplau, L. A. and L. D. Garnets (2000) 'A New Paradigm for Understanding Women's Sexuality and Sexual Orientation', *Journal of Social Issues*, vol. 56, no. 2, 329–50.

Perrons, D., L. McDowell, C. Fagan, K. Ray and K. Ward (2005) 'The Contradictions and Intersections of Class and Gender in a Global City: Placing Working Women's Lives on the Research Agenda', *Environment and Planning A*, vol. 37, no. 3, 441–61.

Peterson, A. M. (2015) 'Maternitet og de castbergske barnelover; lovgivning og konsekvenser, 1900–1915', *Tidsskrift for velferdsforskning*, vol. 18, no. 4, 294–305.

Philipov, D. and H.-P. Kohler (2001) 'Tempo Effects in the Fertility Decline in Eastern Europe: Evidence from Bulgaria, the Czech Republic, Hungary, Poland, and Russia', *European Journal of Population*, vol. 17, no. 1, 37–60.

Phillips, A. (1996) *Monogamy* (London: Faber).

Phoenix, A. (1996) 'Social Constructions of Lone Motherhood', in E. Silva (ed.), *Good Enough Mothering? Feminist Perspectives on Lone Motherhood* (London and New York: Routledge), pp. 175–90.

Pieper, M. and R. Bauer (2006) 'Polyamory and Mononormativity: Results of an Empirical Study of Non-monogamous Patterns of Intimacy', unpublished article.

Pierce, C. (1995) 'Gay Marriage', *Journal of Social Philosophy*, vol. 28, no. 2, 5–16.

Pimentel, I. F. (2001) *História das Organizações Femininas do Estado Novo* (Lisbon: Temas & Debates).

Pimentel, I. F. (2007) *Mocidade Portuguesa Feminina* (Lisbon: Esfera dos Livros).

Pimentel, I. F. (2011) *A Cada um o Seu Lugar: A política feminina do Estado Novo* (Lisbon: Temas & Debates).

Pinheiro, J. (2004) *O Núcleo Intangível da Comunhão Conjugal: os deveres conjugais sexuais* (Coimbra: Almedina).

Pinto, A. V. (2005) 'Intervenção do ACIME para a Inclusão das Comunidades Ciganas', *Rediteia*, 35, 17–43.

Pinto, M. F. (2000) *A Cigarra e a Formiga: Contributos para a Reflexão sobre o Entrosamento da Minoria Étnica Cigana na Sociedade Portuguesa* (Porto: REAPN).

Pisankaneva, M. (2002) 'Reflections on the Butch-Femme and the Emerging Lesbian Community in Bulgaria', in M. Gibson and D. Meem (eds.), *Femme-Butch: New Considerations of the Way We Want to Go* (Binghampton, NY: Harrington Park Press), pp. 135–44.

Pisankaneva, M. (2003) *The Forbidden Fruit: Sexuality in Communist Bulgaria*, Conference on 'Past and Present of Radical Sexual Politics, Socialism and Sexuality', 5th annual meeting at University of Amsterdam, 3–4 October 2003, http://www.iisg.nl/womhist/pisankaneva.doc (accessed 20 December 2017).

Pisankaneva, M. (2009) 'Bulgaria', in C. Stewart (ed.), *The Greenwood Encyclopaedia of LGBT Issues Worldwide* (Westport, CT: Greenwood), pp. 65–78.

Platt, L. (2009) *Ethnicity and Family Relationships Within and Between Groups: An Analysis Using the Labour Force Survey* (ISER: University of Essex, Colchester).

Plummer, K. (1983) *Documents of Life: An Introduction to the Problems and Literature of a Humanistic Method* (London: Unwin Hyman).

Plummer, K. (1995) *Telling Sexual Stories: Power, Change, and Social Worlds* (London and New York: Routledge).

Plummer, K. (2001) *Documents of Life 2: An Invitation to a Critical Humanism* (London: Sage).

Plummer, K. (2003) *Intimate Citizenship: Private Decisions and Public Dialogues* (Seattle and London: University of Washington Press).

Polikoff, N. (2008) *Beyond (Straight and Gay) Marriage: Valuing All Families Under the Law* (Boston, MA: Beacon Press).

Popova, G. (2004) 'Obeztelesenoto tqlo na socializma. Triumfyt na plytta i gospodstvoto na obrazite v obyrnatata perspektiva na publichnostta', in A. Vacheva, J. Eftimov and G. Chobanov (eds.), *Култура и критика*, vol. 4, http://liternet.bg/publish7/gpopova/tialo. htm (accessed 7 February 2018).

Popova, G. (2009) 'Забраненият език – от дискурсивното обезличаване до фактическата асимилац ия на хомосексуалните в България в периода 1945 – 1989', *NotaBene*, vol. 2, http://notabene-bg.org/contents.php?issue=2 (accessed 20 December 2017).

PORDATA (2012) *Database of Contemporary Portugal*, http://www.pordata.pt/Portugal (accessed 17 September 2016).

Porter, M. (2010) 'Gender Identity and Sexual Orientation', in P. Thane (ed.), *Unequal Britain: Equalities in Britain Since 1945* (London: Continuum), pp. 125–62.

Portuguese Civil Code (1966 [1934]) (Coimbra: Almedina).

Povinelli, E. A. (2006) *The Empire of Love: Toward a Theory of Intimacy, Genealogy, and Carnality* (Durham, NC: Duke University Press).

Povinelli, E. A. (2011) *Economies of Abandonment: Social Belonging and Endurance in Late Liberalism* (Durham, NC: Duke University Press).

Prata, A. (2015) 'Contesting Portugal's Bodily Citizenship', in J. Outshoorn (ed.)' *European Women's Movements and Body Politics* (Basingstoke: Palgrave Macmillan), pp. 84–117.

Principe, C. (1979) *Os Segredos da Censura* (Lisbon: Caminho).

Pringle, R. and S. Watson (1992) '"Women's Interests" and the Post-Structuralist State', in M. Barrett and A. Phillips (eds.), *Destabilizing Theory: Contemporary Feminist Debates* (Stanford, CA: Stanford University Press), pp. 53–73.

Probert, R. (1999) 'The Controversy of Equality and the Matrimonial Causes Act 1923', *Child and Family Law Quarterly*, vol. 11, no. 1, 33–42.

Probyn, E. (2005) *Blush: Faces of Shame* (Minneapolis: University of Minnesota Press).

Przeworski, A. and H. Teune (1970) *The Logic of Comparative Inquiry* (New York: Wiley-Interscience).

Puar, J. (2007) *Terrorist Assemblages: Homonationalism in Queer Times* (Durham, NC: Duke University Press).

Pugh, M. (2000) *Women and the Women's Movement in Britain, 1914–1999* (Basingstoke: Macmillan).

Queer Bulgaria (2004) *Анализ на положението на лесбийки, гей мъже, бисексуални, трансексуални и интерсексуални в българското общество*, http://q-bg.org/poz3=bg.php (accessed 5 May 2007).

Qureshi, K., V. J. Varghese, F. Osella and S. I. Rajan (2012) 'Migration, Transnationalism and Ambivalence: The Punjab–United Kingdom Linkage', in P. Pitkännen, A. Içduygu and D. Sert (eds.), *Migration and Transformation* (Heidelberg: Springer), pp. 13–62.

Radicallesbians (1970) *The Woman-Identified Woman* (Atlanta, GA: Know).

Raymond, J. G. (2001 [1986]) *A Passion for Friends. Toward a Philosophy of Female Affection* (North Melbourne: Spinifex Press).

Redman, P., M. Bereswill and C. Morgenroth (eds.) (2010) 'Alfred Lorenzer and the Depthhermeneutic Method', *Psychoanalysis, Culture & Society*, vol. 15, no. 3, special issue, 221–50.

Redmayne, S. (1993) 'The Matrimonial Causes Act 1937: A Lesson in the Art of Compromise', *Oxford Journal of Legal Studies*, vol. 13, no. 2, 183–200.

Reynolds, J. (2008) *The Single Woman: A Discursive Investigation* (London and New York: Routledge).

Reynolds, J. and S. Taylor (2005) 'Narrating Singleness: Life Stories and Deficit Identities', *Narrative Inquiry*, vol. 15, no. 2, 197–215.

Reynolds, J. and M. Wetherell (2003) 'The Discursive Climate of Singleness: The Consequences for Women's Negotiation of a Single Identity', *Feminism & Psychology*, vol. 13, no. 4, 489–510.

Ribbens McCarthy, J. and R. Edwards (2002) 'The Individual in Public and Private: The Significance of Mothers and Children', in A. Carling, S. Duncan and R. Edwards (eds.), *Analysing Families: Morality and Rationality in Policy and Practice* (London and New York: Routledge), pp. 199–217.

Ribbens McCarthy, J., R. Edwards and V. Gillies (2003) *Making Families: Moral Tales of Parenting and Step-parenting* (Durham, NC: Sociology Press).

Rich, A. (1980) 'Compulsory Heterosexuality and Lesbian Existence', *Signs: Journal of Women in Culture and Society*, vol. 5, no. 4, 631–60.

Richardson, D. (1998) 'Sexuality and Citizenship', *Sociology*, vol. 32, no. 1, 83–100.

Richardson, D. (2000) *Rethinking Sexuality* (London: SAGE).

Richardson, D. (2005) 'Desiring Sameness? The Rise of a Neoliberal Politics of Normalisation', *Antipode*, vol. 37, no. 3, 515–53.

Richardson, D. (2018) *Sexuality and Citizenship* (Cambridge, UK: Polity).

Riley, D. (2002) 'The Right to Be Lonely', *differences: A Journal of Feminist Cultural Studies*, vol. 13, no. 1, 1–13.

Ritchie, A. and M. Barker (2006) '"There Aren't Words for What We Do or How We Feel so We Have to Make Them Up": Constructing Polyamorous Languages in a Culture of Compulsory Monogamy', *Sexualities*, vol. 9, no. 5, 584–601.

Robinson, M. (2013) 'Polyamory and Monogamy as Strategic Identities', *Journal of Bisexuality*, vol. 13, no. 1, 21–38.

Robson, R. (2009) 'Compulsory Matrimony', in M. Albertson Fineman, J. E. Jackson and A. P. Romero (eds.), *Feminist and Queer Legal Theory: Intimate Encounters, Uncomfortable Conversations* (London and New York: Routledge), pp. 315–28.

Rosa, B. (1994) 'Anti-Monogamy: A Radical Challenge to Compulsory Heterosexuality?', in G. Griffin, M. Hester, S. Rai and S. Roseneil (eds.), *Stirring It: Challenges for Feminism* (London: Taylor and Francis), pp. 107–20.

Rosas, F. J. M. (1994) *O Estado Novo. História de Portugal*. Vol. 7 (Lisbon: Ed. Estampa).

Rose, J. (1987) *Sexuality in the Field of Vision* (London: Verso).

Rosenbury, L. (2007) 'Friends With Benefits?', *Michigan Law Review*, vol. 106, 189–242.

Roseneil, S. (2000a) *Why We Should Care about Friends: Some Thoughts about the Ethics and Practice of Friendship*, ESRC Research Group for the Study of Care, Values and the Future of Welfare Working Paper.

Roseneil, S. (2000b) 'Queer Frameworks and Queer Tendencies: Towards an Understanding of Postmodern Transformations of Sexuality', *Sociological Research Online*, vol. 5, no. 3, 1–19.

Roseneil, S. (2000c) *Common Women, Uncommon Practices: The Queer Feminisms of Greenham* (London: Cassell Press).

Roseneil, S. (2004) 'Why We Should Care about Friends: An Argument for Queering the Care Imaginary in Social Policy', *Social Policy and Society*, vol. 3, no. 4, 409–19.

Roseneil, S. (2006a) 'On not Living with a Partner: Unpicking Coupledom and Cohabitation', *Sociological Research Online*, vol. 11, no. 3, https://journals.sagepub.com/doi/10.5153/sro.528 (accessed 20 September 2020).

Roseneil, S. (2006b) 'Foregrounding Friendship: Feminist Pasts, Feminist Futures', in K. Davis, M. Evans and J. Lorber (eds.), *Handbook of Gender and Women's Studies* (London: SAGE), pp. 324–43.

Roseneil, S. (2006c) 'The Ambivalences of Angel's Arrangement: A Psychosocial Lens on the Contemporary Condition of Intimate Life', *The Sociological Review*, vol. 54, no. 4, 847–69.

Roseneil, S. (2007) 'Queer Individualization: The Transformation of Personal Life in the Early 21st Century', *Nora – Nordic Journal of Feminista and Gender Research*, vol. 15, nos. 2–3, 84–99.

Roseneil, S. (2010) 'Intimate Citizenship: A Pragmatic, yet Radical, Proposal for a Politics of Personal Life', *European Journal of Women's Studies*, vol. 17, no. 1, 77–82.

Roseneil, S. (2012) 'Using Biographical Narrative Methods and Life Story Methods to Research Women's Movements: FEMCIT', *Women's Studies International Forum*, vol. 35, 129–31.

Roseneil, S. (2016) *The Lesbian C Word: Repudiation and Reversals*, Recognition and Reparation Conference Paper First International Intimate Conference: Queering Partnering, 30–31 March 2016, University of Coimbra, Portugal.

Roseneil, S. and S. Budgeon (2004) 'Cultures of Intimacy and Care Beyond "the Family": Personal Life and Social Change in the Early 21st Century', *Current Sociology*, vol. 52, no. 2, pp. 135–59.

Roseneil, S., I. Crowhurst, T. Hellesund, A. C. Santos and M. Stoilova (2008) *Policy Contexts and Responses to Changes in Intimate Life*, Working Paper 1 (Bergen: FEMCIT), https://eprints.bbk.ac.uk/4436/1/4436.pdf (accessed 20 September 2020).

Roseneil, S., I. Crowhurst, T. Hellesund, A. C. Santos and M. Stoilova (2010) *Changing Cultural Discourses about Intimate Life: The Demands and Actions of Women's Movements and Other Movements for Gender and Sexual Equality and Change*, FEMCIT Working Paper, https://eprints.bbk.ac.uk/4443/1/4443.pdf (accessed 20 September 2020).

Roseneil, S., I. Crowhurst, T. Hellesund, A. C. Santos and M. Stoilova (2011) 'Intimate Citizenship and Gendered Well-Being: The Claims and Interventions of Women's Movements in Europe', in A. E. Woodward, J. M. Bonvin and M. Renom (eds.), *Transforming Gendered Well-Being in Europe: The Impact of Social Movements* (Farnham: Ashgate), pp. 187–205.

Roseneil, S., I. Crowhurst, T. Hellesund, A. C. Santos and M. Stoilova (2012) 'Remaking Intimate Citizenship in Multicultural Europe', in B. Halsaa, S. Roseneil and S. Sümer (eds.), *Remaking Citizenship in Multicultural Europe: Women's Movements, Gender and Diversity* (Basingstoke: Palgrave Macmillan), pp. 41–69.

Roseneil, S., I. Crowhurst, T. Hellesund, A. C. Santos and M. Stoilova (2013) 'Changing Landscapes of Heteronormativity: The Regulation and Normalization of Same-Sex Sexualities in Europe', *Social Politics: International Studies in Gender, State & Society*, vol. 20, no. 2, 165–99.

Roseneil, S., I. Crowhurst, A. C. Santos and M. Stoilova (2016) 'Reproduction and Citizenship/ Reproducing Citizens: Editorial Introduction', in S. Roseneil, I. Crowhurst, A. C. Santos and M. Stoilova (eds.), *Reproducing Citizens: Family, State and Civil Society* (London and New York: Routledge).

Roseneil, S., B. Halsaa and S. Sümer (eds.) (2012) 'Remaking Citizenship in Multicultural Europe: Women's Movements, Gender and Diversity', in B. Halsaa, S. Roseneil and S. Sümer (eds.), *Remaking Citizenship in Multicultural Europe. Women's Movements, Gender and Diversity* (Basingstoke and New York: Palgrave Macmillan), pp. 1–20.

Roseneil, S. and K. Ketokivi (2016) 'Relational Persons and Relational Processes: Developing the Notion of Relationality for the Sociology of Personal Life', *Sociology*, vol. 50, no. 1, 143–59.

Roseneil, S. and M. Stoilova (2011) 'Heteronormativity, Intimate Citizenship and the Regulation of Same-Sex Sexualities in Bulgaria', in R. Kulpa and J. Mizielinska (eds.), *Decentring Western Sexualities: Central and Eastern European Perspectives* (London: Ashgate), pp. 167–90.

Rosenthal, G. (1993) 'Reconstruction of Life Stories: Principles in Selection in Generating Stories for Narrative Biographical Interviews', in R. Josselson and A. Lieblich (eds.), *Narrative Study of Lives* (London: SAGE), pp. 59–91.

Roth, J. A. (1963) *Timetables: Structuring the Passage of Time in Hospital Treatment and Other Careers* (Indianapolis: Bobbs-Merril).

Rothblum, E. D. (1999) 'Poly-Friendships', *Journal of Lesbian Studies*, vol. 3, nos. 1–2, 68–83.

Rothblum, E. D. and K. A. Behony (1993) *Boston Marriages: Romantic But Asexual Relationships Among Contemporary Lesbians* (Amherst: University of Massachusetts Press).

Røthing, Å. and S. H. B. Svendsen (2010) 'Homotolerance and Heterosexuality as Norwegian Values', *Journal of LGBT Youth*, vol. 7, no. 2, 147–66.

Rubin, G. (1993 [1984]) 'Thinking Sex: Notes for a Radical Theory of the Politics of Sexuality', in H. Abelove, M. A. Barale and D. M. Halperin (eds.), *The Lesbian and Gay Studies Reader* (New York, London: Routledge), pp. 3–44.

Rufus, A. (2003) *Party of One: The Loners' Manifesto* (New York: Marlowe & Company).

Rydström, J. (2008) 'Legalizing Love in a Cold Climate: The History, Consequences and Recent Developments of Registered Partnership in Scandinavia', *Sexualities*, vol. 11, nos. 1–2, 193–226.

Rydström, J. (2011) *Odd Couples: A History of Gay Marriage in Scandinavia* (Amsterdam: Aksant).

Sainsbury, D. (1994) 'Women's and Men's Social Rights: Gendering Dimensions of Welfare States', in D. Sainsbury (ed.), *Gendering Welfare States* (London: SAGE), pp. 150–69.

Sainsbury, D. (1996) *Gender, Equality and Welfare States* (Cambridge, UK: Cambridge University Press).

Salling-Olesen, H. and K. Weber (2012) 'Socialization, Language, and Scenic Understanding. Alfred Lorenzer's Contribution to a Psycho-societal Methodology', *FQS – Forum: Qualitative Social Research*, vol. 13, no. 3. http://nbn-resolving.de/urn:nbn:de:0114-fqs1203229 (accessed 20 September 2020).

Santos, A. C. (2013) *Social Movements and Sexual Citizenship in Southern Europe* (Basingstoke: Palgrave Macmillan).

Santos, A. C. (2016) '"In the Old Days, there Were no Gays": Democracy, Social Change and Media Representation of Sexual Diversity', *International Journal of Iberian Studies*, vol. 29, no. 2, 157–72.

Santos, A. C. (2018) 'Repronormativity and its Others: Queering Parental Love in Times of Culturally Compulsory Reproduction', *Analize – Journal of Gender and Feminist Studies*, 11, 199–215.

Santos, A. C., B. Gusmano and P. Pérez Navarro (eds.) (2019) 'Polyamories in Southern Europe: Critical perspectives', Special Issue of *Sociological Research Online*, vol. 24, no. 4.

Santos, A. C. and M. Pieri (2019) 'My Body, My Rules? Self-determination and Feminist Collective Action in Southern Europe', in C. F. Fominaya and R. A. Feenstra (eds.), *Routledge Handbook of Contemporary European Social Movements: Protest in Turbulent Times* (London and New York: Routledge), pp. 196–209.

Saraceno, C. (2014) 'Welfare State Studies in European Sociology', in S. Koniordos and A.-A. Kyrtsis (eds.), *Routledge Handbook of European Sociology* (London and New York: Routledge), pp. 238–51.

Saraceno, C. (2015) 'A Critical Look to the Social Investment Approach from a Gender Perspective', *Social Politics – International Studies in Gender, State & Society*, vol. 22, no. 2, 257–69.

Sarromaa, S. (2011) 'Det Nye og den unge norske kvinnen: diskurser, representasjoner og resepsjoner om ung kvinnelighet 1957–77 og i 2009', Doctoral Thesis, Karlstads universitet.

Sayer, A. (2011) *Why Things Matter to People: Social Science, Values and Ethical Life* (Cambridge: Cambridge University Press).

Schierup, C.-U., P. Hansen and S. Castles (2006) *Migration, Citizenship, and the European Welfare State: A European Dilemma* (London: Oxford University Press).

Schneider, D. M. (1968) *American Kinship: A Cultural Account* (Chicago and London: University of Chicago Press).

Schneider, D. M. (1984) *A Critique of the Study of Kinship* (Ann Arbor: University of Michigan Press).

Schneider, D. M. (2004) 'What Is Kinship All About?', in R. Parkin and L. Stone (eds.), *Kinship and Family: An Anthropological Reader* (Malden, MA, and Oxford: Blackwell), pp. 257–74.

Sedgwick, E. K. (1985) *Between Men: English Literature and Male Homosocial Desire* (New York: Columbia University Press).

Sedgwick, E.K. (1991) *Epistemology of the Closet* (Hemel Hempstead: Harvester Wheatsheaf).

Seidman, S. (2002) *Beyond the Closet: The Transformation of Gay and Lesbian Life* (New York and London: Routledge).

Sender, K. (2004) *Business, Not Politics: The Making of the Gay Market* (New York: Columbia University Press).

Shaw, A. (1988) *A Pakistani Community in Britain* (Oxford: Blackwell).

Shaw, A. (2000) *Kinship and Continuity: Pakistani Families in Britain* (Amsterdam: Harwood Academic).

Shaw, A. (2001) 'Kinship, Cultural Preference and Immigrations: Consanguineous Marriage among British Pakistanis', *Journal of the Royal Anthropological Institute*, vol. 7, no. 2, 315–34.

Shernoff, M. (2005) *Without Condoms: Unprotected Sex, Gay Men and Barebacking* (London and New York: Routledge).

Signorile, M. (1997) *Life Outside – The Signorile Report on Gay Men: Sex, Drugs, Muscles, and the Passages of Life* (New York: HarperCollins).

Siim, B. (1993) 'The Gendered Scandinavian Welfare States: The Interplay Between Women's Roles as Mothers, Workers and Citizens in Denmark', in J. Lewis (ed.), *Women and Social Policies in Europe: Work, Family and the State* (Aldershot: Edward Elgar), pp. 25–49.

Siim, B. (2000) *Gender and Citizenship: Politics and Agency in France, Britain and Denmark* (Cambridge and New York: Cambridge University Press).

Silva, E. and C. Smart (eds.) (1999) *The 'New' Family?* (London: SAGE).

Silva, M. M. and M. Conceição (1943) *Manual de educação moral e cívica* (Porto: Tip. Gonçalves & Nogueira).

Simpson, R. (2006) 'The Intimate Relationships of Contemporary Spinsters', *Social Research Online*, vol. 11, no. 3, 125–36.

Sinha, M. (2014) 'Gendered Nationalism: From Women to Gender and Back Again?', in L. Fernandes (ed.), *Routledge Handbook of Gender in South Asia* (London and New York: Routledge), pp. 13–27.

Skeggs, B. (2003) *Class, Self and Culture* (London and New York: Routledge).

Slettvåg, K. (1980) 'Vi husmødre slutter os sammen'. Fra Hjemmenes Vel – Til Norges Husmorforbund 1898–1915, Hovedfagsoppgave i historie, University of Bergen.

Smart, C. (1984) *The Ties that Bind: Law, Marriage, and the Reproduction of Patriarchal Relations* (London and Boston, MA: Routledge & Kegan Paul).

Smart, C. (2000) 'Stories of Family Life: Cohabitation, Marriage and Social Change', *Canadian Journal of Family Law*, vol. 17, no. 1, pp. 20–53.

Smart, C. (2007) *Personal Life: New Directions in Sociological Thinking* (Cambridge, UK and Malden, MA: Polity).

Smart, C. and B. Neale (1999) *Family Fragments* (Cambridge: Polity Press).

Smith, A. M. (1994) *New Right Discourse on Race and Sexuality: Britain, 1968–1990* (Cambridge, UK: Cambridge University Press).

Smith, B. (1983) (ed.) *Home Girls: A Black Feminist Anthology* (New York: Kitchen Table Press).

Smith-Rosenberg, C. (1975) 'The Female World of Love and Ritual: Relations between Women in Nineteenth-Century America', *Signs*, vol 1, no. 1, 1–29.

Somers, M. R. (2008) *Genealogies of Citizenship: Markets, Statelessness, and the Right to Have Rights* (Cambridge, UK: Cambridge University Press).

Song, M. (2012) 'Making Sense of "Mixture": States and the Classification of "Mixed" People', *Ethnic and Racial Studies*, vol. 35, no. 4, 565–73.

Sotiropoulou, V. and D. Sotiropoulos (2007) 'Childcare in Post-Communist Welfare States: the Case of Bulgaria', *Journal of Social Policy*, vol. 37, no. 1, 141–55.

Spring, J. (2010) *Secret Historian: The Life and Times of Samuel Steward, Professor, Tattoo Artist, and Sexual Renegade* (New York: Farrar, Straus and Giroux).

Stacey, J. (1991) 'Promoting Normality: Section 28 and the Reputation of Sexuality', in S. Franklin, C. Lury and J. Stacey (eds.), *Off-Centre: Feminism and Cultural Studies* (London: HarperCollins), pp. 284–304.

Stacey, J. (2004) 'Cruising to Familyland: Gay Hypergamy and Rainbow Kinship', *Current Sociology*, vol. 52, no. 2, 181–97.

Stacey, J. (2011) *Unhitched: Love, Marriage, and Family Values from West Hollywood to Western China* (New York: New York University Press).

Standley, K. (2006) *Family Law* (Basingstoke: Palgrave Macmillan).

Stanley, L. (1992) *The Auto/Biographical I: The Theory and Practice of Feminist Auto/ Biography* (Manchester: Manchester University Press).

SSB (Statistisk sentralbyrå) (2008a) *Befolkningsstatistikk. Fødte, 2008. Rekordhøy fruktbarhet*, http://www.ssb.no/emner/02/02/10/fodte/ (accessed 11 March 2010).

SSB (Statistisk sentralbyrå) (2008b) *Barnløse menn ved 50-årsalder og kvinner ved 45-årsalder.* Prosent, http://www.ssb.no/samfunnsspeilet/utg/200805/03/tab-2008-12-08-01.html (accessed 20 December 2017).

SSB (Statistisk sentralbyrå) (2009) *Historisk statistikk. Gjennomsnittsalder ved giftermålet*, http://www.ssb.no/histstat/tabeller/3-26.html (accessed 17 September 2016).

SSB (Statistisk sentralbyrå) (2012a) *Personer 18 år og over i privathusholdninger. Andel som lever/ ikke lever i par, etter alder, fylke, kommune og bydel.* 1 January 2011. Prosent, http://www.ssb.no/emner/02/01/20/familie/tab-2011-04-07-14.html (accessed 17 September 2016).

SSB (Statistisk sentralbyrå) (2012b) *Befolkningsstatistikk. Ekteskap og skilsmisser 2011. Færre vigslar, men fleire inngått i utlandet*, http://www.ssb.no/ekteskap/ (accessed 25 September 2012).

SSB (Statistisk sentralbyrå) (2012c) *Inngåtte ekteskap. Ekteskap mellom personer av ulikt kjønn 1950–2011*, http://www.ssb.no/ekteskap/tab-2012-08-23-03.html (accessed 20 December 2017).

SSB (Statistisk sentralbyrå) (2012d) *Andel samboere, gifte og ikke i samliv i ulike aldersgrupper. Menn og kvinner. 1993–2011.* Prosent, http://www.ssb.no/emner/02/01/20/samboer/ tab-2012-05-31-03.html (accessed 25 September 2012).

SSB (Statistisk sentralbyrå) (2012e) *Berekna prosent av ekteskap som vil bli oppløyste når ein går ut frå skilsmisseraten i det einskilde år*, http://www.ssb.no/aarbok/2012/tab/tab-104.html (accessed 7 February 2013).

SSB (Statistisk sentralbyrå) (2018) Table 05707. Beregnet andel ekteskap som vil bli oppløst, forutsatt skilsmissemønster som i det enkelte år (prosent) 1960–2017. https://www.ssb.no/ statbank/table/05707/. (accessed 21 August 2018).

SSB (Statistisk sentralbyrå) (2019) Ekteskap og skilsmisser. Tabell 1. https://www.ssb.no/ befolkning/statistikker/ekteskap/aar-detaljerte-tal (accessed 5 September 2019).

SSB (Statistisk Sentralbyrå) (2020a) Table 06096: Personer 18 år og over i privathusholdninger. Andel som lever/ikke lever i par (prosent) (K) (B) 2005 – 2020. https://www.ssb.no/ statbank/table/06096/ (accessed 20 July 2020)

SSB (Statistisk Sentralbyrå (2020b). Population. https://www.ssb.no/en/befolkning/statistikker/ folkemengde (accessed 20 July 2020).

SSB (Statistisk sentralbyrå) (2020c) Table 06095. Personer 18 år og over i privathusholdninger, etter år, alder, statistikkvariabel og samlivsform. https://www.ssb.no/statbank/table/06095/ (accessed 20 July 2020).

Staykova, R. (2004) 'The Bulgarian Family: Specifics and Development from Liking in the Village Square to Love in the "Chat"', in M. Robila (ed.), *Families in Eastern Europe* (Oxford and New York: Elsevier), pp. 155–71.

Stevens, J. (1999) *Reproducing the State* (Princeton, NJ: Princeton University Press).

Stoilova, M. (2008) 'Bulgaria', in S. Roseneil, I. Crowhurst, T. Hellesund, A. C. Santos and M. Stoilova (eds.), *Policy Contexts and Responses to Changes in Intimate Life*, Working Paper 1 (Bergen: FEMCIT), https://eprints.bbk.ac.uk/4436/ (accessed 20 September 2020).

Stoilova, M. (2009) 'Gender and Generation: Women's Experiences of the Transition from Socialism in Bulgaria', PhD Thesis, University of Leeds.

Stoilova, M., S. Roseneil, I. Crowhurst, T. Hellesund and A. C. Santos (2014) 'Living Apart Relationships in Contemporary Europe: Accounts of Togetherness and Apartness', *Sociology*, vol. 48, no. 6, 1075–91.

Stonewall (2014) *Equal Marriage to Become Law – Thank You!*, https://www.stonewall.org.uk/what_we_do/parliamentary/5714.asp (accessed 10 January 2014).

Strathern, M. (1992) *After Nature English Kinship in the Late Twentieth Century* (Cambridge, UK and New York: Cambridge University Press).

Stychin, C. F. (2006a) '"Las Vegas Is Not Where We Are": Queer Readings of the Civil Partnership Act', *Political Geography*, vol. 25, 899–920.

Stychin, C. F. (2006b) 'Not (Quite) a Horse and Carriage: The Civil Partnership Act 2004', *Feminist Legal Studies*, vol. 14, 79–86.

Sullivan, A. (ed.) (1997) *Same-Sex Marriage Pro & Con: A Reader* (New York: Vintage Book).

Sutherland, E. E. (ed.) (2012) *The Future of Child and Family Law: International Predictions* (Cambridge, UK: Cambridge University Press).

Swindler, A. (2003) *Talk of Love: How Culture Matters* (Chicago: University of Chicago Press).

Syltevik, L. J. (2010) 'Sense and Sensibility: Cohabitation in "Cohabitation Land"', *The Sociological Review*, vol. 58, no. 3, 444–62.

Tatchell, P. (2011) *Gay Marriage Plan Sustains Discrimination*, https://www.petertatchellfoundation.org/gay-marriage-plan-sustains-discrimination/ (accessed 20 September 2020).

Tavares, M. (2000) *Movimentos de Mulheres em Portugal – décadas de 70 e 80* (Lisbon: Livros Horizonte).

Tavares, M. (2010) *Feminismos, Percursos e Desafios. Feminismos em Portugal (1947–2007)* (Lisbon: Texto).

Taylor-Gooby, P. (2009) *Reframing Social Citizenship* (Oxford: Oxford University Press).

Telste, K. (1999) *Brutte løfter: en kulturhistorisk studie av kjønn og ære 1700–1900* (Oslo: Det historisk-filosofiske fakultet, Universitetet i Oslo Unipub).

Thane, P. (2010) *Happy Families? History and Family Policy* (London: British Academy Policy Centre).

The Gay Say (2016) *Gerry Carroll MLA: 'Stormont has let down the LGBT+ community for too long'*, https://thegaysay.com/2016/09/19/gerrycarrollendthevetopetition (accessed 20 September 2020).

Therborn, G. (2004) *Between Sex and Power: Family in the World, 1900–2000* (London and New York: Routledge).

Thomas, W. I. and F. Znaniecki (1996 [1918]) *The Polish Peasant in Europe and America: A Classic Work in Immigration History* (edited by E. Zaretsky) (Urbana and Chicago: University of Illinois Press).

Thurrock.gov.uk (2019) *Marriages and Civil Partnerships*, https://www.thurrock.gov.uk/marriage-and-civil-partnership/example-ceremonies (accessed 20 September 2020).

Todorova, V. (2000) 'Family Law in Bulgaria: Legal Norms and Social Norms,' *International Journal of Law*, Policy and the Family, vol. 14, no. 2, 148–81.

Todorova, V. (2002) 'Grounds for Divorce and Maintenance between Former Spouses, Commission on European Family Law', http://ceflonline.net/wp-content/uploads/Bulgaria-Divorce.pdf (accessed 20 September 2020).

Todorova, I. and T. Kotzeva (2003) 'Social Discourses, Women's Resistive Voices: Facing Involuntary Childlessness in Bulgaria', *Women's Studies International Forum*, vol. 26, no. 2, 139–51.

Traub, V. (1994) 'The (In)Significance of "Lesbian" Desire in Early Modern England', in J. Goldberg (ed.), *Queering the Renaissance* (Durham, NC: Duke University Press), pp. 62–83.

Triandis, H. C. (1995) *Individualism and Collectivism* (Boulder, CO: West View Press).

Trifiletti, R. (1999) 'Southern European Welfare Regimes and the Worsening Position of Women', *Journal of European Social Policy*, vol. 9, no. 1, 49–64.

Trimberger, E. K. (2005) *The New Single Woman* (Boston, MA: Beacon Press).

Tvedt, K. A. and E. Bull (2016) *Arbeiderpartiet. Store Norske Leksikon*, https://snl.no/Arbeider partiet (accessed 25 November 2017).

Tyler, I. (2008) 'Chav Mum Chav Scum', *Feminist Media Studies*, vol. 8, no. 1, 17–34.

UNECE (United Nations Economic Commission for Europe) (2019) *Fertility, Families and Households*, https://w3.unece.org/PXWeb2015/pxweb/en/STAT/STAT__30-GE__02-Families_ households/ (accessed 11 August 2019).

van Hoof, J. (2017) 'An Everyday Affair: Deciphering the Sociological Significance of Women's Attitudes Towards Infidelity', *The Sociological Review*, vol. 65, no. 4, 850–64.

van Rosmalen-Nooijens, K., C. Vergeer and A. Lagro-Janssen (2008) 'Bed Death and Other Lesbian Sexual Problems Unraveled: A Qualitative Study of the Sexual Health of Lesbian Women Involved in a Relationship', *Women & Health*, vol. 48, no. 3, 339–62.

Varela, J. (1999) *Direito da Família* (Lisbon: Petrony).

Vasilev, R. (2005) 'Bulgaria's Demographic Crisis: Underlying Causes and Some Short-Term Implications', *Southeast European Politics*, vol. 4, no. 1, 14–27.

Vedtak om borgerlig vigselsformular (2009) *Lovdata.no*. LOV-1991-07-04-47-§15. FOR-1996-01-19-4263. FOR-2008-12-05-1285 fra 01.01.2009, https://lovdata.no/dokument/SF/ forskrift/1996-01-19-4263 (accessed 5 September 2019).

Verloo, M. (2018) *Varieties of Opposition to Gender Equality in Europe* (New York: Routledge).

Vicente, A. (1998) *As Mulheres em Portugal na Transição do Milénio. Valores, Vivências, Poderes nas Relações Sociais entre os Dois Sexos* (Lisbon: Multinova).

Vicinus, M. (2010) 'The Single Woman: Social Problem or Social Solution?', *Journal of Women's History*, vol. 22, no. 2, 191–202.

Vilar, D. (1994) 'Portugal: The Country of Easy, Illegal and Unsafe Abortion', in A. Eggert and B. Rolston (eds.), *Abortion in the New Europe: A Comparative Handbook* (Santa Barbara, CA: Greenwood), pp. 215–28.

Vodenicharov, P. (2002) 'Любов и брак в? комунистическото общество', in K. Popova, P. Vodenicharov and S. Dimitrovoa (eds.), *Жените и мъжете в миналото* (Blagoevgrad: Southwest University 'Neofit Rilski'), pp. 103–14.

Vollset, G. (2011) *Familiepolitikkens historie – 1970 til 2000*, NOVA rapport 1 (Oslo: Norsk institutt for forskning om oppvekst, velferd og aldring).

Waites, M. (2001) 'Regulation of Sexuality: Age of Consent, Section 28 and Sex Education', *Parliamentary Affairs*, vol. 54, no. 3, 495–508.

Waites, M. (2003) 'Equality at Last? Homosexuality, Heterosexuality and the Age of Consent in the United Kingdom', *Sociology*, vol. 37, no. 4, 637–55.

Walby, S. (2001) *From Gendered Welfare State to Gender Regimes: National Differences, Convergence or Re-structuring?*, Paper presented to Gender and Society Group, Stockholm University.

Walby, S. (2004) 'The European Union and Gender Equality: Emergent Varieties of Gender Regime', *Social Politics: International Studies in Gender, State and Society*, vol. 11, no. 1, 4–29.

Walkowitz, J. (1982) *Prostitution and Victorian Society: Women, Class, and the State* (Cambridge, UK and New York: Cambridge University Press).

Wall, K., S. Aboim, V. Cunha and P. Vasconcelos (2001) 'Families and Informal Support Networks in Portugal: The Reproduction of Inequality', *Journal of European Social Policy*, vol. 11, no. 3, 213–33.

Wallbank, J. (2010) 'Channelling the Messiness of Diverse Family Lives: Resisting the Calls to Order and De-centring the Hetero-normative Family', *Journal of Social Welfare and Family Law*, vol. 32, no. 4, 353–68.

Warner, M. (1991) 'Introduction: Fear of a Queer Planet', *Social Text*, vol. 29, no. 4, 3–17.

Warner, M. (ed.) (1993) *Fear of a Queer Planet: Queer Politics and Social Theory* (Minneapolis and London: University of Minnesota Press).

Warner, M. (1999) *The Trouble with Normal: Sex, Politics and the Ethics of Queer Life* (New York: The Free Press).

Weeks, J. (1977) *Coming Out: Homosexual Politics in Britain from the Nineteenth Century to the Present* (London: Quartet Books).

Weeks, J. (1985) *Sexuality and its Discontents* (London and New York: Routledge & Kegan Paul).

Weeks, J. (1991) 'Invented Moralities', *History Workshop*, no. 31, 151–66.

Weeks, J. (1998) 'The Sexual Citizen', *Theory, Culture and Society*, vol. 15, no. 3, 35–52.

Weeks, J. (2008) *The World We Have Won: Remaking the Erotic and Intimate Life* (London and New York: Routledge).

Weeks, J. (2012 [1981]) *Sex, Politics and Society: The Regulation of Sexuality Since 1800* (London and New York: Longman).

Weeks, J., B. Heaphy and C. Donovan (1999) 'Citizenship and Same Sex Relationships', *Journal of Social Policy*, vol. 28, no. 4, 689–709.

Weeks, J., B. Heaphy and C. Donovan (2001) *Same Sex Intimacies: Families of Choice and Other Life Experiments* (London and New York: Routledge).

Weinstock, J. S. and E. D. Rothblum (1996) *Lesbian Friendships: For Ourselves and Each Other* (New York: New York University Press).

Weisstein, N. (2003 [1969]) *"Kinder, Küche, Kirche" as Scientific Law: Psychology Constructs the Female* (Boston, MA: New England Free Press).

Wengraf, T. (2009) *BNIM Short Guide Bound With the BNIM Detailed Manual. Interviewing for Life-Histories, Lived Periods and Situations, and Ongoing Personal Experiencing, Using the Biographic-Narrative Interpretive Method (BNIM)* (available from tom@tomwengraf.com).

Werbner, P. (2004) 'Theorising Complex Diasporas: Purity and Hybridity in the South Asian Public Sphere in Britain', *Journal of Ethnic and Migration Studies*, vol. 30, no. 5, 895–911.

Werbner, P. and N. Yuval-Davis (1999) *Women, Citizenship and Difference* (London: Zed Books).

Weston, K. (1991) *Families We Choose: Lesbians, Gays, Kinship* (New York: Columbia University Press).

Wiegman, R. (2012) *Object Lessons* (Durham, NC and London: Duke University Press).

Wiegman, R. and E. A. Wilson (2015) 'Introduction: Antinormativity's Queer Conventions', *Differences: A Journal of Feminist Cultural Studies*, vol. 26, no. 1, 1–25.

Wiik, K. A., A. Seierstad and T. Noack (2012) *Divorce in Norwegian Same-sex Marriages 1993–2011*. Statistics of Norway, Discussion papers, no. 723, December.

Wilkinson, E. (2010) 'What Is Queer about Non-Monogamy Now?', in M. Barker and D. Langdridge (eds.), *Understanding Non-Monogamies* (London and New York: Routledge), pp. 243–54.

Wilkinson, E. (2012) 'The Romantic Imaginary: Compulsory Coupledom and Single Existence', in S. Hines and Y. Taylor (eds.), *Sexualities: Past Reflections, Future Directions* (Basingstoke: Palgrave Macmillan), pp. 130–48.

Wilkinson, E. (2013) 'Learning to Love Again: "Broken Families", Citizenship and the State Promotion of Coupledom', *Geoforum*, vol. 49, 206–13.

Wilkinson, S. and C. Kitzinger (2005) 'Same Sex Marriage and Equality', *The Psychology*, vol. 18, no. 5, 290–3.

Willey, A. (2015) 'Constituting Compulsory Monogamy: Normative Femininity at the Limits of Imagination', *Journal of Gender Studies,* vol. 24, no. 6, 621–33.

Williams, F. and S. Roseneil (2004) 'Public Values of Parenting: Voluntary Organisations and Welfare Politics in New Labour's Britain', *Social Politics*, vol. 11, no. 2, 181–216.

Wilson, A. R. (2007) 'New Labour "Lesbian- and Gay-friendly" Policy', in C. Annesley, F. Gains and K. Rummery (eds.), *Women and New Labour: Engendering Politics and Policy?* (Bristol: Policy Press).

Wimmer, A. and N. Glick Schiller (2002) 'Methodological Nationalism and Beyond: Nation-State Building, Migration and the Social Sciences', *Global Networks*, vol. 2, no. 4, 301–34.

Winnicott, D. W. (1965). *The Maturational Processes and the Facilitating Environment* (Madison, CT: International Universities Press), pp. 29–36.

Winnicott, D. W. (1974). *Playing and Reality* (London: Tavistock).

Wokingham.gov.uk (2019) *Wedding Venues and Advice*, http://www.wokingham.gov.uk/births-deaths-and-marriages/marriages-and-civil-partnerships/wedding-venues-and-advice/ (accessed 15 September 2019).

Wolfenden, J. F. et al. (1957) *Report of the Committee on Homosexual Offences and Prostitution* (Wolfenden Report) (London: HMSO).

Wollstonecraft, M. (2004 [1792]) *A Vindication of the Rights of Woman* (London: Penguin Classics).

Woodward Thomas, K. (2015) *Conscious Uncoupling: 5 Steps to Living Happily Even After* (New York: Harmony).

World Bank (2014) *Gender Dimensions of Roma Inclusion: Perspectives from Four Roma Communities in Bulgaria*, Washington, DC, http://hdl.handle.net/10986/17545 (accessed 20 September 2020).

Worth, H., A. Reid and K. McMillan (2002) 'Somewhere Over the Rainbow: Love, Trust and Monogamy in Gay Relationships', *Journal of Sociology*, vol. 38, no. 3, 237–53.

Wright, C. and G. Jagger (1999) 'End of Century, End of Family? Shifting Discourses of Family "Crisis"', in C. Wright and G. Jagger (eds.), *Changing Family Values* (London and New York: Routledge), pp. 17–37.

Wrong, D. H. (1961) 'The Oversocialized Conception of Man in Modern Sociology', *American Sociological Review*, vol. 26, no. 2, 183–93.

Yachkova, M. (2002) *Семейството в България между XX и XXI век: предпоставки, анали?зи, прогнози* (Sofia: ACCA-M).

Yuval-Davis, N. (2008) 'Intersectionality, Citizenship and the Politics of Belonging', in B. Siim and J. Squires (eds.), *Contesting Citizenship* (London and New York: Routledge), pp. 159–72.

Zajicek, A. M. and P. R. Koski (2003) 'Strategies of Resistance to Stigmatization among White Middle-class Singles', *Sociological Spectrum*, vol. 23, no. 3, 377–403.

Zhekova, V. (2001) Репродуктивни нагласи и мотиви за раждане, *Naselenie*, vol. 1–2, 36–55.

Index

civil partnership (*cont.*)
  Civil Partnership Act 2004 (UK),
    53, 57
  Civil Partnership (Opposite-sex
    Couples) Regulations 2019 (UK),
    57
class, 33nn46, 48, 52, 43, 46, 60n14,
  109, 132, 150, 240–1
  middle-class, 17, 29n7, 32n30,
    33n46, 44, 45, 79, 122, 130, 175,
    181, 188n5, 189n15
  upper-class, 6
  working-class, 44, 91n2, 116, 129,
    146, 205
Cobb, Michael, 11
cohabitation, 70, 88, 100–1, 102, 104,
  171, 190, 199, 206–9, 210
  policy/law against 67, 84
  unmarried 46, 47, 49, 50, 63, 71,
    72, 78, 84, 85, 88, 89, 90, 91n2,
    99, 103, 130–3, 139, 141–2,
    144–5, 146, 151, 166, 171, 183,
    184, 197, 219, 221, 238, 247n1
  see also cohabiting couple-form;
    non-cohabiting
Collett, Camilla, 6
colonialism, 16, 17, 40, 96, 97
Coman et al. v Romania, case of, 73
coming out, 153–8, 155, 173, 179, 218
commitment, 55, 125, 133, 165, 175,
  176, 186, 207, 210, 226
  life-long, 89, 116, 139, 177, 217,
    220, 221, 222
  long-term, 85, 178
  moral, 32n37, 50
communist/communism, 38, 40, 62–3,
  65–9, 73–4, 75n7, 141–6, 150,
  153, 158, 160nn1, 5
  see also post-communist/communism
community, 7, 23, 65, 67, 68, 69, 136,
  151–2, 153, 163, 183, 185, 226,
  228, 229, 231n2
  British-Pakistani 134–8
  full membership of, 4, 18
  lesbian and gay/LGBT, 11, 51, 134,
    154–5, 157, 175
  Muslim 135

Norwegian-Pakistani, 163–6, 185,
  221, 225
policing, 69
Portuguese Roma, 190, 191–6, 209,
  221
Turkish-Bulgarian, 221
Turkish-speaking 17
companion/ship, 12, 99, 166, 174,
  177, 222
companionate marriage, 48
Comrade Courts, 67, 69
conservatism/conservative, 11, 54,
  58n1, 59n8, 62, 63, 66, 71, 92,
  95, 121, 143, 157, 159, 181, 196,
  198, 215, 221
Conservative government (Høyre)
  (Norway) 76
Conservative government (UK), 38,
  44, 48, 50–2, 54–7, 58n3
Conservative–Liberal Coalition
  government (UK), 44
conservative welfare regime, 30n19,
  40, 42n6, 62
constraint(s), 19, 63, 118, 121, 138,
  190, 196
contraception, 50, 59n13, 62, 94, 95,
  98, 118–19, 238
convention, 17, 134, 137, 202, 226,
  227, 229
conventional couple/couple-form, 4,
  8, 9, 23, 116, 117, 159, 178, 186,
  201, 204, 211, 230, 231n2, 232,
  233, 234, 238
conventional intimate life/practice,
  48, 115, 173, 177–9, 193, 208,
  221
  see also tradition(al)
conventional middle-class, 33n46
Cook, Hera, 50
Cooper, Davina, 51
corrective labour camps, 68–9
da Costa, Maria Velho, 97
counselling, 125, 171
  see also psychotherapy, 169, 197,
    223
couple courses, 89
couple therapy, 124, 169, 171, 223

coupledom, 3, 5n3, 11, 22, 28, 32n33, 48, 49, 83, 86, 88, 115, 117, 121, 122, 125, 127, 129, 134, 141, 146, 149, 153, 158, 159, 161, 165, 169, 171, 179–82, 184–7, 190, 198, 199, 201, 204, 205, 206–10, 211, 215, 217, 223, 225, 227, 228, 230, 232, 233
  in contemporary Bulgaria, 73–4
  in contemporary Norway, 89–91
  in contemporary Portugal, 102–3
  in contemporary UK, 57–8
couple-form, 4, 6, 8, 9, 10, 20, 23, 27, 29, 32n33, 37, 41, 45, 47, 57, 63, 64–5, 70, 71, 86, 100, 116, 132–3, 153, 159, 209, 216, 229, 230
  cohabiting, 3, 4, 22, 47, 54, 58, 88, 109, 171, 210, 216, 232, 234
  gender-equal, 78
  heterosexual, 3, 4, 28, 39, 43, 44, 45, 48, 54, 62, 69, 71, 72, 74, 159, 207, 216, 225, 234
  male-breadwinner/female-homemaker, 39, 48
  married, 4, 28, 39, 44, 45, 48, 54, 62, 67, 69, 72, 74, 78, 98, 102, 142, 159, 216, 225
  outside the conventional, 4, 20, 23, 37, 45, 57, 81, 109, 149, 207, 210, 211, 225, 228, 230, 232, 233, 234
  procreative, 22, 69, 71, 74, 146, 181, 198
  romantic, 9, 10, 29, 89
  stable, 45, 54, 57, 181, 216, 222
  traditional gendered, 51, 116
  unmarried cohabiting, 46, 47, 88
couple-norm, 3, 4, 5, 12, 22, 23, 24, 26–9, 32n33, 37, 39, 41, 46, 49–50, 62, 63, 66, 84, 88, 89, 101, 104, 112, 115, 118, 127, 132, 136, 138, 139, 141–2, 145, 149, 150, 159, 161, 165, 168, 170, 171, 172, 173, 175, 178, 179, 183, 184, 185–7, 190, 192, 193, 195, 202, 206–11, 221, 224–30, 232–3

beyond the, 232–4
components of, 217–24
interconnectedness with other norms, 224–5
psychosocial workings of, 225–30
couple-normativity, 4, 6, 26–7, 37–42, 54, 101, 216, 232–3
counter-normativity, 201, 222, 224
Cover, Rob, 11
Crowhurst, Isabel, 113n8, 241
'cruel optimism', 230
Custody of Infants Acts, 1839 and 1873 (England and Wales), 45

Daly, Mary, 52
Danielsen, Hilde, 80, 89, 170, 175, 181, 187n3, 188n9
Daskalova, Krassimira, 63
dating, 125, 130, 135, 196, 207
  internet, 135, 171
Davidoff, Leonore, 43, 45, 46, 47, 48, 49
'debit, spousal', 101
Decree no. 1, Article 38, no. 2 (Portugal), 101
Decree on Marriage 1945 (Bulgaria), 64
de facto union (Portugal), 99, 102, 104n10, 192, 205, 210
  see also cohabitation, unmarried
Delphy, Christine, 8
D'Emilio, John, 10
democracy, 16, 17, 40, 97, 98
democratization, 9, 21, 38, 76, 97, 102, 104n4, 205, 209
de-patriarchalization, 37, 39, 77, 97, 103, 186, 215, 220
desire(s), 3, 4, 5, 11, 12, 19, 21, 24, 25, 26, 31n27, 32n38, 33n40, 37, 48, 74, 88, 115, 116, 131, 133, 138, 149, 154, 159, 163, 167, 168, 170, 175, 176, 179, 181, 182, 184, 186, 187, 201, 202, 204, 216, 218, 222, 223, 225, 226, 227, 228, 229, 234
disappointment, 7, 8, 11, 120, 121, 125, 127, 130, 131, 152, 165, 169, 202, 218, 219, 222, 223, 232

Europeanization, 15

European Convention on Human Rights, 234

European Court of Human Rights, 50, 104n8

European Court of Justice, 73

European Economic Community, 98, 209

European norms, 22, 70, 217

European Union (EU), 21, 30n12, 38, 53, 57, 63, 69, 70, 73, 92, 100, 104n13, 211n2, 247n1

European Union Charter of Fundamental Rights, 38, 50, 104n8

Ewald, François, 23, 24, 31n29, 231n4

expectation, 3, 21, 24, 25, 27, 28, 32n37, 33n45, 88, 89, 94, 115, 116, 119, 122, 127, 131, 133, 138, 147, 149, 150, 158, 168, 172, 173, 178, 185, 186, 190, 193, 198, 198, 201, 205, 208, 209, 218, 220, 225

expectation↔injunction, 28, 29, 101, 115, 121, 125, 128, 139, 141, 142, 143, 159, 168, 178, 186, 187, 192–3, 210, 217, 226–9, 232

  dedicated work, 28, 217, 223–4

  family approval, 28, 29, 204, 217–19

  homogamy, 28, 115, 139, 219–22

  marriage/lifelong commitment, 28, 121, 125, 139, 143, 178, 196, 220–2

  romantic love, 28, 29, 168, 173, 222, 223

  sex within the couple, 28, 121, 181, 185, 223

failure, 25, 29, 121, 125, 127, 134, 139, 149, 168, 169–72, 181, 184, 184, 187, 218, 221, 225, 227

family

  'adult worker' model of, 44, 52

  approval, 28, 217, 218, 219, 226

  'of choice', 12

  de-familialization, 38, 40

  de-solidification of, 37

  dual-career, 52

  extended, 3, 33n47, 124, 133, 146, 231n1

  heterosexual, 20, 62

  idealized, 52

  life, 43, 52, 69, 71, 77, 88, 100, 134, 178, 215, 234

  matter, 28, 29, 123, 168, 204, 217

  nuclear, 3, 8, 50, 77, 78, 80, 81, 116, 184, 231n1

  planning, 50, 59n13, 94, 98

  policy, 43, 52, 54, 55, 77, 79, 188n7

  relationship, 31n20, 41n4, 51, 55, 208, 229

  stable, 52, 55, 60n17, 77

  traditional, 37, 47, 95

  values, 12, 55, 60n15

familial, 21

  ideology, 6, 43

  norms, 162

  orientation, 164, 186

  policies, 21, 38, 40

  practices, 19

  relationship, 19

familialism, 10, 40, 41n4, 82, 212n8

Family Code (Bulgaria), 71, 72, 73, 143, 144

Family Planning Act 1967 (UK), 50

'Family Test' 2014 (UK), 55

father(s), 32n30, 46, 49, 54, 55, 61n21, 74n1

  in interviewees' biographical-narratives, 117, 119, 120, 122, 123, 125, 128, 131, 133, 134, 139, 144, 162, 191, 194, 196, 201, 205, 218

fatherhood, 46, 239

Fatherland Front, Bulgarian political organization, 69

FEMCIT, ix, 18, 30nn12, 13, 237

Feminine Portuguese Youth, 94

feminism, 6, 8, 13n2, 20, 47, 51, 78, 96

feminist(s), ix, 3, 6, 7, 8, 9, 12, 13n2, 15, 18, 19, 20, 30nn13, 17, 19, 31n20, 32nn32, 42, 41n4, 97, 210, 228, 230

  activism/movement, 3, 30n17, 39, 40, 44, 97, 98

Law on Protection from Domestic
  Violence 2005 (Bulgaria), 70
Layton, Lynne, 25, 228–9, 231n7
Legitimacy Act 1959 (UK), 49
Leonard, Diana, 8
lesbian, 5, 8, 17, 26, 47, 54, 73, 153,
  154, 155, 156, 160n6, 178,
  189n15, 203, 225, 239
lesbian and gay/LGBT
  community, 51, 102, 154, 155, 175,
    188n11
  liberation, 51, 86
  movement/LGBT movement, 3, 12,
    21, 30n17, 41, 44, 50, 51, 77, 86,
    88, 92, 99, 100, 104n14, 109,
    113n1, 154, 184, 227, 238
  organizations, 63, 72, 102
  politics, 11, 30n17, 53, 73, 177
  rights, 51, 52, 157, 176
  sex, 60n19
lesbians and gay men, 11, 12, 22,
  32n43, 39, 51, 53, 54, 63, 69, 72,
  96, 109, 141, 157, 158, 184, 186,
  240
  differences between, 177, 182–3
  discrimination against, 53, 56, 63
  equality for, 53, 54, 68, 70, 88, 224
Lesthaeghe, Ron, 103, 105n19
liberalism, 16, 17, 50, 80
  late, 20, 45, 58n4, 60n21, 138, 237
  queer, 11
liberalization, 39, 46, 46, 57, 62, 65, 69,
  70, 71, 75n7, 92, 138, 149, 215
Lister, Ruth, 39, 45, 46, 54, 57, 62,
  65, 69, 70, 71, 92, 138, 149, 215
living alone, 3, 84, 90, 161, 166, 234
  see also solo living
living-apart relationship, 5, 58, 103,
  115, 116, 126, 127, 134, 190,
  206–7, 240
  see also non-cohabiting
Local Government Act 1988, 'Section
  28' (UK), 51
lonely/loneliness 13n15, 150, 165–6
Lorde, Audre, 8, 13n3
love, 8, 10, 11, 12, 19, 25, 26, 55, 56,
  65, 81, 85, 88–9, 122, 123, 126,

152, 153–7, 163–8, 172–9, 180–2,
  185, 187, 190, 192, 198, 199,
  200, 204, 215, 223, 228–30, 233
  being in, 163–4, 174–5, 182,
    188n10, 200, 222
  fall in, 122, 123, 132, 164–5, 173–5,
    177, 180–1 185, 201, 204, 222,
    224, 226
  and marriage, 55–6, 88–9, 128–9,
    132, 164, 185, 188n3, 196
  practical, 164, 168, 174
  realistic, 187, 188n10
  relationship, 3, 19, 185, 199, 200,
    206–9, 222
  romantic, 10, 11, 28, 48, 89, 99,
    129, 163–9, 172–9, 185, 186,
    187, 188, 188n10, 192, 196,
    209–10, 217, 222, 223, 226
  story, 188n10, 192
lover, 12, 180, 208
  ex-lover, 12, 13n19, 175, 180,
    188n11
Ludvigsen, Kari, 89
Luhmann, Niklas, 9, 13n5, 18

Maclean, Mavis, 13n4, 51, 52, 231n2
Magalhães, Maria José, 98
Major, John, 50, 60n15
Mann, Kirk, 44, 51
Manual on Civic and Moral Education
  (Portugal), 94
marriage
  age at, 50, 57, 60n14, 89, 90, 102,
    105n19, 143
  arranged, 6, 33n52, 116, 128–9,
    132–3, 140n5, 148, 162–9, 185,
    187, 188n3, 192, 196, 209,
    217–19, 219, 222, 231n1
  ceremony, 61n24, 64
  civil, 64, 65, 88, 95, 100, 143, 145,
    201
  companionate, 48
  compulsory, 7
  de-institutionalization of, 39
  egalitarian, 40, 48
  expectation↔injunction of, 28–9,
    144, 220–2

United Kingdom, 16, 20, 21, 27, 29n3, 33n47, 38, 39, 42n6, 43–61, 68, 73, 80, 84, 98, 102–4, 113n6, 138, 139, 140n3, 153, 177, 187, 211, 215, 239, 240, 241, 247
London, 5, 16, 17, 30n9, 58n1, 61n23, 115–40, 141, 239, 247n1
Universal Declaration of Human Rights, 234
universalism, 40, 81, 230

Varela, João de Matos Antunes, 101
Velotti, Patrizia, 230
Verloo, Mieke, 216
Vilar, Duarte, 94
violence
domestic, 38, 67, 70, 100, 239
against lesbians and gay men/sexual minorities, 39, 41, 71
protection from, 41, 62, 70
sexual, 239, 246
transphobic, 239
against women, 38, 41
see also abuse
virginity, 119, 192
Vodenicharov, Petar, 65, 68, 143
Vollset, Gerd, 84

Waites, Matthew, 52, 53
Walkowitz, Judith, 10
Wallbank, Julie, 54
Warner, Michael, 10, 11, 12, 13n14, 19, 24, 31n21, 160n7
wedding, 84, 98, 118, 133, 142, 162, 163, 169, 183, 192–3, 196
see also marriage
Weeks, Jeffrey, 10, 12, 30n16, 31n21, 43, 47, 49, 53, 58n1, 59n10, 175, 177, 188n11
welfare policies, 38, 39, 40, 44, 137, 234
welfare regime, 19–20, 30nn18, 19, 40–1, 42n6, 58n2, 60n10, 62, 237
welfare state, 20, 39, 40, 44, 49, 51, 52, 57, 60n10, 76–7, 81, 88, 91, 92, 229, 237
'friend-friendly', 234

late liberal, 20, 59n4, 237
'single-person friendly', 234
social democratic, 20, 30n19, 40, 42n6, 59n4, 62, 76–7, 79, 82, 186, 238
system, 22, 137
'woman-friendly', 77
Wengraf, Tom, ix, 110, 112, 114n9, 243
Weston, Kath, 12, 188n11
Wetterberg, Christina Carlsson, 78
Wiegman, Robyn, 12, 13n14, 26–7, 31n25
Wilson, Angelia R., 53
Wilson, Elizabeth, A., 27
Wiik, Kenneth Aarskaug, 90, 189
Williams, Fiona, 39, 44, 52, 60n16
Wilkinson, Eleonor, 32n33, 57
Wilkinson, Sue, 13n17, 54
Wimmer, Andreas, 16
Winnicott, Donald Woods, 229
Wolfenden Report 1957, 49
Wollstonecraft, Mary, 6
women's movement, 7, 18, 30n15, 38, 39, 40, 46, 47, 65, 79, 86, 99, 104n5, 210, 237, 238
see also feminism; movements for gender and sexual equality and change
work
couple as, 28, 89, 124, 170, 181, 187, 217, 223–4, 226
domestic, 97
emotional work, 171, 172
family and, 30n18, 91n4, 92
paid, 31n20, 44, 52, 60n16, 79, 93, 104n5, 119, 153, 179, 191
reproductive, 21
women and, 7, 20, 65, 80, 91n3, 140n5, 146–8, 194
Wright, Caroline, 43, 44, 45
Wrong, Dennis H., 22, 31n27, 32n34

Yuval-Davis, Nira, 8

Zavattini, Giulio Cesare, 230
Zhekova, Vetka, 146
Zhivkov, Todor, 67

Lightning Source UK Ltd.
Milton Keynes UK
UKHW020955300121
377922UK00004B/173